POLITICAL
POWER
and the
GOVERNMENTAL
PROCESS

POLITICAL
POWER
and the
GOVERNMENTAL
PROCESS

by KARL LOEWENSTEIN
with a new postscript by the author

THE UNIVERSITY OF CHICAGO PRESS
CHICAGO & LONDON

CHARLES R. WALGREEN FOUNDATION LECTURES

JA66
L6
1965x

3201
L827

Library of Congress Catalog Card Number: 57-9549

THE UNIVERSITY OF CHICAGO PRESS, CHICAGO & LONDON
The University of Toronto Press, Toronto 5, Canada

© *1957, 1965 by The University of Chicago*
All rights reserved. Published 1957. Second Edition 1965
Printed in the United States of America

To CHARLES W. COLE, *President*

and THE TRUSTEES OF AMHERST COLLEGE

Preface

This book is based on six lectures the author was privileged to deliver under the auspices of the Walgreen Foundation at the University of Chicago in January, 1956. While the publication in book form required the reformulation and amplification of the material, its structure and the sequence of topics are largely identical with the lectures.

The study is a contribution to the branch of political science known as comparative government. In its approach, however, it differs from those traditional in this field; it is not a "country-by-country" description and analysis of political institutions or a "functional" comparison of the related institutions and techniques of different political civilizations. By contrast, this study is a pioneering attempt to establish what lately has come to be spoken of as a "conceptual framework." The political institutions and techniques that operate the different political systems will be analyzed by subordinating them to a single, over-all concept or thought pattern that serves as a compass for the evaluation of the bewildering variety of historical and contemporary patterns of government. This conceptual context to which the discussion is oriented is the exercise of the political power fundamental for all political organizations: Is power concentrated in the hands of a single power holder or state organ, or is it mutually shared and reciprocally controlled by several power holders or state organs?

By design, this undertaking is neither grounded in, nor aimed at, an encompassing and unified political theory of a philosophical —speculative or metaphysical—nature. It should be considered a contribution to the reality of the process of political power.

Unfortunately—and the author is the last not to deplore it—the novel approach to a conceptual framework of the process of political power requires a good deal—certainly too much for the taste of some readers—of terminological clarification and definition. Otherwise the overwhelming mass of empirical data could not be brought under a common conceptual roof. On the other hand, since the study is in the nature of a synthesis, the canvas painted by it is necessarily more or less alfresco. Footnotes are kept to a minimum. For their rather overfrequent references to his own publications dealing with special segments of the general topic under discussion here, the author asks the indulgence of the reader.

Whether or not the present undertaking has successfully woven the complexities and varieties of the process of political power into the fabric of a unifying conceptual frame, others will judge. At any rate, the author is deeply grateful to the University of Chicago Press for the opportunity granted to attempt it.

KARL LOEWENSTEIN

ISTANBUL, TURKEY
April 24, 1965

Table of Contents

Part I

The Political Process
and the Patterns of Government

I. On the Anatomy of the Process of Political Power

The Mysterious Triad

The basic urges that dominate man's life in society and govern the allness of human relations are threefold: love, faith, and power. They are mysteriously intertwined and interwoven. We know that the power of faith moves mountains and that the power of love—ἔρως ἀνίκατε μάχαν (*eros anikate machan*)—is the victor in all battles. But no less innate in the human kind is the love of power and the faith in power. History records what love and faith have contributed to human happiness, and power to human misery. All three forces have this in common: Man can feel and experience them and recognize what they do to him and his environment, but the cognition of their inner reality escapes him. His logical endowment is insufficient to penetrate into their essence. All that humans are able to do in understanding the forces of love, faith, and power is to register and evaluate their manifestations and results. Man can realize what they do, but he cannot grasp what they are. Any ontological definition must fail him because his perception is confined to their externals.

Political Power

Of this triad of societal motivations, power, while operative in all human relations, is of paramount significance for the socio-political realm. Politics is nothing else but the struggle for power. Political science and social philosophy, whose subject matter is politics, could not fail, in recent years, increasingly to accent the power phenomenon. While it may seem surprising that as yet no competent investigation has pursued the role the power element plays, consciously or subconsciously, in the theory of all great political thinkers from Aristotle to Machiavelli, from Montesquieu and Rousseau to Lenin, in the last decades a spate of books has been published that center on the power issue, honoring it either in the title or in the content: Guglielmo Ferrero, Bertrand Russell, Bertrand de Jouvenel, Charles E. Merriam, and Gerhard Ritter, to name only a few of the more distinguished contributors,[1] and a host of others.

Even though in most of these studies the analysis of the power phenomenon is still largely oriented toward the historical inquiry, the focus of political science and philosophy on the role of political power in the process of government clearly indicates the rising dissatisfaction with the strictly "functional" approach, which analyzes the governmental process predominantly in terms of institutional arrangements. More and more, power is being considered the dynamic infrastructure of sociopolitical institutions. It may also seem significant that, in our generation, the emphasis on power as the key for a better understanding of the state society has superseded the scientific interest in the concept of sovereignty that, for so many centuries, had been the foundation of political theory as well as of the application of public law. Today the role of sovereignty has become relegated almost exclusively to the theory of international law and the practice of international relations. Perhaps it is fair to say that sovereignty is nothing else, and nothing less, than the legal rationalization of power as the irrational element of politics. He who is legally entitled to exercise or who ultimately exercises political power in the state community is sovereign.

The questions whether the sudden interest of this generation in the power phenomenon has its roots in the simultaneous discovery of the collective subconscious, and whether it has been stimulated by the application of psychoanalytical research techniques to mass phenomena, may be raised but cannot be answered here. But, in trying to explain the recent eruption of interest in power as the eternal infrastructure of politics, it may be helpful to realize that constitutionalism, a product of the mechanistic and rationalistic thinking of the seventeenth and eighteenth centuries, in itself was nothing else than the revolt of a new social class against the traditional power *mystique* inherent in the control of the state society by the absolute monarchy. In the climate of its original incubation the constitutional theory was bound to the belief that power, as the irrational element of the political process, could be ignored, or at least effectively neutralized, by rational arrangements for its exercise and control. By contrast, in our time the resurgence of the irrational-emotional impulses in the power process may well raise doubt as to whether power can be exorcised by clever functional arrangements.

The Science of "Cratology"

To repeat: Political power is discernible, observable, explainable, and evaluable only by its external manifestations and realizations. We know, or we believe we know, what power does, but we are unable to define its substance and essence. The science of "cratology,"* if it exists at all, is still in its infancy, and it may well be questioned whether it will ever mature to be a reliable tool of human understanding.

It is not surprising that, in the environment of our pluralist society, American political science, for a long time steeped in the behaviorist approach to politics, has been particularly fascinated by the power phenomenon.[2] Formidably ambitious, the "theory of influence" is prepared to apply the measurement devices of behaviorist quantification to what as yet has proved to be the fundamentally unmeasurable substance of political power. Nothing of the mysteries of human attitudes seems sacrosanct to the quantifiers, to whom the only sacrament is the measurement.

* From the Greek κράτος, "power."

The attempt, therefore, to come to grips with the reality of the power phenomenon and its function in the state society by measuring the degree and intensity of reciprocal interactions in the various sociopolitical configurations—roughly circumscribed as the "leader-followers" issue—has little chance of penetrating to the core of the power situation. The most it will be able to accomplish is to demonstrate certain psychological traits of specific individuals or groups in a specific environment, but the conclusions derived from such isolated estimates of collective behavior are conditioned by so many incalculable variables—many of them stemming from the collective subconscious—that the essence of the power reality must remain as elusive as before. This seems to parallel the vain efforts of man directed toward the ontological proof of the existence of a Divine Being: The more He is approximated intellectually, the more He recedes. Revelation by faith is inaccessible to logical proof.

Power and the State Society

The substance of power in the political process, therefore, will not be explained here. For our context the following observations must suffice,[3] and in this context it should be noted that power is used as a strictly neutral, functional, and non-evaluative term, denoting nothing but a factual situation or relationship which is ethically neither good nor evil. Society as a whole is a system of power relations—political, social, economic, religious, moral, cultural, and others. Power is a sociopsychological relationship operating reciprocally between those who hold and exercise power, here called the "power holders," and those to whom it is directed, spoken of here as the "power addressees." Within society the state is the predominant or, at least in certain historical cases, the exclusive organization. Political power denotes, within the state society, the exercise of effective social control of the power holders over the power addressees. Social control, in the narrower sense of contemporary political science, is the policy-making or policy-deciding function and the ability of the power holders to make the power addressees obey the policy decision. The core of every political system, thus, lies in the ideologies, institutions, and techniques operative within the state society for the attainment, exercise, and control of political power.

In the modern democratic-constitutional state the essence of the power process consists in the attempt to establish an equilibrium between the various competitive plural forces within the state society, with due regard to the free unfolding of the human personality. In modern autocracy, whether totalitarian or authoritarian,* social control and political power are monopolized by a single power holder, subordinating the individual to the ideological requirements of the group dominating the state.

These general suppositions, then, may be utilized for analyzing and appraising the functional role the power element plays in the governmental process. Here the first observation is that the power element operates not only between the power holders and the power addressees but also, beyond this, in the relationship among different and several power holders, provided they exist in the particular political system. Second, to understand the nature of the political system in an individual state society, three often closely interrelated stages of the political process have to be distinguished: (1) the designation of the power holders, that is, how political power is gained by the single or the several power holders; (2) how power, once gained, is exercised by them; this is the problem of the assignment to and the distribution of the different functions relevant for community life among the several power holders; and (3) how the exercise of power by the power holders, whether single or several, is controlled. This last and all-important problem of the adequate containment of political power by the interaction of either the several power holders or the power addressees themselves is the core and essence of what historically has become known as the constitutional state.

* For the distinction see below, pp. 55 ff.

The Demonology of Power

At this point our analysis of the power phenomenon is confronted by a basic psychological fact. There is ample evidence of human nature in politics that, unless contained and controlled, power overreaches itself. Rarely if ever is it given to man to exercise unlimited power with moderation and self-restraint. A stigma is attached to power, and only the saints among the power holders—rarely found—are able to resist the temptation of abusing it. If, heretofore, the term "power" has been used here to denote an objective element of the political process without any ethical connotation, uncontrolled power is evil as such. Power carries within itself the seed of degenerating into the lust of power. Unless held in bounds, social control is apt to transform itself into capricious tyranny and arbitrary despotism. Uncontrolled power, therefore, acquires a negative moral accent; it reveals the demonism of the power element and the pathology of the power process. Of this ambivalence of power Aristotle was wholly conscious when he contrasted the "good" with the "perverted" forms of government, the former being instituted for the welfare of the community of the power addressees; the latter, for the selfish benefit of the power holders themselves. The celebrated—and usually incorrectly quoted—epigram of Lord Acton poignantly formulates the pathological implications of the power process: "Power tends to corrupt and absolute power tends to corrupt absolutely."

The Control of Political Power

To prevent this ever present danger inherent in power, the organized state imperatively requires, in the interests of the power holders no less than of the power addressees, that the exercise of political power be contained and restrained. Human nature being what it is, such restraints cannot be expected to operate automatically; they must be carried into the power process from outside. The containment of political power by the containment of the power holders is the crux of what in political history, ancient and modern, appears as constitutionalism. An agreed set of fixed rules, binding the power holders and the power addressees alike, was found to be the most effective device to prevent the abuse of political power by the power holders. The mechanism of such devices, either embodied in a formal document, the constitution, or firmly imbedded in the national mores and conscience, is complex, requiring a full discussion later.*

Beyond this, the issue of the control of the power holders is one of the sociopolitical values or ideologies underlying any specific state society. The authority of the power holders is indispensable for carrying out the purposes of the state society, on the one hand; the liberty under authority of the power addressees is equally indispensable, on the other. The establishment of a harmonious equilibrium between these two basic values presents in a nutshell the eternal quest of man in society. The choices between liberty and authority, thus, are the ideological infrastructure, or the *telos*, of any and all state societies. Liberty of the power addressees is possible only if the exercise of political power by the power holders is adequately controlled. The existence or absence of such controls, their methods and institutionalization, and their degree and intensity characterize the particular political systems and denote the basic differences among them. The process of political power, therefore, is understandable only by way of the analysis of the mechanism for the control of its exercise.

The Political System

By introducing the term "political system,"[4] another avenue to the power phenomenon is opened. In the widest sense, every state with an established relationship between power holders and power addressees in the form of permanent governmental institutions is a political system. Its essential characteristic is found in the apparatus or mechanism through which social control is exercised. In this sense the term "political system," applicable to all states, en-

* See below, pp. 123 ff.

compasses so much as to be practically useless unless the frame is filled with content.

The key to a serviceable distinction among the different political systems is found in the different ideologies and the institutions commensurate to them by which the individual state society functions. All political systems are necessarily operated by institutions and ideologies. Institutions are the apparatus through which the power process functions in a society organized as a state. Institutions, therefore, are all elements or component parts of the state machinery, including, in the contemporary world, government, parliament, courts, administrative staffs, police, and political parties. Ideologies, on the other hand, are the values and value systems that underlie the institutions and determine their *telos*. An ideology may be defined as "a consistent and integrated pattern of thoughts and beliefs explaining man's attitude towards life and his existence in society, and advocating a conduct and action pattern responsive to, and commensurate with, such thoughts and beliefs."[5] Ideologies are incorporations of the supreme values held by influential segments of society or, in a much rarer contingency, by society as a whole. But it is essential to note —and this delineates them from political philosophy or theory— that they impel their adherents to action for their realization. Ideologies, thus, are the *telos* or the "spirit" of the political dynamism of a particular state society.

While these distinctions and definitions hardly break new ground, the relationship between ideologies and institutions generally has not been given the proper emphasis. Institutions of a strictly utilitarian nature are rare indeed; few are indifferent or neutral toward the ideological values of the concrete political organization. While the strictly functional fireman and policeman hardly reflect any particular social value except that of maintaining order and security, most institutions are imbued with the *telos* of an underlying ideology. The ontological approach to the history of political institutions may even claim that sociopolitical ideologies create the institutions serviceable to them. Most institutions are conditioned, generated, and operated by ideology.

From this intimate correspondence of institution and ideology stems the much observed experience that instistutions developed in a specific ideological environment and serviceable to it lose their functional identity when mechanically transplanted to an ideologically different political system. They automatically transform themselves. Elections, parliament, political parties, developed by the political system of liberal constitutionalism for the self-realization of its liberal-equalitarian ideology, change their intrinsic meaning and even their operational utility when applied by a totalitarian political system.

In view of the foregoing observations the term "political system" as used in this study acquires a specific meaning: It is a state society imbued by a concrete ideology—political, socioeconomic, ethical or moral-religious—to which correspond, in turn, specific institutions intended for the realization of the dominant ideology. Political systems, in this sense, are relatively few in number. The historically most significant among them may be mentioned: theocracy, monarchical absolutism based on dynastic legitimacy, constitutionalism (liberal and equalitarian), collectivism (as corporativism, socialism, or communism), and fascism. It is characteristic of the ideology-consciousness of the contemporary process of political power that even political regimes predicated on naked power feel compelled to fly an ideological pennant from their bayonets; its color is usually nationalistic.

Political Systems and Patterns of Government

A "political system" is not coterminous with "forms" or "patterns of government." Being generic, the term "political system," as a rule, embraces various patterns of government linked together by the same or a similar type of ideology and the institutions corresponding to it. Thus, the political system of democratic constitutionalism includes different patterns of government, depending on the interplay of the several power holders in the formation of the will of the state, institutionalized, as the case may be, as presidentialism, parliamentarism with supremacy of the assembly or of the cabinet, assembly government, directory government, and direct or semidirect democracy. All these are inspired by one and the same ideology of the paramountcy of the popular will. The political system of autocracy, on the other hand, dominated by elitist, magico-legitimist, timocratic, proletarian, racial, corporative, or other non-equalitarian ideologies for the conduct of the political process, embraces equally diversified patterns: absolute monarchy, assembly government as practiced by contemporary communism, the personalized dictatorships of fascism and nazism, and the various authoritarian regimes oriented toward neo-presidentialism in which the ideological *telos* is little more than a veneer for the power monopoly of the *de facto* rulers. We may qualify such power structures as horizontal governments because they have no roots in the power addressees.

In the following discussion, therefore, for the sake of terminological precision, the term "political system" refers to the ideological structure, while the term "pattern of government" or "political regime" refers to the concrete institutionalization of the political system in a particular state society.

Shared and Concentrated Exercise of Political Power

At this point a guiding principle can be announced for the identification of the different political systems and for the differentiation of the patterns of government they include. It is the key to the analysis of the power process attempted in this study.

The basic difference between the several political systems consists in whether, in the various stages of the governmental process, political power is distributed among and shared by several independent power holders or whether political power is concentrated in and monopolized by a single power holder, be it an individual person (the "dictator"), an assembly, a committee, a junta, or a party. In the case of the shared and dispersed exercise of political power the political system is qualified as constitutional or constitutional democratic; historically, the two types are not identical.* In the case of the exercise of political power concentrated in a single power holder it is classified as autocratic. There exist, of course, many variants of either type of state organization, and much cross-fertilization between them is frequent, requiring in each individual case an analysis of the actual reality of the power process.

The criterion of shared or concentrated power should be tested by applying it to all stages of the governmental process. Shared power in the designation of the power holders, for example, prevails if an office entailing political power is attained through free elections with competitive candidates and parties. Concentrated power is in evidence if the power holder gains office either by force (conquest or revolution) or by manipulated elections. In its exercise power is shared if, for example, the legislative function is performed conjointly by the government and the parliament or if two houses of parliament partake in it, while concentrated power manifests itself by the legislative monopoly of either the government or the assembly excluding therefrom the other power holders. Control of political power, finally, is shared among the several power holders if, for example, the parliament can remove the government by a vote of non-confidence or if the latter can dissolve the former, leading ultimately to the verdict of the electorate as the supreme power holder. No such reciprocal devices for the control of political power exist under the system of concentrated power.

The basic dichotomy of political systems and the patterns of government included therein would be terminologically best expressed by the pair of opposites, "polycracy" and "monocracy," the former denoting shared and the latter concentrated exercise of political power. However, since the advantage of using precise terms is canceled out by the confusion unorthodox labels may create, in the following discussion the term "constitutionalism"

* See below, pp. 70 ff.

will be used for the configuration of shared power and the term "autocracy" for the political process operated by concentrated power. The term "dictatorship," with which autocratic government is commonly equated, does not always seem apposite, because even autocratic government may have to follow certain constitutional procedures for the exercise of political power; for example, if the policy decision of the single power holder requires formal indorsement by an assembly subservient to him. The term "dictatorship," therefore, may appropriately be reserved for the monopolizing of political power by a single individual without the intermediary of other permanently established institutions. Hitler's Third Reich is a case in point.

On the Power Holders

Who are the power holders? To answer this question, the constitutional lawyer must ally himself with the political sociologist. The reality of the power process suggests a pragmatic distinction between those organs of the state that hold and wield political power by virtue of constitutional investiture—the official, legitimate, visible power holders—and those that influence and determine the power process unofficially, indirectly, and often extraconstitutionally—the unofficial and invisible power holders.

The official and visible power holders are those organs and agencies and their operators that are charged by the "constitution" of the state—normally, though not always, a formalized instrument of government—to perform specific functions on behalf of the state community. The political power they exercise is attached to the office and, only through the office, to its incumbent personnel. Under the political system of constitutionalism power is depersonalized.

In the course of the historical evolution of the state society four such power holders have arisen. (1) The government, the oldest and fundamentally the most indispensable of them all, is charged, within the compass of the constitutional state, with the governmental functions of policy decision and policy execution.* The range of the governmental sphere varies according to the historical period and the specific pattern of government. (2) The assembly (parliament), as the representation of the power addressees, is charged primarily with the legislative and government-controlling functions. Historically, while membership in parliament was confined by a restricted suffrage to the aristocratic, plutocratic, and bourgeois classes, the qualification of the assembly as the representation of the mass of the power addressees remained symbolic at the most. The assembly became a genuine representation of the bulk of the power addressees when, with the extension of the suffrage, its composition corresponded to the political currents within the electorate, as reflected by the political parties. (3) In this case the power addressees themselves, organized as the electorate in the cadres of political parties, rise to the rank of an independent power holder, directly participating in the political process through elections, referendal procedures, and the impact of public opinion on all other established power holders. (4) Finally, the courts are to be considered a legitimate power holder under the exceptional situation when, instead of being merely charged with the subordinate function of applying the law to the disputes arising under them, they acquire the independent right of invalidating legislation indorsed by both parliament and government.

Whether the political parties themselves should be classified as official and legitimate power holders may be an open question. Officially they are not, because most constitutions assiduously ignore them.† But their status as legitimate power holders can hardly be doubted in the modern mass society. Mobilizing and activating the power addressees to function as the electorate, they are indispensable for the power process in all modern state organizations, whether constitutional or autocratic. In the former, they have come to designate the constitutional power holders in parlia-

* For the distinction see below, pp. 42 ff.
† See below, pp. 363 ff.

ment and government, and, in the latter, institutionalized as the single party, they cannot be dispensed with as the tool of social control of the single power holder over the power addressees.

While the official, legitimate, visible power holders can be identified without difficulty in the constitution, the discovery of the invisible, non-official, and non-legitimate power holders requires, in each case, a sociological analysis of the reality of the power process. To locate them is often like opening one of those painted Chinese boxes wherein one finds another, smaller box, containing a third one still smaller, an endless chain of illusion and reality. Wirepullers behind the curtain moving the marionettes on the stage are ubiquitous phenomena of the power process. The *éminence grise* behind the throne of power appears under many disguises, as the priests and confessors possessing the ear and the soul of the absolute monarch, the favorite of the Roman emperor, the grand vizier of the sultan or shah, the mayors of the palace (*Hausmeier*) of the Merovingians, the mistresses of the Roi Soleil, the Rana in Nepal, or the personal confidants and members of the kitchen cabinet of the American presidents. Sometimes their influence on the official power holder is institutionalized in an office, but more often it remains in the twilight of anonymous irresponsibility.

The variety of such extraconstitutional influences on the power process defies classification. However, in our technological mass society a new pattern of the invisible power holders has arisen in the form of the plural groups* and their access to the mass-communication media. The infiltration and penetration of the plural groups and their action spearheads—the pressure groups and lobbies—are, in comparison with previous periods, perhaps the most significant phenomena of the political process in our technological mass society. Now that the mass of the power addressees actively participate as the electorate in the political process, the formation of public opinion, reflecting as well as molding the electorate, has become the most important aspect of the power dynamism of the

* See below, pp. 344 ff.

modern pluralistic society. The individual member of the electorate obtains information on political and socioeconomic facts, together with the ideological equipment for their coherent evaluation, not only from the legitimate power holders—government and parliament—but even more so from the free-wheeling parties and interest groups. The transmission belt for imparting the sociopolitical facts and their ideological interpretation in this electronic age are the media of mass communication. In the contemporary society, therefore, the invisible power holders are the plural groups that command the loyalty of their supporters and adherents and, in addition, those who, in behalf of the plural and interest groups, command and control the media of mass communication through which public opinion and the action of the electorate as the supreme power holder are formed and articulated.

Consequently, the character of a political system is largely determined by whether the access to and the use of the communication media are equally shared by all power holders and plural groups or by whether they are concentrated in the hands of the single power holder and privileged plural groups. In the constitutional-democratic state plural equality prevails in the access to the mass-communication media, while in the political system termed "autocracy" the management of the mass-communication media is monopolized by the single power holder. The subject will be more fully discussed in a later chapter.*

Outline of the Following Discussion

A brief outline of the organization of the book and the sequence of topics conditioned by it may be helpful. The book is divided into three parts. Part I, containing chapters i–iv, presents the pragmatic frame of the process of political power in relation to the process of government. The basic discussion of the power element in politics that has been submitted in this chapter will be followed, in chapter ii, by the analysis of the governmental process proper

* See below, pp. 336 ff.

from the viewpoint of the shared and concentrated exercise of political power. Chapters iii and iv will attempt to classify the various political systems according to the dichotomy of concentrated exercise of political power—called "autocracy"—and of shared exercise of political power—called "constitutional democracy." In this context a functional analysis of the patterns of government that each one of these political systems embraces will be submitted.

The remaining Parts II and III, constituting the bulk of the book, will be devoted to the crucial issue of how, by specific institutional arrangements, the dynamism of the power process can be rationalized and controlled. Part II will be introduced, in chapter v, by an examination of the political constitution itself as the foremost instrumentality of power control. Research into such other control devices as are usually established by the political constitution or its equivalents will follow in chapters v–ix. These may operate *within* a specific power holder—*intra*-organ controls (chap. vi)—or *between* the several power holders—*inter*organ controls (chaps. vii–ix). These types of control devices are bracketed together under the common term "horizontal controls." The pattern of government that prevails in an individual state depends on the specific arrangements of the horizontal controls.

Finally, in Part III the horizontal controls will be contrasted with the "vertical controls," so termed because they operate, not necessarily by virtue of constitutional norms or governmental arrangements, among the different levels of the state society. Each of these devices of vertical control is intended to serve as an effective restraint on the official holders of political power. Under this heading three different situations will be considered: federalism as territorial pluralism (chap. x); fundamental liberties of the individual as areas held inaccessible to all power holders (chap. xi); and the plural groups interposing themselves as shock absorbers between the power holders and the power addressees (chap. xii).

II. On the Anatomy of the Governmental Process

The Necessity of Classifying States and Governments

Looking backward from the vantage point of the present over the expanses of history, one is impressed by the endless procession of state societies that have come and gone and the bewildering variety of governmental techniques they have practiced. Some states are remembered for the excellence of their political institutions to which the historians attribute their accomplishments, others for their deeds alone without evoking admiration for their governmental structure, and still others remain in the twilight, remembered, if at all, only as the chronological links between more remarkable political civilizations.

The urge to classify, by certain rational criteria of similarity or dissimilarity, the variety of states and their forms or patterns of government appears to be more than merely an intellectual curiosity. Political science started with the classification of governments and has never lost interest in it. For this persistent impulse additional reasons exist in our time. Theoretically, a reliable categorization of governmental patterns may, on this shrunken globe, better our understanding of foreign political civilizations and of our own. Practically, an accurate classification of governmental structures may be of value, in a bipolarized world, to distinguish friend and foe. What is called the "free world" is said to enjoy governmental institutions protecting individual freedom, while under the political system qualified as totalitarianism no such freedom can exist. The pragmatic implications of a classification of governmental patterns has become all the more imperative—and increasingly difficult—in view of the deceptive similarity of the political institutions and techniques employed by both the constitutional and the autocratic states: Both operate in an outwardly identical fashion with elections, parties, parliaments, governments, courts, and bureaucracies, and even their instruments of government bear a striking resemblance.

Patterns of government cannot be identified by their constitutionally established institutions and techniques alone. A meaningful classification must be based on the analysis of the political reality of the governmental process which, as a rule, cannot be read from the text of the constitution. Realistic classificatory criteria should be derived from the anatomy of the power process, that is, from the manner by which, in the individual state society, political power is gained, exercised, and controlled.

The Traditional Classifications of the "Forms of Government"

The urge to classify and evaluate state societies in accordance with the type of government they practice is as old as the political thinking of man.[1] If these intellectual exercises had been conducted merely for the sake of *l'art pour l'art* of the political scientist, the labor spent on them through the centuries would have been in vain. But since dissatisfaction with his own political order seems an innate trait of man as a political animal, the effort has been geared to the discovery of qualitative preferences and stimulated by the search for the "best" form of government. Every reputable political thinker engaged in the game ultimately arrived at a differentiation between "good" and "bad" forms of government.

Aristotle.—Of all such attempts, Aristotle's classification of governments has become classic. Following Herodotus and Plato, he utilized an unparalleled comparative material, collected through field investigations by him and his school, to establish the celebrated tripartite division. Focusing on the quantitative criterion of the number of power holders, it distinguishes monarchies, aristocracies, and polities, the latter his appellation for what in modern terms is the constitutional-democratic state. But he was too much a realist and moralist not to recognize the mechanical defects of the purely quantitative approach. The desirable implementation by a qualitative evaluation he found in the "perverted" or degenerate transformations of the "ideal" types: If the power holder or holders use and abuse their power for selfish ends—for the benefit of a single person, of a class or, in the polity, of the mass of the power addressees—instead of for the general welfare, the patterns of rule turn into tyranny, oligarchy, and ochlocracy (or mob rule—his term for democracy), respectively. This systematization, then, was instrumental to the famous Aristotelian cyclicity of the process of political power, reflected by the implacable succession of the patterns of government. But he was wholly conscious of the fact that there is no good and no bad type of the institutionalization of political power as such, its quality depending on the use the power holders make of it.

The "mixed" form of government.—Himself favoring the middle-class polity as the desirable structure of society, Aristotle thereby introduced the sociological element into the study of the patterns of government. Following this cue, some of his most influential successors believed they had found the "best" form of government by grafting the mixture of social classes on the classical tripartism of the number of power holders, each class represented in a different state organ. Polybius, fascinated by the glory that was republican Rome, stands at the beginning of this impressive ancestral line of the theory of mixed government that came to a climax in medieval scholasticism and Thomas Aquinas. Its repercussions influenced the early theory of modern constitutionalism, which developed pragmatically first in Puritan England and was her priceless gift to the political civilization of the West and of the world: the concept of "mixed" government, adhered to by Harrington, Locke, Bolingbroke, Montesquieu, and the *Federalist*, permitted the balancing of political power by blending the social classes with the institutions of government corresponding to them. On the other hand, the absolutists among the political thinkers—Machiavelli foremost, but equally Hobbes and Rousseau and the early ultrademocratic doctrine of the French Revolution—again leaned heavily toward the "pure" forms of government, whether absolute monarchy or total democracy; the latter, in turn, was condemned as tyrannical by Burke, de Tocqueville, Donoso-Cortés, and Burckhardt. But it should be noted that, for both the relativists and the absolutists, the classification of governments was merely ancillary to the purpose of differentiating among the different state societies: the nature of the state society was explained by the pattern of government it adhered to. On this the theories of the classification of governments are nearly unanimous.

Machiavelli.—Tradition has provided us with two separate if interrelated sets of divisions which political theory since has never tired of combining and confronting in more or less ingenious variations. The Aristotelian tripartism was used in a cleverly simplified form by Machiavelli. Perceptibly drawing on the experience of his Italian environment, where republican city-states and postfeudal neo-absolutism lived side by side, he holds that in a principality (monarchy) sovereignty rests with the single power holder alone, whether by right or by might—significantly the *ci-devant* Florentine secretary of state is far more conscious of the power element in politics than any of his predecessors—while in a republic sovereignty is shared by a plurality or collectivity of persons constituting the power holders. But, different from the quantitative nominalism of the older school, Machiavelli, by eliminating aristocracy as a separate pattern and fusing it with the republic, treats aristocracy and democracy as the single category of the republic. They differ in sociological substance but share one and the same governmental pattern.

Subsequently, this monarchical-republican alternative was accepted, without much imagination or challenge, by most political theorists—Hobbes, Rousseau, the French Revolution, and the early liberalism of the nineteenth century, though abandoned by the sociologically oriented Montesquieu—down to the Atlantic Charter, whose famous Article III, that "every people has the right to choose the form of government it wishes to live under," obviously confines the choice to either the democratic republic or the parliamentary monarchy, assuming—perhaps somewhat optimistically—that no nation voluntarily would choose, or could be wheedled against its will into, slavery under an autocracy.

Montesquieu.—Hardly any other political theorem proved to be so tenaciously stationary and reality-resistant as the doctrines classifying the patterns or forms of government. The road to the urgently required reclassification is still blocked by the conventional terminology. Both traditional classifications are utterly useless today and, possibly, were already unrealistic at the time of their conception. Indifferent to the ideological values reflected by the governmental institutions, they refer to the external framework of government only and neglect the actual dynamism of the power process. The defect lies in the fact that the power *mystique* was considered a natural phenomenon of man organized in the state society and that the magic of power was too intrenched in the existence of any and all governments to permit its being counterbalanced and neutralized by institutions designed to limit governmental authority for the sake of human dignity and personal liberty. This is clearly evidenced by the observation that, after the eclipse of ancient constitutionalism in Greece and republican Rome, nowhere outside the Christian West did any semblance of institutions materialize that limited the power of the government. The only possible exception, the Chinese censorate, was ethically rather than politically intended.

It was Montesquieu, whose genius shines more brightly with the progress of time, who visualized the governmental institutions as the organizational frames for the social forces operating in the state societies—the "climate" or the "spirit of the laws"—and came closer to the reality of the power element in government. He implemented the traditional classifications of states, still conceived as determinable only by the patterns of their governmental institutions, in two ways. On the one hand, he ascribed to each of the traditional patterns a moral principle or a social idea (we would say an ideological *telos*): virtue to democracy, moderation to aristocracy, and honor to monarchy. This ideological approach renews and modifies Aristotle's by attaching the qualitative to the quantitative element. Its defects are that his chosen principles did not fit the patterns of government and that his historical material did not support his principles. But his second innovation proved strangely farsighted: From monarchy he split off the separate pattern of despotism, that is, the lawless, capricious, tyrannical exercise of political power by the single power holder. Nobody will hold it against him that he could not anticipate the contemporary tyranny exercised by a collective group organized as a party. Despotism, then, was contrasted with the republican and monarchical patterns, which were grouped together as the "constitutional state," that is, in modern terms, the state under the rule of law. And he added the crowning touch to this new classification by his epochal analysis of the power process itself: the tripartism of the state functions or "powers" and the need, for ideological reasons, to limit them by mutual checks and balances.*

Guglielmo Ferrero.—A more recent and a thoroughly original contribution to the classification stems from Guglielmo Ferrero, the Italian historian whose studies of Roman history and of the revival of plebiscitary Caesarism under Napoleon impelled him toward the significance of the power element in the governmental process. To him the number of power holders is irrelevant. Neither monarchy nor republic as such is instrumental to the value of a political regime. What matters are the sociopsychologi-

* See below, pp. 34 ff.

cal relations between the power holders and the power addressees. To be accepted by the mass of the people, the government must possess legitimate authority. The new dichotomy consists in whether government is legitimate or revolutionary. The psychological approach to the power phenomenon lies in whether or not the government is feared by the people and, vice versa, fears the people. Legitimate government relies on the voluntary consent of the people without fear and force; revolutionary government is forced to rely on compulsion generating fear. Freedom from fear is the freedom to be free; fear enslaves both power holders and power addressees. Although Ferrero himself considered revolutionary government to be the worst type of all, as a historian he could not ignore the fact that revolutionary government may attain legitimacy and, hence, become normalized. When the power addressees, through the lapse of time, have become accustomed to the regime and realize what it actually accomplishes for them, the point is reached at which they accept it as legitimate and live in harmony with it.

None of these classifications seems today wholly satisfactory; none fully corresponds to the reality of the present-day power process. Aristocracy, once universal suffrage had become common, ceased to exist as a separate form of government. Monarchy, once imbedded in the divine-right mysticism, is a mere echo today of its past, as evidenced by the complete rationalization and democratization of the monarchical establishment in western Europe. In the rare cases when it approximates dictatorship, it relies not on the magic of kingship but on the tanks and machine guns of its armed forces. Nor is republican government an unequivocal category; it may be identical with democratic rule, as it frequently is; or it may embody an autocratic and tyrannical exercise of political power, and this renders meaningless the formal distinction between monarchies and republics. The republican form of government has become a frame for the autocratic power monopoly of a single power holder more absolute than the absolute monarch of the past, and yet it is not classifiable as monarchical. Most modern monarchies are as democratic as the democratic republics. By the nominalistic standards of republic and monarchy, Great Britain and Saudi Arabia, for example, would come under the same category, while the republican Third Reich and the republican United States would have to be bracketed together. In short, the traditional classifications are wholly useless today for the evaluation of patterns of government in terms of the realities of the power process by which they are operated.

Such skepticism regarding classifications based on the differentiation of governmental institutions gains additional weight since the recent historical sociology of Mosca, Pareto, Michels, and Max Weber—not to mention Giovanni Battista Vico—has demonstrated convincingly that no causal relationship exists between the structure of the governmental mechanism and the actual location of power. Every state society, regardless of the external institutionalization of its "pattern of government," is controlled by a managerial minority, whether recruited from the official and legitimate or from the unofficial and invisible power holders, who manipulate the strings of the power process in all collective organizations. The discovery of the ruling oligarchy indeed penetrates to the core of the power process. With a single-track mind, the Marxists oversimplified and superficialized a most complex situation into the black-and-white pattern of the capitalist ruling classes and the proletariat. The neopluralist approach to the socioeconomic and political dynamics of the modern technological state society, in turn, is inclined to concentrate on the alleged balancing of the competing social forces and to ignore the existence of a dominant ruling class altogether.

The Sociological Classifications of States

It may be asked whether the sociological approach does not provide a way out of the impasse of the traditional classifications based on patterns of governmental institutions. Could state soci-

eties be distinguished by an analysis of their socioeconomic structures? Every single state society, historical and contemporary,
presents a profile of its own, possesses a specific *Gestalt* composed
of ethnological, geographical, historical, socioeconomic, and other
ingredients. Even within one and the same family of nations Italy
differs from France, Norway from Denmark, Egypt from Iraq.
Yet, when visualized in a global context, some of these state individualities are affinite to certain others in terms of socioeconomic
structure and technological development. Is it possible to find
some common denominators by which to classify state societies
as such rather than grouping them in categories according to their
more or less accidental forms of governmental institutions?

However suggestive the sociological approach may be, categorization based on it transcends our present methodological
equipment. It is obvious that causal relations do exist between the
socioeconomic structure of a state society and the governmental
apparatus it has fashioned for itself. In this sense the Marxian
economic determination of history appears incontrovertible. For
example, the direct democracy of the Greek polis state, actually
an oligarchy, was possible only on the basis of the non-technological slave economy. The Roman Senate in the last two centuries
of the Republic reflected the political and governmental interests
of the new equestrian order. The fragmentation of the state authority in the feudal society had its roots in the self-sufficiency
of the local units. The practice of classical British parliamentarism,
operated in the period between 1780 and 1880 by the upper middle
class, corresponded to the system of economic competition of
early capitalism on which it throve. The managed economy of
Soviet state capitalism cannot be divorced from the technique of
the monolithic institutionalization of power in the single party.

Impressive as the historical material may be, however, it is
insufficient to be transformed into a reasonably accurate ontological theory for a comparative classification of state societies. Moreover, the categories of the ruling classes are too indeterminate to
be used as the elements for a sociological classification of state

societies as such. Certain social determinants of the power process may well be distinguished empirically, such as the militaristic, bureaucratic, capitalistic-plutocratic, industrialist, business, proletarian, bourgeois, squirarchical, agricultural, feudalistic, and clerical-theocratic elements of the social order. It also may well be that each of them is capable of conditioning the institutional superstructure of the state machinery or pattern of government. But in the modern technological state society "pure" or "ideal" types have disappeared almost completely and remain only in such isolated remnants as the agrarian feudalism in some Arab states or the lama theocracy in agrarian Tibet. Even these exceptions are rapidly vanishing as they are exposed to western and communist technologies.

Sociologically, the modern technological state is largely standardized or approaching standardization. All state societies, in this era of a new world revolution, are becoming, or have become, pluralistic frames within which industrial, capitalistic, socialistic, militaristic, bureaucratic, and even clerical ingredients, corresponding to the socioeconomic forces, are inextricably blended and mixed. To ascribe to any single socioeconomic force the character of a, or of *the*, ruling class, or to characterize a state society as "militaristic," "feudal"—a particularly equivocal term—"theocratic," or whatnot, is often a matter of a subjective value judgment rather than the result of the application of scientific standards. The individual observer may be justified in characterizing, for example, the modern American state society as plutocratic; the Wilhelminian German empire as attuned to the interests of the alliance between industry, bureaucracy, and the military establishment; or the Soviet system as proletarian. But all this categorizing is arbitrary—quite aside from the fact that the predominance of a specific plural element in the constantly fluctuating individual state society may be temporary. Consequently, it seems that state societies as such cannot be integrated into a consistent theory of classification.

Shared and Concentrated Exercise of Power as a Basis for Classification

A serviceable classification of states, therefore, can be obtained only by a comparative inquiry into the reality of their governmental structures. On the following pages a new approach is suggested to supply the urgently needed criterion. It is found in the manner in which, in the individual state society, political power is exercised and controlled. Shared exercise and control of political power or concentrated exercise without control are the conceptual framework for the basic dichotomy of the political systems in constitutionalism and autocracy, respectively. The practical test of its usefulness is that all patterns of government, past and present, can be subordinated to the one or the other of these two categories of political systems. It is the advantage of the distinction between constitutionalism as the shared, and autocracy as the concentrated, exercise of political power that it forms the key by which any political regime can be fitted into its proper category. There is, however, an important reservation: since political evolution is no mechanical process, patterns exist which exhibit institutional traits borrowed from both of them.

Constitutionalism.—The constitutional state is based on the principle of shared power. Shared power exists when several independent power holders or state organs participate in the exercise of political power and the formation of the will of the state. The functions assigned to them are subject to reciprocal controls by other power holders. Because it is shared, the exercise of political power is necessarily controlled. It is an elementary truism that, if two minds have to make a decision, one mind alone cannot prevail.

Obviously, it would be inconvenient—and practically it would paralyze the process of political power altogether—if all actions of any power holder were subject to such controls. To be independent, the power holder requires a large amount of autonomy, that is, he must be capable of action without outside interference. *On the degree of autonomy and interdependence of the several power holders depends the specific pattern of government.* Nor can the reciprocal interdependence of the several power holders be completely symmetrical and perfectly matched. As will be discussed in the next chapter, the different patterns of government within the political system of constitutionalism are distinguished by the differential weights that the constitution and the reality of the political process assign to the various power holders. Likewise varying according to the specific institutionalization is the degree of autonomy and interdependence. There is less independence and more interdependence if the government is integrated in the assembly, as under parliamentarism—interdependence by integration—than is the case if government and parliament are practically autonomous though constitutionally required to co-operate—interdependence by co-ordination—as under American presidentialism.

Under the technique of shared and, therefore, controlled power an open power circuit is established within which competitive ideologies and the social forces promoting them circulate freely and on equal footing. The power process, in this political system, is pluralistic and dynamic. Constitutionalism, therefore, denotes a free and equalitarian state society under the rule of law.

Autocracy.—In the opposite political system, on the other hand, only a single power holder exists, be it an individual person ("dictator"), an assembly, a committee, a junta, or a party. Because there are no other power holders independent from him, the exercise of power, instead of being shared, is concentrated in his hands. Nor do effective controls exist. The single power holder's political monopoly is not subject to constitutional limitations; his power is absolute. This political system necessarily can operate only in the closed power circuit that excludes the competition of different ideologies and the social forces promoting them. The political system of concentrated exercise of political power is called "autocracy."

Intermediary configurations.—Complex classifications defeat their purpose, and this dichotomy of autocracy as concentrated and constitutionalism as shared exercise of political power is appealing because of its simplicity. The immediate attribution of a specific political regime to its proper category is often made difficult, however, because elements of the autocratic and constitutional political system are often combined and blended in the course of historical dynamics. Such hybrid or intermediary patterns occur frequently in the transitional stage from one political system to the other, either when autocracy moves toward constitutionalism or, on the return trip, when a heretofore constitutional state adopts the autocratic configuration of power.* These patterns have become increasingly frequent in our time because autocratic regimes are in the habit of masking themselves by procedures and techniques borrowed from constitutionalism, as demonstrated by pseudoconstitutionalism under neopresidentialism, in the Soviet orbit, and in the Latin American *ambiente* in our time. The intrinsic reason for such mimicry lies in the prevalence of the democratic legitimacy of political power. To be respectable before the world and, perhaps, though hard to believe, in the eyes of its own subjects, an authoritarian or autocratic regime feels compelled to bow outwardly to the universally accepted ideology of popular sovereignty. This situation often makes difficult the task of attributing a specific political regime to one or the other of the over-all categories. The text of the constitution being deliberately semantic, in each case an empirical analysis of the reality of the power process is required.†

The Functional Techniques of Constitutionalism and Autocracy

However, certain clues exist for the identification of the political system and the patterns of government it includes. Each political system utilizes political techniques peculiar to it and, as

---

* For a fuller discussion of this complex situation in connection with the authoritarian state see below, pp. 56 ff.

† On the distinction of constitutions as normative, nominal, and semantic see below, pp. 147 ff.

a rule, spurned by the other. The distinction submitted previously between ideologies and institutions* must be implemented here by distinguishing institutions from techniques.[2] Institutions are the organizational arrangements for the performance of the functions assigned to them. For example, the institution of parliament serves for the enactment of legislation and the control of the government; the institution of the armed forces protects external, that of the police internal, security; the courts adjudicate controversies arising in the application of the legal norms.

For the accomplishment of the specific task assigned to it the institution develops specific techniques or procedures commensurate to its specific function. To illustrate: the parliamentary assembly is organized in plenary sessions and committees to accomplish the legislative function. It operates by a specific procedure called "parliamentary" involving motions, competitive discussion and deliberation, and majority votes. No other techniques would accomplish the parliamentary function. The bureaucracy serving the governmental administration—and any bureaucracy, for that matter—operates by assigning specific tasks to its individual members who, while performing them under their own responsibility, remain subject to hierarchical supervision and control by their superiors. Rationalized rules govern appointment and promotion of officials and apply in office routine. The courts perform the judicial function through the techniques of hearings, evidence, legal interpretation, and the mental process of applying the general norm to the individual case. These specific techniques are non-interchangeable. Parliament could not be managed by hierarchical subordination, nor the bureaucracy by political deliberations and majority votes.

It may not always be easy to distinguish between an institution and the technique it employs. For example, the political parties may seem to be simply techniques to mobilize and activate the electorate for political action. At the same time they have become

* See above, pp. 10–11.

definitely a genuine political institution: in the constitutional state they operate the elections and determine the membership of parliament and the political complexion of the government, while in totalitarian autocracies the single state party has become an official institution integrated with the state and the government. The character of a specific pattern of government may often be recognized by the specific techniques by which its institutions are operated. Autocracy and constitutionalism have developed techniques of their own that do not fit into the teleological structure of the opposite political system, and, if transplanted to another political milieu, they fail to produce the expected results.

Prominent among the techniques characteristic of the political system of constitutionalism are elections in which competitive ideologies, represented by the different candidates and parties, vie for the preference of the individual voter, who has a free choice of alternatives. Indispensable also are free votes, parliament's submission to majority decisions, tenure of the officeholder for his legally prescribed term, and mutual consultation and co-operation among the several power holders; in short, patterns of political behavior based on persuasion, compromise, and the give-and-take of reciprocal adjustment demanded by the respect of the majority for the rights of the minority.

The *telos* of the autocratic political system, on the other hand, generates entirely different political techniques. They are predicated on command and obedience—commands issued by the single power holder and obedience given by the power addressees as well as by whatever subordinate organs the single power holder may choose, for the sake of the division of labor, to employ for the enforcement of his commands. The command-obedience relationship is borrowed from the technique of the armed forces and necessarily also governs them in the constitutional state. No army could be operated by deliberative discussions and majority votes, as the anarchist combat groups in the Spanish civil war learned to their peril. Modern autocracies, therefore, exhibit an unmistakably military character. Inherent in the operation of autocracy is the hierarchical subordination of all state officials under the command of the single power holder. In addition, there is the technique of appointment and dismissal at the discretion of the single power holder, extending also to the investiture of the members of pseudoparliamentary assemblies nominated on the single-party ticket or otherwise designated by authoritarian procedures. Consent granted from below is characteristic of the constitutional state order, where it is institutionalized by elections and majority decisions. Compulsion applied from above is the invariable technique of the power process of autocracy. Once again, the dominating technique of command and obedience is often camouflaged by the semblance of elective procedures borrowed from the constitutional milieu, without, however, ultimately affecting the power monopoly of the single power holder.

An Obsolete Concept: The "Separation of Powers"

The fundamental dichotomy of the shared or concentrated exercise of political power suggested here requires a critical reexamination of one of the most celebrated political concepts, fundamental to modern constitutionalism; we refer to the so-called "separation of powers" according to their legislative, executive, and judicial substance. The doctrine of the equation of constitutionalism and the separation of powers found its classical formulation in Article 16 of the French declaration of rights of August, 1789. "Toute société dans laquelle la guarantie des droits n'est pas assurée et la séparation des pouvoirs déterminée, n'a point de constitution." And that there should be three—no more and no less than three—such separated powers was explained with convincing logic by Lally-Tollendal in the Constituante: "Un pouvoir unique finira nécessairement par dévorer tout. Deux se combattraient jusqu'à l'un aurait écrasé l'autre. Mais trois se maintaindriaient dans un parfait équilibre de manière que si deux lutteront ensemble, le troisième, également intéressé au maintien de l'un et de l'autre, se joigne à celui qui est opprimé contre qui opprime, et amène la paix entre tous."[3] The statement is a perfect illustration of the mechanistic thinking which produced the doctrine of the separation of powers. The juncture of the separation of powers with the guaranty of individual liberty is unadulterated Montesquieu, who, in turn, had been inspired by Locke: Only power holders that are independent from one another and capable of mutually checking and balancing themselves—"le pouvoir arrête le pouvoir"[4]—protect thereby the power addressees from the abuse of power by any one of the power holders. From the same intellectual source stems the application of the theory in the subsequent American state and federal constitutions.

Ever since, the separation of powers has been the standard equipment of the constitutional state. Even the vintage of recent constitutions after the Second World War exhibits it loudly and proudly, wholly oblivious of the fact that in the twentieth century the doctrine has become obsolete and devoid of reality. A mere glance at what is today the most common pattern of government, parliamentarism, should have convinced the constitutional medicine men that the legislative and executive power holders are no longer separated, neither in their persons nor even in their functions. The members of the government are members of the parliament; the government is integrated in the parliament. But it is readily granted that old doctrines are not easily discarded and that the reason for the conservatism of the new constitutions lies in the almost insurmountable difficulties of formulating the new power configuration in intelligible constitutional terms.

What the so-called "separation of powers" actually amounts to[5] is nothing more and nothing less than the realization that not only does the state have to perform various activities—the technical problem of the division of labor—but also the power addressees are better off if these activities are performed by different organs: freedom is the ideological *telos* of the separation doctrine. The separation of powers is merely the classical way of formulating the need for the shared and mutually controlled exercise of political power. What is colloquially, if erroneously, spoken of as the separation of *powers* is operationally only the distribution of specific state *functions* among different state organs. The term "powers," firmly established as it is, must, in this context, be understood to be merely figurative. In the following discussion, therefore, "separation of functions" is used in preference to "separation of powers."

One has to bear in mind that the doctrine of the necessity to split up the state functions into their various substantive segments and to distribute them among different exercisers is neither essential to the operation of political power nor a self-evident truth valid from here to eternity. The discovery or invention of the theory of the separated functions was conditioned by time and environment, an ideological protest of political liberalism against the monolithic royal absolutism of the seventeenth and eighteenth centuries. By breaking the Leviathan into its segments, liberal rationalism was out to destroy the state mysticism of the God-ordained absolutism of the crown. It derived its specific flavor from the ideological need of establishing and preserving individual liberty. Only liberal constitutionalism identified individual liberty with the separation of "powers."

It is curious to note that the constitutionalism of antiquity operated without, and often in conflict with, the separation of functions. It is true that both the Greek polis state and the Roman republic assigned specific functions to elected officials. But substantially different functions—executive, legislative, judicial—were often combined in the person of one and the same magistrate. Neither the Greeks nor the Romans seemed to have been concerned or alarmed that, for example, the Athenian *ekklesia* simultaneously exercised legislative, executive, and judicial functions, even though, for practical reasons, these activities were in charge of different groups or committees; nor was the Romans' highly developed sense of justice and fairness offended when the magistrate—consul, praetor, aedile, tribune of the people—combined all three functions in his person. Probably the intrinsic reason for this defect was that ancient constitutionalism cared little for liberty and everything for the equalitarian rule of law. Neither the Greek polis state nor the Roman republic recognized any rights of the individual intangible by, and inaccessible to, the state authority. Different from the ideology of liberal constitutionalism of modern times, the political ethics of the ancients did not call for a separation of functions and their assignment to different state organs.

Political theorists claim to have discovered as early as in Aristotle's *Politics* the nucleus of the modern separation of powers.[6] The Stagirite differentiated three segments or slices—the Greek term is *koiron*—of state activities: *to bouleuomenon peri ton koinon* ("the deliberation concerning common affairs"); *to peri tas archas* ("the organization of offices or magistrates"); and *to peri dikazon* ("the judicial function"). One cannot fail to admire the modernity of the father of political science when he prefaces the apposite discussion by the statement that the different arrangements concerning these three state activities determine the differences between constitutions, that is, in modern parlance, the different patterns of government. Yet the distinction as such fails to correspond to the modern separation of functions that has been read into it. From the discussion following the statement it is evident that what Aristotle attempted—and this by itself is no mean accomplishment—was to analyze the state activities as to their functional substance. There is nothing to indicate that he had observed empirically or desired theoretically that these three segments be assigned to three different organs or persons. This, however, is precisely the ideological meaning of the separation-of-powers doctrine of early liberal constitutionalism. Ancient constitutionalism did not subscribe to the concept of separated powers.

Shared Powers and the Technique of Representation

Whatever merit Aristotle's discovery of the separation of functions—if such it was—may have had, it was lost to posterity. In the millennium and more following the interlude of Greek and Roman constitutionalism, the absolute monarch exercised concentrated power, combining all three functions in his person, by right as well as by might, even though, for practical reasons, he may have delegated them at his discretion to subordinate officials or councils. Concentration of power in absolute government was the invariable rule, isolated exceptions in the medieval city-states in Italy and elsewhere to the contrary notwithstanding. Why, then, did the theory and practice of separated functions and shared powers originate at the dawn of the constitutional period and become a landmark in the political history of man? It is suggested that the concept of shared powers is intrinsically connected with the theory and practice of representation and representative government. The legal essence of representation is that the representatives—whatever the manner of their investiture— are authorized in advance to act conjointly on behalf of their constituents and bind them by their collective decisions. Representative techniques were wholly unknown to antiquity and the Middle Ages until their very end. If the principle had existed before, the astute Roman jurisprudents would have discussed and systematized it.[7] Elections for certain offices with specific functions assigned to them were widely practiced in the ancient constitutional states of Greece and Rome, and the technique was inherited by the organization of the Catholic church and its religious orders, which served as an important transmission belt. But election and representation cannot be equated, though elections are the primary technique of the representative process. Only in the figurative, symbolic sense did the elected magistrates represent the authority of the state community and the mass of the power addressees.

It is, therefore, no mere coincidence that the genuine separation of state functions and their assignment to separated power holders had to wait for the invention, or rather discovery, of the technique of representation. At the end of the feudal period around the turn of the fourteenth century, almost simultaneously in several western European societies—primarily Spain (Aragon, Castile, León),[8] France, and England—representative institutions emerged either by deliberate imitation or, more likely, by the law of convergence. How this came to pass remains one of the most fascinating controversies of political history, and it is all the more puzzling, since analogous representative techniques failed to materialize in any other feudal environment, whether Egyptian, Byzantine, Indian, Japanese, Chinese, or Islamic.[9] Various theories have been advanced from time to time: The romantic theory, naïvely believed by Montesquieu, that representation sprang from the Teutonic woods; the mystical-sentimental assumption that its fountainhead was the Anglo-Saxon soul thirsting for freedom; and the tradition of representative provincial assemblies of the late Roman empire subconsciously surviving in Spain and Gaul. The most recent and possibly the most attractive theory is that of the penetration of the long-established representative techniques of the Catholic church and its religious orders into the secular organization.[10]

Whatever the cause, the fact remains, as clearly demonstrated by the English experience,[11] that at the end of the feudal period, when the crown needed money, the delegates of the financially potent strata of society summoned by the king found it convenient, possibly in view of the primitive communications, to emancipate themselves from the instructions or imperative mandates of their constituents and make their decisions on the spot, relying on their own responsibility, and thereby binding or "representing" the collective communities as whose spokesmen they attended.

Whatever the origin of the representative technique, it must have been instrumental to the sharing of political power between different organs or power holders. During the next centuries the promising germs withered away everywhere in Europe under the impact of royal absolutism, with its increasingly efficient administration by a bureaucracy of professionals trained in Roman law. Only in England did the parliament rise to the rank of a separate and independent power holder representing the moneyed and landed interests. Otherwise not controllable by the crown, and often opposed to it, they claimed their legitimate share in the exercise of political power. By exhibiting wise self-restraint, the institution of parliament survived the period of Tudor despotism. Finally, again for strictly environmentally conditioned reasons, the parliament in the Puritan rebellion and the Glorious Revolution triumphed over the royal prerogative and ascended to the rank of the central power holder of the new state society that had become constitutional.

All this is too well known to require elaboration. It was this power configuration which inspired Harrington, Locke, Bolingbroke, and, finally, Montesquieu and the French Enlightenment to develop the theory of the separated state organs sharing in the exercise of political power. It may seem ironical that, when visiting England (1729–31), Montesquieu misinterpreted the then existing British constitutional order by reading into it a separation of the legislative from the executive function which, on principle at least since William III and Anne and actually after the advent of the Hanoverians, had disappeared, just as Polybius had idealized a Roman republican constitution which at the time of his description was already in the process of disintegration.

In retrospect it appears that the invention or discovery of the representative technique was as decisive for the political evolution of the West and, through it, of the world as the mechanical inventions—steam, electricity, the combustion engine, atomic power—have been for man's technological evolution. Government is indispensable for the organized state society. Only the representative technique permitted the institutionalization of the parliament as a power holder separate and independent from the government.

The independence of the courts, then, was the logical completion of an all-round system of independent power holders. Without the introduction of the representative principle, political power in the western world would have remained monolithic indefinitely, as it remained so in the non-western realm until it was undermined by the fertilization of liberal constitutionalism of the West. Certainly intellectual influences of the Renaissance and Reformation, softening up the traditional *mystique* of unconditional submission to the government, have contributed their full share. But the role of political theory can hardly be overestimated. The palm goes to Locke. By retrospectively interpreting the experience of the Glorious Revolution and projecting it, as a valid generalization, into the future, he dissected the omnipotent Leviathan of state power into its different functional segments and, by this monumental surgery, emasculated it. And hardly less credit goes to Montesquieu, who imparted to the technical separation of state functions and their distribution among different power holders the ideological value of shared powers for the preservation of the liberty of the subjects.

In the world-shaking accomplishment of the prerevolutionary political theory that tried to tame the Leviathan by splitting it up, the tragical elements are not lacking. Tailored to the measure of a relatively homogeneous state society of the preindustrial age, it claimed absolute validity for all future state societies. What Locke, Montesquieu, and, to its dire peril, the French Revolution ignored, or chose to ignore—understandably so because their ideological intent was directed against traditional absolutism—was that all government is power. By rationalizing the governmental process, they were led to believe that power could be neutralized and its demonism exorcised. The terrible answers were first the Terror of the Convention and, after another period of political chaos, Napoleon's dictatorship.

Early constitutionalism was blithely oblivious of the truism that the general will does not operate automatically, that it must be given unified direction by what in modern terms is called "political leadership." Political leadership is nothing else but the conscious exercise of political power. Rousseau's original concept of the general will took the power element for granted; it was totalitarian by definition and implication. But the subsequent mechanistic construction of state and government divided the power process into equipoised segments which were optimistically expected, by virtue of the assumed goodness and co-operativeness of human nature, to play harmoniously together for the promotion of the common welfare. Political experience since the eighteenth century has taught that all state functions are instrumentalities of political leadership. The task of the government is no longer confined, if ever it was, to the execution of the general will articulated by the laws of the assembly. Leadership gives guidance and direction to the general will. Legislation and execution of the laws, instead of being separate or separable functions, are nothing but different techniques of political leadership. And it is consistent with the biology of the power process that political leadership falls to the government, a small and effective body of men capable of producing concerted action, instead of to the assembly, multimembered, cumbrous, and more often than not incapable of producing a unified political will.

The New Tripartism of State Functions

Nothing is more difficult to dislodge than an intrenched thought pattern, and the doctrine of the "separation of powers" is the most hallowed concept of constitutional theory and practice. Moreover, in wrecking the idol, the iconoclast cannot be satisfied with the demolition job. Having jettisoned the ballast of the classical tripartism of the executive, legislative, and judicial functions, he must replace it by a new analysis of the process of political power that is attuned to the realities of the pluralist mass society of the twentieth century. A new tripartism is suggested, based on the distinction between policy determination, policy execution, and policy control.[12]

Policy determination.—Policy determination, or policy decision, refers to the major choices of policy the state community is called on to make. Policy decisions are the fundamental resolves of the community governing its immediate and often its remote future. They pertain to foreign as well as to domestic matters; their objective may be political, or socioeconomic, or even moral when dealing with religious matters. With the border line between the political and the economic substance practically obliterated, the two are inextricably intertwined, and there are hardly any exclusively political policy decisions.

The primary policy decision with which a nation is confronted is its choice of the political system and, within it, the pattern of government it wishes to live under, provided the determination is left to the constituent power of the people and not imposed by force. All constitutions, therefore, are major policy decisions: whether a nation will adopt the constitutional monarchy or republic, parliamentarism or presidentialism. But such instances of the exercise of the constituent power are rare. Otherwise major policy decisions are called for whenever the clash of plural interests and ideologies requires a solution which, more often than not, must be a compromise. Examples in recent political experience are many: the choice between free trade or protection; the attitude of the state toward the religious establishments involving, for instance, the separation of church and state; the educational policy; the alternatives of an economic system of private enterprise untrammeled by government control or of government regulation of business; the welfare state; the relations between labor and management in the productive process; the disposition of the natural resources; socialization and nationalization of segments, or of the entire range, of the national economy; the subsidizing of agriculture; the transition from an agricultural to an industrial economy; fiscal and monetary policies; the tax structure and its influence on the distribution of wealth.

Major policy decisions have become increasingly frequent in the field of foreign relations. Since the border line between domestic and foreign affairs likewise has disappeared, their repercussions on the domestic domain are far-reaching. Examples are: the adhesion to, or secession from, an alliance, or the neutrality toward international combinations; containment of communism; the support of underdeveloped countries; the recognition of a foreign government; issues of national security; disarmament; the attitude toward what is called colonialism and imperialism.

Though in our era of accelerated revolutionary change major policy decisions, whether domestic or foreign, may increase in frequency, they remain relatively rare. In practice it may not always be easy to delineate them from the lesser decisions. But in a pluralist society governed by the interplay of public opinion, the interest the measure arouses in the public and its impact on wide and different layers of the society are indicative of its character as a major policy decision.

It is obvious that the major policy decisions are initiated and formulated by a relatively small number of persons. The sociological law of the predominant role of the elite or oligarchy in the power process of any state society, whatever its political system or pattern of government, applies to the domain of policy determination with added force. Though the policy decision often may be inspired and influenced by the invisible power holders, its formalization and legalization are incumbent on the legitimate power holders, that is, the government and the parliament. It depends on the prevailing pattern of government whether in the policy initiation the government or the parliament takes the lead. But it is inherent in the power process of constitutionalism that at one point in the process they are called on to co-operate.

As a rule the mass of the power addressees is excluded from the initiation of the policy decision, even though in the constitutional democracy they may participate in the subsidiary function of confirmation either directly by referendal procedures or indirectly by elections. The fuller the democratic implementation of the specific political regime, the more the interposition of the electorate into the power process will be insisted on. For this reason constitutional amendments often require popular ratification. But by no means do all constitutional amendments involve major policy decisions, not even in the United States, where the formal constitutional amendment is subject to a special political procedure. Since the Civil War perhaps only the federal income tax and the popular election of senators (Nos. XVI and XVII, 1913) and prohibition (Nos. XVIII and XXI, 1919 and 1933, respectively) come under this category. Most of the numerous amendments of the Swiss constitution, once the policy decision of expanding the federal jurisdiction at the expense of the cantons had been cast at the beginning of this century, were merely subsequent implementations.

Obviously, from the technical viewpoint, the primary instrumentality for the performance of the policy decision is legislation. Invariably all domestic policy decisions require statutory formalization. If the policy decision is initiated by the government, as is the rule, parliamentary indorsement implies shared power: the parliament assumes coresponsibility for the measure. If the parliament rejects or modifies the measure, it exercises policy control over the governmental leadership. In contrast to previous periods, legislation has also become the normal technique for legalizing policy decisions in the field of foreign affairs. Here Locke's third, the "federal," power has a particularly modern ring. Most constitutions require parliamentary confirmation of international treaties. Moreover, since hardly any foreign-policy decision can be activated without financial appropriations, the parliament has another opportunity to share in the policy determination. If, under exceptional conditions, a major policy decision has to be initiated by the executive power holder alone—as was the case with President Roosevelt's destroyer deal, which brought the United States into the war against the Axis—the subsequent normalization of the situation by Lend-Lease duly injected congress into the policy-determination process.

Applying now the category of the policy-decision function to the political systems of constitutionalism and autocracy, one may say that in the former the function is shared by government and parliament with or without subsequent injection of the electorate into the process, while in the latter the single power holder monopolizes the exercise of the policy-decision function, even though, for the pretense of national unity, he may command parliamentary indorsement or popular ratification.

Policy execution.—Policy execution is the instrumentality for the implementation of the policy decisions. The techniques employed extend to the entire range of state activities. Frequently they consist of implementing legislation. The majority of the statutory enactments that fill our statute books either are implementations of antecedent basic policy decisions, applying them to the requirements of community life, or are of a strictly utilitarian character, regulating the normal course of societal relations. Examples of such utilitarian measures couched in legislation are sanitary regulations, weights and measures, and others. Their specific character is that they are value-indifferent and that the plural interests neither condition, nor are affected by, them. Legislation, therefore, has ceased to be a functional category of its own, separate and separable from the other state activities, as was assumed in the old-style tripartism theories.

The most ubiquitous aspect of policy execution—in this sense corresponding to the traditional category of the "executive"—is administration, that is, the application of the policy decisions as well as of the utilitarian regulations of social relations to the requirements of community life. For this purpose policy execution is equipped with a staff—civil service, government bureaucracy— applying the general norms of the legislation to the individual situations. What may be considered the most conspicuous phenomenon of the technological state society of the twentieth century is what has been called the transformation of the legislative into the administrative state. The tremendous increase in administrative intervention of the welfare state in community life necessitated the transfer of large segments of the lawmaking function from the parliament to the government and its agencies. This resulted in the increasing density of contacts between the individual citizen and the state authorities. In terms of volume, administration constitutes the most substantial area of the policy execution and of the state activity as a whole.

Legislation and administration, however, are not the only instrumentalities of the policy-execution function. The judicial function, the third coequal partner of the classical tripartite division, likewise suffers, under the new tripartism, a significant *capitis deminutio*. To the unsophisticated eye of Locke the judiciary did not seem to participate in the power process. When the Two Treatises of Government (1690) were written, the Act of Settlement (1700) had not yet been passed. Nor did Montesquieu feel compelled to raise the judicial to the rank of the other two powers of government and assembly. The famous—and, to many, cryptic—word that the judicial power "devient, pour ainsi dire, invisible et presque nul," acquires a definite meaning:[13] what the judges do is merely to apply the general legal norms to the individual cases before them. Therefore, executing the law much in the same way, if by different techniques, as does the administration, they do not perform an independent function in the power process. Adjudication is basically policy execution. The independence of the judiciary from the power holders, government and parliament, was a political rather than a functional postulate, motivated in England by the desire to curb the royal prerogative and to establish the rule of law. In France the revolutionary constitutions, influenced by the experience with the *parlements*, while asserting the judicial independence with a vengeance, characteristically failed to elevate the judiciary to the rank of a coequal partner of the political process.

The American judicial review, by which the courts, by opposing a decision of both the congress and the president, have constituted themselves a genuine third power holder, is wholly anomalous. Substantially it belongs to the category of policy control and will be discussed at its proper place.*

Applying the category of the policy execution to the political systems of constitutionalism and autocracy, we may say that under constitutionalism, like the policy-decision function, it is shared by the several power holders. The parliament participates in it by legislation, implementing the policy decisions, and by the utilitarian regulations of community life; the government shares in the function by administration through its agencies and staffs; and the courts by adjudicating individual controversies under the laws and checking on the legality of governmental administration in conformity with the authorizing statute. In an autocracy, on the other hand, the single power holder monopolizes also the policy-execution function, with such subdelegations to hierarchically subordinated assistants and auxiliary organs as he may think convenient to establish, without granting them independence beyond his final command and control.

Policy control.—The crux of the new tripartism lies in the third function: policy control.[14] In historical perspective constitutionalism has been the search for the most effective devices for taming and limiting political power, first, of the government alone and, subsequently, of all and any power holders. Rational man is congenitally suspicious of unrestrained power, and for good reasons. The progress of society toward individual self-determination corresponds to the progressive institutionalization of the devices for the containment of political power, and the current retrogression of liberty is reflected in the weakening or elimination of such control devices. The foremost mechanism for the control of political power consists in assigning the different state functions to different state organs which, while exercising them in complete autonomy and under their own responsibility, are ultimately compelled to co-operate to produce the valid will of the state. If

* See below, pp. 243 ff.

powers are shared among several power holders, the individual power holder is restrained and controlled by "checks and balances"; "le pouvoir arrête le pouvoir," in Montesquieu's celebrated formula. How, then, is the control function exercised? The answer depends on the specific pattern of government, and, indeed, the differentiation lies in the degree and intensity with which the various control devices are parceled out among the different power holders. In the formative stages of constitutionalism these controls operated only between the government—crown—and the parliament. Subsequently, the original dualism transformed itself into the familiar triangular power configuration in which the electorate gains a control function of its own as arbiter between the other two. The historical turning point when the electorate entered the political scene came in England with Pitt's triumph (1784) at the general election over the Fox-North coalition.[15] But in England the full recognition of the electorate as supreme power holder had to wait for almost another century, until the democratization of the suffrage by the reforms of 1867 and 1884. The breakthrough of the electorate or "the people" must be attributed to the political theory and practice of the French Revolution. At first the Constituante of 1789 tended toward Montesquieu's elitist concept of representation. But the constitution of the Convention (1793), firmly establishing the principle that a government's authority acquires legitimacy only by the will of the people, introduced universal (manhood) suffrage as the articulation of Rousseau's general will. The nineteenth century never challenged the democratic foundation of the power process, institutionalized by the extension of the suffrage, by free and technically honest elections, and by the free competition of the political parties organizing the electorate as an independent power holder. The control function, thus, devolved on all power holders: government, parliament, and the electorate.

However, before proceeding, it is essential to distinguish *shared* from *controlled* power. Shared power as such amounts to a mutual control of power. If two power holders have to co-operate in the exercise of a function, for example, in the legislative process, neither of them can impose its will on the other. But the sharing of power is not the whole story of the power control. There exist also autonomous control techniques which an individual power holder may exercise at his discretion and independently from the others. The division of the legislative function between two houses of parliament under bicameralism; the requirement of senatorial confirmation of a presidential appointment in the United States; the need for the countersignature by the cabinet of a political act of the monarchical or republican head of state; the mandatory referendum of the people on a constitutional amendment—these are illustrations of control inherent in the constitutional requirement that a political act becomes valid only if the several power holders share in its performance and consummation. On the other hand, there exist specific rights of certain state organs or power holders that are exercised autonomously, subject only to its political discretion. They are optional only, rather than mandatory. Illustrations are: the vote of non-confidence passed by the parliament against the cabinet; the right of the government to dissolve the parliament; the right of the electorate to reject, by referendum, a law passed by parliament and government; the president's veto of congressional legislation; the judicial review of the constitutionality of congressional or parliamentary legislation. All these are autonomous control devices reserved to an individual power holder and exercised independently of the action of another.

The hub of the policy control function lies in the invocation and enforcement of political responsibility. This is the situation in which a specific power holder is accountable, for the conduct of the function assigned to him, to another power holder, for example, the government to the parliament, the parliament to the government, and either of them, or both, to the electorate.

Once again, political responsibility is an invention of modern constitutionalism. Responsibility of an elected official of course was well institutionalized in ancient constitutionalism, for example, in the accountability of the Athenian officials before a quasi-judicial authority;[16] in the various devices for holding the republican official in Rome liable for the performance of his office duties; or, in the remarkable organization of the Venetian oligarchic republic, the permanent non-prescriptible liability of all officials. Likewise in the autocratic environment, the personal responsibility of his subordinates to the single power holder remains an indispensable prerequisite of the power monopoly.

But responsibility as a device of constitutional control, once again, is a British invention. It replaced the previous and cruder forms of criminal liability by impeachment and bills of attainder the parliaments had practiced against the king's advisers and officials. The importance of this device for the constitutional control of political power can hardly be overestimated. It was the rational ramrod of constitutionalism against the mystical submission of the power addressees under the God-ordained authority of the government. Once integrated into the political process, the invocation of political responsibility made it possible to withdraw the legal right to exercise authority from the government or the parliament in power and to remove and renew them constitutionally, that is, without resort to violence.

Political responsibility is institutionalized, according to the prevailing pattern of government, primarily as the parliamentary vote of censure directed against the government, as governmental dissolution of the assembly directed against the parliament, and as elections by which the people confirm or reject the parliamentary and governmental personnel. Political responsibility has become the most effective technique of control exercised by one power holder over another.

To apply now the category of policy control to the political systems of constitutionalism and autocracy: constitutionalism, in addition to being a government under the rule of law, is responsible government. Responsible government is one in which the exercise of political power is reciprocally shared and mutually controlled. The totality of the control techniques are institutionalized in the constitution. The supremacy of the constitution is the capstone of the integral system of political controls.

Autocratic government, by contrast, is characterized by the absence of any techniques by which the political responsibility of the single power holder could be effectively invoked, short of revolution. His power is beyond constitutional limitations. Were he subordinated to any other power holder capable of controlling him, the autocratic system would lose its identity and cease to exist.

III. Patterns of Government in Autocracy

The Key for the Classification of the Patterns of Government

In the preceding chapters the road has been cleared for the distinction, in this and the next chapter, of the various patterns of government within each of the two basic categories of autocracy and constitutionalism that have appeared in the historical evolution of political organization. The key is found in the institutionalization of shared or concentrated exercise of political power.

Autocracy is characterized by the existence of a single power holder who combines, in his jurisdiction, policy decision and policy execution and who, in addition, is beyond effective controls. Constitutionalism, on the other hand, is a political system in which several independent power holders coexist and co-operate. The specific arrangements for the interplay and interaction of the several power holders in policy determination, policy execution, and policy control, by which the will of the state is formed, constitute the essence of the patterns of constitutional government.

However, it should be kept in mind that, although the dichotomy of the political systems is basic, both "autocracy" and "constitutionalism" are generic terms. Within each of the two systems considerable variations in the power configuration occur, depending on the national tradition of the specific state society as well as on the sociopolitical climate of the period. Moreover, there exist transitional and intermediary situations in which a symbiosis has developed, deriving from the fact that one political system has borrowed arrangements indigenous to the other. In spite of such multiple combinations, the basic patterns of government within each of the general categories are surprisingly few.

Amid the tribulations constitutional democracy has faced for a generation and more and with the contemporary resurgence of autocracy, it is easily forgotten that, over the longest stretches of history, unconditional submission of the power addressees under the unchallenged rule of the prevailing power holder was the invariable order of political organization. Periods of relative freedom of the power addressees to fashion their own political destiny were as rare as they were intermittent. The Hebrew communities under the law of God, the glory and misery that was Greek democracy, and the legality-conscious civic virtue of the Roman republic were mere islands in the flood of absolute state power. Thereafter, absolutism, modeled on the Roman and Byzantine imperial establishment, swept over the European world to last for centuries, again briefly interrupted by the oligarchic constitutionalism of the cities of Italy and western Europe until, by a miraculous concatenation of political, economic, and religious incentives, modern constitutionalism dawned in Puritan England. Autocracy of the single power holder, thus, has been the standard pattern of political civilization in Europe. Until modern times it prevailed without interruption outside western Europe, from which constitutional government spread first to the western hemisphere and by now has engulfed the globe.

If, negatively, autocracy is the absence of power shared among several independent power holders and, positively, the concentration of all power in the hands of a single power holder not subject to constitutional limitations, it may seem easy to discern, by these criteria, the autocratic system. However, even though the various applications may seem to operate with similar or identical power arrangements, "autocracy" is an over-all term. Its subdivisions, or patterns of government, are determined by the ideological *telos* on which the power monopoly of the single power holder is predicated. It would serve, therefore, no meaningful classificatory purpose to lump together under the same pattern of autocratic government Byzantine caesaropapism, the Tibetan Buddhist theocracy, and Hitler's Third Reich, all undoubtedly autocratic structures. Their ideological intent no less than their instrumentalities of government are too different to permit a uniform categorization. Moreover, in our time, the prevalence of the professed belief that the legitimacy of all political power is derived from the will of the people has added a novel feature to the political repertory of autocracy: it disguises its autocratic structure by the adoption of pseudoconstitutional institutions and techniques. Rendering the tribute which the ideological climate of our time demands, it pays lip service to constitutionalism, of which, in actual practice, it is the negation. It is this sinister mimicry which makes the prima facie identification of a specific political regime as an autocracy difficult and requires the insight into its actual process of political power.

Authoritarian and Totalitarian Regimes

Hardly any other political term has suffered more from verbal ambiguity and semantic casuistry than "autocracy." Various appellations are in vogue interchangeably: "dictatorship," derived from the classical application of concentrated powers as crisis government in republican Rome;[1] "despotism" and "tyranny," both used as value judgments focusing on the absence of the rule of law rather than on governmental institutions; "police state," because modern autocracy can maintain itself only through enforced regimentation; and, finally, "totalitarianism" and "authoritarianism," often used synonymously. Most of these terms are descriptive-emotional. For a scientific classification[2] of autocratic regimes the differentiation between totalitarian and authoritarian patterns is serviceable and essential.[3]

The authoritarian regime.—The term "authoritarian" denotes a political organization in which the single power holder—an individual person or "dictator," an assembly, a committee, a junta, or a party—monopolizes political power without permitting the power addressees an effective participation in the formation of the will of the state. The single power holder imposes his policy decisions on the community, he "dictates" them to the power addressees. However, the term "authoritarian" refers rather to the structure of government than to the structure of society. As a rule, the authoritarian regime confines itself to the political control of the state without aspiring to the complete domination of the socioeconomic life of the community. The exclusion of the power addressees from participation in the political process is by no means incompatible with the existence of state organs other than the single power holder, in particular an assembly and courts. But it is characteristic of authoritarian government that such separate organs are either wholly controlled by the single power holder or, in case of conflict with him, are compelled to yield. This type of authoritarian organization almost invariably formalizes the power configuration in a written constitution whose norms, because adjusted to the actual configuration of power, are actually observed. Nor is this political regime incompatible with the observation of the rule of law as articulated by the constitution. The rights of the power addressees to life, liberty, and property are secure insofar as they do not affect the exercise of political power as such. The "normative" state lives side by side with the "prerogative" state.[4] Authoritarian regimes do possess an ideology—no state society can exist without such a moral or intellectual self-justification—but more often than not it is neither consistently formulated nor generally insisted on. In most cases the ideology confines itself to defending and justifying the existing power configuration as traditional, or as best suited for the benefit of the state community. Perhaps the most common and convenient ideology of modern authoritarian regimes is nationalism.

Historically, the authoritarian pattern of government is a most important type of political organization. It is found in the transition from royal absolutism to constitutional democracy, on the one hand, and in our time in the retrogressive process from democratic constitutionalism toward the ascendancy of executive leadership, on the other. For example, the constitutionally limited "legitimist" monarchy under the French Charte of 1814,[5] by virtue of its location on the historical crossroads, retained traits of the autocratic power structure of the *ancien régime*, while at the same time bowing to the constitutional experience of the antecedent French Revolution. In the progressive evolution from autocratic to constitutional government it provides an important link. It served as the model for practically all constitutional monarchies until they had transformed themselves into parliamentary monarchies; its pattern persisted in some states—Germany and the Balkans—to the end of the First World War and occasionally even beyond.

Another significant version was the Bismarckian empire, basically an authoritarian regime, although camouflaged behind a façade of democratic institutions and techniques. The Kaiser appointed and dismissed the Reich chancellor at his discretion, without being bound or influenced by the support, or lack of support, of the government, on the part of the democratically elected Reichstag. The Kaiser and his chancellor monopolized the policy-decision function without being subjected to effective control by either the parliament or the electorate. The Reich chancellor could not be removed by a vote of non-confidence of the Reichstag, and the latter was not consulted in the initiation of policy decisions. No established government or opposition parties existed. Parliamentary government was sidetracked. Party dynamics were haphazard and chaotic, the chancellor enlisting changing *ad hoc* majorities for the legislation to execute his policy decisions. Until its very end, by the country's defeat in 1918, the imperial regime remained authoritarian, without effective participation of the power addressees in the political process.

Authoritarian regimes are also characteristic of the retrogressive evolution from full-fledged democracy to neo-absolutism.

They sprouted, in various disguises, all over Europe after the Indian summer of constitutional democracy had paled in the twenties, in most cases as variants of neopresidentialism. They will be discussed later.*

The totalitarian regime.—By contrast, the term "totalitarian" refers to the socioeconomic dynamism, the way of life, of a state society. The governmental techniques of a totalitarian regime are necessarily authoritarian. But the regime does much more than exclude the power addressees from their legitimate share in the formation of the will of the state. It attempts to mold the private life, the soul, the spirit, and the mores of the citizens to a dominant ideology that the various instrumentalities of the power process force on the non-conformists. The officially proclaimed ideology penetrates into every nook and cranny of the state society; its ambition is "total."

It is obvious that a totalitarian state cannot be operated except by the techniques of command and obedience. The foremost instrumentality of enforcing conformity with the ideological tenets is the police apparatus, omnipresent and omniscient, protecting the security of the regime and weeding out potential resistance. By necessity the totalitarian state is a police state; hence the common equation of the two terms. Another indispensable instrument of social control is the single party, serving not only as a voluntary police force on the broadest possible basis but also as the state-directed tool for ideological indoctrination and co-ordination. The single party distinguishes modern totalitarian states from the historical patterns of autocracy. Commensurate to the totalitarian structure of the state society is the closed power circuit. The tyrannical exclusiveness of the official state ideology does not brook free circulation of, and competition with, other ideologies. The outstanding illustrations of modern totalitarianism are fascism in Italy, National Socialism in Germany, communism in the U.S.S.R., the Soviet satellite states—officially labeled "People's

* See below, pp. 65 ff.

Democracies"—and communist China. Their political institutions and governmental techniques of ideological compulsion are too well known to need further elaboration. However, the term "totalitarian" should be used with caution. It rightly applies only to those configurations of political process in which a dominant ideology is instilled by the power holders into the power addressees by an apparatus of compulsion. Where the paramount state ideology is accepted by the power addressees unconditionally and without challenge—by tradition, religious beliefs, unarticulated consent—the regime may be totalitarian in substance but lacks the essential element of deliberate enforcement. We are not entitled to qualify certain ancient autocracies as totalitarian because the *telos* of the state society and the mythos of social control were too deeply imbedded in the minds of the power adressees to require the continuous mechanism of enforcement. Pharaonic Egypt is a case in point: operated under the state-planned economy that the annual floods of the Nile dictated, dedicated to the death cult, deifying its rulers as the incarnation of the Divine, the society was totalitarian in all but name, even though the mechanism of compulsion may have become so integrated in the mores of the community that it evoked no resistance. There are no records of any revolt of the masses for nearly three thousand years. The identical situation of the complete submission of the power addressees to their ruler—religious or secular—prevailed in all pre-Columbian civilizations, and the recent conjecture that the mystery of the sudden collapse of the Maya states may have been due to a popular rebellion against the priests[6] has, from the comparative viewpoint, very little verisimilitude.

On the other hand, the absolutism of imperial Rome, of Byzantium, of the medieval kings and rulers, while undeniably autocratic and authoritarian, failed to meet the totalitarian standards. The *telos* of the state society, rarely articulated in secular terms, was accepted without disagreement by the power holders and power adressees alike and so deeply ingrained in tradition that it required neither ideological formulation nor enforcement. Secular authority and spiritual monopoly of the Catholic church were complementary; religion was an instrument of government, and government a tool of religion. The Galilean was subversive toward the emperor as Savonarola was later toward the state, protecting the monopoly of the Catholic church. Only the Reformation created the legitimate dissenter who, inspired by the new ideology of spiritual and secular self-determination, claimed the right to dissent as an inalienable human endowment. Modern totalitarianism, therefore, with its formidable apparatus of compulsion and conformity, can be properly evaluated only when measured by the standard of legitimate dissent.

The analyst of the realities of the power process will find no insurmountable difficulties to differentiating between an authoritarian and a totalitarian regime. In most cases the criterion lies in the existence or absence of an official state ideology. Most autocracies of the past and many of the present are satisfied with the authoritarian exercise of political power—for the most varied reasons, if for no other than to hold and enjoy power—and do not attempt to infuse by compulsion a dominant state ideology into the masses of the power addressees. Neither Napoleon's authoritarianism, nor that of his nephew, nor Bismarck's rule reveals any traces of totalitarianism; all were either carried by the nearly unanimous consent of the power addressees or at least acceptable to the vast majority of them. In most contemporary authoritarian regimes—Pilsudski's in Poland, Vargas' in Brazil, and the host of the *caudillismo* governments in the Latin American *ambiente*—official state ideologies are either totally lacking or artificial, weak, and ineffective, as in Franco Spain or Peronist Argentina.

Even under the most auspicious circumstances of the state's control of the mass-communication media, integral totalitarianism seems difficult to attain. It requires a particularly virulent and seductive ideology and a favorable political environment and climate. Some nations may be more conditioned for it than others.

Germans, Russians, and Chinese, traditionally authority-minded and submissive to state power, seem to offer a better national predisposition than, for example, the pragmatic Anglo-Saxons and the skeptical Latins. Italian fascism was never more than a thin veneer overlaying native cynicism and ineradicable individualism. And it may well be that integral totalitarianism may prove a passing historical interlude. This is, possibly, the real portent of the process of de-Stalinization and liberalization seemingly under way, since 1953, in Soviet Russia and the significance of the tragedy of the Hungarian revolution of 1956. Perhaps it is impossible to freeze permanently the variety of human impulses in an impermeable mold. Orwell's nightmare may remain the fantasy of a morbid mind.

Finally, it may be asked whether a democratic totalitarianism is feasible, that is, the compulsory subjection of the power addressees to the unanimous acceptance of the democratic ideology. The answer cannot fail to be negative. An attempt in this direction was undertaken by the Jacobins; in spite of its signal failure, it remains one of the most fascinating episodes in the recent political history of man.[7] The essence of the democratic way of life is the free competition, in the open power circuit, of ideologies and the plural forces promoting them, and the enforcement of consent is a democratic *contradictio in adjecto*.

Three Patterns of Autocracy

Absolute monarchy.—Classic among the non-totalitarian autocracies is the absolute monarchy of the European nation-state system. Its legitimacy was rooted in the hereditary claim, unchallenged by the power addressees, of a specific dynasty to the throne. Its supernatural sanctification was reflected by the familiar formula of kingship "by the grace of God."[8] The pattern may be illustrated briefly by its politically most influential application in the French absolute monarchy of Louis XIV, of *l'Etat c'est moi* fame, and his successors. Policy decision and policy execution were monopolized by the king as the single power holder, who ruled and governed beyond any controls by other organs or by the people at large. The power mechanism was so effective that, characteristically, the Fronde failed, while the contemporaneous rebellion of the Puritans against the restoration of royal absolutism attempted by the Stuarts ended in the defeat of the crown. However, constitutional limitations of the French king were believed to exist in the *lois fondamentales du royaume* that reflected the Christian morality of the period and, to some extent, in the intermittent resistance of the courts in Paris and the provinces—*parlements*—against royal arbitrariness; these courts possessed the customary right to render the king's edicts and ordinances executory by registration. If in disagreement with the enactment because of an alleged violation of the *coutume*, they could address objections —the *Remontrance*—to the king, who then could order the registration by *lettres de jussion* and, if the parlement persisted, break the opposition by having himself carried into the court on a litter —*lit de justice*—and command registration which the judges could not refuse.[9] None of these devices proved effective restraints on the king's absolute power, though they helped to stimulate the latent consciousness of constitutionalism. For his policy determination the king utilized consultative councils of dignitaries whose members served at his discretion, and for the policy execution—of considerable impact in a state-directed mercantilist economy—an administrative bureacracy of remarkable ability (*intendants*). Devolution of functions to hierarchically subordinated officials or agencies, however, never amounted to sharing in any degree his absolute exercise of power. It was against this pattern of royal autocracy that the attack of liberal constitutionalism was directed.

On the other hand, in Germany and eastern Europe—Poland and Hungary—the monolithic power configuration of absolutism was mitigated, to some extent and for some time, by the dualistic structure of the state society: the ruler shared power with the organized estates (*Ständestaat*) of nobility, clergy, cities, and, in Scandinavia, farmers. But by the end of the period these corporate elements had become subservient to royal absolutism almost everywhere.

Napoleon's plebiscitary Caesarism.—Napoleon's authoritarian pattern of government merits attention in our context for two reasons: its institutional mechanism presents an authoritarian power configuration administratively just as efficient as that of the *ancien régime*, but it is hidden behind a façade elaborately decorated in the style of the democratic ideology inherited from the antecedent French Revolution.[10] By this skilful mixture, Bonapartism established the pattern for modern authoritarian government. Activating Sieyès' maxim that confidence must come from below but power from above, Napoleon's creative genius realized that political leadership must transcend the mechanics of the governmental process if the general will is to achieve its self-realization. To make authoritarian political leadership acceptable to the French who had gone through the unforgettable experience of the revolution, he camouflaged the monopoly of policy decision and policy execution by pseudodemocratic arrangements of the governmental process which offered to the power addressees the semblance of shared and controlled power. Under the instrument of the year VIII (1799), drafted, in the main, by Napoleon himelf, no fewer than four bodies or assemblies were established. Policy decisions were initiated by the First Consul and his ministers through the Conseil d'Etat, his most felicitous and lasting creation. The Legislative Corps deliberated on the legislative measures submitted to it for policy execution without being permitted to vote on them. Thereafter the Tribunate voted on them without being permitted to discuss them. Later, after the eclipse of both assemblies, the Senate, composed of hand-picked devotees of the regime, whom Napoleon spoiled and by whom, in turn, he was spoiled, became Napoleon's exclusive instrument for policy execution through legislation by *senatus consultum* and administration. The elective principle, dear to the revolutionary tradition, was given lip service by the device of the national list, the apex of a pyramid of indirect elections beginning, at the lowest level, with the elective lists for the *arrondissements* and followed by those established for the *départements:* each of the lists consisted of one-tenth of the members of the preceding one. Eligibility for all assemblies depended upon membership in the national list, removal from which, by fiat of the government, automatically terminated the qualification for public office. The members of the Legislative Corps and the Tribunate were selected by the Senate; the Senate nominees were in practice chosen by the First Consul and emperor.

But this was not all. The very multiplicity of the organs participating in the legislative process destroyed their efficiency. Power was shared to the point of its complete dilution and emasculation. The several assemblies, deliberately isolated from one another, were confined to exercising a specific segment of the legislative process without being able to co-ordinate their functions to the point that they could control the single power holder. The paralysis of powers excessively shared gave full rein to the political leadership of the emperor and his entourage of able advisers and administrators. It functioned so well that even the prolonged absences of the emperor campaigning all over Europe did not affect the smooth operation. When Napoleon had justified the trust of the French nation by his achievements in war and peace as consolidator of the French Revolution, the Tribunate—which had shown itself more obstreperous than the other assemblies—was dissolved and the Legislative Corps condemned to wither on the vine. In addition, he practiced the technique of what was called "*gémination,*" that is, the assignment of identical functions to several organs or persons whose actions mutually tended to control themselves so that the emperor was in the position to pull all strings of the machinery at will. Moreover—and it is from this device that the pattern derives its name of "plebiscitary Caesarism"—

Napoleon created the basis of democratic legitimacy for his rule by submitting his three constitutions to plebiscites (1800, 1802, 1804). Even if their technique had conformed to modern requirements of honesty, which it failed to do, and if they had not been staged ex post facto, there is no doubt that they would have demonstrated the overwhelming indorsement of the regime by the French people.

Neopresidentialism.—Napoleon's authoritarian regime was in his time a unique power configuration, combining, at least in the initial period of operation, the semblance of democratic constitutionality with strict hierarchy in the chain of command. It was bound to disappear with the man who had fashioned it. But it offered to later authoritarian regimes the model for the monopoly of policy decision and policy execution without effective policy controls behind the semblance of democratic legitimacy. It was imitated, still in legitimist disguise, by Napoleon III, with lesser skill and a more articulate opposition, but equally supported by the bourgeois *classe dirigeante* economically benefiting from the regime. Its modern version is the authoritarian pattern of government called neopresidentialism.[11]

The term "neopresidentialism" as used here has practically nothing in common with American presidentialism except the name. It denotes a political regime in which, through specific constitutional arrangements, the chief executive—president—is superior in political power to all other organs of the state. None of them is permitted to rise to the rank of a genuine power holder capable of competing with his factual monopoly or of controlling it. By excluding the power addressees from effective participation in the formation of the will of the state, through a deliberately narrow suffrage and by manipulated electoral procedures, neopresidentialism is basically authoritarian. It does not dispense altogether with a parliament, cabinet, and nominally independent courts, but in the hierarchy of the power configuration they are strictly subordinated to the chief executive. From totalitarianism it is separated by the non-existence or the vacuity of a dominant state ideology. But in general the regime rests on a constitutional basis much in the same sense as the constitutionally limited monarchy: for the formation of the will of the state the existing constitutional procedures are observed.

During the last decades, particularly since the First World War, which witnessed the disintegration of constitutional democracy in many lands where it had been implanted artificially, the pattern of neopresidentialism enjoys an increasing popularity because it guarantees the single power holder the undisputed power monopoly without exposing his regime to the opprobrium of being out of step with the principle of popular legitimacy. Often it proves to be the only alternative to a constitutionless autocracy. It occurs usually either after the experiment with constitutional democracy has failed or, in the opposite direction, as the halfway house on the road from traditional autocracy to a future, more genuine democracy.

Among earlier applications of neopresidentialism are Horthy's rule in Hungary, in the disguise of the traditional legitimist *mystique* of the "Holy Crown," and the regimes of Kemal Pasha in Turkey and of Seipel and his successors, Dollfuss and Schuschnigg, in Austria. Likewise, when disintegrating, the constitutional democracy in Weimar Germany became perverted to neopresidentialism.*

A more recent—and influential—variant of neopresidentialism is offered by the Pilsudski regime in Poland under the constitution of 1935: elective assemblies—Sejm and Senate—continued to function as the democratic blinds, but the elections, based on a highly restricted suffrage of "patriotically" reliable voters, were rigged and the independence of the assemblies curbed to the point where, even if in mutual agreement, they could not overrule the presidential leadership. All organs were carefully emasculated so that they could not interfere with the president.

* See below, pp. 95–96.

The Polish precedent, in turn, influenced the Estonian constitution of 1938 as well as the spurious Vargas constitution of Brazil (1937), which also borrowed heavily from the variant in corporative Portugal under the constitution of 1933. With its attractive feature of being outwardly based on democratic legitimacy, the pattern became particularly popular in Latin America for dressing up, in the new fashion, the old-style indigenous *caudillismo* system, as evidenced by the Perón constitution of 1949, with its significant aspect that the president may succeed himself indefinitely. But its most fitting environment is in new states shedding colonial domination or emerging from their historical setting of monarchical absolutism. Neopresidentialism is the hallmark of Nasser's constitution in Egypt (1956) and of Ngo Dinh Diem's instrument in South Viet-Nam (1956). Its spirit hovers likewise over the Pakistan constitution of 1956 and has visibly come home to roost in Syngman Rhee's perversion of the original model of American presidentialism which the American occupation authorities saw fit to introduce in Korea. Neopresidentialism is tailored to the measure of horizontal governments wishing to hide their naked power behind a pseudoconstitutional or even pseudodemocratic loincloth. Certainly we have not heard the last word on this convenient type of authoritarianism, particularly suitable for the return trip from constitutional democracy to autocracy.

In all these cases the technique of installation follows a uniform pattern, with certain locally conditioned variations. Either the elections for the constituent assembly are rigged and government-controlled, or, where the elections are tolerably honest, the draft of the authoritarian constitution is dictated to the assembly by the man on horseback or, rather, as is the fashion in our motorized age, by the *caudillo* in the Cadillac. Frequently the plebiscite is utilized for confirming a constitution octroyed by the strong man. The desired results can be better produced by manipulated popular emotionalism plus governmental fraud than it could be in an elected assembly subservient as it may be to the presidential power holder. Near-unanimity, invariably engineered by the absence of alternatives, or compulsory voting, or other effective devices of compulsion, is intended to testify, for the benefit of the gullible world, to the democratic legitimacy of the power holders. What is, perhaps, most perplexing is the willingness of American public opinion to accept the spuriously democratic forms of the investiture of such regimes as the genuine article.

When measured by the accepted standards of democratic legitimacy, such neopresidential regimes certainly may seem objectionable. But in fairness it should be realized that on occasion they fulfil a historical mission. Nations awakening, under the impact of the nationalist wave sweeping over the mid-twentieth century, from centuries of unconditional submission to rank absolutism are unprepared for self-government. This is the situation in all new states outside the educational orbit of the British. They cannot be expected to be plunged into full-scale constitutional democracy without risking demagoguery, chaos, and anarchy. Lacking the organic growth of democratic tenets in their intellectual patrimony, few nations inexperienced in the difficult craft of self-rule are capable of pulling themselves up, Munchausen-like, by their own bootstraps. They often stand in need of an extended transitional period of guidance from above, perhaps until a new generation, trained within the confines of a paternalistic authoritarianism, has become acquainted with the technology of modern administration.

Dictators of our time, as these neopresidential rulers may well be called in spite of the constitutional disguise they choose, are certainly a mixed lot. Among them are status quo-reactionaries wishing to perpetuate the privileges of the ruling class to which they belong, as is frequently the case in Latin America, or unmitigated rogues for whom the lust for power is the driving force. But one may find among them also men of vision, personal integrity, and talent who are called upon to play the role of the *deus ex machina* of socioeconomic progress for the benefit of the masses

of the power addressees, as in the cases of Salazar in Portugal—
modestly acting as the perennial president of the council in an
otherwise neopresidential regime—and Vargas in Brazil. And what
Kemal Pasha has done for technological rejuvenation and democratic education in Turkey should not be minimized. On the other
hand, authoritarianism loses its educational rationale when it is
implanted, usually by force, in states heretofore accustomed to
constitutional government, as was the case of Weimar Germany
or Austria, or of Colombia, the Latin American state with the
longest and most ingrained democratic tradition. When this happens, the retrogressive process will reverse itself sooner or later
without fail.

IV. Patterns of Government
in Constitutional Democracy

Constitutionalism and Constitutional Democracy

Even more than "autocracy," "constitutionalism" is a generic term. As a political system it includes several patterns of government, all characterized by the existence of several independent power holders among whom the exercise of political power is constitutionally distributed and who are required to co-operate, by pre-established constitutional procedures, in the formation of the will of the state. However, by the way of introduction, a basic clarification of the term is necessary.

Historically, the meaning of "constitutionalism" is twofold. It refers to both the constitutional and the constitutional-*democratic* political organization. These are by no means identical, and the re-emergence of authoritarian regimes in our time lends weight to the importance of the distinction. To be "constitutional," the state must possess a "constitution," whether formalized in a written instrument or merely imbedded in the national mores. A constitution, in this sense, is a set of fixed norms governing the relations between the power holders and the power addressees as well as the interaction of the power holders in the formation of the will of the state. But the existence of formalized rules for the governmental process does not necessarily imply that the political climate is democratic. It is true that the very first political civilization, the one that literally invented constitutional government, the Greek polis state, happened to be organized as a full-fledged democracy. But states existed long before the dawn of modern democratic constitutionalism that were genuinely constitutional, that is, governed by a fixed set of norms; by no stretch of the imagination, however, could these states be classified as democratic, because the mass of the power addressees did not participate in the political process. Republican Rome, the Italian city-states of the medieval and Renaissance periods, and similarly organized municipalities in western and northern Europe are significant cases in point. England enjoyed constitutional government at least from the time of the Glorious Revolution, yet, until after the Great Reform of 1832, without a democratic basis for the power configuration. And, perhaps most important of all, the constitutionally limited monarchy of the legitimist persuasion, prevailing in most of Europe during the nineteenth century and widely adopted elsewhere, cannot be denied the character of a constitutional state. This pattern not only was non-democratic and even tenaciously resistant to democracy but frequently served as the frame of what in modern terms would be qualified as strictly authoritarian government. The final stage, constitutional democracy, was reached relatively recently when the mass of the power addressees, organized by the political parties as electorate, participated, by the extension of the suffrage and by honest elections, in the political process and rose to the rank of an independent power holder in its own right. This happened in England, France, the United States, and other key states as late as in the nineteenth century. Historically, therefore, constitutionalism was the halfway house between the traditional absolutism of the royal establishment and the classes affiliated with it and the modern era of constitutional democracy.

In our time the term "constitutionalism" has become ambivalent because contemporary autocracy—and in this it differs from similar political systems of the pretechnological past—is in the habit of endowing itself with a written "constitution." As mentioned before, this has become the standard practice in both totalitarian and authoritarian regimes; lip service is paid to democratic legitimacy.

In this strictly nominal sense even autocracies are "constitutional." Whether the power process conforms in substance to the requirements of constitutionalism depends on the actual arrangements for the exercise of political power.* In most cases a "constitution" in an autocratic regime is little more than a compilation of utilitarian bylaws governing the mechanism of government controlled by the single power holder.

The Triangular Power Configuration in Constitutional Democracy

The following analysis focuses on the political system of constitutional democracy and its various realizations as patterns of government. The ideological infrastructure common to all of them is the belief that all power emanates from the people; that government and parliament must conform to and abide by the will of the people; and that free and honest elections offer the open power circuit for competing ideologies and the social forces promoting them. The power configuration is triangular: parliament, government, and people. Political power is shared between the several power holders and is subject to their reciprocal controls.

Since the revolutions of the eighteenth century, several patterns have evolved within this common frame of reference, depending on which of the three power holders is preponderant. However, the "pure" types are relatively rare. Cases of syncretistic combinations in which a specific political regime adopts features characteristic of another pattern are frequent. Such composite arrangements often make it difficult to assign a specific political regime to a concrete pattern of government. Moreover, among the different patterns of government embraced by the political system of constitutional democracy, there is none that could claim to be "the

---

* For the important distinction between normative, nominal, and semantic constitutions see below, pp. 147 ff.

best," the one suitable for all nations. The preference of a nation for a specific pattern seems mysteriously related to its traditions and experiences, for example, the German inclination toward the strong executive or the French fixation on assembly government. What superficially appears to be a bewildering variety of applications of constitutional democracy can be reduced to the following basic patterns:

1. If the people, organized as the electorate, are the preponderant power holder, the pattern of government is known as "direct democracy."

2. "Assembly government" is the name for the pattern in which the parliament as the representation of the people is the ascendant power holder.

3. "Parliamentarism" is the name for the pattern in which an equilibrium between the independent power holders, parliament and government, is attempted by integrating the latter into the former: the personnel of the government—cabinet—are simultaneously members of the assembly. Parliamentarism, thus, is interdependence by integration. In actual practice, however, parliamentarism presents itself in two widely divergent forms, depending on whether the parliament is superior in political power to the cabinet or whether the latter is in a position to control the former. The supremacy of the assembly over the government is reflected by the classical French type of parliamentarism. The ascendancy of the cabinet over the parliament is institutionalized in the British cabinet government.

4. If the independent power holders, government and parliament, are kept separated but are constitutionally obligated to co-operate for the formation of the will of the state, interdependence is achieved by co-ordination instead of integration. In view of the executive leadership implied, this pattern is called "presidentialism"; in the United States it is colloquially if erroneously known as government with "separation of powers."

5. Finally, constitutional theorists are in the habit of assigning to the Swiss governmental system a pattern of its own, for which, because of the collegiate structure of the governmental power holder, the appellation "directory government" is common.

The "ideal type," to speak with Max Weber, of a balanced power configuration would be an arrangement in which the several power holders, or at least the government and the assembly, would confront one another with symmetrically matched powers so that none could dominate the other. This was the mechanistic-equilibristic dream of the political theory of early constitutionalism. It remained a utopian vision to which the reality of the power process never conformed. It appears a biological law of the constitutional state that the center of political gravity continually shifts. It oscillates between the ascendancy of the legislative assembly and the executive leadership of the government. Periods of normalcy tend to increase the weight of the parliament in the political scales; periods of crisis, that of executive leadership. Since the end of the nineteenth century—which practically may be said to have extended to the eve of the First World War—the world has lived in an uninterrupted crisis, reflecting the world revolution under way in the twentieth century. Consequently, the net result is the strengthening of the governmental and the weakening of the parliametary power holder. The phenomenon is universal. Slight deviations from this general experience are conditioned by the specific local situations.

On the following pages each of these five patterns of government within the political system of constitutional democracy will be briefly analyzed. In each case the power process will be filtered through the cadres of the new tripartism of policy determination, execution, and control. However, the three power holders—assembly, government, and people—are nothing but mechanical props unless related to what makes the wheels turn round in constitutional democracy, namely, the political party.

The Political Parties and the Governmental Process

Government in the modern technological mass society is party government, regardless of whether the political system is autocratic or constitutional-democratic. The history of the political parties still remains to be written. As a political phenomenon the political party is three hundred years old, at the most; as an institution of the power process it has existed for perhaps not more than half this time. Under the strict definition modern experience requires, a political party is a combination of persons holding similar ideological beliefs and possessing, for their realization, a permanent organization. Groups joined together, usually in the leader-followers relationship, for the pursuit of common political ends were frequent in the past, but the lack of a permanent organization disqualifies them as political parties in the modern sense. They remained factions, as a rule *ad hoc* clienteles of political leaders, a ubiquitous phenomenon of all constitutional states of the past; occasionally they have even appeared in autocracies. Well-known historical illustrations are the republican and aristocratic factions of the late Roman republic; the "circus" parties of the Blues and the Greens, cruelly suppressed by Justinian and Belisarius in the Nika rebellion (532); the *bianchi* and *neri* in medieval Florence. Significantly, the ruling mercantile oligarchy in Venice saw to it, by a diabolically clever combination of elective and lot devices in the designation of the governing officials and committees, that the formation of factions was made impossible.

Nor were the Roundheads and the Cavaliers of the Puritan revolution or even the Whigs and Tories, originating immediately before the Glorious Revolution, political parties in the modern sense. As late as in the eighteenth century, when constitutionalism was already in full operation, Britain did not possess an organized party system. At the most, she experimented with fluctuating aristocratic combinations that supported or opposed the crown.[1] The Philadelphia convention had no political parties, and the

Federalist never tires of diatribes against the divisive influence of factions.

History imposes the conclusion, then, that a causal relationship exists between the political party and the integration of the mass electorate into the power process by the extension of the suffrage. The party system was bound to remain rudimentary at best, so long as the parliament, based on a selective suffrage, was little more than a closed club of dignitaries representing a homogeneous ruling class. The political party is needed and, indeed, indispensable for organizing and activating the political will of a mass electorate. The coincidence of the mass suffrage and its mobilization by political parties is clearly evidenced by the first appearance of a political party in the modern technological sense, the Jacobins under the rule of the Convention. Here a concrete political ideology was carried to the masses by rationalized organization and propaganda.[2]

In the United States the emergence of genuine political parties had to wait for the Jacksonian period of mass democratization; the American party dynamism was definitely established before the Civil War. But, once again, the credit for the lasting institutionalization of the political parties goes to Britain. In the sixties of the last century first the Liberals—Joseph Chamberlain and the Birmingham caucus—and a decade later the Conservatives under Disraeli followed the inexorable logic of the democratization of the suffrage by establishing permanent party structures that inculcated their ideologies upon the voters by organization and propaganda, attended to the techniques of the electoral process—registration, nomination of candidates, financing of campaigns—and established the indispensable link between the electorate and the parliamentary and governmental personnel. In short, the emergence of political parties signifies the transition from the oligarchic-bourgeois control of the power process to modern constitutional democracy. Next to the discovery of the representative technique, which as such was instrumental to the institutionaliza-

tion of powers shared among several power holders,* the incorporation of the political party into the political process may be considered the most significant invention in the realm of politics.
But the story does not end here. To the autocratic state society
of the pretechnological past, political parties were unknown; they
were alien to its political climate. For the modern mass society
organized in an autocratic political system, however, the political
party in the form of the single state party has become as indispensable as multipartism for the constitutional-democratic state. It
is the organizational clamp holding together power holders and
power addressees. Without the single party, modern autocracy is
inoperable. The unique exception of the Vargas regime in Brazil[3]
confirms the rule. Ephemeral as the experiment was, it had neither
precedents nor imitations elsewhere.

The discussion will proceed now to the analysis of the five
previously listed patterns within the system of constitutional democracy.

The First Pattern: Direct Democracy

Direct democracy is the pattern of government in which the
people, that is, those who by custom or law are recognized as
"active" citizens, themselves attend conjointly, in popular assemblies—the *ekklesia* of the Greeks—or in subcommittees thereof, to
the policy-decision and policy-control functions and even participate in policy execution of a judicial nature. Policy execution as
administration is usually assigned to officials and magistrates
elected, or chosen by lot, for very short terms of office with narrowly circumscribed jurisdiction. A clear-cut separation of executive, legislative, and judicial functions was unknown to, and practically incompatible with, the theory and practice of direct democracy. The pattern was suitable only for relatively uncompli-
cated societies occupying a small territory. Comparative eth-
nology has largely confirmed Tacitus' statement in *De Germania*

* See above, pp. 38 ff.

xi on the primitive Teutonic tribes: "De minoribus rebus principes consultant, de majoribus omnes."

The most famous example of direct democracy's application is in the Greek city-states, where it was in operation for a period not exceeding two centuries; there it was made possible by the existence of a leisure class which was sustained by a non-technological slave economy. While the Greeks enriched mankind in the arts, literature, philosophy, and the natural and the political sciences, their governmental practice proved a failure. They banished their Washington, Themistocles, who, having saved them from Persian imperialism, had to seek a precarious asylum at the court of the archenemy. They ostracized Aristides, his name ever since the byword for honesty in politics. They made Socrates drink the hemlock cup. They were beguiled by Cleon, ever since the byword for demagoguery. They laughed about Aristophanes and themselves, and they ignored Demosthenes' warning against the Philippian fifth column in their midst, only to complete the Aristotelian cycle under the military boot of the Macedons.

The indifferent success of the Greek experience with direct democracy discouraged its repetition. In spite of similar socio-economic conditions, the early Roman republic avoided it. The territorially limited municipalities in medieval Italy and western Europe remained oligarchies. If at times democratic currents occurred,[4] they were not strong enough to convince the ruling classes of the ability of the mass of the power addressees to participate in the political process.

Direct democracy also made its appearance from the thirteenth century onward in certain Swiss peasant communities and cantons; it was subsequently replaced almost everywhere by representative institutions. Where a semblance of direct democracy was permitted to survive—the *Landsgemeinde* still exists in five small and mostly agrarian cantons—it has become a museum piece rather than an effective technique of government. In almost all cantons the regular representative bodies—cantonal councils

(*Kantonsrat*)—prepare the agenda of the popular assembly, and the government council (*Regierungsrat*) conducts the administration. But, even in the cantons with exclusively representative government, the people also participate in the political process by cantonal referendum. The New England town meeting, likewise rapidly dying out, has too limited a jurisdiction to count politically as direct democracy.

However, certain features of direct democracy have experienced a significant resurrection in recent times in referendal techniques applied for both policy decision and policy control. Constitutional theory speaks of this variant as the semidirect or semirepresentative pattern. The electorate participates by referendum in the policy-decision function, particularly where it is mandatory for constitutional amendments, and, in a number of jurisdictions, it may even initiate policy decision to be subsequently approved by government and parliament.*

The Second Pattern: Assembly Government

Of all patterns of constitutional-democratic government, assembly government is the least known to constitutional theory[5] and, by what little is known of it, the most discredited because when it made its first appearance in revolutionary France it was held responsible for Robespierre's dictatorship and the Terror. Yet, in our time, it has experienced a most unexpected and truly phenomenal revival by having become the standard pattern of government in the Soviet orbit. As a pattern of government it is Janus-faced, capable of serving as the organizational tool for democracy and autocracy alike.

The first, obviously accidental, appearance of assembly government coincides with the emergence of modern constitutionalism. The Long Parliament in England (from 1640 to 1649) ruled and governed as the single power holder until subjugated by Cromwell and the army. Failing to rationalize its factual power monop-

* For a fuller discussion of the referendal procedures see below, pp. 263 ff.

oly by a convincing political theory, it provoked violent anti-parliamentarian criticism of the protagonists of incipient democracy, the Independents and Levelers. The famous Agreement of the People (1647) castigated the arrogant absolutism of the legislative assembly and, far ahead of its time, postulated annual elections and other devices for its control. In British constitutional experience assembly government remained merely an episode, unremembered because of its supersession, first by the monarchical restoration and, ultimately, after the Glorious Revolution, by evolving parliamentarism and cabinet government. Locke ignored it, and Montesquieu had no reason for dealing with it or even understanding it.

Assembly government, then, made its first conscious appearance as an authentic pattern of constitutional-democratic government in the French Revolution. Because it was incorporated in the constitution of June 24, 1793, by the Convention, assembly government is known more familiarly as *gouvernment conventionnel*. If the entire course of the French Revolution is visualized as a contest between Montesquieu's cautious concept of elitist representation and Rousseau's principle of radical democratism, the failure of the doctrine-ridden constitution of 1791, carrying Montesquieu's "separation of functions" into the reality of the power process, was bound to be followed by Condorcet's Rousseau-inspired and no less doctrinaire constitutional draft of 1793, on which subsequently the constitution of the Convention was grafted. True to Rousseau's fundamentalism, it was duly ratified by the electorate. Because of the invasion of France by the first coalition, the constitution itself had to be suspended before it became effective. But the revolutionary governments of the Convention lived up to the blueprint in practice. The short-lived experiment ended in the Terror, from which stems the bad reputation it has had ever since, but most unfairly because the government of the Convention contributed its full share to the rescue of France from foreign intervention and saved the revolution from obliteration.

Briefly stated, assembly government amounts to this: the legislative assembly, popularly elected, holds undisputed supremacy over all other state organs, subject only to the sovereign electorate renewing it at regularly recurrent intervals. In contrast to the dual structure of parliamentary government—which, at least in theory, presupposes two independent power holders, the assembly and the government, with reciprocally matching powers—in assembly government the executive is strictly subordinated, the servant or agent of the assembly, appointed and dismissed at the assembly's discretion. The devolution of executive functions to a government or to ministers is of a strictly technical character and does not create rights exercisable outside the instructions and supervision of the assembly. No other state organ is legally in the position to interfere with the autonomy and the power monopoly of the assembly. Consequently, there exists no right of dissolution by the government, though recall by the sovereign electorate may be feasible.[6] Bicameralism is basically incompatible with assembly government. Nor does a chief of state or president, except for strictly ceremonial functions, or a monarchical establishment beyond the control of the assembly fit into the pattern. In short, the pure type of assembly government is undiluted and unadulterated Rousseau, arch-democratic, arch-republican, "monolithic" in the extreme. It presents the strange phenomenon of power concentrated in a democratically elected assembly as the single power holder.

Ever since its introduction by the Convention, assembly government remained a sort of national obsession for the French, appearing as a *deus ex machina* after a revolutionary break or national crisis. The French reverted to it by design in the constitution of the Second Republic in 1848, incongruously blending it with the popularly elected president; more by accident in the government of the National Assembly (1871–75); and almost automatically after the collapse of the authoritarian Vichy regime and the authoritarian interlude of General de Gaulle's Provisional Government. The law of November 2, 1945, governing the period of the drafting of the constitution, remained faithful to the tradition. The first constitution, under communist influence, closely conformed to assembly government. After it had been rejected, for this very reason, by the French electorate in the referendum of June 2, 1946, the Fourth Republic finally adopted the constitution of October 27, 1946, again embodying the classical version of French parliamentarism.

Outside France, assembly government was incorporated in the Swiss constitution of 1848 that was completely revised in 1874.* In the upsurge of democratic fundamentalism after the First World War, assembly government was adopted by all German *Länder* under Weimar (and equally so after 1945 in all four zones of occupation); in the three Baltic states of Latvia, Lithuania, and Estonia; in Austria (at least for the period from 1920 to 1929); and by Kemalist Turkey in the constitution of 1924, in the latter two cases combined with a state president.

Far more important, however, than its appearance in these more or less marginal states is the revival of assembly government in the Stalin constitution of 1936 in the U.S.S.R., from where it spread, after the Second World War, to all satellite states organized as "People's Democracies": Albania, Hungary, Yugoslavia (until 1953), Rumania, and, after brief tradition-oriented interludes, Poland and Czechoslovakia, as well as East Germany, Red China, Outer Mongolia, North Viet-Nam, and North Korea. No communist state fails to conform to this standard pattern.

The adoption of the assembly type of government in the communist sphere of influence is one of the truly puzzling events of recent constitutional history. The question why the communists refurbished a seemingly obsolete and largely forgotten pattern of government this writer, unable to study Russian source material, is not in a position to answer. It may be that the Soviet theorists were attracted by the outwardly arch-democratic character of assembly government, an attraction perhaps responsible also for

* For the Swiss version of assembly government see below, pp. 116 ff.

another communist preference, the plebiscite, likewise a child of the Convention; or, possibly, they adopted it for the more Machiavellian reason that assembly government, by its own biological laws, easily transforms itself into a regime in which a single power holder exercises the monopoly of political power.

There is hardly a more telling demonstration of the cleavage between constitutional nominalism and the reality of the political process than the historical record of assembly government. A multimembered sovereign assembly, rent by party dissensions and intrigues, is technically incapable of the concerted action required for policy decision and policy execution. Effective government is basically oligarchic in structure. It calls for a small compact group of persons willing to take action. An assembly cannot govern. The most it can do is to instal the governing group in the seat of power. Once this has occurred, the Aristotelian shift perverts democracy into autocracy. Assembly government is the archdemocratic rostrum on which autocratic government can be mounted, be it of a single person (dictator), committee, junta, or party. And this may well be the intrinsic reason for the communist preference.

This biological law of assembly government is fully confirmed by the historical record. The Convention fell under the dictatorship of its most effective committees, the Comité de Sûreté Générale and the Comité du Salut Public (et de la Surveillance Générale), respectively, and, in due course, of the latter's chairmen, Danton and Robespierre.[7] The Second Republic, after three years, ended in the dictatorship of Napoleon III, whom the Republic imprudently had raised, by popular vote, to the presidential office. The three Baltic states, after hectic years, turned to authoritarianism, as did Austria after 1929. Mustapha Kemal Pasha (Atatürk), elected four times without opposition on the single-party ticket to the presidency, ran Turkey as a strictly authoritarian regime, succeeded by his prime minister, Ismet Inönü Pasha, with identical prerogatives. Only the German *Länder* under Weimar are exceptions to the rule; but they were politically too marginal to conform to the pattern, being mere subdivisions of the Reich, a unitary government for all practical purposes. The same exception applies, for similar reasons, to the German *Länder* after 1945.

The realization that the Soviet constitution is essentially modeled on assembly government and that this type of government is congenitally conducive to the installation of the strong executive and even autocratic government may help to explain Soviet constitutionalism, at least of the Stalinist period. Prima facie, the document establishes the classic pattern of assembly government: "The highest organ of state power in the U.S.S.R. is the Supreme Soviet of the U.S.S.R." (Art. 30). The Supreme Soviet, bicameral for federal reasons, is an assembly of some thirteen hundred members. However, since it is convened rarely, as a rule twice a year, and only for a few days of sessions to confirm the appointment of the policy-making officials and to ratify the antecedent governmental policy decisions, the traditional pattern has been streamlined by the innovation of the Presidium. Nominally only a permanent standing committee of the Supreme Soviet, it far outranks the latter in actual power. In constitutional practice the legal omnipotence of the Supreme Soviet has been delegated to the Presidium, without, however, affecting the pattern of assembly government as such. The constitution conforms to assembly government also in the position of the Council of Ministers; declared, in Article 64, "the highest executive and administrative organ of state power," it is strictly subordinated, "responsible and accountable," to the Supreme Soviet and its Presidium (Art. 65). Under the logic of the scheme, membership in the Council of Ministers and the Presidium of the Supreme Soviet is mutually exclusive.

Once again, however, the Soviet version is subject to the biology of assembly government. The Council of Ministers or, in reality, its chairman—Stalin himself from 1941 to his death in 1953 —is an organ constitutionally inferior to the assembly; but it has risen to complete domination of all other state organs, the "sovereign" assembly included. This commanding position is enhanced by the permeation of the entire state apparatus by the monolithic single party. The members of its directing group, the Central Committee of the Communist party, occupy the key positions in the Council of Ministers and the Presidium—a situation anticipated by the control of the Jacobins over the Convention—and the members of the Supreme Soviet are elected on a single ticket to which only proven communists or representatives of party-approved groupings have access. It is obvious, under these circumstances, that the Soviet application remains faithful to the intrinsic power configuration of assembly government and that the latter was bound to become the favorite constitutional incarnation of communist autocracy. The closed power circuit sees to it that the will of the people, behind an arch-democratic theory of government, conforms to the interests of the single party and the policy decisions of the ruling party oligarchy.

The Third Pattern: Parliamentarism

Parliamentarism, in its various applications, is by far the most common pattern of constitutional-democratic government today. In contrast to assembly government and presidentialism, both artificially constructed products of political theory, parliamentarism grew organically and pragmatically after the eclipse of the royal prerogative by the Glorious Revolution. Subsequently, the principles of parliamentary government slowly gained recognition: that the king's government—the cabinet—requires the support of the majority of parliament, or at least of the Commons, and that its political responsibility to parliament is best served if its members are simultaneously members of the parliament. Cabinet government developed accidentally—unless one supports the Hegelian interpretation of history as the meaningful operation of the absolute spirit—by the emergence of the prime minister; owing to the inability of the first Hanoverian to understand English, an officer presiding over the king's council was needed. The significant result of the historical process, extending over a century and a half, was the establishment of the cabinet as an independent and quasi-autonomous power holder. At first, in the eighteenth century, it held the upper hand over the parliament by what has been called "government by corruption" (Walpole); later, after the successive electoral reforms of the nineteenth century, it increasingly responded to the electoral will reflected by the general election. Thus, the original dualism of cabinet and crown was converted into the triangular power configuration of Commons, cabinet, and electorate. There was nothing speculative or intentional in this organic process; it just happened, and it took its time to happen.[8]

Parliamentary government is the only one of the standard patterns of constitutional democracy the French Revolution did not try its hand at. With Napoleon's defeat, England had become the leading world power, the citadel of liberal constitutionalism. Parliamentary government, adjusted to the temperament of her people, had spared her the upheavals of the revolution. No wonder it became the model everywhere envied and imitated. It spread to the Continent with the Belgian charter of 1831 and, subsequently, over the globe.

Parliamentarism likewise is a generic term including several widely divergent applications. For its proper understanding three points should be noted. First, the existence of representative or "parliamentary" institutions in a state is not tantamount to its being operated by the parliamentary form of government. Second, parliamentary government is by no means identical with cabinet government. Since the latter is a specific version of parliamentary government, the term as such should be reserved for the British institutionalization. Third, to be qualified as "parliamentary," the governmental structure must possess certain features common to all its variants and not found in any other pattern of government.

Basically, parliamentary government is an attempt to establish between the two independent and separate power holders—assembly and government—such an equilibrium that neither one of them can gain ascendancy over the other. Under this dualism the two power holders share in policy decision and policy execution by legislation. Moreover, since both are endowed with reciprocal restraints and mutual controls—interorgan controls—they also share in policy control. As a dualist power configuration, parliamentarism fitted early constitutionalism not yet perfected by the admission of the electorate as the supreme power holder. This stage was finally reached when the electorate, either in periodical elections or, in the case of dissolution of the parliament, at irregular intervals, determined the political complexion of the assembly and, through it, of the government.

The "ideal type" of this structural arrangement is the complete equilibrium of the two independent power holders, government (cabinet) and parliament, subject to the periodical political reorientation by the verdict of the electorate, each of them endowed with restraining and controlling powers symmetrically matching those of the other power holder. The history of constitutional government since 1789 is nothing but the search for the magic formula by which a stable equilibrium between government and parliament could be established and maintained. The quest has proved unsuccessful. Almost at all times the one or the other of the two power holders weighed heavier on the scales of the power dynamism, and the oscillations between executive leadership and the supremacy of the representative parliament appear intrinsically inherent in the practice of constitutional government.[9]

The following structural elements are common to all variants of genuine parliamentary government.

First, the members of the government or cabinet are, as a rule, simultaneously members of the parliament. In England the principle is based on constitutional custom or convention without statutory formalization. Ever since Walpole, the prime minister has been a member of one of the two houses, and the rule applies by now to all ministers. Most other parliamentary states followed suit.[10] The rationale behind the requirement lies in the fact that the assembly has greater control over its own members than it has over outsiders and can subject them to political responsibility by making them stand up in its midst and account for their conduct of office.

Second, the government or cabinet consists of the political leaders of the majority party or a coalition of parties forming a majority. Since they must be members of the parliament, the cabinet is a committee of the assembly, fused and integrated with it. Although there exists a personal identity between the membership in the cabinet and membership in the parliament, the two power holders are functionally separate and independent. In view of the character of the cabinet as a committee of the parliament, the pattern is appropriately called *interdependence by integration.*

Third, the government-cabinet in itself has a pyramidal structure with the prime minister, president of the council, minister-president, etc., as its apex and recognized leader. Though the degree of ascendancy of the prime minister may vary from one parliamentary regime to the other, the sharing of political power between him and his collaborators in the government has lately sufficiently decreased to allow the generalization that, within the collective group of the government, the prime minister exercises undisputed supremacy over his ministerial colleagues. The power of the government actually is concentrated in the person of the prime minister as its leader.

Fourth, the government remains in power so long as it commands the support of the majority of the members of the parliament. Power is lost if the majority withdraws its support or if the general elections change the majority structure of the parliament.

Fifth, on principle, policy decision is shared by the government and the parliament. Both concur in the legislation implementing the policy decision. In practice, however, their respective share in the initiating of policy decisions—and even the drafting of the statute—depends on the variant of parliamentarism prevailing in the specific state. Policy execution by administration, on the other hand, is intrusted to the government, under constant supervision of the parliament.

Sixth, it is in policy control that the crux of the pattern of parliamentary government lies. To be genuine, parliamentarism must be operated by reciprocal control devices at the disposal of both power holders, the government and the parliament. The most effective instrumentality for the benefit of the parliament is the invocation of political responsibility—a constant contingency—of the cabinet as a whole (collective responsibility) or of an individual member of the cabinet (individual responsibility). The *ultima ratio* of parliamentary control is the vote of non-confidence (censure) carried by the parliamentary majority against the government, or vice versa, the rejection of a vote of confidence requested by the government. Resignation of the government, in this situation, may or may not lead to dissolution of the parliament and to new elections. Contrariwise, the most stringent control device at the disposal of the government is the right to dissolve the parliament and call for new elections. In this case the sovereign electorate serves as the arbiter between the party or parties in opposition to the government and the government itself; if the opposition is victorious at the polls, the electorate is presumed to have disowned the government in power, and the new government has to be formed by the victorious party or party coalition. If, on the other hand, the government majority is returned, the electorate is presumed to have indorsed the governmental policies, and the government remains in power. However, the electoral verdict can be accurately ascertained only in the case of the two-party system.

Dissolution and vote of non-confidence belong together like piston and cylinder. It is their potential reciprocity that makes the wheels of the parliamentary mechanism turn. Where these reciprocal powers are not adequately matched, for example, if the dissolution power of the government is atrophied or, contrariwise, if the power of parliamentary disapproval is limited, the parliamentary system in its authentic form has difficulty operating and may even cease to exist. In the former case—atrophy of the dissolution power—the regime is slanted toward the supremacy of the parliamentary power holder. The government is weakened; the parliament, strengthened. If, on the other hand, the technique of removing a government by a vote of censure is restricted, the regime is slanted toward the supremacy of the governmental power holder. In either case much depends on the prevailing party structure, whether the system is multiparty or two party, and on the degree of internal party discipline, which is naturally greater under the two-party configuration than under multipartism. The choice of these alternatives, by a nation, is neither voluntary nor rational. It is conditioned by national experience and character. A specific variant cannot be enjoined by constitutional provisions.

The reality of the power dynamics offers illustrations for each variant of parliamentarism: the strong assembly and the weak cabinet under classical parliamentarism in France; the strong executive and the weak assembly under the Bonn regime of West Germany; and the complete concordance of cabinet and parliamentary majority in Britain, resulting in the strong cabinet, with the parliament voluntarily subordinating itself to its executive leadership.

CLASSICAL PARLIAMENTARISM: FRANCE

France turned to genuine parliamentarism as late as with the constitution of 1875.[11] In analyzing the French—the classical—pattern of parliamentarism, four different if closely interwoven issues should be considered.

The "dual executive."—The Third and the Fourth republics possess what is called the "dual executive," that is, executive functions are shared by two different state organs, the president of the Republic and the government or cabinet (council or ministers). In reality the dualism is strictly nominal. The president of the Republic lives under the shadow of the president of the council or premier. Having learned their lesson from the Second Republic, the Third and the Fourth saw to it that the official chief of state be elected by the two houses of parliament instead of by popular election, a mode of designation that tempted him, anointed by the democratic oil, to reach out for absolute power. The congenital aversion of the French against the strong executive is rooted in their past experience with the two Napoleons and the near-miss of Boulanger (1889). Strong presidents are resented; parliament makes short shrift of them, for example, by refusing co-operation with Alexandre Millerand (1924). Only Poincaré succeeded because he exercised wise restraint. De Gaulle foundered on the rock of tradition. Even the president's selection of the president of the council, the only autonomous prerogative he retains, is narrowly circumscribed by the party constellations, making him little more than an honest broker.

Cabinet instability.—What, to the superficial observer, appears as the most conspicuous feature—and defect—of classical French parliamentarism is the cabinet instability. Within sixty-five years the Third Republic consumed a hundred-odd different governments; within ten years the Fourth, more than twenty. The causes are psychological and ideological as well as functional. Psychologically, French individualism is responsible for the multiplicity of parties, enhanced, in the Third Republic, by the electoral system based on the majority technique in uninominal constituencies. But the "hexagonalism" of party blocs, under the proportional representation of the Fourth, is hardly much of an improvement. Ideologically, the French earnestly believe in the representative principle inherited from the revolution and in the supremacy of the representative assembly; they abhor governmental regimentation and statism. Of course, less honorable motivations come into play: personal jealousies, rivalries, and ambitions of the political leaders and the strange biological phenomenon that the prestige of even the best cabinet wilts after a short while.

But the functional cause of instability lies in the obsolescence of dissolution. Deprived of its most effective weapon against a recalcitrant assembly, the Damocles sword of dissolution, the government comes under the heel of the parliament. The misuse of the device by President MacMahon—*le seize mai* (1877)— blunted the edge for the duration of the Third, and Premier Edgar Faure's frivolous dissolution of December, 1955, may have the same effect on the Fourth Republic.[12] The absence of the dissolution power, potential or real, shelters the representatives against the vicissitudes of an electoral campaign for the duration of their parliamentary mandate—four years under the Third, five under the Fourth Republic. Under the Third Republic a representative could change his party allegiance without being accountable to his voters, whose memories are as abysmally short in France as elsewhere. Consequently, the party discipline was loose, the deputy being responsible to his conscience only. Matters remained much the same under the proportional representation of the Fourth Republic, which was intended to produce more "monolithic" parties. If formerly the government majority disintegrated by the individual defections of the independent deputies, under the Fourth Republic the cabinets dissolve by the withdrawal of entire parties, or of substantial segments thereof, from the government coalition. Under the Third Republic the inevitable result was the flight of the chambers into the irresponsibility of granting the cabinets vast delegated powers (*pleins pouvoirs*). The Fourth Republic renewed the practice, the explicit constitutional prohibition to the contrary notwithstanding, this time with the blessings of the Conseil d'Etat.* Hence the reformists' clamor for the strengthening of the dissolution power of the government in order to domesticate the assembly and to obtain a stronger executive. Minor procedural reforms—known by the name of the "rational-

* See below, pp. 211–12.

ization of parliamentarism"—were introduced to stabilize the cabinet. The "investiture" of the cabinet antecedent to its final confirmation by the National Assembly aggravated the difficulties in the formation of the new government to such an extent that the constitutional reform of December, 1954, abolished it. Other devices, such as "cooling-off" periods for the final vote on, and increased majorities for, the overthrow of the government, if they have helped somewhat to eliminate surprise tactics, cure symptoms rather than the evil of parliamentary irresponsibility itself.[13]

However grave a defect cabinet instability may be under classical parliamentarism predicated on the supremacy of the assembly, there are attenuating circumstances in the French political regime the foreign observer is apt to overlook: the rock-ribbed stability of the public administration, managed by a competent if overbureaucratic civil service; the protection of the individual against governmental abuse of power by the Conseil d'Etat; the reshuffling of ministerial positions among the same personnel ("replastering"), providing for a continuous supply of experienced political leaders; and, last but not least, the fact that under the Fourth Republic practically every ministerial crisis involved a major policy decision—economics, finances, relations of church and state, foreign policy—in which the parties in the assembly effectively claim their share and refuse to be corralled by a decision of the cabinet. From the viewpoint of our context of the power process, the French take their democracy in deadly seriousness; they believe in the principle of shared power, that is, that different party combinations assume responsibility for the different policy decisions; they abhor being subjected to the monopoly of a single power holder, be it the government or a party coalition. Since the national character cannot be changed, there is little that can be done by a reform of functional arrangements. Numerous as are the prophets of the impending doom of the Fourth Republic, and with it, of classical French parliamentarism, as yet democratic fundamentalism always has succeeded in surviving. And, it may be asked without malice, whether French national policies are really more inconsistent and erratic than, for example, those under the vaunted strong executive leadership of the American presidential system.

A general observation may be in order here: parliamentarism *à la française* seems to be the natural governmental pattern for all democratic republics with multipartism and—this has to be added —without the experience in political co-operation among the parties that has developed in the older parliamentary monarchies of western and northern Europe. The existence of a permanent monarchical head of state may have had something to do with this political stability, though it should not be overrated. The French patterns seem to have an irresistible attraction for states beginning to experiment with constitutional democracy. After the First World War it was almost universally followed by the new states emerging from centuries of autocratic control. Practically everywhere—Czechoslovakia was a notable exception—the constitutions, written in many instances by dogmatic law professors impervious to the lessons of political science, placed the center of political gravity in the assemblies without providing against multipartism and party dissensions splitting them hopelessly asunder. Political crises between government and parliament could not fail to ensue. The chronic paralysis of the policy-decision function invited illegality, with the result that the strong man claimed leadership by force and established an authoritarian regime. This was bound to happen in practically all states recently converted to democracy—Poland, Yugoslavia, Rumania, Bulgaria, Greece, Germany, Austria, and Spain. Since, after the Second World War, the pattern of parliamentary supremacy was repeated in most of the new constitutions, and, understandably, a workable two-party system that seems essential for its smooth operation failed to develop, one can but look with misgiving at the future of classical parliamentarism. To date, several factors seem to have delayed the inevitable crisis: the need for economic reconstruction; the widespread prosperity; and, finally, the threat of communism.

HYBRID PARLIAMENTARISM:
THE DUAL EXECUTIVE

Attempts to obviate the structural defects of the French variant of parliamentarism conditioned by the supremacy of the assembly and multipartism did not fail to materialize. The Weimar constitution in Germany tried out a new power configuration. On traditional parliamentarism—of which the Germans were wholly ignorant—a popularly elected president was grafted. As a power holder independent of the government and the parliament, he was intended to be a counterweight against the popularly elected Reichstag and the cabinet supported by its majority. These contradictory purposes resulted in the fateful misconstruction of the power process under Weimar: the Reich chancellor was appointed and dismissed at the discretion of the Reich president (Art. 53); at the same time he required the confidence of the Reichstag for his conduct of office (Art. 54). These two requirements were mutually compatible only so long as the president and the parliamentary majority—under multipartism always a coalition—agreed on the person of the Reich chancellor and his policies. Once they parted ways, an irreconcilable conflict arose between president and Reichstag majority in which both contestants, because popularly elected, could claim to speak on behalf of the people.

The catastrophe came with the dismissal, by President von Hindenburg, of Reich Chancellor Brüning (May, 1932), although the cabinet still commanded a majority in the Reichstag and the latter's mandate still had more than two years to run. The results are well known: thereafter "presidential" cabinets, possessing the confidence of the Reich president without a semblance of parliamentary support, were substituted for parliamentary government. Weimar had turned authoritarian, and this prior to the final paralysis of the Reichstag by the rapid increase of the antiparliamentarian extremists on the right (National Socialists) and on the left (Communists). President von Hindenburg's illegal overweighting of the presidential, at the expense of the parliamentary, powers was the entering wedge through which Hitler shortly thereafter (January, 1933) could gain power "legally."

A similar situation, with identical results, prevailed in the short-lived Spanish republic under the constitution of 1931. It differed, however, from Weimar in that President Alcalá Zamora was ousted by the Cortes (April, 1936) because he had exceeded his constitutional powers. What Hitler did through the constitution, Franco thereafter accomplished by armed force. The Germans docilely submitted; the Spanish republic resisted for almost three years.

It should be noted, however, that the "dualist" system of parliamentarism, resembling that of Weimar, functions successfully in Finland under the constitution of 1919. The president, popularly (if indirectly) elected, is actually the chief of a parliamentary state. He appoints and dismisses the ministers at his complete discretion, although in accordance with the parliamentary support they command, and replaces them if he finds that they no longer possess the confidence of the Riksdag. No formal acceptance of the cabinet by the parliamentary majority is required, and the president may keep in office even a government which is merely tolerated by the majority. Thus, the squaring of the circle between presidential and parliamentary confidence on which Weimar foundered was accomplished in Finland.[14]

CONTROLLED PARLIAMENTARISM:
THE BONN VERSION

Remembering Weimar, the Bonn constitution introduced an interesting variant of what the Germans think parliamentarism should be. The designation of the government, that is, of the federal chancellor, is performed by a democratically unobjectionable procedure: he is elected to office, "on the proposal of the Federal President," by the absolute majority of all legal members of the Bundestag, the lower house of parliament (Art. 63, secs. 1

and 2). The contingencies provided for the case that the presidential candidate fails to be elected thus far had never been resorted to. Once in office, however, he is practically irremovable during the legislative term—four years—of the Federal Assembly. Such enviable governmental stability, comparing favorably with both Weimar and France, is accomplished by whittling down the right of the government to dissolve the Federal Assembly and the latter's right to overthrow the government by a vote of censure. The presidential discretion to authorize the dissolution as it had existed under Weimar fell by the wayside, deemed incompatible with the strictly ceremonial functions of the federal president.[15] Under Bonn, dissolution is practically impossible. Equally emasculated is the control of the parliament over the government by a vote of non-confidence. The federal chancellor can be overthrown by a vote of the Federal Assembly only (Art. 67) if the parliament, at the same time, elects his successor (the so-called "constructive" vote of non-confidence). This contingency can arise, if at all, only if one of the parties in the government coalition joins the opposition and is strong enough to transform it into a majority. During the first three legislative periods of the Federal Assembly this situation did not arise and could hardly have arisen because of the prevailing party constellation. Multipartism still persists; but it has become considerably attenuated and is even said to approximate the two-party system or, rather, a one-and-a-half-party system because of the numerical ascendancy of Chancellor Adenauer's Christian-Democratic party and its allies. This the Social Democrats, steadily polling not much more than one-third of the total vote, were unable to match, even though in 1956 there were substantial defections from the government majority coalition. In the first legislative period of the Federal Assembly (1949–53), Dr. Adenauer was safe because the coalition stuck tightly together. In the second period (after 1953) he held an absolute majority of his own Christian Democrats whom he controlled with an iron hand; he could afford to lose two of his coalition partners in 1956.

Cabinet stability under Bonn, thus, to date is as strong as in Britain, practically assuring the incumbency of the chancellor for the duration of the legislative period. But here the comparison with Britain ends. So strong was the hold of the chancellor that opponents as well as followers complained about his authoritarian conduct of the office. Cabinet stability has been bought at a heavy price indeed: the democratic process is stifled; the parliamentary majority is subservient; public opinion has no influence whatsoever on the government majority, protected in its mandate by proportional representation, and even less on the government, protected against loss of office by the difficulty of finding a successor. While avoiding the frying pan of governmental instability, the Bonn regime has fallen into the fire of an emasculated parliamentarism. In substance the regime is "demo-authoritarianism," at least for the duration of the legislative period.[16] Policy decision is monopolized by the chancellor alone, the unchallenged master of his cabinet; it is translated into legislation by the disciplined parliamentary majority at his command, and there is no gainsaying that there hardly exists elsewhere a group of parliamentary technicians more hard-working and conscientious. There are no effective means of policy control except the general elections every four years. The system in vogue is hardly appropriate to teach the Germans how to operate authentic parliamentarism—or genuine democracy, for that matter.

The Fourth Pattern: Cabinet Government

In striking contrast to France, parliamentarism in Great Britain and the nations following the British model signifies the undisputed ascendancy of the government—prime minister and cabinet —over the parliament or, more precisely, since the Parliament Act of 1911 (1 & 2 Geo. V, c. 13), over the House of Commons.

British parliamentarism has undergone considerable transformations. During the eighteenth century the unreformed House of Commons, whether Whig or Tory, could usually be manipulated by the cabinet with the support of the crown. Genuine parliamentarism began to function normally only after the Great Reform of 1832, which extended the suffrage to the propertied middle classes. For a short while, during the fifties and sixties of the last century, British parliamentarism unmistakably tended toward the superiority of the Commons over the cabinet. Between 1852 and 1868 a turnover of cabinets took place, resembling, if remotely so, the later classical French parliamentarism. No fewer than nine cabinets came and went, some of them of very short duration. In a number of cases the fall of the cabinet was caused by splits in the majority party; neither Liberals nor Conservatives maintained party discipline. The Commons conducted themselves as an exclusive club with a socially homogeneous membership, impervious to the control of either the electorate or the cabinet. Nor did the defeat of the government in power require the dissolution of the Commons.[17] But the supremacy of the Commons over the cabinet was temporary. It changed radically with extention of the suffrage to the working classes in the second Reform Bill of 1867. By the emergence of organized mass parties the new mass electorate was integrated into the political process. For the last eighty years British parliamentarism has presented a triangular shape, the three corners being the electorate, the Commons, and the cabinet. But in this constellation the electorate and the cabinet hold positions of equal strength, the House of Commons being reduced to the function of a transmission belt for the will of the electorate to reach the cabinet; by itself it is inferior in real political power to either one of the others. The power dynamism functions between the electorate, determining the majority party and its official leader as prime minister, and the cabinet rather than between the cabinet, designated by parliament, and the House of Commons. Invariably, a defeat of the cabinet on a matter it considers vital leads to the dissolution of the Commons, whose lifespan, in accordance with the acceleration of the democratic process, was shortened, in 1911, from seven to five years.

The main features of the British version of parliamentary government may be summarized thus:

1. It is predicated on the existence of two alternating parties possessing even chances in the long run of becoming the majority party at the general elections. This traditional situation suffered a temporary interruption when, with the rise of Labor, the dilemma of a three-party configuration presented itself (1923–31). After several minority governments (1923–24 and 1929–31) the realistic British solved it by eliminating the third party of the Liberals and returning to the two-party system, which alone makes cabinet government possible. For the same reason the British people stubbornly adhere to the majority technique in (mostly) single-membered constituencies. Resisting the temptation of proportional representation, they prefer a workable government and the unavoidable inequalities of majority elections to a mechanical equality involving the risk of unstable governments. Population shifts are largely remedied by a periodical redistribution of seats.

2. The cabinet is a relatively small committee, composed of the leaders of the majority party. All its members and the other ministers, that is, members of the government who are not members of the inner circle of the cabinet, must be members of the parliament. The majority of them sit in the Commons; the share of the Lords in the composition of the cabinet was statutorily regulated by the Ministers of the Crown Act of 1937 (3 Edw. VIII and 1 Geo. VI, c. 38).

3. The official leader of the majority party winning the general elections is the prime minister designate. He is the undisputed leader and superior of his cabinet, whose members he chooses at his discretion. His position vis-à-vis his cabinet is so commanding that, in actual practice, in the triangular power configuration he has eclipsed the cabinet. He determines the policy decisions and the manner by which they are to be executed. How far he accepts the advice of his colleagues in the cabinet depends on his personality and prestige. A minimum degree of consultation implying shared power is secured by the otherwise rather elastic rules gov-

erning the cabinet's procedure. But policy determination is monopolized by the prime minister to such an extent that his role is sometimes spoken of as "constitutional dictatorship." However, this qualification is far off the mark. The British cabinet system is prevented from sliding into authoritarianism by the self-restraint of the prime minister and the cabinet; by their respect for the rights of the opposition which, by a turn of the political wheel, may become the government and retaliate; and, most of all, by the sensitiveness of the government to public opinion.

4. In view of the concentration of policy decision in the hands of the prime minister and his cabinet, the Commons are granted only that degree of participation in the policy execution by legislation that the prevailing political climate of public opinion demands. By themselves, the Commons share in the policy decisions only to the limited extent that they confirm in principle those previously taken by the cabinet. The rejection of a major legislative plan indorsed by the government would lead to dissolution and the arbitration of the electorate between Commons and the cabinet. No such contingency of a Commons majority disowning its cabinet has arisen since the eighties of the last century. This situation implies that legislative initiative is strictly monopolized by the government. No bill unless indorsed by the government can reach the statute book. The legislative initiative of the private members—that is, deputies of both parties not belonging to the cabinet and ministry—has almost completely vanished; it is limited to non-controversial improvements of the existing laws.[18] The government has complete control over the entire legislative process; the drafting of the bills is undertaken by the ministerial bureaucracy primarily of the Treasury; agenda and timetable of the Commons are arranged to suit the governmental legislative planning. However, less to avoid retaliation in case the pendulum has swung to the other end than in deference to democratic fairness, the legislative business is conducted in loyal co-operation with the leaders of the opposition.

5. Policy control, on the other hand, is vested in both houses of

the parliament and in the electorate. Within the Commons it is primarily the opposition, less frequently also the backbenchers of the government majority, which acts as the semaphore of public opinion and the people at large. The reports that the representatives bring back from their weekly visits to their constituencies and relay, through the party whips, to the leadership are an important control device.

The outwardly most conspicuous control technique, however, is the daily practice of question time. Questions addressed to the individual ministers serve most of all the purpose of checking on the administrative side of policy execution which otherwise—a universal phenomenon of the transformation of the legislative into the administrative state not confined to Britain—tends to emancipate the administration more and more from the effective control of the Commons. The House of Lords likewise, though politically emasculated since the Parliament Act of 1911, has its share in policy control through its more leisurely conduct of the legislative business and its frequent high-level debates on major policies. In general, the imponderables of a free democratic environment constantly attune the majority, the cabinet, and the prime minister to public opinion. By-elections, which during the normal five-year term of the Commons may reach a figure of forty and more, are straws in the political wind closely observed by government and opposition until, finally, the general election serves as the ultimate test. Its time is determined by the prime minister. If even British politicians are not above giving the electoral wheel a slight push in their favor by choosing the politically most opportune moment for the dissolution and the granting of tax favors to the voters, in the last analysis the electorate, on the day of reckoning, is in the habit of giving the government and its critics of the opposition a fair deal. The electoral laws see to it as far as it is humanly possible that all competing parties have equal chances of victory and defeat.

6. The British parliamentary personnel is still one of the best existing, if no longer the elite it used to be in the nineteenth cen-

tury; the great majority of them are men of intelligence, integrity, and experience. How does one account for the truly amazing phenomenon that these elected representatives submit like good soldiers to the commands of their superiors? The key for the understanding of British cabinet government lies in party discipline. Its motivations are several. Party loyalty induces the member of parliament to toe the party line even at the expense of sacrificing his personal convictions. Rare indeed are the occasions when the government, in co-operation with the opposition, permits a free vote, as, for example, on the reform of the prayer book or the abolition of the death penalty. Party loyalty pays: the member can hope to retain his seat only by and through the party; independent candidates have practically disappeared since the Labor party abolished the university seats (1948). Common sense teaches the individual member that only party discipline secures the smooth operation of the system as it exists, providing for effective governmental leadership, effective legislative performance, and effective democratic control which respects the rights of the opposition and guarantees fair play between the alternating parties. And, finally, the threat of dissolution underscores all other motivations: if the government's majority should break and the cabinet be defeated on a policy decision declared vital by it, dissolution is the inescapable consequence. New elections compel the member to the expenses of a new campaign and expose him to the vicissitudes of the electoral gamble. He is proud of his seat and does not want to lose it. Hence he obeys the whips and votes as they tell him. The overriding strength of the party discipline was highlighted by the Suez crisis in November, 1956, which split the nation and with it the Conservative majority in the Commons wide open. Yet the threatened "revolt of the backbenchers" failed to materialize. The party machine worked overtime. In the decisive vote of December 6, 1956, only fifteen members of the government party placed a token opposition on record by abstaining.

From the viewpoint of the process of political power, cabinet government should be recognized as a fusion of the two independent power holders, cabinet and parliament, into a single power mechanism in which the two organs are practically integrated. It is, in essence, interdependence of the two power holders by integration. The counterweight lies in the continuous control of public opinion, represented by the opposition, and the recurrent general elections. Easily one of the most successful patterns of government of our time—and, possibly, of all times—it is predicated on the existence of two, and not more, competing and alternating parties, with the electorate holding the balance between them.

Cabinet government found application in those British Dominions—Canada, Australia, New Zealand, South Africa—which either inherited from England the two-party structure or imitated it. Temporary three-party configurations always tend to yield to the traditional two-party system. But its suitability for effective government under the rules of democratic fair play is such that it can function successfully also in politically more mature nations given to multipartism. In these cases, where two-partism does not exist organically, it can be created artificially by the device of several parties joining, for the duration of the parliamentary term, to form a stable government coalition confronted by an equally stable government opposition. This is the situation in the Scandinavian states—whether, as in Sweden and Norway, the Socialists have an absolute majority or, as in Denmark, even a minority government is formed—and in Belgium and Holland, both of which are able to combine stable cabinet government with multipartism. While all the nations mentioned have long experience in responsible self-government, even newer states of multiple-party structure and more violent political temper have had the good fortune to adopt the cabinet pattern of government. This is true in Eire and Israel, both significantly trained in the British school of politics. And it may be noted that in most of these instances proportional representation, alleged to increase the chances of multipartism, does not stand in the way of the successful application of cabinet government. However, it demands of the nation practicing it, if not a large measure of socioeconomic homogeneity —which is helpful—at least a high degree of political responsibility and self-restraint, qualities that cannot be created by constitutional arrangements alone.

The Fifth Pattern: Presidentialism

The American reader does not need a detailed presentation of the American pattern of government. All the following discussion sets out to do is to apply to it, within the conceptual framework of shared exercise of political power, the new tripartite categories of policy determination, policy execution, and policy control.

The American government is commonly spoken of as one with "separation of powers," a designation lately refined to "separated and co-ordinated powers." Abroad, because of the belief in the dominant position of the president, it is better known as "presidential government" or "presidentialism." As has been pointed out previously, the term "powers," figurative rather than structural, should be replaced by "functions," denoting different areas of state activity.

The early concept of a strict and rigid separation of functions, used by both the American and the contemporaneous French constitutional theory and practice, appears an artificial product, period- and environment-conditioned by the speculative rationalism of the Enlightenment. It was nurtured by the infusion of Newtonian mechanistic premises into the sociopolitical realm and inspired by the belief that the equilibrium established between the several power holders will result in the permanent harmony of the state society. The assumption that the power holders in equipoise would voluntarily dedicate themselves to co-operation for the common welfare was psychologically unsound. It neglected, to its peril, the demonism of the power dynamism. The coexistence of several power holders in rigid isolation was an unworkable illusion, as clearly demonstrated by the French constitution of 1791, which attempted to apply Montesquieu's separation of functions to a practical test.

THE PRINCIPLE: INTERDEPENDENCE BY CO-ORDINATION

There is no more fitting prescription for the American variant of the separated functions than Thomas Jefferson's statement: "An elective despotism was not the government we fought for; but one which should not only be founded in free principles, but in which the powers of government should be so divided and balanced among the several bodies of magistracy, so that no one should transcend their legal limits, without being effectually checked and restrained by the others."[19] The fifty-five men of the Philadelphia convention were better advised than their brethren of the French National Assembly. Bent on avoiding legislative despotism as well as executive absolutism, they built into their plan of the power process several independent power holders, linking them together by mutual co-ordination. To achieve this end, two different and, to some extent, even conflicting principles were applied: in line with the prevailing constitutional theory the state activities were divided into three distinctive areas, and each area was assigned to a different "body of magistracy," the executive to the president, the legistlative to the congress, and the judicial to the courts. In each area the respective power holder was granted autonomy and the monopoly óf action not to be infringed on by any other power holder. This was the principle of specialization in the exercise of the assigned function. However, well aware that rigid isolation of functions necessarily must lead to constant deadlocks between the power holders and could completely paralyze the political process, they required that, at certain specified "points of contact," the several independent power holders must be co-ordinated in such a manner that only by their co-operation could the specific state activity assigned to an individual power holder achieve constitutional validity. This is the principle of co-ordination.

The power mechanism as a whole presents itself as the *interdependence* of the several power holders *by co-ordination*. It differs fundamentally from the interdependence by integration governing the parliamentary pattern: under the latter, government and parliament are inextricably wedded and welded together; they cannot perform their functions without the antecedent or subsequent action of the other power holder. Interdependence by co-ordination, on the other hand, means that the independent power holders function autonomously within their respective sphere of action but that, at pre-established points of contact, they have to co-operate. The requirement of co-operation implies the sharing of power.

The details of the co-ordination of president and congress are too familiar to demand more than the briefest of summary. They are few in number and located at strategic points of the political process. The president shares in legislation by putting his signature on the congressional bill or withholding it (veto). If overridden by a two-thirds majority, the veto fails to impede the congressional legislation. The Senate participates in the presidential conduct of foreign policy by treaty ratification and in the presidential appointive function by confirmation of the nomination. In both cases the presidential act can be permanently negated. Judicial review, another point of contact, was not included in the original plan. The courts were confined to the application of the statutes conjointly enacted by congressional adoption and presidential signature.

Outside and beyond these instances of constitutionally required co-ordination there are other extra-constitutional mutual influences of the independent power holders. Foremost among them is the fact that the president in his capacity of leader of his party influences the attitude of his party in congress. Congress, as the dispenser of the purse, injects itself into the entire sphere of the presidential action that requires appropriations. The president, through his party friends in congress, may initiate legislation. The senator influences the appointments and the patronage dispensation of the president within his state.

RECIPROCAL INDEPENDENCE OF
THE POWER HOLDERS

The crucial distinction, however, of the presidential from both assembly and parliamentary government lies in the reciprocal independence of president and congress from each other. The president is in no manner accountable to congress. Or, to use the parlance of parliamentarism, political responsibility, enforceable by a vote of non-confidence or the rejection of legislation considered vital, does not exist. Regardless of what the congress majority may think of the president—and at times this may be preciously little—it cannot remove him from office. This may be done eventually, at the expiration of his four-year term, by the electorate. Nor can congress force the resignation of a member of the president's cabinet. Impeachment, never an effective device of control, has become obsolete.*

Corresponding to the irremovability and irresponsibility of the president, congress likewise stays in office for its appointed term. Regardless of how much the president disagrees with its majority —and at times this may reach considerable dimensions—congress cannot be dissolved by him. The reciprocal political immunity and autonomy is indirectly written into the constitution (Art. II, Sec. 6, clause 2): "No Senator or Representative shall, during the time for which he was elected, be appointed to any civil office under the United States, . . . and no person holding office under the United States, shall be a member of either house during his

---

* See below, pp. 199–200.

continuance in office." The constitutional incompatibility of the governmental office and the parliamentary mandate is the nub of the American political regime. By peremptorily excluding any personal identity between a member of congress and of the governmental administration, interdependence by integration, which is the core of parliamentarism, becomes strictly impossible. The system separates the power holders from one another and confines their co-operation and co-ordination, their sharing in the exercise of power, to the constitutional and extra-constitutional points of contacts between them.

Since the several power holders thus are kept in isolation from one another, it would seem that deadlocks between them and the paralysis of the entire state machinery would constantly threaten. That this did not happen during the early years of the American republic was largely due to a socially homogeneous agrarian state society of the pretechnological age operated by an equally homogeneous oligarchy. That it failed to happen afterward, when the United States entered the age of industrialization and democratization, is due to the emergence and function of the political party, unforeseen and thought undesirable by the founding fathers. The political party became the missing link between the several constitutionally isolated power holders. It is the lubricating oil of the entire state machinery without which the latter would have run into unbreakable deadlocks. The party is the transmission belt for the translation of the political leadership of the chief executive into congressional action.

It was practically true in the past, and theoretically may still be true today, that, if the incumbent of the presidency has at his disposal reliable majorities in both houses—as was almost invariably the case in the past at the beginning of a new presidential term until the tradition was broken in the elections of 1956—he is in a position to co-ordinate the presidential with the congressional policies. Under particularly auspicious circumstances of the two-party structure, the American system of government, then, may in practice come close to the cabinet-parliament variant of parliamentarism.

However, this has ceased to be the normal situation, if ever normal it was. One would think that, because of the constitutional separation of the independent power holders, for the smooth functioning of the power mechanism party discipline is well-nigh indispensable: the president can fulfil his mission of political leadership only if his majority in both houses of congress follows him loyally through thick and thin. Otherwise, the opposition party, under the two-party configuration, might play havoc with his policies. This, however, is just not the case. Quite aside from the sociological structure of the American two-party system—in important aspects entirely singular—the function of the parties differs under the presidential system from its counterparts in other patterns of government. There are two principal reasons for the inability of the president to impose his will on congress. First, it happens frequently in the mid-term elections that the president's party loses the majority in one of the two houses, and it even happens not infrequently that the president is confronted by two houses in which the opposition holds the majority. Second, American congressional parties are distinguished—or cursed?—by lack of party discipline. There may be cogent sociopsychological reasons for this habit; in particular, the Senate is composed of ninety-six superindividualistic prima donnas unwilling to subordinate themselves to any outside direction. Moreover, many members of congress may use the party for attaining office, but some of them could win their seats even as independents. The main reason, however, for the absence of party discipline is that, as under classical French parliamentarism, dissolution is unavailable to the government. The congressmen are just as irremovable from their office as is the president himself. This motivation may be less potent for the members of the House of Representatives with a term of two years—unusually short for any legislative assembly— than for the senators with a six-year term. With party discipline the American system would probably function much in the same way as parliamentary government in Britain; without it, it does not make much difference whether there are, under presidentialism, only two, or three, or more political parties in the legislature, as demonstrated by the experience in Latin America, where it has become evident that the customary multipartism does not weaken the legislature nor the two-party configuration strengthen the president.

To these another aspect must be added: for the last twenty years, at least since the end of the New Deal, the American two-party system actually has transformed itself into a sort of hybrid multipartism. The two-party frame still stands firm for the elections of the president and of congress, the ephemeral exceptions of third parties in both instances amply confirming the rule. However, for the last two decades the traditional two-party dynamism has revealed deep fissures once the elections are over. Both the Republicans and the Democrats lack political homogeneity. The Republicans are split into the liberal and the conservative factions, and the Democrats are even more divided into the progressives in the North and the arch-conservatives in the South, and this not only because of the unliquidated heritage of the Civil War. This situation results in the constantly fluctuating legislative majorities in congress, with its familiar phenomenon of cross-voting, again much resembling French parliamentary habits. Dissidents of the government party join the opposition, and defectors from the opposition vote with the government party. The conditions of near-anarchy prevailing in today's congress tend to enhance the difficulties of presidential leadership, neither party loyalty nor party discipline supporting it. Moreover, with the almost complete disappearance of presidential patronage because of the institutionalization of the civil service, this formerly potent instrumentality of presidential persuasion—a cousin twice removed of Walpole's government by corruption—has lost most of its cutting edge.

AMERICAN GOVERNMENT AND THE NEW TRIPARTISM

Hardly any other pattern of constitutional-democratic government has moved farther away from its original concept than American presidentialism. The most superficial glance at the political dynamics reveals the obsolescence of the classical tripartism of separated executive, legislative, and judicial functions. A more realistic perspective is gained by the application of the new tripartism of policy determination, policy execution, and policy control.

The general picture is as follows: In the majority of cases policy determination is initiated by the president; occasionally, however, congress is the spark plug. Whatever the initial source, the president is compelled to share the actual decision on major policies with congress, often on the latter's own terms, because of the need of implementing a policy decision by legislation and, almost invariably, because of appropriations. The appropriations committees stare icily at every move the administration plans to make. By contrast, it just does not happen that a policy decision of the British cabinet is frustrated by the Commons, in spite of their financial prerogatives. The money they wish is granted. It happens frequently in this country. Even in foreign policy, the function specially assigned to the executive, congress cannot be cheated out of its share if appropriations are needed, quite aside from the required ratification of treaties by the Senate. Policy execution, again the specific domain of the president in terms of the constitution, is likewise shared between the president and congress because of the requirement of implementing it by legislation and appropriations. Finally, policy control has become, under the American pattern of government, an all-round machinery. It is here that the famous checks and balances come into operation. Against congress the president uses the veto, and, contrary to the earlier stages of the American republic, it is being used with increasing frequency against legislation disapproved by the executive on political grounds. Through what the veto has become, the president practically claims a share in the legislative function proper, beyond the original intent of the constitution. For its part, congress has at its disposal a vast repertory of controls of the administration and uses them increasingly: along with the constitutionally established "points of contact"—senatorial confirmation of political appointments and ratification of international treaties— the appropriating and the investigating functions have come into prominence. Checks and balances are no longer confined to the instances constitutionally provided for.

The people, organized by political parties as the electorate, also share in the policy-control function. However, because the president cannot be removed by a vote of non-confidence or congress by dissolution, the controlling function of the electorate is erratic and intermittent. Quiescent during the term, it is activated only at the time of the elections, unalterably fixed to take place in the first week of November every two and four years. By-elections are rare and seldom considered indicative of political trends. From the viewpoint of intensified democratic control the otherwise objectionably short term for the members of the lower house is a blessing in disguise. Congress and the president are less sensitive to the vibrations among the grass roots than, for example, the British cabinet and Commons and far more accessible to the stupendous articulateness of the pressure and interest groups than their British counterparts.* It is only in the second session of the legislature that the antennae of the individual congressman become increasingly attuned to the electoral mood in his constituency.

Finally, the all-round system of controls includes also the judiciary, a unique phenomenon of the American pattern. In due course the courts, primarily the Supreme Court, injected themselves into the power process by claiming, or usurping, the right to invalidate congressional legislation because of its alleged incom-

* See below, pp. 354 ff.

patibility with the constitution. Transcending the policy execution ordinarily incumbent on the judiciary, the Supreme Court exercises the control of policy decisions that were jointly indorsed by congress and the president. Although the American pattern of government can no longer be imagined without the institution of judicial review,* the injection of the judiciary into the power process is wholly anomalous under the original concept of the mutually independent power holders, and this all the more since the court, while constantly intervening in the operation of the others, itself is exempted from control by the electorate.

Seen in its functional context, the American pattern of interdependence by co-ordination is neither presidentialism nor congressional government. Whether it inclines to the one or the other configuration depends on the personality in the White House. Woodrow Wilson in the eighties of the last century could appropriately describe the political regime after the Civil War as congressional government. Legislative supremacy at that time came close to the situation in France. The American system turns into genuine presidentialism only under the leadership of a strong personality: the older Roosevelt, Wilson, and Franklin D. Roosevelt. Since then, under both the Truman and the Eisenhower administrations, it has slipped back into the mold of congressional government. Foreign observers, for example, in contemporary France, who believe that the American system per se offers a guaranty against the hazards of parliamentary supremacy[20] misunderstood the power dynamism in the United States just as badly as did Montesquieu in his misinterpretation of the English government under the early Hanoverians.

It is hardly an exaggeration to describe the American pattern of government as the most difficult of all in actual operation, particularly if coupled with the complexities of federalism, an equally difficult arrangement of conflicting power interests. That it worked at all is a near-miracle, explainable only by the abundance

* The subject will be further discussed below, pp. 243 ff.

of a nation that could afford a cumbrous and wasteful governmental system. But its educational value should not be minimized. By virtue of the inherent interdependence by co-ordination, it trained the American people in the necessary art of political compromise, the noise and odor of our politics to the contrary notwithstanding. And in times of crisis—civil or foreign war, economic dislocations—the American pattern of government always succeeded in streamlining itself. The center of gravity shifted to the president without forcing him to resort to illegality, and congress always voluntarily submitted to presidential leadership.

No wonder that, when transplanted into a foreign environment, American presidentialism failed to take roots. For European constitutionalism, incongruously grafting the American loan of the independent and popularly elected president on parliamentarism, it was the kiss of death. The Second French Republic, Weimar-Germany, and republican Spain are cases in point. Marginal states, like Finland, are exceptions, but in such cases the president accepts the facts of parliamentary dynamics. On the other hand, more than a century and a half of imitated American presidentialism in Latin America fell far short of the expectation to provide for constitutional continuity and good government. Almost everywhere the American-inspired presidency served as the rostrum on which the Latin American brand of authoritarianism, *caudillismo*, was mounted. Either the primacy of the presidential position became a power device for an ambitious individual supported by the armed forces, landed oligarchs, and the church, or, in line with the recent political climate, it acquired a quasi-plebiscitary hue catering to the masses revolting against agrarian feudalism. More often than not a military junto dominates without any ideological pretenses. It appears in pseudoconstitutional disguises or struts about without constitutional trappings as naked power. Only in a few politically more advanced nations, with the nucleus of an independent middle class, did American presidentialism work tolerably well, as, for example, in Argentina and Brazil until 1930, in Colombia until 1948, and in Mexico during the last thirty years. More recently, American presidentialism has lost much of its magic even in Latin America.[21] Chile possessed from 1891 to 1925 a full-fledged parliamentary government under which cabinet instability and *détournement du pouvoir* closely resembled the last decades of the French Third Republic and for the same reason that the president lacked the power of dissolution. In 1925 Chile returned to a modified presidentialism which, however, retains certain features of parliamentarism: the congress is in a position to balance presidential supremacy, and the cabinet cannot govern without parliamentary support. The constitution proved serviceable in hectic times. Similar attempts to reconcile presidentialism with parliamentary government, as in Cuba (1940), Venezuela (1947), and Guatemala (1945), were short lived, terminating in unconstitutional junta autocracy. Experiments with American presidentialism in Asia are either inconclusive, as in the Philippines (constitution of 1935), or downright discouraging, as in South Korea (constitution of 1949).

In short, the American pattern of government, whether labeled "presidentialism," "separation of powers," or "of separated and co-ordinate functions," is an almost unique national experience of the American people, more blessed by Providence than any other nation in the history of man. The miracle of the American republic happened, not because of its constitution, but in spite of it.

The Sixth Pattern: Directory Government in Switzerland

Switzerland presents to the student of comparative political institutions a pattern of government *sui generis*, notwithstanding the fact that the design of the constitution of the Swiss confederation of 1848—completely revised in 1874—closely follows the assembly type of government. Once again one is struck by the cleavage between the constitutional intent and the political reality.

The Swiss political regime of today has nothing in common with the classical model of the French Revolution. The center is occupied by the Federal Assembly (Bundesversammlung), which Article 71 declares to be "the supreme power holder" (*oberste Gewalt*) of the Confederation. It is composed of two houses, the lower called the National Council (Nationalrat), and the upper the Council of States (Ständerat); the latter is the federalistic organ deliberately following the American precedent, without, however, possessing the superiority over the other house of the American Senate. On the other hand, the federal government—the Federal Council (Bundesrat)—consists of a group of seven men elected, like the lower house of parliament, for a term of four years by both houses of parliament sitting together as the Federal Assembly (Bundesversammlung). In contrast to the nominally omnipotent Federal Assembly, the Federal Council is described by the constitution (Art. 95) merely as the "highest executive and directing authority (*Behörde*) of the Confederation." It is noteworthy that these provisions almost literally correspond to Articles 57 and 64 of the Soviet constitution of 1936, another pure type of assembly government. According to the theory of assembly government underlying the constitution, the Federal Council is merely the subordinate agent of the parliament and not an independent power holder in its own right.

The actual power configuration does not conform to the American concept of separated functions, although it is sometimes, if erroneously, likened to it. Nor is the Federal Council in any sense a party cabinet as under parliamentarism, though its members are chosen by the parliament from among the party leaders. From this it is removed by the fact that the office of the federal councilor is incompatible with the parliamentary mandate. However, the members of the Federal Council attend the plenary meetings and commissions of both houses of parliament and take part in the debates. What is characteristic of parliamentarism is absent in Switzerland: the Federal Assembly cannot force, by a vote of non-confidence, the resignation of the government as a group or of an individual member. This is at the same time a significant deviation from the archetype of assembly government. To the latter, however, conform the inability of the government to dissolve the assemblies and the non-existence of a state president. The chairman of the Federal Council, an annually rotating function, has merely the title and exercises the ceremonial functions of the president of the Confederation.

The natural history of assembly government could not fail to assert itself in due course also in its application to Switzerland. True to the pattern, the Federal Council developed into the strong executive dominating the other power holders. Instead of remaining the subordinate agent of the omnipotent parliament, it rose to the commanding stature of political leadership unchallenged by the assembly. For this development beyond the word and the intent of the constitution several factors are responsible: the Federal Council is a coalition committee of the major parties which distribute the seven seats among themselves according to a prearranged key; more recently the Socialists—now alternating with the Liberals as the strongest party and long excluded by the bourgeois parties—are also represented. But, once elected, the Federal councilor conducts his office irrespective of his previous party affiliation, guided exclusively by the welfare of the Swiss state. He is chosen for his administrative and organizational competence and not because of his position as a prominent party politician. Constitutional convention has it that he may remain in office as long as he wishes to serve, thus providing Switzerland with a group of quasi-permanent governmental experts unparalleled elsewhere. Corruption is practically unknown in this happy land.

The characteristic organizational feature of the Federal Council is that the governing committee or directory—and it is from this institution, traceable back to the French constitution of 1795, that the Swiss pattern of government takes its name—assumes, by virtue of the constitution, collective responsibility for its performance before the parliament and the country.*

Policy decisions are initiated by the Federal Council, and the country expects this. The federal assemblies, as a rule, follow the political directives of the government and translate them into legislation as policy execution, even though legislative proposals may emanate also from either house. The respect for the political leadership of the Federal Council is such that the customary policy controls of the parliament are attenuated almost to the vanishing point. In this respect Switzerland is almost a happily underdeveloped country. Rarely is the Federal Council disowned by the parliament; if this happens, the government abides by the parliamentary decision.

However, by design of the constitution—and this is another unique feature thoroughly compatible with assembly government under popular sovereignty—policy control over both the government and the parliament, the center of political gravity, is shifted to the people as a voting collectivity, constitutional custom still stubbornly granting the franchise to the males only.[22] The voters have to pass on all constitutional amendments, more frequent in Switzerland because of the incessant extension of the federal jurisdiction to permit a largely government-controlled economy in a landlocked country without natural resources except hydroelectric power. The people also share in the policy-control function by the right to demand, on every bill passed by the legislature, a subsequent ratificatory referendum. They may even take the lead in policy decision by popular initiative—frequently resorted to— to induce the federal authorities to attend to a matter by legislation. In recent years the most noteworthy exercise of the referendal democracy was to restore the constitutional right of the people to pass on all legislation.†

The original version of assembly government, thus, has been

---

* See below, p. 169.   † See below, p. 225.

converted in Switzerland into a power process in which the government exercises undisputed political leadership, counterbalanced by the continuous policy control of the voting electorate.

The Swiss directory pattern of government is a non-repeatable experience of a politically mature, socially homogeneous, emotionally stable, and even-tempered nation. Only Uruguay experimented with a similar collective government—the so-called *colegiado*—under the Batlle constitution (1917) from 1918 to 1934; thereafter the country returned to modified presidentialism. Collective government reappeared under the constitution of 1951: the presidency was abolished and replaced by a National Council of Government, composed of nine members (*colegiado integral*) (Arts. 149 ff.). In both instances the collegiate executive was intended to minimize the excesses of presidential power customary in Latin America and to integrate the opposition—for generations Uruguay has operated with a two-party system—into political responsibility.* The first tryout period of collegiate government is generally considered successful. Conclusions on its recent repetition are premature.[23]

* See below, p. 366.

Part II

The Control of Political Power I
The Constitution and Its
Horizontal Controls

V. The Constitution

The Constitution, Basic Instrumentality of Power Control

Whether a political system is to be classified as autocratic or constitutional-democratic depends on whether effective techniques exist through which the power holders share in the exercise of political power and are subject to the control of the power addressees acting in their capacity as the supreme power holder. Human nature being what it is, it cannot be expected that the power holder, or holders, by voluntary self-restraint, will protect the power addressees and themselves against the destructive abuse of power. Devices for the containment of power do not exist or operate automatically; they must be created deliberately and built consciously into the power process. It took political man many centuries to realize that the good society, in which he possessed rights and in which these rights were secure, was conditioned on the containment of the power holders, whatever the legitimation—factual, religious, or legal—of their social control. In time this purpose appeared to be served best by articulating the restraints society wished to place on the power holders in the form of a set of fixed rules—the "constitution"—limiting their exercise of political power. The constitution, thus, became the basic instrumentality for the control of the power process.

ON THE TELOS OF THE CONSTITUTION

Every state society, whatever its social structure, possesses certain commonly shared convictions and established conduct patterns which, in the Aristotelian sense of the *politeia*, may be called its "constitution."[1] They reflect, whether articulated or not, the principles on which the relationship between power holders and power addressees is based. In the process of social control of the earlier stages of political civilization, secular government was identified with the religious values and institutions of the community. Political power was exercised by the rulers as the representatives and incarnators of the supernatural to which the power addressees submitted traditionally and voluntarily. But in due course the mythological era came to an end. Man's consciousness of himself as a free individual awoke, challenging the mystical legitimation of the political power of the rulers and demanding that obedience to political authority be rationalized. While the Hebrews still believed that the limitations of political power were in concordance with the law of the Lord, binding rulers and ruled alike, it is the immortal gift of the Greeks to have proceeded to the secularization and rationalization of the power process. With it, constitutional government was discovered.

The history of constitutionalism is nothing but the quest of political man for the limitation of the absolute power exercised by the power holders and the effort to substitute for the blind acceptance of factual social control the moral or ethical legitimation of authority. This was found in the consent of the power addressees to the exercise of social control by their rulers and, correspondingly, in their active participation in the political process. The limitations on naked power were to be secured by the agreement of the state society on certain definite rules for the conduct of the political process. It was believed this purpose would be served best if several power holders mutually shared and co-operated in the exercise of political power, instead of one power holder monopolizing it all. Where powers are shared, government is limited and, being limited, is restrained and controlled. The embodiment of these principles and rules is the ontological constitution of a state society, whether merely imbedded in the convictions of the people without explicit formalization—the constitution in the substantive sense of the term—or contained in a written document—the formal concept of the constitution. When Haile Selassie's constitution of Ethiopia (1931) says in Article 5, "In the Ethiopian Empire supreme power rests with the Emperor," it cannot claim to be a genuine constitution in the substantive sense, since it fails to institutionalize shared and limited government.[2]

The *telos* of any constitution, in the ontological sense, must be seen in the articulation of devices for the limitation and control of political power. In this sense the ideological intent of any constitution is twofold: to liberate the power addressees from the absolute social control of the rulers and to assign to them their legitimate share in the power process. To achieve these purposes, the exercise of political power was to be based on certain rules and procedures to which the power holders were to be compelled to conform. In historical perspective, therefore, constitutionalism, and in particular modern constitutionalism, is a product of the liberal ideology. In the modern mass society the only practicable device for the participation of the power addressees in the political process is the technique of representation, at first symbolic but later real.*

ON THE SUBSTANCE OF THE CONSTITUTION

The desire to articulate and formalize the basic ordering of the state society in a written document—a constitution in the formal sense—as a gapless system of fundamental norms is a relatively late development of constitutionalism. It was not postulated by ancient—Greek and Roman—constitutionalism. For Plato and Aristotle and in Greek political theory the *politeia* remained the constitution in the substantive sense. Even the sophisticated lawyers of the late Roman republic, foremost Cicero and the Stoics, while fully conscious of the superiority of a higher law over statutory legislation, did not claim that the fundamental norms governing the community should be written as substantive *leges*, let alone

* See above, pp. 38 ff.

that they should be codified. Such a procedure actually would have destroyed the essence and the meaning of the "higher law" and put it on the level of mere ephemeral state legislation.

The demand for a written and unified documentation of the fundamental norms arose as late as in the Puritan revolution, in opposition to the claim of absolute and unlimited authority of the Long Parliament. Its inspiration was religious—the biblical concept of the covenant. It was in the seventeenth and, more insistently, the eighteenth centuries that, under the powerful stimulation of the social-contract concept, the term "constitution" assumed its modern connotation. It came to signify a single document, containing the fundamental law of the state society and imbued with its specific *telos*, designed to curb the arbitrariness of the single power holder—at that time usually, though not invariably, an individual person, the absolute monarch—and to subject him to restraints and controls. For this purpose, to use the verbal imagery of the period, the Leviathan was tamed by splitting his heretofore monolithic sovereignty into different segments or departments, to each of which a specific state activity was assigned; this was the principle of the differentiation or specialization of state functions. To this was added a second correlative: each department should exercise the function assigned to it independently from the others; this was the principle of functional independence. It raised the department to the rank of an independent state organ or power holder. The organic unity of the state, then, was achieved by combining these specialized and autonomous power holders in joint action for the formation of the will of the state. All these arrangements, carefully planned in advance, were then to be incorporated in a single document, enacted with specific solemnity, called the "fundamental law," the "instrument of government," or the "constitution."

These functional principles did not spring to life like Minerva from Jupiter's head; they evolved slowly, by trial and error. But, after the vast experimentation of the English, American, and French revolutions, constitutional experience reached the stage where there could be agreement on certain minimum requirements of any formalized constitutional order.

The following elements are considered the irreducible minimum:[3] (1) There should be a differentiation of the various state functions and their assignment to different state organs or power holders, to avoid concentration of power in the hands of a single autocratic power holder. (2) There should be a planned mechanism for the co-operation of the several power holders. These arrangements—the "checks and balances" familiar to American and French constitutional theory—imply the sharing and, being shared, the limitations of the exercise of political power. (3) There should be a mechanism, likewise planned in advance, for avoiding deadlocks between the several autonomous power holders to prevent one among them, when the constitutionally required co-operation of the others is not forthcoming, from solving the impasse on his own terms and, thereby, subjecting the power process to autocratic direction. When, under the impact of the democratic ideology of popular sovereignty, constitutionalism had reached the point where the role of the ultimate arbiter of conflicts between the instituted power holders was assigned to the sovereign electorate, the original concept of liberal constitutionalism had been perfected as democratic constitutionalism. (4) There should be a method, also planned in advance, for peaceably adjusting the fundamental order to changing sociopolitical conditions— the rational method of constitutional amendment—in order to avoid the resort to illegality, violence, and revolution. (5) Finally, and this occurred at an early date in the evolution of constitutionalism and indicates its specific liberal *telos*, the fundamental law should also contain the explicit recognition of certain areas of individual self-determination—the individual rights and fundamental liberties—and their protection against encroachment by any and all power holders.* Next to the principle of shared and, therefore, limited power these areas inaccessible to political power have become the core of the substantive constitution.

* See below, pp. 315 ff.

Observations on the Historical Evolution
of Constitutionalism

The differentiation between the substantive and the formal constitution, leading to the codification of the fundamental principles of the state society in a single written document, took its final shape in the rational climate of the Enlightenment. However, the existence of a written constitution and constitutionalism are not identical. Previous political civilizations had lived under constitutional government without feeling the need of articulating the limitations in the exercise of political power. They were imbedded in the national consciousness and mores, honored by the rulers and the ruled.

The Hebrews.—The first of the nations practicing constitutionalism were the Hebrews. Flavius Josephus coined for their political civilization the name "theocracy." Ever since, the term has been applied to a political system in which the subjects live, or claim to live, under the rule of the divine authority of which the power holders on earth, whether priestly or secular, are merely the agents and representatives. The pattern was common in the ancient oriental empires where religious and secular values were fused, if subconsciously, into a coherent ideological frame with corresponding institutions. Theocracy appeared, under different names and forms, in the Islamic world, in Buddhism and Shintoism. Its foremost illustration in Europe was Calvin's Geneva. The pattern of government still survives today in Tibet.

For the theocratic establishment of the Hebrews it was characteristic—and in this lies one of the decisive elements of political history—that the ruler, far from being absolute and endowed with arbitrary power, was limited by the law of the Lord that bound rulers and ruled alike. This was their substantive constitution. Possibly echoing the pharaonic reformation of Ikhnaton in Egypt, the Hebrews were the first to emphasize the limitation of secular power by the moral code, and much of the eloquence of the Scriptures is dedicated to enjoining justice on the rulers, reminding them of their moral obligation to their subjects, lest the wrath of Yahweh-Jehovah visit their sins on the entire community. Politics, thus, were a function of theology, and secular power was a trust under the Lord. As the recognized voice of the public conscience, the prophets arose to resist unjust and unwise rulers who deviated from the path of the law—in the history of man the first legitimate opposition against established authority—justifying their rebellion against government unmindful of the law by the moral constitution of the state society. For more than two millennia the Bible, beyond its paramount role as the ethical code, has remained the standard canon for the evaluation of secular government, and there is hardly any subsequent political theory that can not draw its arguments from the Scriptures.

The Greeks.—In two brief and brilliant centuries there emerged in the glory that was Greece a fully constitutionalized political civilization. By one of those miracles in which the history of government is rich, this exceptionally talented nation progressed, almost by a single step, to the most advanced pattern of constitutional government: constitutional democracy. The direct democracy of the Greek polis states in the fifth century is the only known example of a political system with the complete identity of the rulers and the ruled in which political power was equally divided and evenly shared by all active citizens. For the lasting impact the Greeks made on the political development of the western world, it matters little that the polis state was rather a rule of the oligarchy of a relatively small leisure class resting on the infrastructure of a slave economy.

All Greek political institutions reflected their ingrained aversion to concentrated and arbitrary power and their almost frantic devotion to democratic fundamentals. The different state functions were widely dispersed among different officials, organs, or magistrates; the latters' powers were hedged in by ingenious controlling devices. Prominent among these were the following: Officeholders were designated by lot; short terms and rotation of office were prescribed; officeholders were not re-eligible; all active citizens had access to the public offices, for no qualifications were required except for certain offices in charge of technical functions. To these instrumentalities of unmitigated democracy were added the legal institutions of proscription and ostracism, directed against public figures whose popularity was feared to endanger the democratic structure of the state. Political power, thus, was rationally shared and, therefore, effectively controlled.

However, democratic fundamentalism was driven to the point where the assembly of the active citizens (*ekklesia*) was held to be omnipotent, without any constitutional limitations except those inherent in the moral traditions of the community. The virtues of the Greek direct democracy turned into its vices. It ultimately foundered because the sovereign people proved incapable of restraining their own sovereign powers. At no time in their checkered history did the Greek city-states, Athens least of all, attain internal stability. Their very form of government, together with the fickleness of their national character, proved the fertile soil of what they feared most: stasis, or, in the words of Professor McIlwain, "the lack of equilibrium, the condition of disharmony in a state."[4]

The Roman republic.—The Roman republican order, lasting much longer—from the fifth to the end of the second centuries—presents the classical illustration of a state society which was profoundly constitutional without committing the error of excessive democratism. The assemblies, no fewer than four, rather than reflections of democratic functions, were institutionalizations of the historical social structure. If they did not entirely wither away, they eventually lost their roles as political centers of the power process.[5] The republican organization was a political system with complex devices of checks and balances for the sharing and containment of the political power by the established magistrates. An elaborate repertory of reciprocal restraints existed: intra-organ controls, such as the collegiality of the higher and highest magistracies, annual terms of office, and prohibition of immediate reelection; and interorgan controls, purposefully interlocking the various power holders; for example, the intercession of the popular tribunes with illegal acts of the other, and even the consular, magistrates; the participation of the Senate, which in due course rose to the real center of political power, in the designation of the officials; and, the most modern solution for crisis government, the institution of the constitutional dictatorship, established, basically, for limited purposes and, invariably, for limited periods.

Republican constitutionalism, for all times the classical model of constitutional government that is non-democratic, disintegrated in the civil wars of the first century B.C., leading to Caesar's rule, a monarchy in all but name.[6] It was consummated through the cumulation of the major republican offices in his person, without limitation in time, and his skilful manipulation and corruption of the Senate. Republican Caesarism, then, was stabilized and legitimized in the Principate of Augustus. Finally, all republican and constitutional residues were swept aside by the Dominate. Subsequently, the Roman political civilization was exposed to the influence of oriental, later particularly Sassanian, governmental techniques and theocratic ideologies. In its final form the imperial establishment became the model pattern of monarchical absolutism with strong theocratic overtones, predicated on the virtual fusion of religious and secular authority in the person of the emperor. In the Byzantine empire it perpetuated itself, as caesaropapism, for another millennium.

And yet the influence of republican constitutionalism, if more symbolic than real, continued in the dogma of the *lex regia*, according to which the fountainhead of the absolute power of the monarch is the original transfer of political authority to him by the people.[7] The tradition of republican legitimacy runs like a subterranean river through ancient and medieval political thought; it breaks to the surface in Azo and, through the latter's influence on Bracton, enters the blood stream of English political tradition.

England and the Puritan revolution.—The second, the modern, stage of constitutionalism begins with the Puritan revolution in England and its repercussions in the British colonies in the New World.[8] A unique constellation of circumstances was responsible for the transformation of the absolute into the constitutionally limited monarchy. With the destruction of the Armada, the national emergency that had compelled the parliament to submit to the leadership of Elizabeth had disappeared. The foreign dynasty of the Stuarts succeeded to the throne. Men of substance were sent to represent the borough constituencies, which, carrying the burden of taxation, claimed their share in financial legislation. Religious dissenters asserted their rights of spiritual self-determination against the ironclad ecclesiastical rule of the established church. The new middle class in parliament resurrected its "ancient and indubitable rights and privileges" that had become submerged, though not forgotten, in the long years of Tudor despotism. No longer satisfied with the inarticulate premises of a constitutional society, which the Stuarts were only too prone to ignore, the new Commons insisted on the reality of the traditional limitations of the crown and demanded their share in political power. The momentous struggle ended with the triumph of the parliament over the crown in the Glorious Revolution of 1688, and this at a time when the absolute monarchy, free from constitutional limitations, had reached its zenith everywhere else in Europe.

It is in this period that the first written constitutions make their appearance.[9] If the colonial charters are neglected because they were granted by the crown, the most prominent among the constitutional documents autonomously enacted was the Fundamental Orders of Connecticut (1639). Theoretically, the most influential in England proper was the Agreement of the People (1647), which, though never a formal legislative act, must be considered the first blueprint of a full-fledged modern constitution. Finally,

Cromwell's Instrument of Government (1654) is the first valid written constitution of the modern state, preceding even the *Regeringsform* in Sweden (1663). But the British permanently abandoned the concept of a written basic law. Beginning with the legislation before and after the Glorious Revolution—Habeas Corpus Act (31 Car. II, c. 2 [1679]), Bill of Rights (1 Will. and Mary, sess. 2, c. 2 [1688]), and Act of Settlement (12 & 13 Will. III, c. 2 [1700])—they were content with statutory regulations of their fundamental order, which popular conviction endowed with no less constitutional sanctity than if they were embodied in a formal constitution. Ever since, the proud tradition of constitutional government without a written constitution has persisted in England; today she is the only one of the major states that dispenses with it.

THE UNIVERSALISM OF THE WRITTEN CONSTITUTION

The final triumph of democratic constitutionalism solemnized in a written document started in the New World, first with the constitutions of the American states in rebellion against the English crown and then with their federal constitution in 1787. For a long time French political theorists, nurtured by the concepts of the social contract and popular sovereignty, had advocated a written constitution. The demand erupted with full force in the French Revolution. Sieyès' inventive mind, expanding Rousseau's dogma, expounded the theory of the *pouvoir constituant* as belonging by right to the nation and applied it skilfully to the practical tasks of the hour by assigning it to the Third Estate as the true representation of the nation. For a century and more, political theorists had urged the rationalization of the process of political power by limitations of royal absolutism and the relocation of the power center from the crown to the people and their representatives. This demand became epitomized in the establishment of a formalized constitutional document. It was the seal on the new social order and believed to be the guaranty that once and for all constitutional government could be nothing but democratic constitutionalism sanctified by a written constitution.

The third and, to date, last stage of constitutionalism is the universalism of the written constitution. Logically, it follows from the precedents of the American and French revolutions. Constitutions sprouted in the wake of the victorious tricolor. After the interlude of Napoleon's autocracy, which eagerly conformed to the new fashion, the technique of the written constitution spread to the Continental monarchies. Yielding to the irresistible pressure of public opinion, they either granted their people a constitutional document (the "octroyed" constitution) or were compelled to do so. All these constitutions established representative institutions that restricted the royal prerogative. In some cases these instruments were grafted on the traditional dualism of the crown and the estates. Among them the most influential was the "legitimist" Charte of 1814 in France. The constitutions of the early nineteenth century are the bridge between monarchical absolutism and democratic constitutionalism, a transitional institutionalization of the pragmatic compromise between tradition and revolution. The turning point, ushering in the contemporary version of the monarchical establishment in conformity with democratic constitutionalism, was the Belgian *charte* of 1831. It squared the circle between the royal prerogative and popular sovereignty by the henceforth sacred formula inherited from the French Revolution: "All powers emanate from the people" (Art. 25).

The written constitution offered the frame within which, in the following generations, the complete democratization of the process of political power could be accomplished. With the extension of the suffrage from the propertied oligarchy to the entire adult population with completely democratic representation, the electorate rose to the rank of the supreme power holder to whom all other instituted power holders—parliament, government, crown —had to submit. From Europe the written constitution conquered the globe. For the last one and a half centuries it has become the symbol of nationhood and statehood, of self-determination and independence. No nation emerging from foreign domination in the successive waves of nationalism that have swept the world since the French Revolution has failed to give itself, often with a great deal of travail, by a free act of original creation, a written document embodying the fundamentals of its future existence. Sovereignty of the people and the written constitution have become ideologically and practically synonymous.

THE PROCEDURE OF CONSTITUTION-MAKING
AND CONSTITUTIONAL AMENDMENT

In line with the concepts of popular sovereignty and the original *pouvoir constituant* of the sovereign people, a standardized and even stereotyped procedure has evolved for the framing and the adoption of the written constitution.[10] A national assembly or *constituante* is elected by the entire people for this specific task. More frequently in recent times, the final ratification by the sovereign people has been mandatory. The rationale behind this is that the supreme law of the land acquires, by being indorsed by the sovereign people, a higher sanctity. To date in the history of constitution-making, the electorate has disowned the work of its freely chosen representatives in the national assembly only once; this occurred in the rejection of the first constitution of the French Fourth Republic in 1946. Not infrequently, however, the work of the national assembly has been confirmed by unimpressive majorities of the electorate, occasionally amounting, together with the abstentions, to a minority of the electorate. This occurred with the French second constitution of 1946 and the Uruguay constitution of 1952.

Likewise, constitutional amendment, as a rule, is subject to more difficult procedures than ordinary legislation. The techniques applied are most varied. In some cases parliament must vote on it according to specific procedures and pass it by qualified majorities;

in others the participation of the electorate in the amending process is mandatory, and they are called on to confirm the amendment either by a referendum or by the election of a new parliament. The details do not require a full discussion here.[11]

It is safe to say that the written constitution has become the most common and universally accepted phenomenon of the contemporary state organization. So deeply implanted is the conviction that a sovereign state must possess a written constitution that even modern autocracies feel compelled to pay tribute to the democratic legitimacy inherent in the written constitution. But what the American and French revolutions expected to have established once and for all as the symbol and realization of government in a free society has become, in our time, the frequent and convenient cloak for naked power. By no means, therefore, does the existence of a formalized constitutional document make a state "constitutional," except in the most nominal sense of the term.

Classifications of Constitutions

OBSOLESCENCE OF THE STANDARD CLASSIFICATIONS

The total number of constitutions enacted since the late eighteenth century has never been established accurately, and no "register" of constitutions exists.[12] By now, if the instruments of the member units of federal states are included, they must have reached a substantial four-digit figure. Latin America holds the record in the number of constitutions enacted: the Dominican Republic had twenty-five, Haiti had twenty-two, and Bolivia had fifteen within a century and a half before 1952.[13] Since that time the turnover has been even greater. In Europe, France and Greece compete for the dubious honor; the former, including also the *lois organiques,* can pride itself on at least sixteen since the revolution; the latter has had at least ten since 1821.[14]

A glance at this plethora of written constitutions reveals that their functional arrangements still conform to the standard pattern that emerged with the first appearance of constitutions at the end of the eighteenth century. All divide the state functions into the legislative, executive, and judicial departments and assign them to different state organs or power holders. All of the recent vintages profess belief in the sovereignty of the people, including those of regimes that have become notorious for their nondemocratic conduct of the power process. The majority of them add a bill of rights to the frame of government. Without exception all establish electoral procedures for at least the representative assembly, and some for the designation of the supreme executive organ also. The proverbial man from Mars, when confronted with these documents, would not imagine that behind the structural and often verbal identity of these provisions is hidden a vast differentiation of the actual power dynamism.

While the deceptive identity of the functional mechanics stimulates the need for a classification of written constitutions, the very standardization contributes to the difficulty of the task. Once again, the classical categories that political science is in the habit of dragging like iron chains for a generation and more prove wholly inadequate. For the iconoclast willing to wreck the stock-in-trade classifications of the textbooks, it is sufficient to review them briefly:

1. To distinguish between the written and the unwritten constitution is beside the point. Practically all constitutions of today are written, and the class of those unwritten is represented only by Great Britain, New Zealand, and Franco Spain. Prior to the communists' seizure of power, Hungary also belonged to this group. A state without a written constitution is by no means constitutionless. While Britain traditionally disdains the assemblage of the basic constitutional conventions in a single document, much of the fundamental order is articulated in statutory form, beginning with the legislation of the Glorious Revolution and lead-

ing to the series of the Representation of People Acts since 1832, the Parliament Acts of 1911 and 1949, the Ministers of the Crown Act of 1937, and others. However, the complete absence of a written instrument of course cannot be equated with the existence of an unwritten constitution. Constitutional vacuums of this kind are characteristic of contemporary autocracy. For example, Hitler's Third Reich deliberately dispensed with a formal constitution, the Weimar insrtument having virtually ceased to exist with the passage of the presidential emergency ordinance of February 28, 1933, which suspended the basic civil liberties indefinitely. In Latin American states, likewise, the revolutionary rule of a junta or the military may dispense with a written instrument. A special case in point was Vargas' rule in Brazil (1937–47); the constitution of 1937 was stillborn, superseded at once by a suspending clause and the state of siege.[15] Such interregnums are usually terminated by the adoption of a new constitution, with or without the manufactured consent of the power addressees. Periods without constitution may also occur on the return trip from the authoritarian to the democratic constitutional state, as exemplified by the post-Perón regime in Argentina, which canceled the Perón constitution of 1949 without immediately re-enacting the previous instrument of 1853. A similar situation prevailed in Colombia after the ousting of the military dictatorship of Rojas Pinilla (1957).

All states with a written constitution possess also constitutional law in statutory form and a vast body of unformulated constitutional usages and practices. This situation led to the useful distinction in Continental jurisprudence between formal constitutional law, incorporated in a single document called the "constitution," and material or substantive constitutional law, consisting of statutes and constitutional conventions.

2. Another of the traditional classifications distinguished flexible and rigid constitutions, according to the mechanics of the amending process. In practice, the distinction largely coincides with that

between the written and the unwritten constitution, because the constitutional norms embodying the latter can be modified by simple legislation. Again this approach is highly formalistic and unrealistic. The written constitution adjusts itself to social change not only by formal constitutional amendment but also by constitutional usage, conventions, and interpretation on the part of the government agencies, the parliament, and the courts. For example, under the United States constitution the formal amending procedure, designedly made difficult to provide stability, has been used since the birth of the Republic only twelve times, if the first ten amendments are omitted, as they should be. Yet constitutional usages and the judicial interpretation of the Supreme Court certainly have modified it beyond the recognition of its framers. Contrariwise, the fundamental norms of the British unwritten constitution, seemingly easy to amend by simple statute, have remained relatively stable; the inevitable changes were accomplished by modifications of the unwritten conventions. Since even in states with a written constitution formal constitutional amendment is no longer the foremost instrumentality for establishing the harmony of the document with social change, the amending procedure has lost its importance as a criterion for classification.

3. Other traditional classifications actually refer more to the patterns of government they embody than to the constitutions themselves. The distinction between a monarchical and a republican political regime is familiar. If this criterion were applied, Great Britain and Sweden would have to be listed in the same category with Saudi Arabia or Nepal, which makes the classification obviously meaningless. The distinction between the parliamentary and the non-parliamentary executive is another example of the differentiation of patterns of government rather than of the constitutions proper: in this case American presidentialism and the French Charte of 1814 would be grouped together, with equally unsatisfactory results. Other standard classifications focus on rather marginal features or institutions, such as whether the

chief executive is elected by parliament or the electorate at large, or whether the legislature is uni- or bicameral. 4. Finally, there remains the distinction between the federal and the unitary state organization. It certainly has retained more validity than most others, but, as will be shown later,* this approach also has lost much of its realistic value because of the progressive erosion of the federal principle in traditionally federal states. What seems needed, therefore, are new, more substantially oriented, classifications of written constitutions. The following are suggested.

ORIGINAL AND DERIVATIVE CONSTITUTIONS

The "original constitution" is understood to be an instrument of government which embodies a new, truly creative, and, hence, "original" functional principle for the process of political power and the formation of the will of the state. The term "derivative constitution" denotes a constitutional pattern which largely borrows from existing constitutions either at home or abroad, adjusting them to the national environment. Whether a constitution is genuinely creative or merely imitative depends, of course, on the value judgment of the observer. However, few will characterize the French constitution of 1946 as truly creative, while there exist justifiable differences of opinion concerning Weimar.

Original constitutions are relatively and absolutely few. Through the years the art of constitution-making has exhibited little inventive imagination, owing to the intrinsically conservative character of political man, understandably averse to violent breaks with the past. A sort of *vis inertiae* forces constitutional reform more often than not into the traditional channels of the national experience. Moreover, experiments with constitutional innovations are dangerous. Only large-scale social revolutions are likely to produce new constitutional patterns.

As original in this sense may be characterized the following

* See below, pp. 285 ff.

constitutional patterns: British parliamentarism—interdependence by integration; the American constitutional system of presidentialism—interdependence by co-ordination; the French constitution of 1793, launching assembly government on its career; the Napoleonic constitutions, introducing plebiscitary Caesarism; the French Charte of 1814, establishing the constitutionally limited monarchy of the legitimist ideology; the Belgian *charte* of 1831, reconciling the monarchical principle with popular sovereignty; and the Russian "Soviet" constitutions of 1918 and 1924. Possibly Pilsudski's constitution of Poland (1935) may be included also, since it institutionalized neopresidentialism. Constitutional gourmets may add Gabriele D'Annunzio's delightfully poetic and monstrously unworkable vision of a corporate state society under the *Statuti della Reggenza Italiana del Carnero* (Fiume) of 1920,[16] or the Chinese Kuomintang constitution of 1931, with its five Yuans as power holders. Practically all other written constitutions are more or less derivative in the sense that they appropriate features from other constitutional patterns and tailor them to fit the national requirements.

To this natural process of syncretism, through which the dynamics of constitutional history operate, one may attribute another seldom-observed phenomenon: Constitutions are subject, like feminine apparel, to fashions and styles conditioned by the political climate of a specific period. Hence they appear in clusters or families, all members of which can trace their linear ancestry back to a mother constitution that has transmitted to its progeny common traits. Often the "originality" of a specific constitution is revealed in the incidence and frequency of its imitation by other nations in search of a formula for constitutional national destiny. Among the families of constitutions, therefore, must be mentioned those sired by an original constitution mentioned above. But, curiously, strictly derivative constitutions, which are little more than composites of features on loan from other instruments of government, also often exert a tremendous influence on other nations engaged in the exercise of their *pouvoir constituant*. Examples are the French constitution of 1791, its failure at home notwithstanding, and that of 1875; Germany's ill-starred Weimar constitution of 1919; and, finally, the wholly imitative constitution of the U.S.S.R. of 1936.

IDEOLOGICALLY PROGRAMMATIC AND UTILITARIAN CONSTITUTIONS

As another promising approach to a more realistic classification an analysis of the ideological substance of the various instruments is suggested. One would be tempted to distinguish constitutions that are ideologically "charged" or "programmatic" from those that are ideologically neutral or strictly utilitarian. Since the *telos* of early constitutionalism was the limitation of absolute power and the protection of the power addressees against unreasonable and arbitrary power holders, all constitutions of the late eighteenth and the early nineteenth centuries are necessarily colored by the liberal ideology. Its influence was latent in the distribution of functions among the several power holders under reciprocal control and patent in the inclusion of a bill of fundamental rights.

Once liberal constitutionalism had become generally accepted in the western world and no longer seemed to require specific emphasis, another type appeared. It presents a strictly utilitarian frame of government, confined to the mechanics of the governmental process without blatant or even latent ideological overtones. Such instruments of government are perfect reflections of the rational optimism of the nineteenth century, which took the irresistible progress of constitutionalism for granted. An illustration is the Bismarckian federal constitution of 1871, which is nothing more than bylaws regulating the conduct of the governmental business by the high-level state organs. Its ideological inspiration equals that of a telephone directory; any reference to fundamental rights, always alien to German tradition, is conspicuously absent. But the absence of programmatic embroidery suggests to the constitutional sociologist its intrinsically authoritarian *telos* and character. Likewise, the contemporaneous constitution of the French Third Republic of 1875 was merely a bundle of instructions for the relations of the instituted power holders, and a skeletal one at that. If the document was silent on individual rights, the Declaration of Rights was at least the underlying supra-constitutional assumption.

What such ideologically neutral constitutions set out to do is to offer, without any ideological preferences, a functional framework within which all sociopolitical forces of the community are expected to compete, provided they utilize the existing institutions and respect the prescribed mechanics of the power process. One of the most recent of such predominantly utilitarian constitutions is that of the French Fourth Republic of 1946, which refers to the liberal ideology only in passing in the preamble.

In our age, which calls itself "ideological," once again, as in the eighteenth century, the climate of public opinion has become more ideology-conscious. Into many recent constitutions the ideological intent has infiltrated to such an extent that, now, a constitution does not seem fully dressed unless it is dressed up ideologically. These constitutions are often veritable catechisms rather than business codes for the rational conduct of the governmental process. This aspect may also help to explain the change, for the worse, in draftsmanship; their verbosity is a far cry from, for example, the succinctness of the American or the precision of the Belgian constitutions. An outstanding illustration of the ideologically conditioned constitution is that of Mexico of 1917, with its emphatic orientation toward a socialist society. While other nations commemorate the birth of their fundamental order by giving its date as a name to a street or square, there is no other country which so honors a specific article, the one hundred and twenty-third, containing the principle of the social welfare state. Weimar, rather promiscuously, blended liberal and social ideologies. More and more the classical bill of liberal-individual rights is being implemented and extended by socioeconomic rights of the people that require for their fulfilment positive action on the part of the power holders.* If the Soviet constitution of 1936 is still ideologically reticent—the socialist accent is confined to the rights and duties of the citizens (Arts. 118 ff.)—the Hungarian constitution of 1948 bristles with references to the toilers, workers, proletarians, and the like. The constitutions of Portugal (1933), Austria (1934), and Eire (1937) use Christianity, meaning Catholicism, in their mastheads. The Bonn Basic Law stipulates, at a prominent place in the introduction to the frame of government proper (Art. 20, sec. 1), the ideological principle that "the Federal Republic of Germany is a democratic and social federal state under the rule of law," repeating the social element in Article 28 when enjoining the same principle on the *Länder*. In all such cases the ideological infrastructure has more than merely declaratory force; it is of a normative character and confronts the constitutional lawyer with the altogether novel obligation of judging the political process by its conformity to its ideological values and premises.[17] If the trend persists, it may well necessitate a corresponding approach to the classification of constitutions.

The Perversion of the Constitution by Modern Autocracy

The foregoing suggestions, focusing on the content and substance rather than on the external mechanics of the constitutions, may be useful for a new classification, but they have a fundamental defect in common with the standard classical categories. They fail to take into account what must be considered the most significant phenomenon in the recent practice of the written constitution. If originally the formalized document served to limit the exercise of political power for the sake of the liberty of the power addressees, today the existence of a written constitution no longer *ipso facto* implies the guaranty of shared and, thereby, limited power. More and more the device of the written constitu-

---

* See below, pp. 323 ff.

tion is consciously used to disguise authoritarian and totalitarian political systems. In many cases the written constitution is nothing but a conveniently deceptive camouflage for the installation of the concentrated power of a single power holder. The constitution has become denuded of its intrinsic *telos* of institutionalizing the shared exercise of political power.

There is little comfort in the fact that constitutional democracy, in defeat, scored a Pyrrhic victory: no political system of today can afford to flout openly the democratic ideology that all power emanates from the people and that its exercise is legitimate only if in conformity with their will. Intellectually, at least, the civilized world has graduated from authoritarianism. The nostalgic protestations of the elitist fringe notwithstanding, it is axiomatic that the people are the ultimate source of political power. Even Hitler had his Goebbels exalt the Third Reich as an "ennobled" democracy, whatever this, or similar semanticisms, may mean. A written constitution imbues any political regime with a sort of respectability. The Machiavellians have come to realize that the democratic credo is the shingle under which they can pursue their sinister trade. The written constitution thus has become the protective coloring for the operation of naked power. If the externals of the democratic process are faithfully proclaimed in a written constitution, the internals matter little, except for the people deprived of its substance. Autocracy in the mid-twentieth century defiantly sails under the false flag of democracy. The constitution is a rose by any name. By a sleight of hand the modern authoritarians perverted the constitution from an instrument of freedom into a tool of oppression. Its original *telos*, the sharing of political power by several power holders to limit absolute power, has been transformed into its opposite.

The historical honor for having deliberately invented the metamorphosis of constitutionalism for his own authoritarian ends goes to Napoleon,* if not to the precedent set by Julius Caesar. Hence derives the appellation "Caesarism" or "Bonapartism"[18] for

---

* See above, pp. 63 ff.

authoritarian rule disguised as democratic constitutionalism. After the experience of the French Revolution, no government could claim to be legitimate unless it derived its power from the will of the sovereign people. But neither in Caesar's nor Napoleon's time did organized political parties exist. The technical invention that authoritarianism needed in order to succeed in the technological society was the single or state party. Through it, the plurality of several power holders could be nominally maintained but subordinated to the single power holder, an individual person, junta, committee, assembly, or party. The single party dominates all established power holders and state organs, including the members of the governing group itself, the assembly, courts, army, and bureaucracy. Once the competition of the rival sociopolitical forces has been eliminated in the closed power circuit, the constitution becomes meaningless. At most, it remains a functional frame for the conduct of governmental business by the party-controlled power holders.

A glance at certain recent instruments called "constitutions" suffices to show the progressive obliteration of the original concept of the written constitution. An increasing number of states, without being constitutional in any but the most nominal and semantic sense, flaunt elaborate written constitutions adorned with all the trimmings of a full-fledged constitutional democracy. During the nineteenth century, Latin America was the preferred region where autocracy masqueraded as constitutional government. Today, however, the practice of garnishing rank autocracy by a written constitution is flourishing in many lands. Some of them are long-established states; others are just emerging from feudalism and colonialism into nationhood. Among the former are more than half the Latin American nations; among the latter are practically all the Arab states, together with Iran, Afghanistan, South Korea, and South Viet-Nam. The perversion of the written constitution for autocratic purposes is most common, however, in the communist orbit: in the Soviet Union, its satellites in Europe and Asia, and Red China. Everywhere such constitutions were enacted with much pomp. But the fountain of the constituent power of the sovereign people is polluted from the start by the novel—or, for the historian, not so novel—practice of manipulation from above.* In our technological age autocracy has perfected itself to the point that it can even bend the fundamental law at will.

A final question may be asked to which no answer can be offered: Why do these regimes go through the motions of democratic legitimacy? Why do they need constitutions, elections, and all the paraphernalia of the constitutional democracy? Is it to deceive the world at large, their own people, or themselves? Does the modern autocrat expect, by enacting a constitution, to gain more diplomatic respectability, or has he become in time a victim of his own tricks, so that he believes in them? The Napoleonic plebiscites, in spite of their crudeness, reflected rather accurately the indorsement of the regime by the majority of the people. For his nephew the assumption of popular support is more doubtful. Neither of them, however, could ignore the powerful magic of the French Revolution. The election that brought Perón into power was honest, at least technically. But Mussolini, Goebbels, Perón, Ngo Dinh Diem, Nasser, and *tutti quanti* are modern men and no fools. They cannot believe in what their constitutions proclaim and their elections produce.

The "Ontological" Classification of Constitutions

With the radically changed role of the written constitution in mind, it is suggested that a new approach to the classification of constitutions is necessary. To avoid the more fashionable term "existential," the new analysis may be called "ontological."[19] It is proposed to differentiate constitutions as to their normative, nominal, and semantic character.[20]

The normative constitution.—The ontological approach, instead of analyzing substance and content, focuses on the concord-

* See below, pp. 270–71.

ance of the reality of the power process with the norms of the constitution. It proceeds from the recognition that a written constitution does not operate automatically once it has been adopted by a nation. A constitution is what power holders and power addressees make of it in practical application. To a large extent, the paramount issue of whether the specific power arrangement of a constitution becomes effective depends on the sociopolitical environment it is destined to serve. If a full-fledged constitutional democracy is implanted without antecedent political education into a state just emerging from traditional autocracy or colonial tutelage, it would be a near-miracle if it were to take roots at once. To be a living constitution, that is, lived up to in practice by power holders and power addressees, a constitution requires a national climate conducive to its realization. The tradition of autocratic processes must have sufficiently atrophied in the minds of governors and governed to give constitutional government a reasonably fair chance. To be living, it is not enough that a constitution be valid in the legal sense; to be real and **effective, it** must be faithfully observed by all concerned; it must have integrated itself into the state society. If this is the case, a constitution may be spoken of as *normative:* its norms govern the political process, or the power process adjusts itself to the norms. To use a homely simile: the constitution is like a suit that fits and that is actually worn.

The nominal constitution.—However, the normativity cannot be taken for granted; it requires verification by practice in every single case. Even though legally valid, a constitution that is not lived up to in practice lacks existential reality. In this case the constitution may be described as *nominal.* The situation must not be confused with the well-known phenomenon that constitutions as written differ from constitutions as actually applied. If at the beginning was the word, the word changes its meaning as soon as it is put to the test of reality. Constitutions change not only by formal constitutional amendment but also and even more by an imperceptible metamorphosis of the established norms through political usages and habits. What the nominal constitution implies is that the existing socioeconomic conditions—for example, lack of political education and training, absence of an independent middle class, and other factors—militate, for the time being, against the complete concordance of the constitutional norms with the exigencies of the power process. The factual state of affairs does not, or not yet, permit the complete integration of the constitutional norms into the dynamics of political life. Perhaps the adoption of a constitution, or of this kind of constitution, was premature, but the hope exists, supported by the will of power holders and power addressees, that sooner or later the reality of the power process will conform to the blueprint. The primary objective of the nominal constitution is educational, with the goal, in the near or distant future, of becoming fully normative and actually governing the dynamics of the power process instead of being governed by it. To continue the simile: the suit, for the time being, hangs in the closet, to be worn when the national body politic has grown into it.

The semantic constitution.—Finally, the instances are unfortunately increasing, both in number and in the importance of the states affected, in which the constitution is fully applied and activated, but its ontological reality is nothing but the formalization of the existing location of political power for the exclusive benefit of the actual power holders in control of the enforcement machinery of the state. While the primary function of the written constitution is that of limiting the concentration of power and permitting, within the constitutional frame, the peaceable competition of the social forces of the community, the mobility of social dynamics is eliminated by the type of constitution referred to here. The power configuration is frozen in the interests of the Powers That Be, be it an individual person (dictator), a junta, a committee, an assembly, or a party. This pattern may be spoken of as a *semantic* constitution. The actual operation of the power process would not be noticeably different if no formalized constitution existed at all. Instead of serving for the limitation of political power, it has become the tool for the stabilization and perpetuation of the grip of the factual power holders on the community. The peaceable, non-revolutionary change in the location of political power is impossible. To apply our simile: the suit is not an honest suit at all; it is merely a cloak or a fancy dress.

Whether a constitution is to be characterized as normative, nominal, or semantic cannot be decided, as a rule, from its text alone, particularly since constitutions are usually silent on some of the most essential aspects of the power process, such as the electoral system, political parties, and plural groups. In each case insight into the realities of the power process is required. The nominal and the semantic type always pretends to be normative. Moreover, the discovery of the ontological quality of a specific constitution is made difficult by the deceptive similarity of the political institutions with which all governments operate. This cannot be otherwise. With slight variations, the machinery of social control is identical everywhere. Constitutions are instructions concerning the conduct of the power process; they cannot individualize and become treatises on national psychology. Particularly difficult is the distinction of the nominal from the normative constitution. But at least there are certain unmistakable criteria for recognizing a semantic constitution: a state president can perpetuate himself in office; he is empowered to veto the actions of the legislature without ultimate recourse to the electorate; the representative assembly is wholly or in its majority nominated; the confirmation of policy decisions is left to plebiscites instead of to a freely elected parliament; elections are conducted on the single-party ticket.

It is impossible to submit here a complete survey of the areas of constitutional normativism, nominalism, and semanticism in the ninety-odd states of today. The general statement must suffice that the normative constitution is the rule in western states with an established tradition of constitutional government and a relatively high degree of socioeconomic homogeneity. Normativism enjoys an unbroken record in Great Britain; in the western and northern monarchies; in the British Dominions; in Switzerland; and in the United States. France, Italy, Germany, and Greece have always reverted to it after revolutionary interludes. But also newer state societies, particularly those trained in the British school, such as India, Ceylon, Eire, and Israel, strive hard and not without success for the scrupulous observance of their western and often complex type of constitutions. It testifies to the strength of the normative tradition that the Nationalist government of the Union of South Africa has recently been engaged in a bitter and tenacious struggle to remove the obstacles to their ideology of white supremacy by constitutional methods, if often debatable, rather than by naked force. In other instances of constitutions in the British educational orbit—in Burma and Pakistan—and likewise in Indonesia—the constitution does not yet seem to have advanced from the nominal to the normative stage. Turkey is a special case; here a formerly strictly semantic constitution has been converted, for the time being, into a normative one.

The nominal constitution, on the other hand, has its natural habitat in states where western democratic constitutionalism has been implanted into a colonial or feudal-agrarian social order, without antecedent intellectual incubation or political maturation. The absence of an economically independent and intellectually self-confident middle class also plays an important role. Literacy still appears to be the indispensable prerequisite for the proper functioning of a normative constitution, in spite of the radio and the techniques of electoral symbolism employed as substitutes. Latin America has the traditional *ambiente* for the nominal constitution. But here the record of genuine normativism, if spotty at times, persists at least in Argentina, Brazil, Chile, Colombia, Uruguay, Mexico, and Costa Rica. The novices in constitutional government in Asia and Africa will have to pass through an extended apprenticeship in the nominal constitution before they can graduate to constitutional normativism.

Finally, the semantic constitution does not seem to have a specific breeding ground. It may appear anywhere. In the past the constitutions of the two Napoleons set the pattern. The instruments of most of the neopresidential states belong to the category. The "ideal type" of the constitution abused in order to intrench the power of the ruling clique is presented by the constitution of Cuba of 1952, proclaimed by the dictator Fulgencio Batista after his *coup d'état*.[21] Practically all Islamic states, with the possible exception of Lebanon—which is half-Christian—and Turkey, have perfect constitutions of a strictly semantic character. The ruling cliques, whether dynastic, feudal-oligarchic, or plutocratic, hardly ever pay more than scant lip service to the letter, let alone the spirit, of their constitutions. The practice of contemporary totalitarianism varies considerably. Mussolini was satisfied with perverting the existing Carlo-Albertian constitution of 1849 to the point where it offered no limitations to his personal regime. Therefore, he took care to observe superficially the constitutional procedures, but he committed the error of the apprentice sorcerer in retaining the institution of the monarchy, which ultimately, together with his own creation, the Fascist Grand Council, was his undoing. Hitler was more realistic and honest: he never thought of fettering his despotism by even a semantic constitution.

The semantic constitution, disguised as the ultrademocratic pattern of assembly government, has become the common practice in the Soviet orbit. The Stalin conception of the written constitution was merely static; it registered the factual power configuration without pretending to be a frame for a future change in the location of power.[22] It stabilized and perpetuated the existing power configuration of formal assembly government, factually dominated by the Communist party, which, in turn, was under his absolute control. The formula proved convenient for the other communist autocracies wherever they could implant themselves, even in nations with a substantial tradition of constitutional government like Hungary and Czechoslovakia. Whether the transformation of the Soviet political system that has been under way since Stalin's death presages the gradual transition from a strictly semantic to a nominal or even a normative constitution is hard to tell. The indications are that, while the power circuit may remain ideologically closed for a long time, the liberalization of the governmental control and the establishment of a semblance of the rule of law may well help to dismantle the semantic constitution. Even then, Soviet constitutionalism will hardly approximate western constitutional democracy. Moreover, the historical experience that an autocratic regime by domestic liberalization destroys itself may no longer be applicable. From 1789 until the appearance of the Soviet Union, none has lasted long enough to allow a new generation to grow up under it.

It is frankly admitted that the classification of constitutions as normative, nominal, and semantic can be little more than a pioneering attempt in need of further refinement and precision. It may at least have the merit, however, of breaking away from the wholly unrealistic traditional categorizations and of corresponding more to the experience of our time.

The Devaluation of the Written Constitution in the Constitutional-Democratic State

Constitutional democracy in the mid-twentieth century is in a state of crisis. Even in states with a fully integrated constitutional order the written constitution has suffered a serious functional devaluation and loss of prestige.[23] Its luster has visibly paled. Two interrelated problems may be bracketed together. The first centers on the observation that, in states that traditionally have had a normative constitution, it is no longer so scrupulously obeyed by the power holders themselves as it once was; it is not treated in a way that befits the supreme law of the land. The second is the alarming indifference of the mass of the power addressees to their instrument of government, a psychological attitude that ultimately may lead to the atrophy of their constitutional conscience.

DELINQUENCIES IN THE APPLICATION OF THE CONSTITUTION

If it is accepted as the underlying premise of democratic constitutionalism that the constitution, as enacted by the constituent power of the sovereign people, is binding on both power holders and power addressees until changed through the constitutionally provided procedures, it should be expected that the constitution as written is fully normative and integrally applied by the power holders—government, parliament, and courts. But there are cases on record in which the power holders, indifferent to constitutional injunctions, are openly delinquent in their constitutional duties.

Such delinquency must not be confused with another common phenomenon: in the continuous competition among power holders in the political process, each of them will attach to the constitutional norm he has to apply the interpretation that seems best suited for his specific interests. For example, a federal government may claim jurisdiction under the constitution at the expense of the member states, or vice versa; a parliamentary investigating committee may extend its powers beyond the proper limits; or the government may refuse to produce evidence requested by the parliament—in all these cases there exist legitimate constitutional controversies, even though the specific interpretation may be branded as a violation of the constitution by the opponents and may even be so attested judicially. But no delinquency in constitutional duty on the part of the power holders is involved; on the contrary, each contestant claims for its conduct the support of the constitution.

What is meant here by delinquency is the situation of an essential constitutional provision being deliberately and consistently not applied or activated. It remains a *lex imperfecta*, a dead letter, at variance with the supposedly binding force of the basic law. The reasons for such non-compliance vary. A constitutional provision may have been unworkable to begin with. In most instances, however, the reasons for non-compliance are strictly political: the belief of the government in power that the provision, if applied, would run counter to its specific interest; the aversion to it of the party constellation controlling the legislative assembly; socioeconomic pressures against its activation; or factors of foreign policy. Removal of the objectionable norm by constitutional amendment may often be impossible because of the lack of required majorities or may even be more impolitic than the tacit non-observance.

A comprehensive study of this phenomenon is lacking. The following selected cases will help to illustrate it. On the precedent of the French constitution of 1791 (Art. 39), many constitutions declare the parliamentary deputies to be representatives, not of the constituency from which they are elected, but of the entire nation, and explicitly prohibit the imperative mandate.[24] Yet, with the emergence of political parties, it has become common practice to subject the representatives to more or less rigid party discipline under which they are compelled to vote as dictated by the party leadership or party caucus. Thus, the constitutionally prohibited imperative mandate is reintroduced in practice.

The Japanese constitution of 1946, appropriately styled the "MacArthur constitution" because enacted by fiat of the American occupation authorities, solemnly stipulates (Art. 9, sec. 2) that "land, sea, and air forces never will be maintained." Yet, under American pressure, Japan has been steadily rebuilding her military potential under the semantic label of "National Police Force." A controversy about this has been raging for years without being solved legally.[25] Prior to the elections of 1956, the majorities required for a constitutional amendment to repeal the provision altogether were lacking in either house and thereafter still in the Senate. All that has been done is the establishment of a study commission.

The French constitution of 1946 explicitly prohibits (Art. 13, sentence 2) the delegation of legislative functions. Nonetheless, the injunction is openly flouted by government and parliament; the practice of *pleins pouvoirs* has again infiltrated into parliamentary government and is now even condoned and sanctioned by the Council of State.*

In Italy the Constitutional Court, prescribed by the constitution of 1948 (Arts. 134 ff.) as the capstone of the rule of law, could not be established for eight years, partly because the parliamentary parties would not agree on the persons of the five judges parliament has to nominate and partly because the successive cabinets were unwilling to surrender the police powers they exercised under literally scores of fascist enactments palpably illegal under the constitution. When, in 1956, the court at long last was established and promptly invalidated the objectionable legislation, the cabinet of Premier Segni supinely disregarded the judicial decisions and continued to apply the illegal acts, possibly remembering President Jackson's famous dictum after *Cherokee Nation* v. *Georgia* (5 Pet. 1 [1831]): "John Marshall has made the decision, let him enforce it." Only after the respected Chief Justice Enrico de Nicola had temporarily resigned in protest did the government honor the constitution and discontinue the illegal practice.

The division of Italy into regions prescribed by the constitution (Arts. 114 ff.) has remained, for the most part, unestablished until today, and this in spite of constitutional injunctions (Arts. VIII and XVII of the Transitional Provisions) that their statutes had to be submitted within a year.†

Belgium's participation in supranational organizations was clearly unconstitutional until, in 1954, a constitutional amendment remedied the situation.[26]

The adhesion of the German Federal Republic to the European Defense Community treaties, involving the establishment of a new German army for which no constitutional authorization existed, led to one of the most momentous constitutional and judicial con-

---

* See below, pp. 211–12.   † See below, pp. 301–2.

troversies of recent times, and the violation of the Bonn Basic Law planned by the Adenauer government was later indirectly admitted by creating, through constitutional amendment (1954), the federal jurisdiction that had been lacking before.[27]

The Weimar constitution prescribed the enactment of a statute implementing the celebrated Article 48, the constitutional basis for the emergency legislation of the earlier period of the Weimar regime and of the "constitutional" dictatorship of the cabinets after 1930. It was never enacted by the Reichstag, with the result that the emergency powers of the president were extended far beyond their original intent and, in due course, became the entering wedge through which Hitler could "legally" establish his autocratic rule. Likewise the constitutionally prescribed statute implementing Article 21, section 12, of the Bonn Basic Law to regulate the internal organization of the political parties was never enacted; neither the government nor its majority parties were sufficiently interested to insist on it.

The Swiss, a people renowned for their loyalty to constitutional-democratic processes, were engaged for thirty-odd years in the practice, openly admitted to be unconstitutional, of using the so-called "urgent federal resolutions" for purposes for which neither the letter nor the spirit of the constitution destined them. Only in 1949 was the return to constitutional legality forced by the people upon the reluctant federal authorities.*

And, finally, it must be reported regretfully, in the United States, a country which prides itself on its faithfulness to the constitution, the normative character of the supreme law of the land is not invariably observed. Congress, in 1920, deliberately failed to comply with the constitutional injunction (Art. I, sec. 3, clause 2) of periodical reapportionment. This may appear as a minor delinquency, however, when compared with the situation that has developed after the crucial school desegregation decisions of the Supreme Court in 1954: if certain states opposed to desegregation

* See below, pp. 225 ff.

—Virginia, North Carolina, Georgia—still honor the constitution by circumventing and side-stepping it, others—Mississippi, Alabama, Louisiana—blandly ignore it by professed non-application.

THE EROSION OF THE CONSTITUTIONAL CONSCIENCE

The foregoing examples of deliberate non-compliance with the basic law even in states with an otherwise fully normative constitution may seem trivia except to sticklers in constitutional legality. Perhaps they are. But they are also straws in the wind pointing to the decay in the prestige of the written constitution which once, in the early period of constitutionalism, possessed a quasi-supernatural quality far beyond its usefulness as the rationalization of the political process. The unvarnished truth is that the written constitution has become emotionally and intellectually estranged from the power addressees.[28] The constitution means precious little to the proverbial common man. Only a microscopic fraction of the people in all countries is sufficiently interested to have read, let alone absorbed, it. Constitutional law has become a secret science for the initiated; knowledge of it is confined to a minority of the professionals in legal practice and in the government bureaucracy. This can hardly be otherwise. Constitutions have become increasingly complex. Policy decisions are the domain of the politicians; for their translation into policy execution the constitutional technicians and specialists are called in. Yet the decline of interest in their constitution on the part of the masses of the people and, attendant thereon, the loss of prestige it has suffered are impressive and alarming facts. The well-constructed written constitution, at the time of its first emergence, was considered the magic formula for the ultimate happiness of the good society. Today, manipulated by the professional politicians, it has ceased to be a living reality for the mass of the power addressees.

There are, of course, degrees of popular attachment to, and, vice versa, of indifferent disenchantment with, the constitution. Evidently a constitution requires time to integrate itself in the mind of a nation. The older it has become, the more the community has learned to live with its virtues and vices. By merely being in existence over an extended period, a constitution exerts a powerful educational influence. The processes of adjusting it to social change likewise have repercussions on the constitution-mindedness of the people. Frequent amendments may blunt it. There is no parallel to the singular phenomenon of the American constitution which, beyond its somewhat strained symbolism as a national myth, has served, and still serves, for the peaceful adjustment of the power process to the competition of socioeconomic forces represented by parties and plural groups. This fortunate situation is, of course, causally related to the fortunate socioeconomic conditions of a continent of abundance and to the freedom—until the atomic age—from the danger of external aggression. In retrospect it is a transparent patriotic distortion to attribute the absence, in this country, of insoluble class conflicts, let alone of the class struggle, to the existence of the constitution. Rather the reverse is true: the continued congruity between the constitutional form and the socioeconomic substance could be preserved because the functional mechanism of the power process was arranged in such a way that no single power holder could gain ascendancy over the others, and no social class could be denied, in the long run, its legitimate share in political power. Labor had to fight a long uphill battle against capitalism, which dominated public opinion and was intrenched in the Supreme Court, but in the peaceful revolution of the New Deal the constitution permitted its rise to the position of an equal partner in the productive process. With the exception of the Civil War, no major social conflict challenged the loyalty to the constitution, and the constitution, if somewhat battered, survived that ordeal. By contrast, to the sober Swiss, who are no less dedicated to constitutional government than the Americans, the constitution is neither sacrosanct, as evidenced by the frequency of constitutional amendments, nor emotionally supercharged with symbolism.

Perhaps it is fair to state that outside the United States in a few, actually merely a handful, of the older western constitutional-democratic nations the written constitution has retained a reasonable degree of psychological attachment based on strictly utilitarian motivations. These countries include the western and northern European monarchies, Switzerland, and, of the British Dominions, at least Canada and Australia. In them the constitution is a useful and reliable frame within which the struggle for power is conducted. But what value does the written constitution have in the host of older and newer state societies trying their hands at constitutional self-determination after ages of indigenous autocratic or foreign colonial rule? What value do the French, probably the world's politically most sophisticated people, attach to the existing constitution when they observe the rapid turnover? And what good did it do Weimar to have the constitution (Art. 148, sec. 3, sentence 2) prescribe that every pupil, upon the termination of his course of studies, had to be handed, free of charge, a copy of the constitution?

It is hard to believe that the constitution means anything anywhere to the little man ground between the upper and the nether millstones. He is indifferent to "his" constitution, because it is indifferent to him. The masses of the people are enlightened enough to hold themselves entitled to a modicum of social justice and economic security. But the most letter-perfect constitution is incapable of satisfying these desires, the pretentious bills of socioeconomic rights to the contrary notwithstanding. The constitution cannot bridge the gap between poverty and wealth. It cannot provide food, housing, clothing, education, and recreation, the bare essentials of life. Hence, everywhere state societies are irresistibly driven toward the welfare state. Moreover, the substance of the written constitution has become stagnant. The vital issues affecting the daily life of the people are no longer decided by constitutionally established organs but by the pressure groups and the political parties ignored by the constitution and often operating outside its frame.* Wages and conditions of work, on which

* See below, pp. 344 ff., 362 ff.

the life of the majority of the common people depends, are negotiated by the oligarchs of plural groups—the associations of entrepreneurs and the trade unions. The total indifference, if not hostility, of the mass of the power addressees toward "their" constitution seems justified: what constitutions spell out in complex and tedious detail—the interplay of the power holders in the political process—does not concern the common man; what constitutions gloss over are the essentials of his daily existence. The propagandized ideological premises are to him empty promises. The constitution has failed to do what he expected most; it has failed to establish a social order that is shock- and crisis-proof. Even the current full employment is vitiated by the vicious inflation. There is a tragic irony in the fact that now, when the written constitution is nearly universal and has reached its quantitative zenith, it is at the qualitative nadir of its prestige.

Perhaps the causes for the present ambivalence of western constitutionalism lie deeper than in the cleavage between the functional arrangements for the power process in the constitution and its integration in the minds of the people. The traditional assumption of the written constitution that, confining itself to the mechanics of the formation of the will of the state, it can be neutral toward the sociopolitical realities of the power process, that it can and must accommodate within its frame any sociopolitical system, appears as much the by-product of liberal relativism as the concept of the written constitution itself. Western constitutionalism still adheres to the naïve optimism of its ideological founding fathers that all that is needed is to give the people a good constitution and they will use it for their good. The crude materialism of the semantic constitutions of the Soviet orbit at least demonstrates that a deliberately chosen socioeconomic pattern of the state society requires a commensurate institutionalization of the power process in the constitution. State socialism or communism is as incompatible with a liberal constitution as the latter with integral state socialism and communism. It seems highly doubtful that a constitution can be neutral.

Two distressing conclusions follow from the cleavage between the constitutional mechanics and the realities of the daily life of the power addressees. Everywhere, with the exception of the few stable western democracies referred to before, the masses of the people are alienated from the instituted power holders. They distrust the governments and their encroaching bureaucracies; the parliaments and their bickering and selfish parties; the courts and their judges and, with them, their constitutions. On the other hand, the disharmony between the advertised ideological premises of the constitution and the inadequacies of the daily existence of the masses of the power addressees increases the temptation to escape from the "freedom" of their constitutional order, which fails to satisfy their needs, into the eschatological panacaeas of the Pied Pipers. The crisis of the written constitution, therefore, significantly reflects the crisis of the constitutional-democratic state of our time.

The reader may find this analysis too pessimistic and even dated when he observes the unprecedented material progress and prosperity that exist at present in many parts of the world and considers the vastly perfected methods for warding off and blunting a world-wide economic depression, breeder of revolutionary discontent. But he should bear in mind two things. First, the written constitution, as the primary instrumentality for the control of political power, is no longer the infallible guaranty of shared and, thereby, limited power; it no longer protects against the recurrence of autocracy. With diabolical skill modern autocracy has perverted it into an instrument of unlimited power; already more than two-fifths of the world's population are living under semantic constitutions. The group of genuinely democratic nations is constantly shrinking. Second, even in the remaining constitutional-democratic states, with few exceptions, the masses of the people have become visibly estranged from their constitutions. More and more the constitutional processes are being superseded by the extra-constitutional dynamism of the plural groups with which the life and happiness of the individual citizen is inextricably inter-woven. The revitalization of the constitution in the minds of the power addressees appears of crucial importance for the ultimate survival of the constitutional-democratic society. How this can be accomplished—whether to bring the people to their constitutions by educational means or, rather, to bring the constitutions to the people by reforming and modernizing them—this is something the author is unable to visualize.

VI. Intra-organ Controls

The preceding chapter attempted to demonstrate that the purpose of the written constitution is to limit the concentration of absolute power in the hands of the single power holder by distributing the various state activities among several power holders. Sharing in the exercise of power, these different state organs are constitutionally required to co-operate in the formation of the will of the state. By being distributed and shared, power is limited and controlled. The present chapter will analyze the technical and institutional devices established by the constitution by which the several power holders are individually limited and reciprocally controlled in the performance of the functions assigned to them.

Intra-organ and Interorgan Controls

The techniques of control are structurally of two kinds. If the control devices operate *within* the organization of an individual power holder, they are spoken of as *intra-organ* controls. If, however, they operate between the several interacting power holders, they are called *interorgan* controls. The terms "intra-organ" and "interorgan" controls are modeled on the familiar distinction of the American constitution between intra- and interstate jurisdiction. Intra- and interorgan controls together form the category of *horizontal* controls. Obviously, the horizontal categorization requires completion by, and contrast with, the vertical structurations of the power process. These are controls at work between the totality of the constituted power holders conducting the governmental process, on the one hand, and other sociopolitical forces of the state society, operating on a territorial, plural, or even individual basis, on the other. A fuller discussion of the vertical controls is reserved for chapter xii. The foregoing terminology is less forbidding than it may appear at first sight. Perhaps it can be clarified thus: If the politically organized state society is visualized as a layer-cake-like pyramid rising vertically upward from the electorate as the basis to the constitutional power holders—the government, the assembly, and the courts—horizontal controls are those that operate on the same level of the governmental process, either within an individual power holder as intra-organ controls or between the several power holders as interorgan controls.

While interorgan control is fairly obvious, exemplified as it is by the control the president exercises over congress through his veto power, intra-organ control—of which the bicameral organization of the parliament is a pertinent illustration—requires further discussion.

All conscious acts of the political process are performed by individual persons. No institution or office operates automatically or is self-executing without the interposition of the action of an individual person or several such persons.

However, an essential characteristic of constitutional government is the "depersonalized" exercise of political power,[1] that is, power is institutionalized. Depersonalized or institutionalized power is vested in the established institution or office as such, irrespective of the person, or persons, operating it. Power attaches to an individual or several individuals because they are the legally designated incumbents of an institution or office. Power derives not from the individual but from the institution or office whose functions the individual exercises.

Personalized power has been the natural configuration of the political process in primitive and preconstitutional societies. An individual distinguished by prowess (Achilles), cunning (Odysseus), experience (Nestor), or leadership (Agamemnon) is able to exercise power without any other legitimation than his personal aptitude or charisma. Today, in the fully organized and continuous state society, personalized power has largely disappeared. It is confined to revolutionary situations in which the established constitutional order temporarily has ceased to function properly. The familiar term *régime personnel* usually refers to either the temporary concentration of naked power, without legal institutionalization, in an individual or a group of power holders *de facto* or, in a more figurative sense, to the successful exploitation of his institutional position by a forceful individual.

Power holders who are incumbents on established institutions are either an individual person—a monarch, state president, prime minister, or single judge—or a plurality of individual persons who co-operate, by determinate procedures, in the performance of the function assigned to the institution—an assembly, a cabinet, a collegiate court. Though the members of such collective groups perform the function as individuals, the performance acquires reality and validity only by their collective action. The number of members in these collective groups varies, and it is the quantitative element of membership which characterizes the group as an assembly, committee, junta, directory, or presidium. But always their numbers are arithmetically fixed and determinable. This criterion distinguishes such organized collective groups from other collectivities with an indeterminate number of members, such as the electorate or the political party. An institutionalized power holder is always characterized by the fact that the membership of the persons composing it is numerically determined. The only exception to this rule is the electorate.

The realization that a function of the political process may be performed by an institution consisting of a plurality of members is essential for the understanding of the term "intra-organ controls." In these situations the exercise of a function is constitutionally attributed to, divided among, and shared by, several individual persons. Intra-organ controls, therefore, can become operative only in the case of a collectively organized, multimembered power holder—a parliament, a cabinet, an appellate court. They are existentially excluded when a state function is constitutionally vested in a single person holding the monopoly of its monistic exercise. The following discussion will first deal with intra-organ controls and then with interorgan controls. Intra-organ controls pertain to the executive, legislative, and judicial power holders.

Intra-organ Controls of the Executive Power Holder

In the autocratic state where political power is concentrated monolithically in the hands of a single power holder, intra-organ controls cannot and do not exist. The policy decision of the Egyptian pharaoh, of the Roman emperor of the Dominate, of the absolute monarch of the European nation-state system in the sixteenth century, and of a Hitler or a Stalin was not restricted in itself by intra-organ controls, even though the pharaoh may have been guided by his priests and oracles, the Roman emperor by his high officials, Louis XIV by his advisory councils or his mistresses, Hitler by his cronies, or Stalin by his party sycophants. This influence on the power process was not institutionalized; it remained incidental and accidental, depending exclusively on the whim and the will of the autocrat. Factually and legally, the single and supreme power holder in an autocracy is omnipotent, subject to neither intrinsic nor external controls.

Collegiate organization.—On the other hand, intra-organ controls of the executive government are a common feature of the political system of constitutionalism. For operational efficiency the policy-deciding function must be concentrated in the hands of a single person or at least a very small number of individual persons. All policy decisions are necessarily oligarchic. Of all constituted power holders, the executive—government—is potentially the most dangerous for the freedom of the community. One of the technical devices to obviate the danger is the collegiate organization. Says the wise Anatole France in *L'Île des Pingouins:* "La jalousie est une vertu des démocraties et garantit des tyrants." Psychological reasons have always induced constitutional government to favor the collective organization of the executive. For example, the kingship in Sparta and other pretechnological states was dual; nine archons with equal powers held the highest administrative office in Athens. All Roman magistrates were collegiately organized—consuls, praetors, aediles, quaestors, and tribunes of the people; even the constitutional dictator had a *magister equitum* attached to his function, substituting for him in the field and at home. Co-emperorship was a standard pattern in the late Roman empire even though jurisdictional collisions were avoided by the geographical separation of their respective areas of power.

The dual executive.—The dual executive is a characteristic of many constitutional democracies of today. The dualism between the crown (or state president) and the government (or cabinet) stems from the constitutionally limited monarchy of the early nineteenth century. It was carried over into the parliamentary monarchy and imitated in the establishment of the parliamentary republic. While in the past the crown and the government actually had to co-operate in the formation of the will of the state, nowadays a real sharing of political responsibility and, with it, of political power no longer exists. Power has shifted from the nominal head of the state to the real executive power holder, the government or cabinet. The chief of state, whether monarch or elected state president, has become completely eclipsed by the minister-president and his cabinet supported by the majority in parliament. The power of the monarch and the republican state president is wholly neutralized by the constitutional requirement, for all their political acts, of countersignature by the cabinet; the cabinet thereby assumes political responsibility for them. The participation of the chief or head of state in the political process has been reduced to strictly ceremonial, symbolic, and representative functions. Only the choice of the prime minister is left to him, and it, in turn, is conditioned and restricted by the existing party constellation. The moral influence on the government, however, of an experienced monarch or state president may often be of such persuasive force as to amount to a factual intra-organ control without being so considered legally. Various efforts—in France in 1848, in Germany-Weimar, in republican Spain—to restore an effective dualism of the executive by strengthening the presidential position and/or introducing the popular election of the chief of state invariably led to throwing parliamentary government out of kilter and slanting it toward presidential authoritarianism.*

The Swiss Federal Council.—The real executive agencies in constitutional-democratic states are organized, without exception, on a multipersonnel basis which in practice may or may not amount to a collegiate exercise of the executive functions. The outstanding illustration of constitutionally organized collegiality in a governing group, in which the members have an equal share in the function, is the Swiss Federal Council. Although the governmental tasks are administratively distributed among seven different departments, the theory behind the federal government, faithfully observed in practice, is that all policy decisions emanate from the Federal Council as a body. Its members assume the corporate responsibility for them. Consequently, the Federal Council arrives at its resolutions by unanimity. Differences of party approach and of individual opinions are adjusted by mutual compromises.

The structure of the cabinet.—The structure of the cabinet under parliamentarism fails to present a uniform pattern. The ideal type is that of a closely integrated team of ministers in which the prime minister (minister-president) assumes leadership as *primus inter pares* without dominating his colleagues. However, the center of gravity inevitably has shifted to the prime minister, the cabinet being hierarchically subordinated to him. This relationship is reflected by his prerogative, now unchallenged in most parliamentary states,[2] of freely selecting the individual ministers, subject, in multiple-party cabinets, to the prevailing party configura-

* See above, pp. 95–96.

tion; the nominal chief of state can no longer refuse the prime minister's appointments of his ministerial collaborators. The British prime minister, by convention, actually operates the cabinet according to his will; some do so more authoritatively than others, but every prime minister directs the cabinet and the ministry and gives them the stamp of his personality. In general, collective responsibility has become a fiction of parliamentary theory: the prime minister assumes responsibility for himself and the entire cabinet.

In Germany the commanding position of the chancellor—the "chancellor principle" traditional under the empire—is faithfully repeated by the later constitutions: "The Reich chancellor determines the political directives [*Richtlinien der Politik*]" (Weimar, Art. 56; Bonn, Art. 65). Ministers selected by him must be appointed by the president. The Bonn instrument explicitly centers parliamentary responsibility on his person alone. It cannot be invoked against the cabinet as a whole or an individual minister (Arts. 67 and 68), a factor which contributes to the authoritarian complexion of the Bonn regime. Nonetheless, the collective organization of the cabinet cannot fail to influence the conduct of policy of even the most strong-willed leader, who will utilize the consultative techniques offered by the cabinet organization to his advantage.

By contrast, the leadership position of the president of the Council of Ministers in France is much weaker. His policy decisions are far more dependent on collective agreement than in either Britain or Germany. The constitutional requirement that his actions be countersigned by the individual minister affected (Art. 47, sec. 4) is an effective intra-organ control in view of the fact that he is the leader of a coalition cabinet. Since it is composed of the delegates of the political parties participating in the government, the parties' consent to all major policy decisions is indispensable. In practice, therefore, the French cabinet is marked by its plural character. Agreement has to be bought by concessions to the partners, and, if conflicts cannot be reconciled, the parties withdraw support, and the cabinet breaks up. This is the primary cause of cabinet instability in the Fourth Republic.

What is called the "cabinet" in the American presidential system is actually a more or less informal aggregation of the heads of the departments and other presidential advisers and is wholly lacking in collective capacity. In making his policy decision, the president may solicit and accept advice from his official family or his "kitchen cabinet," but he alone assumes responsibility for them. If an American cabinet operates as a team, it is a psychological rather than a constitutional phenomenon.

"Collective leadership" in the Soviet orbit.—Finally, the present context invites comment on the striking transformations the Soviet political system has undergone since the death of Joseph Stalin (March, 1953). There is, of course, no precise knowledge of things politic in the Soviet Union; there are only varying degrees of ignorance. Yet there are strong indications—long suspected by the West and confirmed by the revelations of the twentieth congress of the Communist party (February, 1956)—that the one-man dictatorship of the mad tyrant has been converted into a collegiate organization, and "collective leadership" is precisely the official label under which the new power configuration in the U.S.S.R. and her satellites is being advertised. Immediately upon Stalin's unlamented departure a sort of directory government emerged, on whose personnel the successor group must have agreed in advance. At first the ruling committee was under the leadership of Malenkov as chairman of the Council of Ministers. Once Beria, a member of the original group, who may have aimed at the continuation of the monolithic Stalinist power structure, had been forcibly eliminated, the collegiate structure continued under Marshal Bulganin in the same official capacity. At the present time, with due reservations commensurate to a still autocratic system, it may be said that the collective technique has been firmly established in the Soviet power center. In the ruling directorate the various socio-

political forces share in the power apparatus: the Communist party, represented by its first secretary, Khrushchev; the political professionals and the non-political technicians of the Council of Ministers, represented by its chairman, Bulganin, and including the economic (Mikoyan) and the diplomatic (Shepilov, subsequently Gromyko, replacing Molotov) sectors; and, finally, the armed forces, represented by Marshal Zhukov.

The fundamental change, in comparison with the monolithic exercise of power in the Stalinist era, seems to lie in the fact that, even though Khrushchev may have gained ascendancy in the ruling group and appears to have considerably strengthened it by the spectacular purge of July, 1957, the policy decisions must be arrived at by mutual agreement and can no longer be imposed by a single individual, whatever his specific power potential at a given time. Power, so it appears, is shared, at least to a certain extent. Collegiate techniques seem to have attentuated whatever hierarchical ingredients a gigantic power structure like that of the Soviets necessarily contains.

The reasons for this momentous reversal in the outstanding autocracy of our times can be stated only hypothetically. In the first place, it is psychologically understandable that the new ruling group should wish to protect themselves against the vicissitudes of personal insecurity that had been the lot of the upper hierarchy of the Stalinist regime. In the second place, profound changes in the social stratification of the Soviet state society may have made a broadening of the power structure at the top advisable and even necessary. Not only have a new generation and a new middle class made their appearance but the new stratum of the professionals, technicians, managers, and scientists may have proved too important, in view of the global competition the Soviets are engaged in, to allow the perpetuation of their complete exclusion from a reasonable share in power. The history-conscious observer is reminded of the Napoleonic regime: the revolutionary doctrinaires were replaced by the professional technicians, the Saint-Justs and

Robespierres by the Cambacérèses and Molliens. De-Stalinization and the dismantling of the "cult of the personality"—history will see to it that the propagandistic excesses of these processes are corrected—must be visualized as the corollaries of the current process of depersonalization and institutionalization of power in the Soviet Union.

All these aspects appear to be a reflection of the progressive consolidation of the regime in which the relevant sociopolitical forces of party, technical bureaucracy, and army are balanced, if precariously, in the collegiate organization of the ruling directory. With the advent of a new generation, the Soviet political system may have reached the point where it can afford a certain degree of liberalization. Again one is reminded of the Napoleonic experience: the apparent restoration of a modicum of personal security and legality in the Soviets brings to mind the parallel phenomenon of the firm establishment of the rule of law under the Napoleonic administration after the excesses of the revolutionary period. However, an approximation to the western pattern of constitutionalism will remain impossible as long as the ideological power circuit remains closed. Once it is opened, an autocracy loses its inner cohesion.

Intra-organ Controls of the Legislative Power Holder

The assembly or parliament is commonly spoken of as the "legislative power holder," though the parliament, in addition, performs the equally important task of policy control. Intra-organ controls pertaining to its function are of three kinds. First, the assembly must be organized and managed in such a way as to enable it to exercise the assigned functions without outside pressure or interference from other power holders or extra-constitutional forces. This situation is here called the "requirement of functional independence." Second, the internal management of the assembly must be such as to protect the minority against the tyrannical control of the majority. Power must be equitably shared between them. This situation is here called "functional autonomy."* Third—the most significant intra-organ control—the legislative function as such is split between two separate branches which mutually check and control themselves. This is the institution of bicameralism.

FUNCTIONAL AUTONOMY OF THE ASSEMBLY

Functional autonomy lies in the principle of internal self-government of the assembly and the techniques for its realization. It implies the parliament's unrestricted direction of the arrangement and management of its internal affairs, usually fixed by its Standing Orders. The assembly must be free to exercise discipline over its members and to protect the conduct of the parliamentary business against any extraneous interference on the part of the government or other power foci, including even the electorate. It is here that the principle of shared powers—shared between the majority and minority parties and among the different political parties—comes into play. Various devices of intra-organ controls and shared power customarily guarantee an equitable participation of all parliamentary groups and of the individual members in the parliamentary process. The officers of the assembly, freely elected by it, are enjoined by the Standing Orders to display complete impartiality toward all parties and members. The members of the managing directorate of the assembly—the "bureau" or the speaker and his associates—are evenly distributed among the parties. While, under the two-party system of the United States, the speaker is taken from the majority party, in Britain he is staunchly nonpartisan and retains office in the successive Commons irrespective of the change in the majority party. He is even returned unopposed. In multiple-party states the presiding officers are equitably distributed among the several parties.

Minority protection is significantly preserved in the legislative planning and in the arrangement of the agenda of the assembly.

* For the differentiation of functional independence and functional autonomy see below, pp. 186–87.

Special institutions of the assembly—the Conference of the Presidents (of the commissions and of the political parties) in France, the *Ältestenrat* in Germany—see to it that railroading of legislation by the government majority is avoided and that the parties have their fair share in the debates. Even in Britain and in the Dominions following the British practice, where the government possesses quasi-dictatorial powers over the timetable, the agenda, and the general conduct of the debates, the rights of the minority, by mutual arrangements of the party whips, are scrupulously protected. The parties also share equally in the committee work. In the United States the majority party always holds the majority in the committees and, thus, is in a position to override the minority. By contrast, in England committee membership usually is divided evenly between the two major parties, and in France it is assigned in accordance with the proportional strength of the parties in the assembly.

Similar intra-organ controls are the standard practice of the constitutional-democratic state in the conduct of the parliamentary debates proper. It is true that in England the closure, the strongest weapon of the government, in the last analysis operates for the benefit of the government and, with it, the majority party. But, again by mutual agreement, the minority is granted sufficient opportunity to present its viewpoint. A unique phenomenon in this context is the institution of filibuster in the American Senate: the independence of the individual senator is respected to such an extent that, if at all, only qualified majorities can call a halt to the oratorical marathon, much to the detriment of the legislative process of the United States as a whole. The maximum of intra-organ controls cannot always be equated with its optimum.

However, the degree of parliamentary autonomy and independence varies from one pattern of government to another.[3] It is hardly exaggerating to say that the pattern of government under which the specific state operates depends on the extent to which the parliament is able to exercise internal autonomy. The control of the parliament over the legislative process is least effective in Great Britain; the cabinet monopolizes it to the point of complete subordination of the majority party and emasculation of the private members' share in it. It is more extensive, if still largely subordinated to the government, in Germany and Switzerland. It matches the government's influence and is even superior to it in France; it is fully autonomous in the United States, where the government wholly lacks effective influence on, let alone control over, the parliamentary procedure and is confined to the president's indirect methods of subtle persuasion and pressure.

MINORITY PROTECTION BY
QUALIFIED MAJORITIES

To transform the multiplicity of individual opinions into the common will, multimembered corporate organizations apply the technique of the majority vote. As corporate bodies, the representative assemblies of constitutional democracy conform to the majority principle.[4] However, to keep the mechanical majority from exercising naked tyranny over the minority, the technique was refined, apparently for the first time by the Catholic orders: In certain major policy decisions the corporate will must manifest itself by a more impressive degree of consent in the form of qualified or special majorities—two-thirds, or any other convenient arithmetical fraction—of the entire body. Qualified majorities, thus, are an important instrumentality of intra-organ control, providing for a more equitable sharing of power and limiting the majority by an effective protection of the minority. When the level of consent for the formation of the common will is raised, a minority of considerably less than half the members can prevent action. The psychological element is added: the more stringent the numerical requirements, the more convincing the expressed corporate will of the assembly and the greater the willingness of the outvoted minority to accept it.

Qualified majorities have been the standard equipment of the democratic constitutions since the American and French revolutions. They are particularly favored for the constitutional amendment but are also used for other major policy decisions. For example, the Weimar constitution prescribed qualified majorities in no fewer than five instances. Frequently they are also enjoined by the Standing Orders of the parliaments for important matters of internal parliamentary management, such as elections.

A somewhat attenuated version of the technique consists in the requirement of an absolute majority for certain votes; that is, at least half the legal members of the assembly must participate in, and of these the majority must agree to, the vote. Such provisions have been introduced recently in the course of what has been called the "rationalization of the political process,"* for example, for the election of the state president and the investiture and the removal of the cabinet.

BICAMERALISM AS INTRA-ORGAN CONTROL

Politically the most important and functionally the most effective intra-organ control built into the legislative power holder is bicameralism. The legislative function is shared between two separate and mutually independent assemblies of varying nomenclature but often called the "lower house" and the "upper house."[5] Being constitutionally empowered to pass separately on each bill, they are in the position of reciprocally checking, restraining, and controlling each other. This situation of shared power was graphically alluded to by Washington and Jefferson at the breakfast table: The Senate is the saucer that cools the coffee in the cup of the House.

The institution of the dual legislature originated in England. For many centuries the House of Lords represented the landowning aristocracy and the plutocratic elements assimilated to it, the House of Commons, until the full effect of the electoral reforms of the nineteenth century had made itself felt, the upper-

* See below, pp. 197–98.

and middle-class bourgeoisie. In terms of sociopolitical stratification it can be said that the Lords represented roughly the conservative and the Commons the progressive elements of the nation. The British two-chamber model was imitated by the constitutionally limited monarchy elsewhere; in most states a hereditary or government-appointed upper house was the conservative counterweight against the lower chamber, which was elected at first on the basis of property qualifications but later by a more or less universal suffrage. The principle of bicameralism was also accepted, without challenge of its utility, by most of the parliamentary republics.

Nor has the popularity of the bicameral organization suffered much in recent times. In the democratic upsurge after the First World War a relatively small number of the new constitutions preferred the unicameral organization; these included those of Turkey, the Baltic states, and the German *Länder*. The latter adhered to it also after the Second World War, with the sole exception of Bavaria, whose constitution of 1946 is adorned with a strictly advisory Senate. All Central American states, with the exception of Nicaragua and Panama, have become converted to unicameralism. Of the states created after 1945, Israel, Indonesia, South Korea, and South Viet-Nam joined the unicameral camp. Member units of federal states likewise frequently dispense with a second chamber, for utilitarian reasons. But in the United States the example of Nebraska was not followed by other states. More recently only New Zealand (1949)[6] and Denmark, in her new constitution of 1953, passed from the bicameral to the unicameral column. However, faithful to the principle of assembly government, which does not jibe with a split personality of the sovereign legislature, all Soviet satellite states are unicameral. The U.S.S.R. itself, because of its federal structure, adheres to the two-branch model, the Soviet of the Nationalities being of even less significance than the Soviet of the Union. Yugoslavia, likewise a federal state, has two, or rather, under the constitution of 1953, three chambers. As can be seen, all unicameral states are either small in size or of marginal political importance.

The reasons for the perseverance of the bicameral tradition are varied. For federal states the two houses are obviously indispensable because they offer the member units the opportunity of sharing in the policy decision and policy execution of the central state. Otherwise the retention of the bicameral structure has convincing political reasons, partly to preserve the influence of the conservative classes affiliated with the crown and partly, again in the interests of the propertied classes, to restrain the reform impetus of the lower, popularly elected chamber. More recently, in line with the progressively recognized importance of pluralism, the upper house has become a useful laboratory for the integration of economic and vocational interests into the political process.*

Once democratic theory and practice had proceeded to the point where all power holders had to be directly or indirectly designated by the will of the electorate, the non-elective membership basis, whether hereditary or appointive, was replaced by elective procedures. Here the Belgian *charte* of 1831 set the pattern. But, with the progressive democratization of the state, in time a new difficulty arose: if both houses are elected on the same, or a similar, electoral basis, the party constellation in either house tends to be identical or similar, and the intra-organ control inherent in the concurrent participation of two houses in the legislative process may be largely canceled out. To avoid such mechanical duplication of the electoral will, a vast repertory of rather artificial devices for the differentiation of the two houses has been developed. All of them are intended to preserve, without violating the democratic principle, the traditional character of the upper house as the more conservative branch by providing for a personnel of greater maturity, selectivity, and stability. Some of these techniques operate in the electoral process proper. These include: direct election of the lower branch and indirect election by an

* See below, p. 375.

electoral college of the upper branch; co-optation of the members of the upper house; designation by the member units in federal states; designation by professional or territorial (regional or provincial) groups instead of constituencies based on population alone; integral election of the upper house, or of a determined portion of its members, by the lower; choosing of candidates from certain socially elevated groups to insure a superior caliber of membership; higher age requirements for the suffrage and the eligibility of members of the upper house; periodic renewal of part of its members; different periods of legislative terms and different times for the elections; and different size, in which case the upper house is usually the smaller of the two. Finally, differentiation is sought by attributing different powers to each house.

But, whatever the device or the combination of devices chosen, the contingency cannot be peremptorily ruled out that the two houses, failing to agree, may be deadlocked. This danger is obviously greater if the two houses possess equal powers, and it is still more enhanced if the two chambers have a different membership basis and are correspondingly divergent in social structure. To keep the state machinery going, one of the two must yield, and democratic theory demands that it is the upper chamber which must do the yielding. Here the taming of the Lords in England in the constitutional crisis of 1910/11 proved of decisive influence on the position of the second chamber generally. In the twentieth-century process of integral democratization the lower house was bound to become the center of political gravity. Consequently, during the last decades, the bicameral system has approached the unicameral solution, at least in the non-federal states, in the sense that the upper chamber is granted, at the most, a suspensive veto on the policy decisions of the lower house. This is the solution of the French Fourth Republic. In contrast to the equal powers the Senate and the Chamber of Deputies enjoyed in the Third, the National Assembly of the Fourth Republic, when there is a conflict, prevails over the Council of the Republic, whose share in the legislative function is pared down to that of a mechanism delaying the National Assembly. Bonn adopted an identical solution for all conflicts except those over matters affecting the states or *Länder* rights, where the veto of the Federal Council is absolute. Japan (constitution of 1946) conforms to the trend. Of recent constitutions, only that of Italy (1948) saw fit to establish two chambers with completely identical powers.

Whatever the concrete situation, elaborate mechanics have to be built into the constitution to resolve deadlocks between the two houses and make the will of the lower house prevail. Most common is the requirement that only qualified majorities of the lower house can override the resistance of the upper chamber. This appears a sufficient intra-organ control on what otherwise would be the legislative omnipotence of the lower house. Other techniques for the adjustment of differences and conflicts between the two branches include conferences or conciliation committees composed of an equal number of members of either house; intervention of the electorate as arbiter through referendum or the mandatory dissolution of the lower house or of both houses; and joint sessions of both houses in which the upper one, with its usually smaller membership, is the loser unless it can muster sufficient support among the members of the other chamber.

A synoptical review of the recent development of bicameralism warrants the conclusion that the institution, historically and functionally intended to serve as an intra-organ control for the sharing of legislative power, today is undergoing a process of erosion. For the federal state it may remain indispensable as a method for insuring the participation of the member units in the federal political process; but federalism by itself is a pattern whose usefulness, in our time, is declining.* The continued ascendancy of the Senate under American presidentialism remains an almost unique phenomenon, owing to its longer term, smaller size, more extensive constitutional attributes, and established prestige. In the unitary

* See below, pp. 294 ff.

state, however, the net result of the integral democratization seems to be almost everywhere the irreversible *capitis deminutio* of the upper chamber, regardless of its mode of designation, and the final ascendancy of the lower house. The traditional financial prerogatives of the lower house anyway tend to slant bicameral structures toward the superiority of the latter.

Nonetheless, even with the powers and functions of the upper branch severely trimmed, the institution of bicameralism retains its usefulness as an effective intra-organ control over potential excesses of the lower house. While it can hardly be denied that the regurgitation of the same legislative material by two separate houses may often be waste motion, there is no gainsaying the fact that quite often the requirement of qualified majorities to overcome the resistance of the other chamber may stop an unwise policy decision, or at least mobilize public attention to the point that the ultimate decision actually will reflect the will of the majority of the people. Frequently also—though not in all juris-dictions—the injection of the politically less preoccupied upper house may improve the legislative product; the emasculated House of Lords is a case in point. As an essential element of intra-organ control, bicameralism has lost little of its original rationale.

Intra-organ Controls of the Judicial Power Holder

Finally, the operation of intra-organ controls within the judicial function deserves brief mention. No less a man than Montesquieu speaks of the judicial power as "la puissance de juger si terrible parmi les hommes."[7] The very independence of the judiciary, mainstay of constitutional government, carries with it the danger of its abuse. Independent and subject only to the law, judges are beyond the control of any other power holders, be it the govern-ment, the parliament, or the electorate, and should be impervious even to the influence of public opinion. Yet judges are human and, as other mortals, exposed to the temptations of unlimited power. Hence the imperative need for techniques of self-restraint built into the judicial function to protect the individual before the bar of justice against the caprice of the bench. All legal civilizations, therefore, possess certain intra-organ controls of the judiciary.

Conspicuous among them is the collegiate organization of the courts. Several judges, who are required to decide a case by majority rule, are less apt to commit a judicial error or to partake in a miscarriage of justice than a single judicial mind. Multimembered courts throughout the entire judicial organization, therefore, are the standard rule in France, the states influenced by the Roman law of the French codes, and also in the Soviet orbit. In the Anglo-Saxon nations, on the other hand, the single judge obtains, as a rule, at least in the first instance. But even a multimembered court in whose judgment several judicial minds concur may err in the evaluation of the factual evidence or in the application of the legal norms to them. This danger is obviated by the requirement, uniform in all legal civilizations, of granting an appeal against the decisions of the first instance. Often, at least on points of law, a further review is granted by a court of cassation or a supreme court. Adjudication by a single court exists only in the exceptional cases of serious crimes against the security of the state, but in these cases the accused invariably is protected by the intra-organ control of being adjudged by a multimembered court. The Anglo-Saxon practice of the jury, not considered essential for due process in countries under Roman law and even in England on the decline, serves the same purpose of intra-organ control and the sharing of judicial powers; the accused is granted the privilege of being adjudged by his peers instead of by professional judges alone. Intra-organ controls, thus, are as essential for the proper administration of justice according to law as they are common.

VII. Interorgan Controls between the Parliament and the Government

Techniques and Patterns of Interorgan Control

The second aspect of the general category of horizontal controls will now be discussed. *Inter*organ controls refer to the reciprocal relations among the several and independent power holders. As has been explained previously,* what distinguishes the political process of the constitutional state from that of autocracy is the distribution of the various state activities among several independent power holders who, in turn, are constitutionally required to co-operate in the formation of the will of the state. This dynamism of the interaction and interplay of the several power holders in the political process constitutes the interorgan controls. They are basically of two kinds. First, the power holders are constitutionally enjoined to perform a specific function in conjunction; for example, in the United States an international treaty acquires validity only by senatorial confirmation of the antecedent conclusion by the president. In this case the power holders share in the exercise of the function and mutually control themselves. Or, second, the individual power holder is constitutionally authorized to intervene, at his exclusive discretion, with the operation of another power holder and, thereby, counteracts it; for example, the president may veto a congressional bill. In the first contingency co-operation is mandatory; in the second, optional. But the effect is identical: control is exercised over the other power holder. Both types operate as interorgan controls.

* See above, pp. 29 ff.

It is in the *technical arrangement* of interorgan controls—whether the controls at the disposal of the respective power holders are evenly matched or whether one power holder prevails over the others in the political process—*that the criterion for the "patterns of government" has been found.* Interorgan controls are strongest under parliamentarism (interdependence by integration); they are still effective, if to a lesser extent, under American presidentialism (interdependence by co-ordination); they are weakest, or non-existent, under assembly government. Needless to say, in actual practice these generalizations are merely frames for endless variations. The specific weight an individual power holder gains in the political process depends on numerous variables that defy systematization.

Democratic constitutionalism, operating with four power holders—the government, the assembly, the courts, and the electorate—presents four patterns of interorgan controls: (1) the controls of the assembly over the government; (2) the controls of the government over the assembly; (3) the controls of the judiciary over the assembly and government; and (4) the controls of the electorate over the other power holders. However, as a rule, the independent judiciary is exempted from control. This fourfold division will be the basis of the following discussion.

In actual political life, however, it is the interplay and interaction between government and parliament that constitute the core of the power process. The participation of the electorate is intermittent, being displayed only on the occasion of the general election. Likewise the intervention of the courts in the political process is confined to states that legalize judicial review over legislation—a minority—and allow the control of governmental administration by the courts—the majority. By contrast, the power contest between government and parliament is permanent and continuous. The history of constitutionalism since its inception has been nothing but the perennial quest for the magic formula to establish the ideal equilibrium between government and parliament; it has never been discovered and, possibly, does not exist. Its closest approximation is cabinet government in Britain, and, under it, as the appellation implies, the cabinet governs and the parliament confirms. The constitutional state has always oscillated between the superiority of the government and the ascendancy of the assembly, the government rising to the commanding position in periods of crisis, the parliament regaining its stature upon the return to normalcy. Fluctuations in the power dynamism were usually reflected in the swing of the ideological pendulum back and forth from liberty to authority, two concepts equally difficult to reconcile in a permanently harmonious equilibrium.

Before the four types of interorgan controls can be analyzed systematically, another aspect, historically and politically of prime importance, has to be pointed out. To perform properly the function assigned to him, the individual power holder must be free not only from direct intervention but also from indirect pressure, not provided by the constitution, that may be exerted on him by another power holder or by forces extraneous to the constitutional process. This aspect is spoken of here as "functional independence." If mandatory co-operation with another power holder in the performance of a specific political act and discretionary authorization to intervene with such performance are the positive aspects of interorgan controls, the preservation of the functional independence of the individual power holder is their negative aspect. Functional independence must be guaranteed to every single one of the instituted power holders—the assembly, the government, the courts. If, for example, the government controls the parliament by bribing a substantial portion of its members— Walpole's "government by corruption" is a case in point—the assembly is no longer free to exercise the representative mandate as a trust of the community. Judges exposed to dismissal by the government disapproving their decisions are no longer free agents of the judicial process under the rule of law.

In modern times, however, with the rise of the political parties, functional independence of both the parliament and the government has undergone a complete transformation. Both are continually exposed to the extra-constitutional intervention of the parties in the power process and actually dependent on them. Moreover, both parliament and government are increasingly subject to the more or less subtle influences of the organized plural groups.

The First Pattern: Controls of the Parliament over the Government

FUNCTIONAL INDEPENDENCE OF THE ASSEMBLY

For a member of parliament to divest himself completely of his professional, religious, or class antecedents is humanly impossible, and indeed the ideal assembly should constitute the microcosmos of the totality of the sociopolitical forces of the community. But, if the power process is to be conducted in conformity with the constitution, it is at least necessary for the parliament's functional independence to be adequately protected against governmental pressures.

Freedom of the parliament from the government was hard to win and still requires eternal vigilance, as demonstrated by its decay in contemporary autocracy. Having been for centuries the paramount political system, absolutism of the crown and the classes affiliated with it surrendered its monopoly of political power only after a bitter struggle. The primary objective of early constitutionalism was to emancipate the assembly from governmental control over the composition of its personnel and the conduct of the legislative function. In England the goal was reached only after the extension of the suffrage and the redistribution of seats in the Great Reform; in other countries, correspondingly later.

The principal positions that had to be secured in the fight for functional independence may be summarized thus:

1. The elimination of governmental influence on the selection of the parliamentary personnel, exercised through slanted electoral laws and unscrupulous intervention in the electoral process. This was accomplished by the democratization and neutralization of the electoral techniques. A fuller discussion of this all-important situation will follow later.*

2. The elimination of governmental ascendancy in the legislative process through the appointment of the members of the assembly. The technique of governmental appointment was inaugurated by Napoleon I, who designated the members of all branches of the legislature; Tribunate, Legislative Corps, and Senate. But its specific locale was in the upper houses or "first" chambers, composed either of hereditary incumbents or of members appointed by the government. These were naturally inclined to side with the government. To redress the balance, either the nominated upper house was replaced by an elected assembly or, where the former continued to exist, its political weight in the legislative process was curbed.

3. The elimination of governmental control over the sessions of parliament (convocation, adjournment, and dissolution). By extended periods of parliamentary non-activity the government could rid itself of parliamentary control. Charles II ruled without parliament from 1629 to 1640. Subsequently the Triennial Act (1643) and the Septennial Act (1715) made such practice impossible. The final solution was either the complete self-determination of the assembly over the time and duration of its meetings or their fixation by constitutional prescription, as exemplified by the United States (Amendment XX) or the French Fourth Republic (Art. 9). Dissolution, however, the strongest interorgan control of the government over the parliament, remained at the discretionary disposal of the former.†

4. The elimination of governmental influence on the conduct of the parliamentary business itself, a practice exemplified by the

* See below, pp. 269 ff.   † See below, pp. 213 ff.

designation of the presidents of the Legislative Corps and the Senate by the government of Napoleon III. This was finally accomplished by the recognition, now standard under all constitutions, of the unabridged internal self-government of the assembly.

5. The elimination of adverse pressures of the government against the members of parliament during the exercise of their mandate. This is guaranteed adequately by the parliamentary immunities, for a long time recognized by all democratic constitutions. The privileges of irresponsibility and inviolability protect the members from any liability, criminal and otherwise, for acts committed in the performance of their representative functions and from harassment (arrest, prosecution) on the part of the government. In the autocratic states of our time the relinquishment of these privileges by terrorized or subservient majorities facilitated the removal of duly elected members of the opposition from the assembly and vastly contributed to the enslavement of the assembly.

6. The elimination of property qualifications and other restrictions on the eligibility of the members that habitually favor the governments supported by the propertied classes. Democratization of the access to the assembly broke the previously existing monopoly of the landowning and plutocratic classes in parliament and integrated the lower classes into the political process. The same purpose was served by granting the members of parliament salaries and, in some jurisdictions, even pensions; this by now has also become the standard practice in all constitutional states.

7. The prohibition of the simultaneous incumbency of the parliamentary seat and certain occupations. These so-called "incompatibilities" are of cardinal importance for the functional independence of the assembly and are instrumental to the removal of indirect governmental influence on the parliamentary personnel. Among the incompatibilities, the simultaneous holding of a parliamentary mandate and a position as government official or civil

servant, even if on leave of absence for the duration of the mandate, is of such political importance even today that it requires some comments.

Not only may a public official have an undue advantage over his competitors as a candidate for the parliamentary seat but, once in parliament, he is understandably disinclined to oppose the government on which his future career, after his return to the service, is dependent. For this reason incompatibility of public office and the representative mandate is the invariable practice of the Anglo-Saxon countries; in the United States it is enforced by constitutional injunction (Art. I, sec. 6, clause 2); in England and the Dominions following the British pattern it is enjoined partly by statutory regulation, partly by convention. However, in the British orbit the strictly political, that is, the ministerial offices, are excepted; otherwise the parliamentary system, based on the integration of the responsible governing group into the parliament, would be impossible, as is, in view of the constitutional prohibition, the introduction of parliamentarism in the United States. On the Continent, on the other hand, public officials on leave constitute an important segment of the parliamentary personnel. The practice is traditional in France, though to a lesser extent under the Third and Fourth republics than, for example, under the Orleanist monarchy after 1830, when the government could control whatever majorities it needed by relying on its officials elected to parliament and appointing other members during their term to lucrative government positions. The practice is also so deeply intrenched in Germany that remedial efforts of the occupation authorities after 1945 could not eradicate it. Substantial numbers of the deputies of the Bundestag and of the *Land* parliaments are government officials, a situation that could not fail to distort and dilute German parliamentarism. Some jurisdictions (Britain for a long time and, more recently, France) have also created incompatibilities between the parliamentary mandate and certain economic ties that may influence the representative freedom of the deputy, such as positions in banks and industrial enterprises engaged in government business and holding government contracts. 8. Another indirect technique of the government to gain favor with, and influence over, the members of the parliament is what is generally called "patronage." The border line between outright corruption, as practiced, for example, in Italy before 1918 and still rampant in certain Latin American countries, and mere patronage is difficult to draw. If corruption is deemed reprehensible in civilized nations, patronage, under various disguises, is legitimate and thoroughly respectable. With the improved morality of the assemblies, the constant vigilance of the press, and the jealous competition of the political parties, straight corruption has lost much of its former bite. The range of patronage likewise has become narrower. For example, in the United States, where it had been the twin brother of the spoils system, it is now largely confined to the upper crust of the policy-making governmental positions, because the vast majority of appointments has come under civil service regulation. But it still is not entirely banned from congress; senators and representatives can be kept in a benevolent mood by assigning military installations or government contracts to their bailiwicks. Similar more or less subtle hand-out techniques are not unknown to most states in Continental Europe.

However, all these aspects of the functional independence of the assembly from the government may seem minor when compared with the substance of the assembly's function, namely, to enact legislation. To be factually independent from the government, the parliament would have to monopolize the entire legislative process. In particular, in line with Royer-Collard's famous dictum, "Initier la loi, c'est gouverner," the assembly would have to have exclusive control over the planning of the legislative program, especially over the initiation of legislation. Though conforming theoretically to the traditional concept of the "separation of functions," this postulate has become, in political practice, wholly unrealistic and obsolete for two reasons. In the first place, as has been pointed out,* the assembly's primary function is not legislation as such; rather it is the participation in policy decision, execution, and control. Legislation, in the technical sense incidental to all three of them, is no longer isolated or isolable from the other attributes of the assembly. In the second place, in the modern mass society, government is party government; the political party is the iron clamp holding parliament and government together. The power process, whether operated through interdependence by integration or interdependence by co-ordination, hinges on the dependence of both government and parliament on the party dynamism. Consequently, the theoretical postulate of the complete functional independence of the parliament has become eclipsed by the fact that the government in our time dominates the legislative process in degrees varying as to the specific patterns of government: absolutely in Britain; with a greater amount of shared powers in France, Germany, and Switzerland; and least, but still with a degree of effectiveness, in the United States.

CONTROL INSTRUMENTALITIES OF THE PARLIAMENT OVER THE GOVERNMENT

Turning now from the negative aspect—freedom of the assembly from governmental influence—to the positive control devices at the parliament's disposal, three areas may be distinguished here: (1) the designation of the executive power holder; (2) the political control over the conduct of the governmental functions; and (3) the removal of the government. These three aspects, however, are not always neatly separable in practice.

Designation of the government.—The manner by which the holder of a political office has attained it cannot fail to influence his subsequent conduct in office, even though no constitutional or legal obligations may exist between the officeholder and those responsible for his elevation to office. From this rule the chief of

* See above, pp. 42 ff.

state is not exempted. Only the hereditary monarch—so claim the advocates of the monarchical principle—is completely independent, because he owes his position to dynastic legitimacy alone.[1]

For the president of a republican state two methods of designation are the rule: either the chief of state is elected by the people and remains responsible to them only—he is neither designated nor removable by the assembly—or, as is the near-general rule in the parliamentary republic, the state president is elected by the parliament. Austria and Finland are the only countries in Europe where the president is elected by the people. It is almost axiomatic that parliamentary government is allergic to the popular election of the president and that, if combined, these heterogeneous elements do not blend. This experience was confirmed by France in 1848, when the popularly elected president was incongruously grafted upon assembly government, and by Weimar Germany and republican Spain, where the president designated in the same manner ran into irreconcilable conflicts with the parliament. But it is equally axiomatic that the state president elected by the assembly remains more submissive to it than one deriving his mandate from popular election, and this in spite of the fact that the chief of state usually is irremovable during his constitutional term and that otherwise he is not subject to any formalized controls by the assembly. The continued deference of the president toward the assembly has sociopsychological rather than legal reasons: in the first place, the assembly is in the habit of preferring one of its own members to an outsider; in the second place, a president seeking re-election is always careful not to antagonize his future constituents.

Under parliamentary government the assembly designates the premier or minister-president as the actual governmental power holder, who then chooses his cabinet either at his discretion (under bipartism) or in conformity with the party configuration (under multipartism). The investiture of the head of the cabinet is performed either through direct election by the assembly (Germany-Bonn) or by approving through a vote of confidence the person nominated, again in line with the party configuration, by the chief of state (monarch or republican state president); this is the situation in Britain and France. In either case, the mode of parliamentary designation cannot fail to have decisive influence on the subsequent conduct of government by the minister-president and his cabinet: they remain under the continuous control of, and at any time may be removed by, the parliament. Method of designation and continued control are thus complementary, since parliamentary government is basically interdependence by integration. The minister-president and his cabinet, being members of the assembly and in continuous confrontation with it, are dependent on the support of the parliamentary majority for the conduct of office. In the Swiss directory pattern, on the other hand, the designation of the Federal Council by the federal assemblies deviates from the rule of assembly government: the government remains completely independent from the assembly in the exercise of the governmental function.

Routine political controls of the assembly over the government. —The foremost interorgan control of the parliament over the government, common to all patterns of constitutional democracy, is the rejection of legislation sponsored directly or indirectly by the government and its equivalent, the denial of appropriations requested by the government. Under parliamentarism such adverse action of the parliament normally would lead to the resignation of the government if the rejected measure is considered politically vital. However, under the British variant of parliamentarism—cabinet government—the Commons can practically neither reject a government bill nor refuse the requested financial supply. All the opposition may do is to move, as a symbolic device of control, for the reduction of the salary of the cabinet member with whose conduct of office it is dissatisfied; the action is invariably unsuccessful. Under presidentialism likewise the rejection of a measure operates as an effective interorgan control on the chief executive, though he is irremovable during his legal term: accepting defeat, the president must abandon or change his policy. Again the Swiss directory system differs: by no means does the rejection of a proposal of the Federal Council by the federal assemblies entail loss of prestige, let alone lead to the resignation of the Federal Council as a whole or its individual member responsible for the specific measure.

Among the other customary instruments of political control of the assembly over the government are the following: (1) Through questions and interpellations the governmental conduct of office is scrutinized, criticized, and controlled. No government, however safe its majority, can easily disregard them. (2) The congressional investigating committees have gained particular importance, at least in the United States, during the last decade, perhaps less by the malpractices they actually uncover than by the undesirable publicity to which they expose the administration. In England parliamentary commissions, often organized as royal commissions and including politically disinterested persons outside the parliament, are primarily fact-finding agencies. In France and Germany the investigating committees have not integrated themselves into the political process.[2] (3) Potent interorgan controls exist in all constitutional-democratic states in the form of the parliamentary ratification of international treaties previously concluded by the executive power holder in charge of foreign policy, insofar as they involve national legislation. (4) In the United States, the senatorial confirmation of presidential nominations for judicial, military, and civilian policy-making positions is also an effective control; the fitness of the nominee is often subjected to severe scrutiny.

The government is incessantly exposed to the barrage of criticism from the opposition and, frequently, also from its own supporters. The debates in the plenary sessions and committees and on special occasions, such as the address to the throne, offer current and extraordinary opportunities for such voices critical of governmental conduct. The government is constantly in the ring and has as much to take as it can dish out. Here the compulsory membership of the ministers in the assembly is the technical key of interdependence by integration of the parliamentary pattern. The presence of the ministers facilitates the effective confrontation of the political leader and the responsible heads of the department with their critics in the assembly. In most presidential states in Latin America and likewise in Switzerland, the ministers sit—without voting rights—in the assembly, and, where this is not required constitutionally, they may be summoned to be questioned and held to account.

Removal of the government by vote of censure.—In patterns with a fixed term of the executive power holder the assembly is deprived of legal means for compelling the government to withdraw from office, barring impeachment. Only under exceptional circumstances can public opinion in the United States induce the president to retire an individual member of his official family, as occurred, for example, under the first Eisenhower administration for serious misconduct in office ("conflict of interests"). But the decision is always the president's; congress exercises extreme restraint and is constitutionally as well as politically incapable of forcing his hand.

Contrariwise, under parliamentarism—and this is a crucial difference between the two patterns of government—the parliament, or rather the party majority in the assembly, can invoke at any time the political responsibility of the cabinet and force its resignation. Parliamentary confidence in the government and governmental responsibility to the parliament are reciprocal and complementary, the obverse and the reverse side of the same coin. Political responsibility is the pivot on which parliamentary government hinges, and loss of confidence the Damocles sword that dangles over any government unless it enjoys so watertight a majority that it can weather any storm.

This strongest weapon against the cabinet at the disposal of the assembly—the threat of removal—is exercised by a formal vote of non-confidence (censure) or by one of its equivalents, the rejection of a vote of confidence sought by the cabinet or the rejection of a policy measure declared vital by the government for its continuation in office. If the prime minister, having lost or being about to lose the confidence of the party majority in parliament, feels convinced that the electorate will support his person or the policies he represents, he will counter the threat of removal by the threat of dissolution of the parliament or proceed to actual dissolution.

Of the three kinds of ministerial responsibility—criminal, civil, and political—only the last has remained of practical importance. Likewise the distinction between collective and individual responsibility of the cabinet, at times much belabored by constitutional theory, has lost most of its practical value, since the minister-president assumes responsibility for himself and the entire cabinet as well as for its individual members. However, to save his cabinet as a whole, or to strengthen it, he may divorce himself from an individual member (the case of Sir Samuel Hoare in England, 1936), and an individual member may resign voluntarily because of disagreement with the cabinet's policies (the case of Pierre Mendès-France in France, February, 1956).

It is interesting to note that the functional core of the parliamentary pattern—confidence of the parliament in the government and responsibility of the government toward the parliament—having grown organically, is not specified, except in the most general terms, in the constitutional documents and has successfully defied any institutionalization by enforcible constitutional norms. Only since the First World War have the rules of the parliamentary game been subjected to a certain degree of articulation and streamlining, the so-called "rationalization of power."[3] Various devices were inserted in the constitutions: "cooling-off" periods between the motion for a vote of censure or of confidence and the actual vote on it, as an attempt to eliminate the nuisance of

surprise or "snap" decisions which, in connection with interpel-
lation, were a frequent cause for the fall of cabinets under the
French Third Republic, and qualified majorities both for the
investiture, by vote of confidence, of the cabinet and for its
removal by adverse action of the parliament. These devices are
intended to make the fate of the cabinet less an object of the
caprice and intrigues of the politicians and more the result of
mature consideration by the majority of the assembly. Pertinent
examples are offered by Italy (constitution of 1947, Art. 94, sec.
5) and France (constitution of 1946, Art. 49). A similar device
for rationalizing the parliamentary dynamics was the so-called
"investiture" under Article 45 of the French constitution: under
this provision the president of the Council of Ministers, designated
by the president of the Republic after negotiations with the parties, had first to obtain the approval of the National Assembly for
his program (by simple majority) and afterward to be formally
invested by the absolute majority of the members of the assembly.
The artful device increased the difficulties of forming a cabinet
and was repealed by constitutional amendment in 1954. The most
stringent of all measures to stabilize the cabinet is the requirement
of the Bonn constitution of the "constructive" vote of non-
confidence which succeeds only if combined with the simultaneous election of the successor-chancellor.*

These efforts to solidify and rationalize the dynamics of parliamentary government, sensible as they may seem prima facie, contributed little to the stability of French cabinets. They fall rarely
through a vote of non-confidence but rather through the disintegration of the party coalition behind the cabinet. But it is only
fair to point out that in other multiple-party regimes, even where
no single party holds an absolute majority (as was the case in Italy
before 1953 and in Germany between 1957 and 1961), the fatality
rate of cabinets is not much higher than under the two-party
systems, as evidenced, for example, by Belgium, Holland, Den-

* See above, pp. 96 ff.

mark, and others. It is the political maturity of a nation and its ability to compromise political differences, rather than artificial constitutional arrangements, that provide for a stable government capable of attaining and exercising political leadership.

Removal of the state president by impeachment.—In view of the dual character of the executive power holder customary under parliamentarism, a distinction should be made between the nominal head or chief of state (monarch and state president, respectively) and the actual governmental power holder, the cabinet. In general, the chief of state occupies a position as safe as that of the American president. The monarch is beyond the reach of political responsibility because of the fiction that "the king can do no wrong"; the republican state president, because of the requirement of the ministerial countersignature for all his political acts by which the cabinet assumes responsibility on his behalf. Exceptions to the irremovability of the state president occurred in Weimar Germany (Art. 43) and republican Spain (Art. 83), which provided, without invoking the impeachment procedure, for the removal of the president by a combined action of the parliament (Reichstag and Cortes, respectively) and the electorate. The remedial device makes sense only in political regimes where the state president is endowed with more than ceremonial or symbolic-representative functions. It was used successfully in Spain (1936) against President Zamora, who was alleged to have overstepped his constitutional powers.

The *ultima ratio*, finally, for the parliament to rid itself of an incumbent on the presidential office who has become obnoxious to it but is constitutionally irremovable during his term is the impeachment, or the exercise of what by a misnomer the French call "political justice." It may be used against the republican state president and in certain jurisdictions also against the ministers; in the latter exceptional case, however, it is only an *ex post facto* penalty for politically objectionable conduct of office invoked after the minister has relinquished his position.[4] The impeachment is a genuine interorgan control of the assembly over the executive power holder. The indictment is invariably instituted by the lower house of parliament, while the trial itself is conducted either by the upper house (France, Third Republic; United States) or by a judicial agency composed of professional judges as well as parliamentarians (High Court of Justice in France, Fourth Republic) or of judges alone (Federal Constitutional Court in Germany-Bonn). In spite of the painstaking efforts of some recent constitutions to judicialize the institution in line with the rule of law, the impeachment everywhere has become practically obsolete. Stemming from the formative period of constitutionalism when the Stuart parliaments used it as a retaliatory weapon against the advisers and ministers of the crown, it has lost its rationale in parliamentary states with the development of the political responsibility of the cabinet. But even in presidential regimes where the irremovability of the chief execuitve may justify an extraordinary interorgan control of the assembly, its psychological value, let alone its political utility, is non-existent. Again the good people of Switzerland are on the side of the angels: no impeachment procedure against the Federal Council is provided.

In this context it is proper to note that the position of the traditionally irremovable monarch, in our time, is no longer unconditionally secure. Thrones have collapsed everywhere since the First World War, and even in nations where the monarchical institution enjoys undiminished respect the incumbents are no longer absolutely safe. The abdication of Edward VIII (1936) in England, while public opinion was divided, was enforced by the cabinet fully supported by the majority of the Commons, and Leopold III of Belgium had to resign (1950) under the pressure of the parliamentary majority supported by the majority of the people, against the resistance of the cabinet.[5]

The proper understanding of the power process can be obtained only by considering the reciprocal controls of the government over the assembly, which will be discussed in the next section.

The Second Pattern: Controls of the Government over the Parliament

The problem of the functional independence, so important for the position of the assembly in relation to the government, has no counterpart relative to the government. Complete independence of the government from the assembly signifies authoritarianism and autocracy. Contrariwise, in the constitutional-democratic state, functional independence of the government from the parliament is impossible. Modern government is party government. No constitutional government, regardless of the specific pattern, can govern against the opposition of the majority in parliament. At no time is the government in a position to emancipate itself completely from the support and, with the support, from the control of parliament. Nonetheless, the government always occupies the privileged position in the power process. To govern presupposes the assumption of political leadership. These factors provide the technical, moral, and intellectual basis for political leadership: the relatively small number of persons engaged in the policy-deciding function; the greater selectivity prevailing in their designation; the more compact cohesion of the governing group; and their willingness to accept political responsibility. It is from the government rather than from the multimembered assembly that the mass of the power addressees expects leadership. To the public the government is more visible, more tangible, than the mostly anonymous collectivity of the parliament. What the government does is always news. Moreover, the government disposes of the power apparatus of the state. Regardless of the specific pattern of government, the political process necessarily is slanted toward the ascendancy of the government. In the organized state executive leadership is natural.

The institutionalized controls the government today has at its disposal over the parliament can be grouped in two main areas: (1) influence of the government on the parliament's legislative, including the budgetary, prerogatives and (2) influence on the operation and existence of the assembly as a legally functioning power holder as a whole—the right of dissolution. If the third and historically so important avenue by which government could aspire to the domination of the assembly—the influence on its personnel structure—has become legally blocked by the elaborate defense mechanism the assembly in time has built up for its protection,* it does not mean that the government has abandoned its indirect efforts to obtain a composition of the parliamentary membership favorable to its policies and unfavorable to the political opposition. Today this aim is served merely by different methods. The electoral process and the laws governing it remain the traditional battleground of the never ending struggle for political power between the government and the parliament. A fuller discussion of this all-important subject will follow at a later point.†

GOVERNMENTAL   INFLUENCE   ON   THE
LEGISLATIVE   PROCESS

The ideal type of the strict autonomy of the several power holders would forbid governmental intervention in any stage of the legislative process—initiation, drafting, deliberation, and passage. This, however, is at variance with the realities of the political process. Nothing is more revealing of the obsolescence of the traditional tripartite "separation of functions" than the government's position in the legislative process. The government must necessarily assume political leadership for policy decision, which is essentially legislation, and responsibility for policy execution, likewise frequently cast in legislative form. Instead of being aloof from the legislative process, the government is closely integrated in it.

However, the government's role varies according to the specific pattern of government. In authoritarian states its monopoly over all stages of the legislative process is firmly established. Where permitted to exist, the assembly is reduced to a subsidiary body, if not to a rubber stamp. In constitutional democracies the intensity

* See above, pp. 187 ff.   † See below, pp. 270 ff.

of the government's participation depends on the specific pattern of government. At one extreme is cabinet government in England and the Dominions. Government control is quasi-authoritarian in substance though based on voluntary subordination of the parliament. Planning and initiative of the legislative program are monopolized by the cabinet; the initiative of the private members of both parties is nearly extinct. Complete control of the cabinet over the agenda is coupled with the disposal over parliamentary time, leading if need be to the curtailment of debate by drastic measures of closure ("the guillotine"). At the other end is the United States: governmental influence on the legislative program, the calendar, and the timetable of congress depends on the strength of presidential persuasion, even when the president's party commands a majority. The president lacks any constitutional authority to demand priority for his program, and, in addition, the Rules Committee of the House of Representatives occupies a near-dictatorial position that has no parallel in other assemblies. France, under the Third and Fourth republics, presents a situation between these two extremes, which may be characterized as the mixed system: program, calendar, and timetable are under the autonomy of the assembly, acting through the Conference of the Presidents. But the ascendancy of the parliament is attenuated by the influence the leaders of the government coalition parties exercise on the Conference and also by the representatives of the government coalition in the important committees. In Germany-Bonn, Bundestag and federal government share in the legislative programming in recent years about equally, but drafting of practically all politically important legislation is undertaken by the ministerial bureaucracy, and the government proposals enjoy a strict priority. In Switzerland, finally, the control of the Federal Council over the legislative process comes close to that in Britain, though parliamentary initiative is given considerably more leeway.

Significant for the increasing leadership of the government is also the management of the budgetary and financial prerogatives of the parliament. Historically the Commons' control of the purse strings was the leverage for the transformation of the absolute into the constitutionally limited monarchy and of the latter into the parliamentary monarchy. However, these historical prerogatives have been whittled away to the point of no return. The mastery of the British cabinet over the finances is as undisputed as that over the legislation. Nowadays the mother of parliaments swallows the governmental budget hook, line, and sinker. On the other hand, in France, land of classical parliamentary supremacy, the Chamber of Deputies and the National Assembly have retained their financial autonomy to the largest possible degree, with the powerful Finance Committee as the center of political gravity. However, the constitution of 1946 (Art. 17, sec. 2) sensibly restricts expenditures requested during the debates for which no revenues have been provided. In the United States the executive budget is the invariable practice. Congress, however, jealously reserves for itself and frequently exercises the right to reduce governmental requests for appropriations while remaining, on the whole, amenable to presidential wishes for revenues.

INFLUENCE OF THE GOVERNMENT ON COMPLETED LEGISLATION

The traditional separation of functions between the executive and the legislative power holders would imply that the legislative product completed by the assembly be final and no longer subject to governmental control. This, however, is not the case: under parliamentarism governmental control over legislation passed by parliament is reduced almost to the vanishing point, for the obvious reason that, with interdependence by integration, all legislation is at least government approved if not government sponsored. If the parliament would pass a bill of vital importance against the opposition of the cabinet, the latter would resign. On the other hand, interorgan control of the government over the completed legislative product is strongest under presidentialism, interdependence by co-ordination.

The following types of relationship between government and parliament with reference to completed legislation have developed historically:

1. The unconditional finality of the assembly in the legislative process is the logical solution of assembly government, first stated by the French constitution of 1793 (Art. 59). No further act of confirmation by the executive is required. This is also the invariable constitutional pattern in the Soviet orbit, because of the party identity of government and assembly. Characteristically, it prevails also under the assembly type of government in Switzerland: acceptance or rejection of a bill by the federal assemblies is final.

2. Under parliamentarism a formal validation of parliamentary legislation is required by the head or chief of the state, the crown or the republican state president, respectively. In the former case it is called "royal assent" (England), "sanction," or "promulgation" (Belgium, Art. 69); in the case of the republican state president it is always called "promulgation" (France, Third and Fourth republics; Germany-Weimar and Germany-Bonn). The constitutional theory holds that promulgation cannot be refused by the head of the state because the cabinet, by countersignature, has assumed political responsibility for it. The British crown has not refused to grant royal assent since Queen Anne's rejection of the Scotch Militia Bill (1707). It is unthinkable today; the crown would certainly lose its cabinet and, possibly, the throne.

3. The president of the republic may withhold promulgation, always covered by the approval of the government, until a referendum has been held on the bill, thus injecting the verdict of the electorate as the supreme power holder. Under Germany-Weimar (Art. 73, sec. 1) the president could call for the referendum on his own initiative, always protected by the countersignature of the Reich chancellor. In Eire (constitution of 1937, Art. 27) the presidential initiative for the referendum is dependent on the petition of specified portions of the Senate or the Oireachtas. None of these devices has ever come into operation.

4. The government may be accorded the right of the suspensive veto against the legislation passed by the assembly. This device, first introduced for the benefit of the crown in a constitutionally limited monarchy by the French constitution of 1791 (Art. 117), went by the name of "refusing the royal sanction" and subsequently was much imitated by similar regimes. However, the most prominent role the suspensive veto plays is under American presidentialism. It is also deemed compatible with the parliamentary power process, for example, in Czechoslovakia (constitution of 1920, Arts. 47 and 48). In France, under both the Third and the Fourth republics, it has been pared down to the presidential request for a second consideration by the chambers (the so-called "*renvoi*"), without, however, requiring for the latter's second deliberation qualified majorities. Dormant under the Third, it has been reactivated under the Fourth Republic.[6]

5. Finally, the executive power holder may be endowed with the absolute veto against legislation passed by the assembly. This device, signifying the authoritarian slant of constitutional government, prevailed in the French Charte of 1814 as the right of the royal sanction and even under the Orleanist parliamentary monarchy; it died hard in the Continental limited monarchies (for example, Prussian constitution of 1850, Art. 62), even though it had become a dead letter before its ultimate extinction. The absolute veto of the executive is being conveniently resurrected in contmporary neopresidentialism, which takes no chances even when the assemblies are entirely appointed or controlled by the government.

The veto is still of practical importance within the frame of the pattern of government based on interdependence by co-ordination, primarily in the American presidential system. The *Federalist* (Nos. 69 and 73) treated the institution of the veto as a genuine interorgan control, a "shield of the Executive" and a "salutory check on the legislative body," calculated to guard the community against "the effects of factions." The founding fathers were perennially preoccupied with the dangers of what to them was democracy. If the presidential veto was originally intended primarily as a restraint on "improper," that is, technically defective, laws, it changed its meaning radically after the review of constitutionality had shifted to the courts. The history of the use of the veto sheds light on its transformation into a potent instrumentality of the president for claiming his share in congressional policy decision, which the constitution had withheld from him. Applied most sparingly in the period before the Civil War, it became thereafter a legitimate interorgan control at the disposal of the president against legislation which appeared to him politically unwise or undesirable. Franklin D. Roosevelt and Harry S. Truman used it with deliberation to increase presidential leadership when other means of persuasion administered to congress during the deliberative stage of the bill would not suffice to prevent the passage. Since the qualified majorities to override the presidential veto are only obtainable under exceptional circumstances, the president, through the veto power, has become an energetic partner in the legislative process instead of confining himself to being the faithful executor of the congressional will. This accretion to the presidential power seems to match the recent increase in congressional power through withholding appropriations, a reflection of the almost automatic equalization of the respective power potentials of president and congress under the American constitution.

LEGISLATIVE POWERS OF THE GOVERNMENT

In this context of the relationship between government and assembly in the legislative process another development that tends to increase the ascendancy of the government over the parliament deserves attention. The government not only participates in the legislative process but actually exercises the legislative function, either autonomously or by delegation. Delegation of legislative powers by the assembly to the government has become a universal phenomenon in the technological age. This most significant change in the power dynamics derives from the transformation of the legislative into the administrative state. The demands for government intervention in the socioeconomic process have enormously increased, and, correspondingly, the area of self-determination of the private citizen has shrunk. More spheres in which private initiative once prevailed have come under state control. The net of governmental regulations thrown over the individual has become denser; his contacts with administrative authorities, more frequent and intricate. What concerns the individual is less how the law is written than how he fares when it is applied to him.

The ordinance-making function.—Within the frame of the delegation of legislative functions several frequently interconnected situations have to be distinguished. In its original, more narrow, sense legislative delegation refers to the authorization of the government by the assembly to enact rules and regulations for the execution of the parliamentary statute, generally spoken of as the "ordinance-making function" of the government. It is either granted the government by a parliamentary statute or considered implicitly inherent in the function of policy execution and administration assigned to the government. The reasons for this practice, familiar to all patterns of government, are self-evident: the assemblies, recruited largely from among amateurs turned politicians and usually lacking experience in the ever increasing complexity of modern administration, are incapable of attending to the technical details that make a statute applicable to the life of the community. Moreover, pressure of time on parliament, which can hardly perform properly its legislative share in policy determination, together with the need for flexibility in applying the statutory rules to the changing conditions, and, finally, the exigencies of emergency or crisis government* necessitate the transfer of the executory, implementing, and ordinance-making function to the professionals of the governmental bureaucracy and the staffs of the civil service, better qualified for these tasks than a multimembered assembly of politicians.

* This aspect will be dealt with below, pp. 217 ff.

The situation in England is illustrative of most other countries:[7] lawmaking functions are delegated by parliament to the King-in-Council, that is, the cabinet, enunciated by orders-in-council; to ministers and heads of departments; to local authorities and public corporations; to rules committees; and even to autonomous non-governmental bodies, such as professional associations. The terminology applied in each case varies and is wholly accidental. In France and Germany both allocation and nomenclature of the ordinance-making function are far better systematized. In the United States, after the Supreme Court in an early decision[8] had sustained the right of congress to delegate the function of "filling in the details" of a statute, the courts have insisted on, and the congress has complied with, the requirement of "intelligible standards" to which supplementary rules and administrative actions must conform.[9]

The lawmaking or rule-making function thus delegated must be exercised strictly within the limits of the enabling statute and in conformity with it. Parliamentary control over the use the government and the administration make of the legislative powers delegated to them necessarily can be intermittent only and remains far from effective. To subject, therefore, the governmental rule-making power to continuous judicial control has become one of the basic postulates of the state under the rule of law. The function of the courts, in this context, is to see to it that the executory ordinance does not overstep the limits set by the statute for its implementation (*ultra vires*) and to safeguard the citizen, with due regard for administrative discretion as required by flexibility, against the arbitrariness of the administering government officials.*

Enabling acts and "pleins pouvoirs."—Aside from referring to rules implementing and executing the parliamentary statute, delegated legislation has a wider and politically more ominous meaning. In this sense it signifies the situation in which the parliament, embroiled in political dissensions and, hence, frequently incapable of attending to the legislative function, devolves it by a sweeping

* See below, pp. 240 ff.

authorization (enabling act) to the government. It is distinguished from the transfer of the ordinance-making power in that the delegation pertains to subject matters ordinarily considered the exclusive domain of parliamentary legislation. This delegation of the legislative power is a complete reversal of the constitutional assignment of the various state activities to different power holders in that it substitutes the executive for the legislative power holder. The government, thereby, is granted an ascendancy in the legislative process far beyond constitutional normalcy. Decree laws under enabling acts have the rank of ordinary parliamentary statutes and therefore can amend or repeal existing statutory law. This phenomenon is known in France, Belgium, and elsewhere as *pleins pouvoirs*, authorizing the cabinet to issue decree laws in place of parliamentary statutes, and in Germany and elsewhere as enabling acts (*Ermächtigungsgesetze*), authorizing the government to enact ordinances in the place of federal statutes. The practice failed to develop either in Britain or in the United States, except in crisis periods,* partly because it is at variance with the Lockian maxim of "delegata potestas non potest delegari" and partly because it is not required by the mechanics of the two-party structure.

The rationale of such sweeping transfers of the legislative function to the government is primarily political, though technical considerations may also come into play. The parliament as a whole, or the parties forming the government coalition, are unable to agree on a policy decision as such (for example, a program of economic reform) or are incapable of converting it into the legislation required for its execution (for example, a complex civil service law). By the force of political circumstances, therefore, they confer the legislative function on the smaller group of the government believed to be more qualified to act expeditiously and effectively, and, at the same time, they devolve political responsibility for the policy decision on the government.

* See below, pp. 224–25.

Enabling acts and *pleins pouvoirs* vary considerably as to scope and substance. They are granted either for a specific purpose, for example, the protection of the currency, or without any substantive specification; in the latter case they amount to the complete abdication of the legislative function by parliament. Delegated powers are granted for short or long periods but never indefinitely. Parliamentary control is formally maintained by the customary requirement that the government must submit decree laws to the parliament for eventual repeal, a contingency that has hardly ever arisen. However, the balance between government and parliament may be restored in time, because *pleins pouvoirs* are bestowed only on a specific government supported by a specific party combination and never devolve automatically on a successor cabinet. They lapse with the cabinet to which they have been given. But a cabinet endowed with *pleins pouvoirs* is usually safe, for the duration of its mandate, from being overthrown.

France is the traditional land for the practice of encompassing delegation of legislative powers to the government.[10] Originating during the First World War as a measure of crisis government, the delegation of *pleins pouvoirs* was frequently resorted to in the postwar period. Beginning with the premiership of Doumergue in 1934, they became a regular feature of the political process and, before and after the outbreak of the Second World War, often the normal method of legislation. The majority of legislative reforms since the thirties were enacted by decree legislation, and parliament never exercised its nominal right to repeal them. Without them France would have fallen into anarchy. To forestall the repetition of the experience considered unconstitutional, if politically necessary, the constitution of 1946 explicitly prohibited the delegation of legislative powers (Art. 13, sec. 2), but to no avail. The practice reasserted itself with a vengeance in the form of sweeping enabling acts, authorizing the government to undertake large-scale reform measures in the fields of finances, economics, civil service, and even judicial organization for which the politically split parliament could not bring itself to assume responsibility. Moreover, the practice was now blessed by the Conseil d'Etat.[11] In comparison with its use in the Third Republic, the technique was somewhat systematized and subjected to certain interorgan controls: the government requires for the individual decree the advice (*avis*) of the Conseil d'Etat, the highly respected judicial agency completely independent from the govenrment, or, under certain circumstances, the concurrence of the Finance Commission of the National Assembly.

Enabling acts were also a familiar feature in the early crisis years of the Weimar republic. Because of the implicit deviation from the constitutionally provided legislative procedure, their passage required the majorities prescribed for constitutional amendment. Later the federal government preferred the more convenient and less controllable ordinances enacted under the emergency powers of Article 48.*

In this connection an interesting innovation of the Italian constitution of 1947 (Art. 72, sec. 3) may be mentioned: bills can be drafted and passed by special parliamentary committees in which the parties are proportionally represented. The widely practiced devolution of the legislative function to such miniature parliaments has given excellent results, without disturbing the normal balance of interorgan controls.[12] At any time prior to the final approval of the bill by the committee either the government, or one-tenth of the members of parliament, or one-fifth of the members of the committee may request the transfer of the bill to the parliament itself. The procedure is an interesting combination of inter- and intra-organ controls built into the legislative process.

To restate briefly what influence the practice of delegated legislation has on the dynamism of reciprocal interorgan controls: By assuming—with the consent of the parliament—the authority to legislate by decree, the government usurps, for extended periods, the domain constitutionally reserved for the legislative power

* See below, pp. 222–23.

holder. By this abdication the parliament deprives itself of its legitimate share in policy determination and policy execution. Its interorgan control over the government is reduced to the nominal right of rescinding the governmental decree. The loss of the power potential of the assembly is the gain of the government. Executive leadership is bought at the expense of the principle of shared powers.

DISSOLUTION OF THE PARLIAMENT

The dissolution of the parliament,[13] either of both houses simultaneously or of the lower house alone, is germane only to the parliamentary pattern of government. It is structurally incompatible with both the assembly government—except as autodissolution, never resorted to—and the presidential patterns. If, in the armory of interorgan controls, the vote of non-confidence is the strongest weapon of the parliament toward the cabinet, the right of the government to dissolve the assembly and call for new elections is the matching counteraction of the government toward the parliament. Within the frame of authentic parliamentarism these two devices, at least since the second half of the nineteenth century, belong together like hand and glove. The process of political power revolves around them. Since the advent of mass democracy the logical sequence of the vote of non-confidence is the dissolution of parliament to obtain the verdict of the supreme power holder, the electorate, as the arbiter between the cabinet and the parliamentary majority hostile to it. In addition to the solution of a conflict between the executive and the legislative power holders, dissolution may also be resorted to by the government solely on the assumption that the present party complexion of the parliament no longer reflects the genuine will of the nation. Two other constitutionally provided applications of dissolution, namely, conflicts between the two houses of parliament and the ratification of an antecedent constitutional amendment passed by parliament, do not belong to the same category of interorgan controls at the disposal of the government.

Where the dissolution power is effective, a vote of non-confidence or one of its equivalents, if carried against the cabinet, invariably leads to dissolution. This extreme point, however, is rarely reached in parliamentary states. As a rule, the threat of dissolution is sufficient to prevent the fall of the cabinet. The institution of dissolution as such, therefore, constitutes the core of the power dynamism of the parliamentary state. Its mere existence tends to make the cabinet strong; its absence, weak. This conclusion is fully proved by comparing the divergent development of the parliamentary institutions in Britain and France. In England the ever present threat of dissolution with its inevitable electoral risks closes the ranks of the majority party behind the government and gives the cabinet the whip hand over the Commons. Contrariwise, in France the dissolution power of the government has atrophied. The mere existence, therefore, of the governmental power to dissolve the assembly blunts the edge of the vote of non-confidence and similar devices to remove the cabinet from power.

The dissolution as an institution to solicit the arbitration of the electorate in conflicts between the government and the parliamentary majority evolved slowly. It will be remembered that, historically, the dissolution served the English crown to rid itself of a recalcitrant House of Commons. Later, in the eighteenth century, the device was used more often than not by the crown and the cabinet to secure, by hook and crook, a favorable majority in the new elections. In the period between the first and the second reforms in England a defeat of the government in the Commons—unlike other parliamentary states, the British upper house never possessed the right to overthrow a cabinet—did not always result in dissolution. Either a prime minister struck by a vote of non-confidence endeavored to reorganize his majority through dissidents of the opposition party or the leader of the opposition assumed responsibility forthwith without an antecedent dissolution and confirmation by new elections. Only with the full democratization of the suffrage did the triangular power configuration evolve in which the electorate in the general elections decides which of the two political parties and which of the party leaders should govern. The British practice set the pattern of dissolution in most other parliamentary states since the second half of the nineteenth century.

Much of the effectiveness of the dissolution in producing a genuine verdict of the electorate depends on the prevailing party structuration—whether bipartisan or multipartism—and on the technical system by which the general elections are conducted. It is most clearly indicative of the electoral will under the two-party system or a party configuration approximating it and least so under multipartism. The dissolution can approximate the referendum only in the rare instances when definite and discernible issues, on which the parties are clearly divided, are at stake in the general election. Obviously, this can happen only under the two-party system. Dissolution under multipartism rarely allows a definite interpretation of the will of the electorate.

In addition, the straight majority technique usually results in a clear-cut expression of the electoral will, while proportional representation with its proliferation of political parties tends to obscure it. Moreover, under proportional repesentation the dissolution is less capable of effectively producing a verdict of the electorate, because the party cadres tend to become frozen under it and because an emotional upsurge of the electoral will—a landslide—is less likely to occur. Under the majority technique even slight changes of the electoral climate may be reflected in changing majorities.

To minimize the danger that the government may abuse the dissolution device, its most powerful interorgan control, and permanently outplay the parliament, the institution is often hedged in by certain restrictions. Among these may be mentioned the following: (1) Most constitutional democracies prescribe in their constitutions that, within a specified period after dissolution, new elections be held and, after another specified period, the new parliament be convened. (2) For the dissolution of the lower house the consent of the upper house is required (for example, France, Third Republic, Constitutional Law of February 25, 1875, Art. 5); this interorgan control tends to stay the hands of the government when the upper house likewise suffers extinction by simultaneous dissolution. (3) The constitution enjoins that the dissolution must not be repeated "for the same cause" (Weimar constitution, Art. 25); this provision was grossly violated by the two successive dissolutions of the Reichstag (July and November, 1932) by the "presidential" cabinet of von Papen, exercised only in order to increase the hopeless minority supporting the government. (4) The dissolution may be prohibited within a constitutionally determined period after the preceding general election. This is the situation under the French constitution of 1946 (Art. 51), with the additional restriction that even thereafter it is permissible only if two ministerial crises have been occasioned by a vote of non-confidence. The provision, with the single exception of 1955 mentioned before, remained a dead letter if for no other reason than the fact that most French cabinets fall by internal disintegration of the party coalition supporting the government rather than by formalized disapproval of the National Assembly. (5) Only exceptionally is the prime minister's discretion in deciding on the dissolution restrained by an intra-organ control exercised by the chief of state. As a general rule, the state president is constitutionally bound to grant the cabinet the dissolution it requests. In the constitution of Eire of 1937 (Art. 13, sec. 2), however, the president may refuse, "in his absolute discretion"—that is, he is not bound by the advice of the *taoiseach* (prime minister) and may act without the latter's countersignature—a dissolution if the prime minister "ceases to retain the majority in the Dáil Eireann." All these devices must be visualized as intra- or interorgan controls to blunt the edge of the dissolution weapon in the hands of the government.

On the other hand, the complete discretion of the prime minister in choosing the proper moment for the dissolution operates to the benefit of the government. Actually, during the last fifty years, very few of the British Commons have reached the legal end of their five-year term, even when the cabinet enjoyed an absolutely safe majority. The prime minister is at liberty to select the moment most propitious for the retention of his majority in the ensuing elections, and he may even, in anticipation of the campaign, legitimately tip the scales by measures passed to curry favor with the rank and file of the electorate; among these, tax reductions and salary raises enjoy special popularity.

From the viewpoint of constitutional theory, the dissolution is the capstone of the democratic power process under parliamentarism: it places issues and men squarely before the supreme power holder, the electorate; it solves conflicts between the government and the party majority of the parliament; it resolves otherwise unbreakable deadlocks between the executive and legislative power holders. Some constitutions, therefore, endow the people themselves, contending that the existing parliament no longer corresponds to their true will, with the right to demand a dissolution by initiative and referendum, even against the opposition of the government and its majority in the assembly. It was attempted, without success, in Prussia in 1932. In the case of the popular initiative the dissolution is turned from an interorgan control operating between government and parliament into another type of interorgan control operating between the electorate against government and parliament together.

CRISIS GOVERNMENT

This survey of the interorgan controls of the government toward the assembly would be unrealistic without including that significant phase of the power process generally characterized as "emergency" or "crisis government." The optimistic assumption of classical constitutionalism that the constitution would remain, at all times and under all circumstances, the supreme law of the land and the unalterable frame for the conduct of the power process failed to materialize. After a steady march toward the normalcy of the constitutional order under the rule of law during the nineteenth century—truly the century of progress and order—came the twentieth, the century of irrationality and violence intensified beyond precedent by new techniques of mass indoctrination and emotionalization. For a generation and more, at least since the outbreak of the First World War, the world has been living in a permanent revolution, a succession of major crises interrupted by brief spells of deceptive normalcy. The revaluation of all values by the present world revolution surpasses in range, scope, and intensity the great revolutions of the past. Technology revolutionalized the entire fabric of the life of the individual and the community, socioeconomic, political, and moral. No state society, whether of the East or the West, whether in Europe, Asia, or the New World, has been exempted therefrom. Over large parts of the world, crisis government has become the rule rather than the exception. It is a recurrent phenomenon of the constitutional-democratic state not likely to disappear in the era of competition between totalitarianism and the values of a free society. For many of the recent transformations of formerly constitutional states into autocratic or authoritarian regimes, the impact of a crisis situation, either real or assumed, has been responsible.

The natural agency to take over in an emergency or crisis situation is the government. Since the normal procedures of parliamentary and party-conditioned action in a crisis may seem, and often are, too slow, cumbrous, and politically inexpedient, the duty and with it the right of leadership devolves on the relatively small, homogeneous, and compact governing group. "Videant consules ne detrimentum capiat res publica."

The assumption of leadership in an emergency by the governmental power holder is often, if obliquely, spoken of as "constitutional dictatorship."[14] Projected against the systematization of the power process that underlies our discussion, crisis government is the temporary supersession of the technique of powers shared among several power holders, who are endowed with reciprocal controls, by the deliberate concentration of power in the hands of the executive power holder, and the suspension, for the duration of the emergency, of the normal interorgan controls of the assembly toward the executive power holder to the benefit of the latter.

It is impossible to find accurate legal criteria for what constitutes a crisis or emergency situation which would justify, and even dictate, the installation of crisis government. Any legal definition would defeat the essential purpose of crisis government, namely, the mobility of the government in coping with it. The casuistic reference of the American constitution (Art. I, sec. 9, clause 2) to rebellion and invasion in which the writ of habeas corpus is suspendable testifies to the strictly externalized approach to the problem by the constitutional theorists of the eighteenth cetnury. An emergency may be partial, affecting merely a sector of the community, such as a natural catastrophe, or total, affecting the welfare of all. The emergency may, but need not, be reflected by actual disturbances of the normal public order. The mere threat of social unrest may suffice for its reality. Crisis situations arise from the most varied causes. Aside from man-made catastrophes which, in the nuclear age, may assume unimaginable proportions, its main causes, in our revolutionary time, are socioeconomic dislocations of the normal order of things—the "depressions," the political paralysis of the normal constitutional process, and, most important of all, the threat of civil or foreign war and war itself. In all these cases the very existence of the state society may be at stake.

Whatever the cause of the crisis situation, it presents a crucial problem for the constitutional-democratic state: how can its impact be dealt with by constitutional procedures designed for the normal political situation? And, if the answer is that it cannot: how can a crisis government be established and conducted that is allowed enough freedom to cope with the crisis situation but not so much that it is able to establish unbridled authoritarianism? The great danger inherent in crisis government is that selfish men can pervert it for selfish purposes of naked power. What restraints on the exercise of crisis government, therefore, should remain in operation to avoid the danger of its abuse? It is prima facie obvious that the courts are disqualified to decide on the existence of the emergency situation and the necessity of the establishment of the crisis government, even though they may be called on, in certain jurisdictions, to prevent the excesses in its exercise. The decision that a crisis situation exists always must be left to the political authorities as a political question. No well-constructed constitution of our time can afford to ignore the exigencies and potentialities of the crisis situation and fail to reconcile it, insofar as it is possible, with the principles of a free socety under the rule of law.

Three basic solutions for dealing with the crisis situation strikingly reveal the divergence of political civilizations. These are as follows: (1) in the absence of a specific constitutional authorization the government assumes extra-constitutional emergency powers and, eventually, seeks parliamentary indemnity for them; (2) constitutional or statutory provisions, enacted in anticipation of the emergency, equip the government with extraordinary powers; and (3) crisis government is established by an *ad hoc* transfer of delegated powers from the parliament to the government.

General emergency powers were assumed by the theory of the constitutionally limited monarchy, following the precedent set in the French Charte of 1814 (Art. 14), to be implicitly inherent in the governmental function. This doctrine, under the label of *Notrecht* ("state of necessity"), was generally accepted down to 1918 in Germany.[15] Bismarck, in the famous constitutional conflict between the crown and the government with the Prussian diet (1862–66), under which the Prussian constitution was practically suspended, resorted to this solution; after the victorious war against Austria he obtained indemnity from the new parliamentary assembly. Traces of the state of necessity appeared in France briefly at the beginning of the First World War.[16] Today it is wholly repudiated by western constitutionalism.

Where statutory or constitutional norms exist under which the government may exercise emergency powers, a distinction has to be made between arrangements under which the government may use them at its own discretion, without antecedent authorization of the parliament, and those under which the legislature decides that a state of emergency exists and permits the government to operate under its rules. A familiar device in constitutional democracies is the declaration of the state of siege. Its essence is that the government, in certain internally or externally conditioned emergency situations, is authorized by the assembly to assume, for the duration, quasi-dictatorial powers, usually combined with the subordination of the civilian authorities to military command and the establishment of martial law. In France the state of siege, regulated by the laws of 1878 and 1916, is established exclusively by parliamentary statute; if declared by the government while the chambers are not sitting, they are convened automatically within two days. Likewise the lifting requires a parliamentary statute. The same holds for the state of urgency, newly created by a law of 1955. However, the state of siege is rarely resorted to in Europe and practically is no substitute for the ordinary constitutional procedures. The American parallel is martial law. As a rule it is decreed, in exceptional cases such as natural catastrophes or social unrest, by the state governors. Lincoln, during the Civil War, is the only president who has resorted to it; but, to preserve congressional control, he was sharply rebuffed by the Supreme Court in the famous *Ex parte Milligan* case.[17]

In Latin America the *estado de sitio* (or *de assemblea*), on the other hand, is the customary method for the assumption of complete governmental control in real or pretended emergency situations. With their perennial political turbulence, violent power struggles among cliques, factions, parties, and classes, and the traditional impotence and incompetence of the legislatures, the Latin American nations are the classical land for presidential dictatorship under the protective coloration of the constitution.[18] For *caudillismo* the state of siege is the most convenient vehicle and the standard procedure for the establishment of authoritarian government. In the majority of the constitutions, however, the declaration of the state of siege is left to the decision of the legislature, while in others its establishment is at the discretion of the president. In either case, the result is the transfer of the legislative powers to the executive; the suspension of the fundamental guaranties; the installation of military rule; and the near-complete exclusion of parliamentary and judicial control. In fairness it should be noted, however, that in a number of Latin American states with a greater degree of constitutional stability—among them are Chile, Uruguay, and Mexico—the concentration of power in the executive is more confined to genuine emergency situations and exercised under a more effective interorgan control of the legislature.

The most famous—or infamous—illustration of crisis government authorized by the constitution is offered by Article 48, section 2, of the Weimar constitution. It conforms, in a modified form, to the German tradition of the state of necessity. Formally the Reich president, factually the Reich chancellor and his cabinet, were authorized to take appropriate measures for the restoration of public security and order. These emergency powers usually took the form of governmental decrees (*Notverordnung*) in the place of ordinary legislation. Neither the Reichtstag nor the courts could challenge the emergency powers as to their need and as to the adequacy of the measures taken under them. They were limited neither in time nor in scope. For the duration of the emergency the seven most important fundamental guaranties could be suspended. Residual interorgan controls of the parliament consisted, on the one hand, in the provision that all measures had to be submitted to the Reichstag, which could rescind them; this occurred a single time (1930), with the result that Chancellor Brüning dissolved the Reichstag and forthwith re-enacted them. On the other hand, the chancellor's political responsibility toward the parliament remained intact, an ineffective control because a Reichstag that could not muster sufficient majorities for legislation was incapable of overthrowing the government.

During the first turbulent years of the young republic, Article 48 was used for genuine crisis situations, primarily for the suppression of internal disorders, much in the same way that the state of siege (*Belagerungszustand*) of the imperial constitution was used. However, with the rapid economic deterioration through inflation, the emergency powers under Article 48 were converted, against the constitutional intent, to instruments of the government for dealing with socioeconomic matters deemed urgent (finance, unemployment, labor, etc.), and this concurred with sweeping enabling acts granted the cabinet by the Reichstag. These the government found less expedient because they had to be authorized by often hesitant parliaments and, in addition, were subject to passage by the qualified majorities required for constitutional amendment. After a brief period of deceptive stabilization, the economic situation deteriorated again. In addition, after the elections of 1930 the Reichstag had become incurably split between the center parties and the extremists to the left and the right. Emergency decrees under Article 48 became the ordinary method of legislation, completely replacing the parliamentary legislation. Both Brüning and the following "presidial" cabinets governed with the emergency powers under Article 48 until the republic finally collapsed. The suspension of the seven fundamental rights under the decree of February 27, 1933—repealed only by the Allied authorities after the defeat—became the "Magna Carta of the concentration camp."

In the Anglo-Saxon nations provisions for crisis government are not spelled out in the constitutions. The policy decision as to whether an emergency situation exists and to what extent it requires the concentration of legislative and executive powers in the hands of the executive power holder is shared by government and parliament. The customary technique used for crisis government is the delegation of emergency powers to the government through enabling acts and the grant of *pleins pouvoirs*. Not every such grant indicates the existence of a genuine crisis situation, since the delegation of legislative decree powers has become a current method of streamlining the legislative process.*

The delegation of emergency powers occurs generally either by statute, in anticipation of a situation requiring them, or *ad hoc* when a crisis situation has actually arisen. An example of the former technique is the Emergency Powers Act of 1920 (10 & 11 Geo. V, c. 55) in Britain, intended to secure the essentials of community life in internal emergencies. The powers delegated to the government, if wide, are strictly limited in time and remain subject to rigid control by the parliament. The measure was practically applied only once, on the occasion of the general strike in 1926. Otherwise emergency powers are granted the government by the parliament only in the case of an immediate crisis situation. In the First World War they were given by the Defense of the Realm (Consolidation) Act of 1914 (5 & 6 Geo. V, c. 8) and its various extensions, and in the Second World War by the Emergency Powers (Defense) Acts of 1939 (2 & 3 Geo. VI, c. 62) and of 1940 (3 & 4 Geo. VI, c. 20) and subsequent enactments. Moreover, the technique of delegated crisis legislation was used also in peacetime, first by the Conservatives when dealing with the economic crisis of 1931 and after; later, after 1945, by the Labor government to facilitate the adjustment to peace conditions and the socioeconomic reforms pursued by the Labor majority.

The identical technique of delegating emergency powers to the president is used in the United States. Only Lincoln, in the short interval between Fort Sumter and the convocation of congress in

* See above, pp. 208–9.

July, 1861, resorted to extra-constitutional emergency powers. In the First and Second World Wars congress granted the president, in his capacity as commander-in-chief as well as chief executive, sweeping authorizations to deal with the various aspects of national defense and the conduct of the war, pertaining to war production, transportation, communications, price controls, and other fields. Of those granted President Roosevelt, the most important were the First War Powers Act of December 18, 1941 (55 Stat. 878), and the Second War Powers Act of March 27, 1942 (56 Stat. 176). They were discontinued after the cessation of hostilities and re-enacted, in part, as a stand-by measure in connection with the Korean war.

In England during the Second World War such sweeping delegations amounted to a factual "constitutional dictatorship" of the prime minister and the war cabinet composed of both parties. The corresponding weakening of parliamentary control was justified by the deadly peril the country was exposed to. In the United States, however, congress never abdicated and, while giving the president full rein to conduct and win the war, otherwise retained its constitutional interorgan controls over the government, often to the point of challenging presidential leadership.

Nor was Switzerland in a position to deal with emergency situations without measures of crisis government. The Swiss constitution, otherwise so distinguished by its circumspection, fails to give the Federal Council emergency powers either in war or in peace. Nonetheless, the oldest democracy granted the Federal Council twice—on the occasion of the First World War (decree of the federal assemblies of August 3, 1914) and of the Second (decree of August 30, 1939)—emergency powers for the duration. In particular the second measure, with its practically limitless delegation, surpassed anything enacted in other constitutional democracies. Both delegations were clearly unconstitutional on several counts: federal usurpation of the cantonal jurisdiction; assumption of legislative powers by the government; suspension

of fundamental guaranties, quite aside from the illegal withdraw-
ing of federal legislation from the challenge by referendum.[19] In
addition, emergency powers were delegated to the Federal Council in peacetime also, to enable the government to deal with the
economic crisis in the early thirties and again to cope with the
threat of German and Italian aggression in the late thirties.

While these legislative delegations operate for the benefit of the
government in crisis periods, Switzerland, for thirty years, was
plagued by a camouflaged type of emergency legislation by which
the federal authorities—the federal assemblies together with the
Federal Council—entered into an unholy alliance to the disadvan-
tage of the supreme power holder, the sovereign people. What
made the practice particularly obnoxious was that it was used in
peacetime.

Under the constitution of 1874 the people were granted the
optional referendum, by the request of thirty thousand citizens or
eight cantons, on any law enacted by the federal assemblies, provided it was not declared urgent by them. Thus, it was left to the
federal parliament to withhold enactments declared urgent from
the participation of the electorate in policy decision and policy
execution. For the first fifty years the federal parliament used the
authorization sparingly; after the First World War, however, the
number of urgent measures that went into force surpassed those
against which the referendum was permissible. The situation was
repeated in the economic crisis years of the thirties. Urgency
legislation almost became the normal method of legislation. In
many instances the urgency was debatable, and, what was worse,
the enactments frequently involved violations of the constitutional provisions, in particular those pertaining to the constitutionally guaranteed economic freedom. But the parliament found it
convenient to cheat the sovereign out of his right to say "No."
The result was widespread dissatisfaction concerning the undermining of the constitution and the rule of law.

No fewer than four popular initiatives were launched to force the reluctant federal authorities back to constitutional normalcy and legality. Three, in 1936 and 1938, failed, but the fourth effort, in 1949, was successful. Upon popular initiative and ratification by subsequent referendum, a new article (89 bis) was inserted into the constitution. The authorization of the federal assemblies to declare enactments urgent is maintained, but it can be challenged by popular initiative and referendum. However, on those urgent measures which are constitutional as to substance (*verfassungskonform*), the referendum is merely optional. These are distinguished from substantially unconstitutional urgent legislation (*die sich nicht auf die Verfassung stützen*), for which the referendum is mandatory within one year after passage of the measure, and, if rejected by the people or the cantons, it loses validity. The interesting fact, for our context, is that unconstitutional measures are not only possible; they are even permissible under the constitution![20] In actual practice the new regulation amounts to the grant of constitutional crisis powers to the government and parliament.

To restate the situation: crisis government, whatever its legitimation, seriously affects the normal conduct of the political process and nullifies, to a varying extent, the operation of the normal interorgan controls for the benefit of the executive and to the detriment of the legislative power holder. But, since crisis has come to stay, constitutional democracy will have to live with crisis government.

VIII. Interorgan Controls of the Judiciary over the Government and the Parliament

Our discussion will proceed now to the third of the four patterns of interorgan control on which the practice of the modern constitutional-democratic state is predicated.*

Judicial Independence

Independence of the judiciary in the exercise of the functions assigned to it from any interference whatsoever on the part of any power holder is the capstone of the constitutional-democratic state under the rule of law. In many constitutions, old and new, the formulation has become standard: "The judges are independent and subject only to the law" (Prussia, constitution of 1850, Art. 86; Germany-Bonn, Art. 102, sec. 1). The rationale for judicial independence is obvious: unless protected against any extraneous influences or pressures, the judge is not in a position to administer justice impartially according to law. The law, as supplied to him in the legal norms enacted by the constitutionally designated political agencies or as found by him in the common conscience of the community, is his master, and only the law.

Judicial independence in the traditional sense has a personal and a functional connotation. It implies, first, that the judge, regardless of the method of designation to the office, cannot be removed from it during good behavior except for cause (*quamdiu se bene gesserint*); this is the celebrated formulation of the first statutory recognition of the principle in the Act of Settlement of 1700 (12 & 13 Will. III, c. 2). Removal for cause can be accomplished only

* See above, p. 185.

by a formalized procedure: a resolution of both houses of parliament in England; impeachment in the United States;[1] or conviction by a disciplinary court composed of judges or officials in the Continental states. Compulsory retirement on account of age does not conflict with the principle of tenure.

Judicial independence implies, second, that in the performance of his judicial task the judge must be free from whatever influence or intervention could be brought to bear on him from outside, be it the government, the parliament, the electorate, or public opinion. In deciding the individual case at hand, he must not be subject to orders of the government or, in particular, of the minister of justice, where existing—this was the malpractice of the Nazi regime during the last war (*Richteranweisungen*).—He must not be subject to the parliament or even to a higher court of the judicial hierarchy. The remanding of a case by the court of appeals for retrial in the lower court, the ordering of a new trial by a court of revision in conformity with its binding interpretation of the law, and also the observance of the rule of *stare decisis* where it prevails are merely corollaries of the legal order under which adjudication is conducted and not influences extraneous to the judicial process.

Judicial Monopoly of the Courts

Moreover, the principle of judicial independence leads inevitably to the claim that the legally constituted courts must enjoy the monopoly in the exercise of the judicial function. This not only implies the illegality of any extraordinary or exceptional tribunal unless duly authorized by the constitution but also excludes any non-judicial agencies of the government or parliament from adjudication. The former practices of justice by parliament in the form of a bill of attainder or by fiat of the crown (*Kabinettsjustiz*) are no longer permissible. Applied to more recent situations the judicial monopoly excludes the arrogation of judicial functions by parliamentary investigating committees or any other intervention of non-judicial agencies in the administration of justice. A flagrant violation occurred, for example, in 1898 in France, when the Chamber of Deputies, in the passion aroused by the Dreyfus case, adopted a resolution that transferred the trial for revision against the conviction of the military court from the Criminal Senate of the Cour de Cassation, to whose jurisdiction it belonged under the criminal code, to the plenary session of the court, because the former was suspected of sympathies for the unfortunate victim of military arbitrariness.[2] Nor does the United States have a clean record on this score, as evidenced by the case of *Ex parte McCardle*.[3]

Two exceptions to the rule of the judicial monopoly may be noted. Both confirm it and are, on the whole, of minor importance: the jurisdiction of the House of Lords as the highest instance of appeal[4] still exists. But, as a rule, it is exercised, in the place of the assembly itself, by a three-man quorum composed of legal professionals, the Lords in Ordinary, and such peers as hold, or have held, the highest legal offices. The "Law Lords," whose maximum number was fixed at nine by the Appellate Jurisdiction Act of 1947 (10 & 11 Geo. VI, c. 11), are appointed for life by the crown, that is, the cabinet. Those members who hold, or have held, certain high judicial offices, for example, the lord chancellorship, may also participate in the trial. For all practical purposes this group constitutes a supreme court for the United Kingdom. The other residue of parliamentary justice, the trial by the House of Lords, in the first instance, of peers and peeresses for treason and felonies was abolished by the Criminal Justice Act of 1948 (11 & 12 Geo. VI, c. 58). The other exception to the monopoly of the constituted courts is the exercise of political justice (impeachment) left to the parliamentary bodies. This may be justified by the political nature of the alleged offense for which strictly professional judges may appear less qualified than men experienced in political life. Today the institution has become practically obsolete.*

* See above, pp. 199–200.

A special situation of judicial competition on the part of another power holder arose with the assignment, attendant on the current transformation of the legislative into the administrative state, of judicial or quasi-judicial functions to non-judicial agencies, for example, governmental departments and boards in England and the independent regulatory commissions in the United States. Their decisions, however, have been brought under the control of the courts on appeal, and, thus, the judicial monopoly has been ultimately restored.*

Principal Patterns of the Designation
of the Judicial Personnel

Because of the complete independence of the judiciary from all other power holders, the method of designation to the judicial office is of crucial importance. The common sociopsychological experience that the incumbent in an office remains indebted to those responsible for his designation holds specific dangers in the case of the judicial function. In particular, if the designation has been influenced by political considerations, the beneficiary is exposed to the human temptation to repay his debt by a pliable conduct of his office. In the course of historical development various patterns of designation have appeared, of which the following may be mentioned:

1. In prerevolutionary France the judicial office was purchased. Wealth, the socioeconomic basis of the leisure class, was believed to produce a cultural elite, which was held to be the guarantor of an impartial administration of justice. In due course the upper stratum of the judicial personnel in the *parlements* evolved into a veritable nobility of the robe, with vested and even hereditary rights. It not only operated as one of the few interorgan controls on the royal absolutism but also presented France with an administration of justice which was by no means the least accomplishment of the *ancien régime*. History in time modified the harsh

*See below, pp. 242–43.

verdict of the Revolution; the venality of office did not necessarily connote the venality of the individual judge.

2. The democratic theory favored the popular election of judges. The experience with it of the early French Revolution proved most discouraging, and it was soon abandoned in favor of governmental designation. Today popular election of judges is practiced in the majority of American states, in a number of Swiss cantons, and for the judges of the first instance in the Soviet orbit. This mode of designation does not meet with uniform and unqualified success. If combined with short terms, it is intrinsically at variance with judicial independence, because the judge seeking re-election may be inclined to curry favor with his voters or the party politicians manipulating them. Various reform devices in the United States—bipartisan nomination, indorsement by the bar associations, extended terms of office—have failed to remove completely the taint of political bias attached to this method.

3. In certain jurisdictions the judges are elected by the parliament. The outstanding illustration is Switzerland. Under the constitution (Art. 107) the members of the Federal Tribunal (at Lausanne) are elected for a six-year term by the two houses of the legislature in joint session (Art. 92); they are re-eligible and in practice almost always re-elected if they wish. The original appointment is not altogether free from political overtones insofar as the Federal Assembly sees to it that all major parties, the two religious denominations, and the three official languages are properly represented. However, the system provides the country with a professionally satisfactory and a politically wholly unbiased highest judiciary. On the other hand, parliamentary election is easily susceptible to political abuse or influence. In the Soviet orbit all judges above the first instance are elected by the assemblies. The technique cannot be considered conducive to guaranteeing genuine judicial independence, partly because of the implicit requirement of political and ideological conformity of the candidates with the political regime and partly because of the

institution of recall by the parliament, which is logically connected with parliamentary appointment and always threatens, should the incumbent fail to toe the official line. Parliamentary election prevails also for the designation of the members of the Federal Constitutional Court of the Bonn regime, to which judicial control of the constitutionality of legislation is intrusted.* One half the members are elected (constitution, Art. 94), by the Federal Assembly (Bundestag) by a very complex indirect procedure designed to minimize political considerations and one half by the Federal Council (Bundesrat) directly by a two-thirds majority.

4. The United States offers the most famous illustration of the pattern of designation shared by the government and the legislature: the president nominates the candidates; the Senate confirms their appointment. Senatorial rejection being very rare, the presidential selection usually prevails, but sometimes only against strong opposition. Nonetheless, the participation of the Senate in the appointive procedure constitutes an important interorgan control over the government. A similar combination of governmental and parliamentary appointment is adopted by the Bonn constitution (Art. 95, sec. 3; Art. 96, sec. 2) for the installation of the members of the higher federal judiciary. The appointive function is exercised by a judicial election committee (*Richterwahlausschuss*) composed of the federal minister of justice and, for federal reasons, the ministers of justice of the *Länder* (now, with the Saar, ten), and an equal number of members of the Federal Assembly (Bundestag). An interesting variant, which combines governmental appointment with the participation of the elected political bodies and the judicial estate itself, prevails with excellent results in Belgium (Art. 99): the king, that is, the government, appoints all judges except two categories: the members of the courts of appeal and the presidents and vice-presidents of the courts with original jurisdiction are appointed by the crown from two double

* See below, p. 255.

lists of candidates, one presented by these courts themselves, the
other by the provincial councils. For the members of the Court
of Cassation, likewise, double lists are presented to the king by
the court itself and by the Senate, respectively. In addition, every
candidate must be nominated on both lists.

5. The traditional and most commonly used device for the
designation of the judiciary is appointment by the government.
It prevails, for example, in Great Britain and the Dominions, in
most Latin American states, and in general in the Continental
states of Roman-law civilization that follow the French precedent.
More recently the technique has been refined by being combined,
particularly for the promotion from a lower to a higher judicial
office, with a sort of in-service co-optation through which the
judiciary itself as a corporate body participates in the procedure.
The last two patterns deserve some additional observations.

APPOINTMENT BY THE GOVERNMENT

Two distinctly different systems exist here, geared primarily to
the unity or dichotomy, respectively, of the bench and bar.[5] In
the Anglo-Saxon jurisdictions bench and bar are considered
merely as the two branches of a unified legal profession. The
appointment to judicial office is made from among the ranks of
the most prominent practitioners of the law (England, the Dominions) or in the United States the appointees may also be, in
addition to reputed practicing lawyers, high-ranking government
officials (attorney-general or solicitor-general); law professors,
or politically deserving persons (members of congress or state
governers). Contrariwise, in the Roman-law civilizations of the
Continent, following the French pattern, the strict division of
bench and bar prevails. From the start the judicial career is separated from that of the practicing lawyer and remains so throughout. Change-over from one to the other legal career is extremely
rare. When, under Weimar, an eminent practitioner was appointed president of the Court of Appeals in Hamburg, it created

a sensation. Entrance into the judicial career is gained by competitive examinations—the same that practicing lawyers have to take —while in the Anglo-Saxon countries merely the passing of the bar examination, regardless of the result, is required; in the United States even this is not stipulated by the federal constitution. The issue of judicial promotion from a lower to a higher court, so crucial in the Continental system, hardly arises, since appointment to a specific judicial position is usually for life, and promotions to a higher court, though they occur, are not regularly expected or striven for. Moreover, the salaries of the lower and higher courts in the Anglo-Saxon countries are reasonably high and relatively equal regardless of the rank of the court. In Continental Europe and Latin America, however, the upper rungs of the judicial ladder are reached only by judges who, by professional competence and personality, have demonstrated beyond reasonable doubt their fitness for the top positions of the judicial hicrarchy. It should also be remembered that in Continental Europe there are far more judges per capita of the population than there are in the United States or England and that, while in the latter countries the highest social prestige attaches to a judgeship, in Continental Europe government service is at least equal in social esteem to the judicial position.

Political considerations in the appointment to judicial office and, even more so, in the promotion from a lower to a higher court cannot be excluded in either the Anglo-Saxon or the Continental system. In England and the majority of the Dominions—with the exception of the Union of South Africa under the Nationalist governments—appointment by the crown, that is, the cabinet, without any participation of parliament whatsoever did not result, at least for the last generation, in the infiltration of politics or favoritism into the judiciary. Political partisanship in the appointment does exist elsewhere, possibly more open in the United States and more subtle under the Continental system. It cannot fail to color the subsequent conduct of the judicial office. That judges are more conservative than other professionals is a fact of life, since the law in itself is conservative and necessarily static until changed. If the American federal judiciary, at least at present, is on the whole politically neutral, this is a credit to the persons on the bench rather than to the method by which they are designated. Moreover, subservience to the government is one of the least noticeable defects of the federal judiciary, even though the Supreme Court has shown itself at times not above the suspicion of preferences conditioned by class and ideology, reflected by its collective jurisprudence and that of individual members.

Under the Continental judicial career system, on the other hand, for a long time and not long ago, neither the first appointment nor the promotion to the higher positions was free from political considerations. In a number of states the judges are quasi-public officials. Where, as in most Continental jurisdictions, the judge serves successively on the bench, in the office of the public prosecutor, and in the ministerial bureaucracy, he can never develop the mentality of independence from the government; even on the bench he remains a public official who is dependent on the Ministry of Justice's good will for promotion and for the desirable positions. The government could see to it that the judiciary remained both sociologically homogeneous and well disposed toward its policies. For example, in Prussia until 1918 members of the lower classes, if appointment could not be denied them on account of their examination results, found the ascent in the service steeper than aspirants from the ruling classes. Socialists were even refused the first appointment. Most of these discriminations, however, disappeared with the progressive democratization of the political process.

IN-SERVICE CO-OPTATION

More recently, strenuous efforts have been undertaken to achieve the political neutralization of the process of appointment and promotion. A novel designation pattern is being evolved in which governmental appointment is replaced by a technique of judicial co-optation with which elements of parliamentary participation are combined. The Superior Councils of the Magistrature of the French (Art. 83) and the Italian (Arts. 104 ff.) constitutions may serve as examples. These bodies are designed to eliminate governmental influence so far as is humanly possible. The judiciary itself is injected into the promotion procedure to guarantee its fairness and objectivity. In both cases the Superior Council of the Magistrature, under the chairmanship of the president of the Republic himself, is composed of members partly elected by parliament, partly by the judicial order as such; under the Italian regulation the judiciary designates two-thirds, the parliament only one-third, of the total membership. The Council is charged with promotion procedures in addition to discipline of the magistrates and supervision of the administration of the courts (not to be confused with the administration of justice proper).

Of all designation techniques practiced today, perhaps the most perfected is that for the Council of State in France, under the noteworthy reform legislation of 1945 and after. It is an outstanding example of professional in-service co-optation that secures complete freedom from political bias both in the access to and in the promotion within the judicial career. The personnel of this most distinguished of French courts are the professional elite. These judges are absolutely free from governmental influence in the exercise of their judicial duties. This freedom is all the more remarkable, since the members are frequently on loan from the court for the fulfilment of administrative tasks, and a constant cross-fertilization takes place between the administrative services proper and the court. The entrance to the service is obtained by special training and a highly competitive process of personal qualification. Promotion is dependent on professional ability attested to by the most prominent members of the court itself.[6]

There is no ideal type of judicial designation that not only would exclude political considerations but also would offer a fool-

proof method for selecting only candidates who, by their professional ability and integrity of character, would guarantee to
bring into office only the best talent available. Each of the various
systems has its merits and demerits; none can be considered uniformly applicable to all legal civilizations. Each is tradition-bound;
none can fail to have deep repercussions on the performance of
the administration of justice. In general—but this statement may
be oversimplified and open to challenge—while popular election is
the least satisfactory method, appointment by the government appears to be the most adequate, whether or not it is combined with
parliamentary participation. From the viewpoint of interorgan
controls, however, two negative aspects should be noted: political
considerations in both appointment and promotion can hardly
ever be wholly neutralized, not even if the parliament shares in
the appointive power. And, governmental appointment, at least
in the systems of Continental career service, tends to make the
judiciary more government-minded, more of a caste than it is in
Anglo-Saxon states, where bench and bar are considered a unified
profession. Having never stood up in his practice against the
government, the Continental judge is inclined to conduct himself
rather as a public servant than as a self-reliant, independent dispenser of justice. On the other hand, the technique of judicial
co-optation breeds the corporate judicial mentality—*esprit de
corps* at its best, caste spirit at its worst—though this mentality
may not be totally absent in the Anglo-Saxon countries where the
judges are taken from the bar.

Interorgan Controls of the Judiciary

Within the configuration of the power process the judiciary
occupies a unique position. If judicial independence implies the
freedom from any interorgan controls on the part of any other
power holder, the judiciary should also be denied any intervention
in the operations of the others. The judicial function should be
confined to policy execution and not extend to policy decision

and policy control. This was the original concept of Montesquieu. Various emphatic passages in the *L'Esprit des lois* (Book XI, chap. 6) leave no doubt whatsoever that he considered the judiciary strictly subordinate to government and assembly, merely a secondary branch of the executive function and a separate "power" only in the limited sense that the judicial action is performed by distinct agencies or persons. All the judge was called on to do was to apply the law, as it was furnished him or as he found it, to the individual controversy at the bar.

However, since the eighteenth century, the judicial function has undergone a momentous transformation. Judicial independence still continues, as it should, to shield the courts from any interference in the exercise of their functions by the other power holders. But this isolation is no longer reciprocal. One of the most significant phenomena in the evolution of the constitutional-democratic state is the rise of the judiciary to the position of a genuine third power. In the Anglo-Saxon countries this situation had existed for a long time, though definitely not from the beginning of either the British version of constitutionalism or in the early American republic. In the Roman-law civilizations on the Continent it was a long time in coming because its road was barred by the ideological concept of the king as the fountainhead of justice. But the recent crop of constitutions—Germany–Bonn, Italy, France, as well as, for example, India and Pakistan—make deliberate efforts to give the judiciary a stature in the power process not inferior, and in certain cases even superior, to that of the traditional power holders, the government and the parliament. In line with this novel development the courts are accorded strong and effective interorgan controls in their own right toward the other power holders. These are primarily of three kinds: (1) the right of the courts to supervise and control the administrative activities of the executive as to their conformity with their statutory basis; (2) the judicial review of the constitutionality of legislation indorsed conjointly by government and parliament; and

(3), in certain jurisdictions, the arbitral decision over jurisdictional conflicts concerning the functional performance of the other power holders; this latter development is frequently spoken of as the "judicialization of political power."

JUDICIAL CONTROL OF PUBLIC ADMINISTRATION AND ADMINISTRATIVE JUSTICE

The first area of interorgan controls at the disposal of the judiciary is what is commonly spoken of as "administrative justice."[7] This comprises the decision of controversies concerning the actions of the agencies of public administration that affect the status, property, and liberty of the citizens. To these traditional objectives of judicial protection have been added, in line with the increasing bureaucratization of the state, the disputes concerning the organization of the administrative services and the rights of the administrative staffs—civil service—employed by them. The main problem inherent in administrative justice is whether it is to be administered by the ordinary or by special "administrative" courts.

Administrative justice before independent courts—independent in the sense that they are impartial toward the government appearing before them as a party—by now has become an accepted feature of the state under the rule of law and, indeed, its foundation. For a long time, even genuinely democratic states, benighted by the doctrinaire assumption of the complete separation of functions, resisted the adjudication of the administrative disputes by the ordinary courts. Strictest non-intervention of the courts with the governmental operation was enjoined by the instruments of the French Revolution.[8] Napoleon broke with the tradition. His Conseil d'Etat was charged with the preparation of administrative decisions, and the lower *Conseils de Préfecture* were assigned corresponding jurisdiction on the departmental level. However, to protect his officials against interference by the ordinary courts, the famous Article 75 of the constitution of the year

VIII (1799) stipulated that the agents of the government should not be liable for acts relating to their conduct of office except by authorization of the Conseil d'Etat, under the assumption, subsequently confirmed by practice, that the latter would be cautious in granting it. It was mainly this provision which aroused A. V. Dicey's hostility to administrative justice in England. The provision was repealed by the Government of the National Defense (1870) only after Napoleon III's fall. Elsewhere it persisted much longer, for example, as the *Vorentscheidung* in Prussia until 1920.

The credit for having made administrative justice respectable goes to the Third Republic. It established the dual judicial system of the ordinary (civil and criminal) and the administrative courts and also a "Tribunal of Competence" to decide conflicts of jurisdiction, positive as well as negative, between the two branches. The French pattern was widely accepted on the Continent, in Latin America, and elsewhere, for example, in Japan. In France proper it culminated in making the much-envied model, the Conseil d'Etat, the highest organ of administrative justice. In the Anglo-Saxon nations, on the other hand, the supervision of the conformity of the actions of the public administration with the statutory norms, including the allegation of the action of the officials to be *ultra vires*, remained basically under the jurisdiction of the ordinary courts. The persistent controversy as to whether the disputes between the public administration and the citizens should be handled by special administrative courts or by the general ordinary courts has lost much of its significance today. The initial fear that government-appointed courts would be partial toward the government when it appeared before them as a party has been dispelled in all states where administrative courts exist, since they are just as independent as the ordinary ones. And it is no longer disputable that, by their special training and experience, they are better qualified to deal with the technicalities of administration and administrative law than are the ordinary courts.

The issue of administrative justice gained momentum with the current transformation of the legislative into the administrative state. In particular, the advent of the welfare state in its manifold disguises resulted in the proliferation of administrative agencies, deeply affecting the daily life of the power addressees and reaching into every socioeconomic corner of the community. A revolutionary change in the power pattern took place. In its relations to the citizens, the executive, acting as public administration, rose to the commanding position in comparison with the legislative power holder. The overburdened parliament can merely outline the general principles of a policy decision and leave its implementation by executory norms to the executive and its administrative agencies. The technical device is the delegation of the rule-making power to the government and administration.* The control by the parliament of the vast bureaucracy which inevitably arose is nominal at best. The task, of unprecedented proportions, of protecting the citizen against the danger of uncontrolled delegated legislative powers shifted to the courts.

But this was not all. In addition to the norm-creating function, the administrative agencies increasingly assumed, either on the basis of explicit parliamentary authorization or by implicit necessity of the administrative process, the right to issue judicial or quasi-judicial decisions of administrative controversies in their respective jurisdictional fields. Many administrative bodies exercise simultaneously, and often through the same personnel, lawmaking, administrative, and judicial functions, a situation that would make Montesquieu turn in his grave and, in addition, appears to compete seriously with the judicial monopoly of the courts. No greater danger has threatened the rule of law of the democratic state for a long time.

The battle is joined but not yet won. For its outcome the venerable issue of administrative versus ordinary courts is less important than the need for bringing all legal disputes ultimately under the jurisdiction of a genuine and genuinely independent court. The solutions attempted in the three key states—France,

---

* See above, pp. 208 ff.

United Kingdom, and the United States—differ, though they move in the same direction. Of all constitutional democracies, the best protection of the citizen against illegal action of the administration is afforded in France. The Conseil d'Etat developed a vast armory of effective remedies against administrative measures alleged to be at variance with their statutory basis—*recours pour excès de pouvoir* and *exception d'illégalité*—and even against the abuse of administrative discretion—*détournement du pouvoir*. In addition, it carefully distinguishes between a *faute personnelle* of the official and a *faute de service* for which, in general, he is not personally liable. In England, the classical land of resistance against administrative law and justice, remedies against *ultra vires* action of the officials are granted by the ordinary courts. By the Crown Proceedings Act of 1947 (10 & 11 Geo. VI, c. 44) at long last an ancient loophole of governmental escape from responsibility was finally plugged: the crown, that is, the government, can no longer rely on the immunity against being sued in its own courts, and it is made liable for omissions and commissions of its agents. However, the citizen's armor of protection against the state has fissures: not only is the array of remedies still chaotic and disorganized and lacking a clear systematization of administrative justice but also parliament itself, that is, the government controlling parliament, not infrequently precludes judicial control of administrative action. On the other hand, in the United States judicial recourse is available against administrative acts before the ordinary courts, and, since the Administrative Procedures Act of 1946 (60 Stat. 237), it is also available on appeal against the judicial decisions of the so-called "independent" regulatory commissions that combine rule-making, administrative, and judicial functions. The rule of law, thus, has been restored.

JUDICIAL REVIEW OF LEGISLATION IN THE UNITED STATES

An altogether different vista is opened by the right of the courts—assumed, usurped, or explicitly granted—to appraise the conformity of legislation, enacted conjointly by parliament and government, with the constitution and to deny it validity if it is found to violate the supreme law of the land. This aspect of the judicial function exceeds by far the legitimate domain of the courts, which is policy execution. Constitutional review is substantially policy control, and, if it prevails against the other power holders, it is actually policy decision. By claiming and exercising judicial review, the courts cease to be simply the policy-executing organ and become a power holder equal, if not superior, to the other politically constituted power holders.

The idea that the judiciary was authorized to frustrate the action of the assembly and the government was wholly alien to the theorists of early constitutionalism. It is interesting to note that Montesquieu, who was himself a judge and had sufficient occasion to observe the operation of the *parlements*, failed to discover the theoretical impact of their right to deny registration to the royal ordinances that were held to contravene the *coutume* of the province they presided over judicially. Neither in Book XXVIII, which deals with the judicial estate, nor in his basic discussion of the judicial power as "pour ainsi dire invisible et presque nul" (Book XI, chap. 6), referred to previously, does he face the issue. That the judicial "power" could set itself up in opposition to government and legislature never entered his mind. Nor did the *Federalist*, in Hamilton's famous discussion of the judicial power (No. 78), disagree: "The judiciary, by the nature of its functions, will always be the least dangerous to the political rights of the Constitution because it will be least in a capacity to annoy or injure them. . . . The judiciary . . . has no influence over either the sword or the purse, no direction either of the strength or of the wealth of the society, and can take no active resolution whatsoever. It may truly be said to have neither FORCE NOR WILL but merely judgment. . . . It proves incontestably, that the judiciary is beyond comparison the weakest of the three departments of power." At this point Hamilton cites Montesquieu's passage referred to above. It is true that immediately following this emphasis on the "feebleness" of the judicial power, which he wishes to see shored up by "permanency in office . . . justly regarded as an indispensable ingredient of its constitution," he delivers his celebrated discourse on the "perplexity respecting the rights of the courts to pronounce legislative acts void." There is no need to enter into the controversy as to whether or not this supports the argument that the founding fathers envisaged judicial review as a legitimate province of the judiciary. The whole context of this passage says no less and no more than that the right legally to interpret the constitution is inherent in the judicial function and not in the "superiority of the judiciary over the legislative power."

Be that as it may, judicial review of congressional legislation appeared in the young republic in the first quarter of the nineteenth century by virtue of John Marshall's intent to enlarge the federal jurisdiction. The judges thereby became a third power, a phenomenon without historical precedent if one ignores the hardly apposite parallels sometimes adduced of the *graphae paranomon* of the Athenian democracy, the *fueros* in the late feudal environment of Spain (Aragon and Navarre), and the *droit d'enregistrement* of the French *parlements* under the *ancien régime*.

The theory and the practice of judicial review in the United States, in particular of the Supreme Court, are too familiar to merit elaboration. Our discussion concerns only its double-barreled role as an interorgan control of the judiciary toward both the congress and the president. Judicial review is by far the most conspicuous and distinctive feature of the American pattern of government, so much so that the pattern has been variously described as "judiciocracy" or "government by the judges,"[9] and the Supreme Court has been called the "third chamber of the legislature." This was foreshadowed by Jefferson's angry protest against Marshall: "The court as the ultimate arbiter of all constitutional questions would place us under the despotism of an oligarchy." For the locus of judicial review within the compass of the political process it is significant that, while the first case when Marshall exercised it (*Marbury* v. *Madison*, 1 Cranch 137 [1803]) pertained to a federal law, the second and historically more fundamental application in *McCulloch* v. *Maryland* (4 Wheat. 316 [1819]) referred to the federal structure, by striking down a state law on the basis of the supremacy-of-the-constitution clause in Article VI. From the start, hence, judicial review occupied the area of federal-states relations; it was subsequently used frequently, though not always, for expanding the federal jurisdiction at the expense of the states. This points up the fact that in every federal organization an agency for adjudicating disputes between the central state and the member states is indispensable.[10] Otherwise the federal structure would disintegrate. Consequently, the federal-states relations are a legitimate domain for judicial review. The typical issue arising in federal organizations is whether a federal statute trespasses on the jurisdiction reserved to the member units or whether legislation of the latter poaches on the preserves of the former. All federal organizations, without exception, possess appropriate judicial institutions, even when the constitution generally stipulates that federal law takes precedence over state law (e.g., Weimar, Art. 13, sec. 1).

The second area within which judicial review may legitimately operate is that of the protection of civil liberties and fundamental rights uniformly valid for all power addressees. Often intimately related to the federal-states relationship, its rationale is no less unchallengeable in unitary states. In this domain judicial review still remains, in the majority of cases, within the policy-executing function. What the court does here is, basically, to apply the norms guaranteeing civil liberties to either legislative or administrative infringements, a none-too-difficult task if, as is the case in the United States, the fundamental rights are guaranteed unconditionally and not, as is the habit elsewhere, only "within the limits of the law," in which case judicial review has no legitimate leverage.* In exercising judicial review, the courts draw the line between the relative interests of an orderly and secure community life and the claims to absolute freedom of an individual or a group. Issues of policy determination may be involved, but not necessarily. In the school desegregation cases of 1954,[11] contrary to political appearances, no genuine policy decision was involved. What the Supreme Court did was merely to reinterpret its own previous jurisprudence in *Plessy* v. *Ferguson*[12] and to harmonize it with the substantive and literal intent of the constitution.

It is in the third area of application that judicial review as interorgan control becomes most controversial, namely, when the judges claim the right to evaluate a socioeconomic policy decision of the political power holders—government and parliament—as to its substantive merits or demerits. It is true that approval or disapproval of policy decisions is undertaken always under the protective coloration of the supremacy of the constitution, which the judge is duty-bound to uphold. This argument, often restated (as, for example, in *United States* v. *Butler*[13]), is a semantic camouflage—convenient as it is unassailable—of the fact that the Supreme Court, often sharply divided, sets itself up as the sovereign arbiter over congress and president, both popularly elected and accountable to their constituents, which the Court decidedly is not. If applied to policy decisions, judicial review amounts to judicial policy control, theoretically not inherent in the judicial function; and, since a negative verdict kills the legislation, judicial review actually may become the substitute for the policy decision of the political departments. It matters little that the Supreme Court refrains from formally invalidating a statute; its inapplicability to the case in hand implies, under the rule of *stare decisis*, its final demise.

The invasion of the policy decision function by the Supreme Court can be verified by a glance at the recent use of judicial

* See below, pp. 321 ff.

review as the instrumentality of judicial interorgan control. In the period between 1890 and 1936 the Supreme Court, by using certain stretchable terms of the constitution, in particular the due process clause of the Fifth and Fourteenth amendments and the commerce clause, was able to impose on the nation the economic ideology of laissez faire against government regulation of business and to nullify the approximation to social justice called for by progressive majorities in state legislatures and congress. It culminated in the resistance of the "nine old men" against the peaceful social revolution of the New Deal. After 1937 the incidence of judicial review on congressional and governmental policy determination declined steeply, partly because the cleavage between the Court and public opinion reflected by legislation had narrowed, partly because of the intervening renovation of the judicial personnel. In the period after the end of the Second World War the accent of judicial review was on liberty rather than on property. In the protection or non-protection of civil liberties the Court, more than may seem warranted by its tradition, yielded to the pressure of government, congress, and public opinion emotionalized by the impact of the ideological conflict on the American way of life. In the conflict between internal and external security and the principles of American freedom, the Court, at least until recently, often preferred the former to the latter.*

It should be noted, however—and herein lies another singularity of the American system of judicial review—that the Court, in the exercise of policy control by judicial review, observes certain self-limiting restraints which, singly and taken together, tend to attenuate what otherwise would amount to complete judicial supremacy. Judicial intervention is restricted to genuine "cases" and "controversies," in contrast with advisory opinions and anticipatory decisions *in abstracto*. The assumption prevails that the congressional will must be respected unless it clearly violates the constitution as interpreted by the Court. Finally and most important

* See below, pp. 334–35.

from the viewpoint of interorgan controls, the courts refuse to deal with the so-called "political questions," often the hub of the policy-decision function. The principle that political questions are non-justiciable, referred to as early as *Marbury* v. *Madison*,[14] has constituted a bar to judicial review for more than one hundred years.[15] Roughly comparable to what in France are *actes de gouvernement*, in England, acts of state, but considerably less encompassive than what the German constitutional theory calls *justizfreie Hoheitsakte*, a political question in the United States is authoritatively defined as "a question relating to the possession of political power, of sovereignty, of government, the determination of which is vested in Congress and the President, whose decisions are binding on the courts."[16] Among the non-justiciable issues are the conduct of foreign affairs by the executive; what constitutes the "republican form of government" guaranteed, under Article IV, to the states; and, with certain qualifications, matters pertaining to the electoral laws of the states.

Visualized within the context of interorgan controls, the judicial review of the constitutionality of legislation concurrently passed by the politically constituted power holders appears an anomaly, structurally incompatible with the distribution of functions among the several power holders. A single power holder, whose establishment is neither democratic nor free from political vitiation, arrogates to himself the right to frustrate and overrule the policy decisions of the other power holders, popularly elected and controlled; yet he himself, by virtue of tenure, is not exposed to reciprocal controls on the part of the other power holders, including the electorate. Congress and the president are rarely in a position to overrule the Court by new legislation because they have to conform to the interpretation of the constitution by the Court.[17] In most cases the objection to congressional-presidential policy decisions can be removed only by constitutional amendment, as was the case of the income-tax amendment (1913).

The foregoing objections to judicial review are submitted from the viewpoint of the necessary reciprocity of the interorgan controls on which the process of political power in constitutional democracy is balanced. They should not be construed as a denial of the usefulness of the institution under the American pattern of government. Judicial review has become integrated into it to such an extent that foreign observers consider it more characteristic than even the alleged "separation of powers." In our political climate with its hectic fluctuations, it is as much a counterweight against congress as the reciprocal controls of the vote of nonconfidence and dissolution between parliament and government under parliamentarism. What harm it may at times have done is far outweighed by its protection of the citizens' liberty against the ever present danger of congressional encroachment. The elimination of judicial review from the American pattern of government is unthinkable. If it could be accomplished at all, it would be possible only by the elimination of the supreme-law-of-the-land clause of Article VI, and this would destroy the constitution itself.

JUDICIAL REVIEW OUTSIDE THE UNITED STATES

Considering the environmental conditions of judicial review in the United States, it is hardly surprising that the institution, much observed and even envied abroad, met with indifferent success when tried abroad.[18] Much of the failure may be ascribed to the pattern of government in which judicial review was intended to operate. Obviously, it is essential for the proper functioning of a federal organization as the device for adjusting interfederal jurisdictional controversies. In this sense it has implanted itself in Canada and Australia. But there are exceptions: in Switzerland the Federal Tribunal (Bundesgericht) has been denied the right to review federal legislation but is authorized to check on the compatibility of cantonal with federal law. Under the German empire (constitution of 1871, Art. 76) it was the Federal Council, a political body, which upon request had to decide controversies between the member states. In unitary states, on the other hand, judicial review may appear appropriate for the presidential pattern of government, based on interdependence by co-ordination, while it can hardly fit into parliamentarism, interdependence by integration. It is wholly incompatible with assembly government. Needless to state, the concept of a court uncontrolled by the government, let alone controlling the government, is inconceivable in autocratic and authoritarian regimes. In addition, existing habits and experience likewise militate against judicial review in various legal civilizations.

Judicial review is alien to the political tradition of England not only because no written constitution exists with which the statute could be compared but also because of the paramountcy of the king-in-parliament. French aversion to any intervention of the judiciary with the legislative function dates back to the Revolution: the constitution of 1791 (Art. 157) forbade any "immixture" of the judiciary with the legislative (or executive) functions. This prohibition was motivated partly by grievances under the *ancien régime* and partly because the separation-of-powers concept was taken seriously. Since the French experience influenced many subsequent constitutions, judicial review was ignored during most of the nineteenth century. The courts did not feel entitled to it and did not claim it, with few and sporadic exceptions, as in some Latin American states with federal organization. The "professors' " constitutions after the First World War revived the academic interest in the institution, without, however, vitalizing it anywhere but in Austria.[19] Under Weimar the Supreme Court (Reichsgericht) did not proceed beyond mild obiter dicta. Not a single statute was invalidated, though there existed substantial doubts about the constitutionality of not a few. The Reich State Court (Reich-Staatsgerichtshof) (Art. 19) dealt primarily with federal-state or interfederal constitutional controversies (*Verfassungsstreitigkeiten*) and was denied the judicial control of federal legislation as such.

It was only in recent constitutions after the Second World War that, with the rising interest in American institutions, judicial review began to enjoy increased popularity. If the French Fourth Republic confined itself to a mere gesture, the German and Italian constitutions made serious efforts to vitalize the institution by the establishment of special courts with a monopoly of adjudication. Outside Europe under the new constitution of India (1948), likewise a federal organization, the application of judicial review is visibly inspired by the American precedent.[20]

Of the host of technical problems that emerged in the experimentation outside the United States, the following should be noted: judicial review may be preventive—forestalling a statute held violative of the constitution either as to procedure or substance from entering into force—or it may be remedial, depriving an unconstitutional statute of its validity. Preventive action is incumbent on the political agencies but could also be assigned to the courts by advisory opinions binding the other power holders. Remedial action is basically the task of the courts but could also be assigned to a political agency not identical with the one that enacted the challenged legislation. In the case of review by the courts, three sets of problems arise. Should it be assigned to the ordinary courts or to a special court? There are also different solutions for initiating the procedure; this may be done by a party affected by the statute held unconstitutional, by certain specified state organs, or by the courts ex officio. Finally, solutions have to be found concerning the invalidated statute: should it be treated as unconstitutional *ex tunc*, that is, beginning with the time it was enacted—regardless of the concomitant invalidation of vested rights created meanwhile—or only *ex nunc*, that is, beginning with the declaration of unconstitutionality?

The following types of judicial review, both by non-judicial agencies and by the courts, have been practiced.

The parliament.—The parliament that has enacted the statute in the first place is least suited to act as the custodian of the constitution. Rabbits are usually not the most reliable guardians of the vegetable garden. The assembly, or its majority, cannot reasonably be expected to reverse itself. Sieyès' proposal of the Jurie Constitutionnelle, a political body, found its practical application in Napoleon I's Sénat Conservateur of the constitution of the year VIII and was imitated by the Senate of the constitution of 1852 of Napoleon III, in both authoritarian regimes a futile semantic gesture. The parliament as the judge in its own case was adopted by the equally semantic constitution of the German Democratic Republic (East Germany) of 1949 (Art. 66): a Constitutional Committee was established by the People's Chamber (Volkskammer), consisting of members of all parliamentary groups in accordance with their numerical strength in the assembly, together with three judges of the Supreme Court and three law professors. A statute can be challenged only by certain public agencies, namely, the assembly (at least one-third of its members), its presidium, the president of the Republic, the national government, and the assemblies of the *Länder* (prior to their abolition by the "Democratization" Statute of 1952).[21] The opinion of the committee is advisory only, the final decision being left to the assembly. The procedure is politically so tainted as to be valueless, but it conforms to the repudiation of the separation of powers by the communist doctrine.

A Constitutional Committee for the review purposes was also institutionalized in the constitution of the French Fourth Republic (Art. 91): it is composed of three ex officio members, namely, the president of the Republic, the speakers of the two chambers, and ten members elected by the parliament (seven by the National Assembly and three by the Council of the Republic) who must not be members of it. The committee is charged to consider whether an individual statute would have required the form of a constitutional amendment in order to be valid. No formal declaration of unconstitutionality results. The procedure, if requested by an absolute majority of the Council of the Republic, is set in motion by a joint request of the president of the Republic and the speaker of the Council of the Republic. The investigation of the committee, however, pertains only to the political institutions (Titles I–X of the constitution) and excludes *a limine* the preamble containing fundamental guaranties and social rights. The institution, embryonic as it is, has to be understood as an intraorgan control device for protecting the Council of the Republic against encroachments by the National Assembly. This was confirmed by the single instance to date in which the Constitutional Committee was called on to function (1948).[22]

The president.—Another solution to prevent an allegedly unconstitutional statute from entering into force is the presidential veto, customary only under the presidential system and permissible also in neopresidential regimes. The American president may of course use his veto for the explicit reason that he holds the bill to be unconstitutional. In parliamentary states the head of the state (monarch or president), as a rule, is not in a position to inject himself into the procedure. If he were to utilize his duty of promulgation* as a substitute for constitutional review, he would place the cabinet in the contradictory situation of first supporting the bill in parliament and subsequently assuming responsibility, by the countersignature, for its veto by the state president. However, an interesting variant has been adopted by the 1937 constitution of Eire (Art. 26): The president, after consultation with the Council of State, may refer a bill (except money bills) to the Supreme Court for a decision on its constitutionality. Promulgation is meanwhile suspended. If, within sixty days, the Supreme Court sides with the president, the bill cannot be signed by him; otherwise his signature is mandatory.

Constitutional review by the courts.—Quite aside from the political objections to the injection of the political departments in the procedure of testing the constitutionality of a statute, the main difficulty lies in the fact that, in the vast majority of cases, the un-

* See above, p. 205.

constitutionality does not exist prima facie. As a rule, it will be brought to the surface in the litigation of the parties affected by it before a court. The most practicable solution, therefore, is to leave the decision to a judicial organ in a judicial procedure. Here the institutionalization varies considerably. Either the function is assigned to the ordinary courts, reaching, on appeal, the Supreme Court; this is the situation in the United States and other countries, such as Australia, Canada, and Argentina. Or a special constitutional court is endowed with the monopoly of constitutional review; its members are designated with particular care to secure professional competence and political impartiality. Outstanding illustrations are the Constitutional Court in Austria, before and after the Nazi interlude, and that provided by the Bonn constitution (Art. 100): when any court considers a federal law unconstitutional that is pertinent to its decision, the pending lawsuit is suspended and the question referred, for a binding decision, to the Federal Constitutional Court (Bundesverfassungsgericht), or, in the case of a *Land* law, to the respective *Land* Constitutional Court.

Considerable variations exist also as to who may set the procedure in motion, whether any citizen as party in a pending lawsuit or only specified state organs: the government; certain percentages of the legislature of the central state or of the member units; the ordinary courts before which the law is challenged; or the tribunal itself which renders the decision. The regulation in Austria may serve as an illustration: the Federal Constitutional Court is faced with the issue of constitutionality (1) on the request of a provincial government; (2) if the issue was raised before the court itself; or (3) if it arose before the Supreme Court or the Supreme Administrative Court, provided they resolved to bring the question before the Federal Constitutional Court. Practically the procedure depends on the initiative of an official agency

There are differences also in the manner in which the issue of and the individual litigants have no direct share in it.

constitutionality is raised. If the attack is directed against the statute as such (*par voie d'action*, spoken of as *abstrakte Normenkontrolle* in Germany), the court may annul the law; if the unconstitutionality is alleged in a lawsuit (*par voie d'exception*), the court may deny its applicability to the case in hand without formal declaration of unconstitutionality. Where *stare decisis* exists, the effect is likewise the final elimination of the law from circulation. Another difficult problem is whether all provisions of a constitution are of equal rank to constitute the yardstick for the validity of legislation. The courts are compelled to distinguish between the positive norms of the constitution and its merely programmatic promises, a difference closely related to the distinction between the normative and nominal content of a constitution.*

A preferential evaluation of these variants of judicial review depends on the viewpoint of the observer rather than on objective standards. To some, the concentration, in a special tribunal of the highest competence and experience, of so important a function as the judicial interorgan control over government and parliament may seem preferable to its being shared by all courts, high and low. The monopoly of a single court may seem more economical than to wait until after years of litigation conflicting opinions of lower courts are adjusted by the Supreme Court. To others, wide dispersion of the right to challenge legislation has its advantages over confining the initiative to the state organs or the judicial agencies themselves. Certainly the American practice may not appear everywhere the most desirable one. Much will depend on the prevailing pattern of government and the national attitude toward the judiciary in general.

The "Judicialization of Political Power"

To many the control of the compatibility of legislation with the constitution is a legitimate function of the judiciary because it

* See above, pp. 147 ff.

serves the maintenance of the state under the rule of law. An entirely different political philosophy, however, underlies recent efforts in Bonn-Germany and, to a lesser extent, also in Italy to build the judicial power up to the point where it occupies the commanding position above the other power holders as the supreme arbiter of the political process. Under the Bonn constitution the Federal Constitutional Court (Bundesverfassungsgericht) is authorized to decide, in the forms of the judicial process, controversies (*Verfassungsstreitigkeiten*), not between individuals—this is the task of the ordinary courts—but between the state organs and power holders themselves. The peg on which this authority of the Constitutional Court hangs is again its right and duty to interpret the constitution, because every power holder claims to rest the legitimation of his political action on a constitutional norm. But, since often the substance of the controversy is political, the function of the Constitutional Court by necessity assumes political character though disguised in judicial form. The jurisdiction extends to what elsewhere are considered non-justiciable "political questions" and *actes de gouvernement*. The situation has been variously described as the ' judicialization of political power," leading, it is alleged, almost inevitably to the "politization of the judicial process."[23]

Under the Weimar constitution (Art. 19) a federal constitutional court, the Reich Staatsgerichtshof, was assigned the task of adjudicating controversies of a public nature within a *Land*, if no corresponding *Land* court existed, and between the *Länder* and the federal state. In general, therefore, its jurisdiction confined itself to the interfederal relations. The "public" nature of the controversy was determined by the parties participating in it: the power holders (government and parliament) themselves, political parties as such and as parliamentary groups, municipalities, churches, and all other legal persons recognized by public law. Under these headings the constitutional court of Weimar unfolded a vast activity and contributed measurably to the adjustment of controversies that were often of a political nature. However, in the field of federal-state relations there were limits to its usefulness. When the court was called on, in 1932, to decide a major power conflict between the conservative Reich government of von Papen and the socialist-controlled coalition government in Prussia, it meekly yielded to the Reich government by bending the constitution in its favor.[24]

The Weimar instrument deliberately refrained from extending the jurisidiction of the court to controversies arising between state organs or power holders on the federal level. This gap—if such it was—was filled by the Bonn Basic Law (Art. 93, No. 1). The Federal Constitutional Court was assigned the duty to "interpret the constitution on the occasion of controversies concerning the extent of the rights and duties of a supreme federal organ." This assignment implemented the customary jurisdiction, arising out of the federal structure as such, of a federal supreme court concerning the compatibility of (federal and *Land*) law with the federal constitution (Art. 93, No. 2) and concerning the rights and duties of the federal state and the member states under the constitution (Art. 93, No. 3). The jurisdiction of the court is stretched so far that German constitutional lawyers seem to doubt whether there are any non-justiciable, because political, issues left, except such top-level decisions as the declaration of war, the recognition of a foreign government, or the dissolution of the Bundestag.

The Federal Constitutional Court has been engaged, since its inauguration in 1951, in a constructive activity for the maintenance of orderly constitutional procedures in the fields of the protection of civil liberties, the demarcation of federal-state relations, and the vitalization of the democratic-social state society, proclaimed by the Basic Law (Art. 20, sec. 1).[25] All this was imperatively required by the liquidation of the legacy of the Third Reich and the needs of reconstruction. The court assumed the role of the stern governess to keep order among the unruly *Länder*, whose natural appetites were stimulated by the share-the-wealth philosophy of the constitution and whose selfishness was encouraged by the trickeries of an overcomplex federal organization. But the Weimar experience repeated itself. In the politically highly charged controversy between the Adenauer government and the Social Democratic opposition concerning the legality of the European Defense Community treaties under the constitution,[26] the court, after more than two years of futile procrastination wrapped up in legal technicalities, evaded its judicial responsibility and refrained from making any decision at all. Perhaps such judicial self-restraint was wise, if damaging to its prestige. Confronted with the realities of the power process, the court found impotence the better part of judicial wisdom. If the decision had gone against the government, it would have frustrated a major policy decision and, most likely, led to the court's emasculation by constitutional amendment.

The Italian constitution likewise (Art. 134) assigns to the Constitutional Court jurisdiction in conflicts between the "powers of the state," in addition to those between the Italian state and its regions and between the regions themselves. As yet these assignments have not become operative, the first because of the lack of time—the court was established as late as 1956—the second because the abortive pseudofederalism of the Italian republic did not require judicial intervention.[27]*

The novel approach to the solution of political conflicts involves considerable danger for both the judicial and the governmental process. The advocates of the judicial arbitration between the political power holders contend that, in the state under the rule of law, all political acts of whatever power holder must conform to the constitutional norms, and to appraise the extent and to interpret the content of constitutional norms are the legitimate functions of a supreme constitutional court. This approach is incontrovertible. But, against this, one may hold that the intervention of the court tends to obliterate the border line between the

* See below, pp. 301–2.

administration of justice and the conduct of the political process. The politically responsible power holders, government and parliament, are exposed to the temptation to devolve a controversial policy decision to the court. The judges, in turn, are compelled to substitute, in the disguise of a judicial decision, their political value judgments for those of the responsible power holders. To establish a court as the supreme arbiter of the power process—and this is the core of the "judicialization of politics"—would, in the last analysis, convert the system of government into a judiciocracy.

The German experience under both Weimar and Bonn suggests that attempts at the "judicialization" of the power process can be successful only if no vital interest of the major power holders is adversely affected. If the right to overrule a policy decision of government and parliament is assigned to the courts, the danger threatens either that its decision will not be obeyed—to the detriment of the rule of law—or that the governmental policy decision will be replaced by a judicial action which, though formally couched in constitutional terms, is basically a political action. In the conflict between the rule of law and the right and duty of the government to govern, both will suffer. Moreover, what would happen if the conflict to be judicially decided is one affecting the court itself? *Quis custodiet custodes?* Who is to decide? Grave constitutional crises may result, as evidenced by the struggle between the Roosevelt administration and the "nine old men," or between the Nationalist government and the Court of Appeal in the Union of South Africa (1951–56) concerning the statutory implementation of the apartheid or "white supremacy."[28] The maximum of interorgan controls in the power process cannot always be equated with its optimum.

IX. Interorgan Controls of the Electorate over the Government and the Parliament

Finally, the fourth and last of the patterns of interorgan control operative in the constitutional democracy* will be discussed. Constitutionalism culminates in constitutional democracy. It was achieved by the gradual extension of the suffrage and, with it, of the access to political office, from the privileged classes to the entire adult population. Constitutional democracy is the political system under which the totality of "the people," organized as electorate and mobilized, for political action, by the political parties, freely participate in the power process. The electorate rises to the rank of the supreme power holder, ultimately controlling both government and parliament.

The electorate participates in the political process either indirectly, by electing the persons and parties in parliament and government to whom the policy decision is intrusted, or directly, by referendal and plebiscitary procedures.

Elective Procedures

Elective procedures serve, in the first place, for the designation of the power holders in government and parliament by the electorate. Such designation may be performed directly or indirectly. The direct designation of the chief executive is characteristic of the presidential pattern of government and its variants. The electorate, in a mass society necessarily following party directives, determines by direct vote the person of the state president. Anoint-

* See above, p. 185.

ment by the democratic oil endows the popularly elected state president with a specific prestige.

Direct designation of one of the power holders, the parliament, is characteristic of all patterns of government in constitutional democracy. It is accomplished by directly manifested preferences for specific persons and political parties who, in the open power circuit of competitive ideologies, present themselves for the choice of the voters. Under parliamentary and assembly government, however, the other power holder, the government, is designated indirectly: the representatives of the parties elected to the assembly determine the person holding the prime ministership and, through him, those holding other governmental positions. In nations which practice the two-party system the election actually determines directly the person or persons of the government, because the leaders of the victorious party automatically are called into office. In Britain and the states following the British pattern the general elections attain a plebiscitary character. In states with a multiple-party system, unless an individual party obtains a clear majority, the designation of the governmental power holders remains indirect, because the ultimate investiture depends on the agreement of a party coalition.

By electing specific parties, or persons representing them, to the assembly and, through these intermediaries, designating the incumbents of the governmental positions, the electorate actively participates in the power process. By this action it determines the future policy decisions. By re-electing a party majority or certain persons to the assembly, the electorate exercises retroactive policy confirmation. By refusing to re-elect a majority party or specific persons in the parliament, the electorate exercises retroactive policy control. The injection of the electorate into the power process becomes particularly manifest when elections take place after a dissolution of the parliament: the electorate becomes the arbiter of a policy controversy between the government and the majority of the parliament or between the parties of the parliament.

Referendal Procedures

Under the classical concept of representative government the political process was predicated on the interplay of the assembly and the government. The acceptance of universal suffrage has transformed this situation. The triangular configuration of the power process, operating between parliament, government, and the electorate, suggested additional techniques of participation of the latter beyond the elective procedures. Great efforts have been devoted, in particular in the sophisticated constitutions after the First World War, to the fullest possible integration of the electorate as the supreme power holder into the political process through referendal procedures. The referendum serves as an instrument of policy control when it approves or disapproves an antecedent policy decision of the government and parliament. If combined with popular initiative, it may even amount to a policy decision, subsequently to be confirmed or disapproved by parliament and government. The political parties intervene also in the referendal process. Experience with the institution, however, reveals that in it the voter follows the party line less consistently than he does in elections. With the advance of political education he begins to learn how to appraise for himself the merits and demerits of a proposal. Moreover, while the parties are indispensable for personnel selection, their guidance is less cogent for the individual voter's referendal decision.

Three different if often tangential areas of referendal participation of the electorate may be distinguished: (1) the constituent function, (2) the legislative function, and (3) the plebiscite.

THE PARTICIPATION OF THE ELECTORATE IN THE CONSTITUENT FUNCTION

In this area again two different applications are to be noted: the referendum on the "form of government" and that on constitutions and constitutional amendments.[1]

In recent times, prior to the drafting of a constitution by a constituent or national assembly, the people occasionally have been called upon to decide on their future "form of government," that is, in practice, whether they prefer a republic or a monarchy. This happened, for example, in Italy (June 2, 1946) and Bulgaria (September 8, 1946). In both cases the referendum turned against the monarchy, accurately reflecting the will of the people, because the dynasty was identified with defeat. In Greece, where the issue of monarchy versus republic was at stake several times within the last generation, the result usually depended on which side was in control of the electoral machinery. However, in view of the fact that "monarchy" is a multi-faceted concept subject to different applications in practice, it may seem preferable to leave the decision to a national assembly elected for this task rather than to the voters, as was the case in Tunisia (July, 1957).

The first instrument of government completed by a constituent assembly and submitted to the electorate for approval was the French constitution of June 4, 1793. Its submission was an application of Rousseau's doctrine of the people confirming the social contract. Napoleon likewise saw to it that his three constitutions of 1799, 1802, and 1804 and the Acte Additionnel of 1814 were submitted to, and duly approved by, the people. In the nineteenth century, possibly because it had become tainted by radical and dictatorial abuse, the constitutional referendum lost favor with the Powers That Be, who preferred final adoption by a national assembly. An exception is Switzerland, whose constitution of 1848 and its total revision of 1874 were ratified by both the majority of the electorate and the cantons. In the ultrademocratic ground swell after the First World War approval of a new constitution by popular vote became more fashionable, particularly in Latin America (e.g., Chile, 1925; Uruguay, 1942, 1952), in some of the German *Länder* under Weimar (Baden, 1920), and later in the Philippines (1935) and in Puerto Rico (1952). After the Second World War even referendum-shy France resorted to it twice, the first time (June 2, 1946) to reject the first constitution and again to adopt the second constitution (October 27, 1946). The constitutional referendum enjoys suspicious popularity in autocratic and authoritarian regimes of our time not only in the Soviet orbit but also in such neopresidential regimes as South Viet-Nam (1956) and Egypt (1956). The obvious reason for this preference is less the ultrademocratic procedure than the fact that a popular vote can be manufactured by propaganda and constraint with more ease than can approval by the more rational process of a representative assembly.

However, the submission of constitutional amendments to the people for approval or disapproval has become quite common. Popular ratification has been mandatory in Switzerland since 1848. Doubtless more cumbersome and less expedite than parliamentary adoption, the method did not prevent the Swiss from adjusting their liberal instrument of government to the requirements of the service and welfare state. If, in general, the people have shown themselves conservative and rejected more amendments than they approved, in the long run no reasonable constitutional reform failed to reach the statute book. In Switzerland the people may also set a policy decision in motion by popular initiative. The final abolition of the malpractice of the "urgent federal resolutions" was due to such an initiative.* However, the relative popularity the constitutional referendum enjoyed in the post–World War I constitutions was not maintained after World War II. In the constitution of the French Fourth Republic (Art. 96, sec. 6) it is thinned out to the remote contingency of an otherwise unbreakable deadlock between the two chambers. In Italy (constitution of 1947, Art. 138) it plays a strictly subsidiary role and is excluded entirely if the two houses pass the amendment by a two-thirds majority. Under Bonn it is conspicuous by its absence, understandably so after it had remained a dead letter under Weimar (Art. 76, sentence 4). The constitutional referendum is widely practiced in the states of the American Union, but its usefulness is often marred by an over-

* See above, pp. 225 ff.

technical phraseology which the average voter is unable to grasp and the accumulation of proposals at the time of the biannual elections.

THE LEGISLATIVE REFERENDUM

Switzerland, again, supplies the most favorable environment for the submission to a referendum of legislation enacted by the parliament and for the initiative of legislative proposals by the people. The frequency with which the Confederation and the cantons resort to the technique has earned the Swiss pattern of government the appellation of a "semidirect" government. The institution achieved striking results in integrating the electorate in the process of policy decision and policy control.

In the euphoric Indian-summer climate of constitutional democracy after the First World War the legislative referendum figured in numerous new constitutions without, however, attaining anything like the importance it had acquired, over the years, in Switzerland. The techniques varied: either the legislative referendum confirmed or rejected an antecedent parliamentary enactment, or the proposal was initiated by the electorate, subsequently to be either adopted by the parliament to become law or, in the case of parliamentary rejection, submitted to a final referendum. The referendal procedure could be initiated either by a specified minority of the parliament, or by the president, meanwhile suspending promulgation of the measure in question, or, in federal states, by a specified number of the member units. The general impression, outside Switzerland, is that the institution has not become integrated into the power process. So little was it used in the interwar period that the majority of the post–World War II constitutions ignored it altogether. Certainly the most recent vintage of constitutions is less democratic than the preceding one. The power process again is monopolized, except for the elections, by the party oligarchies controlling parliament and government.

THE PLEBISCITE

In common parlance the term "plebiscite" is used for a variety of acts of popular participation in the political process, becoming even a synonym for elections. However, even though the appellation has become generally accepted for votes on the "form of government," it should be reserved for popular votes on non-constitutional and non-legislative matters. In most cases the plebiscite denotes a popular vote on a territorial issue—the modification of the external or internal state boundaries or the change of sovereignty for an entire territory.[2]

Another child of the French Revolution sired by Rousseau, the territorial plebiscite was at first frequently used for the legalization of foreign conquests and annexations and, more sporadically, for purposes of national self-determination during the nineteenth century. Its most constructive application was to consummate the Italian unification. But a veritable rash broke out after the First World War, when, under the flag of self-determination proclaimed by the Paris peace treaties, it was employed, on several occasions under international supervision, to straighten out long-festering minority issues (in Upper Silesia, Carinthia, the Saar [1935], and elsewhere). In most of these cases an ethnical minority was asked to decide whether to retain its existing political allegiance, join another state considered more consanguineous, or become an independent political entity. The plebiscite found fewer advocates after the Second World War and was used to settle the ensuing territorial changes in only a few cases, for example, again in the Saar territory (1955), which decided to exchange its status as a quasi-independent state for the reincorporation into Germany. By contrast, the Maltese (1956) declined by a popular vote to accept the closer integration into the United Kingdom offered them by the British government. The Kashmir issue, disputed between India and Pakistan, was never submitted to the test because of India's adamant refusal.

Changes of territorial sovereignty are, of course, policy decisions of the first order. To deny a people the decisive voice in matters of political allegiance would be tantamount to flouting the democratic legitimacy in which the contemporary state society is said to be grounded. Yet, in the light of experience, it may seem that, even if the vote is technically impeccable, the value of the territorial plebiscite as the arch-democratic manifestation of the popular will is vitiated by the excessive emotionalization of the population immediately concerned as well as of the states that are to gain or to lose by the result. A representative assembly specifically elected to decide on a change of territorial sovereignty may seem preferable. But the coloration of the democratic ideology inherent in it has become so convincing to the minds of the statesmen and people of today that rational arguments against the territorial plebiscite, much as they are supported by experience, will hardly detract from its appeal.

Moreover, suspicion against the intrinsic value of the territorial plebiscite is aroused by the preference for it that autocratic and authoritarian regimes exhibit. Hitler staged it with resounding success in the annexation of Austria (1938). The Soviets likewise used it as a convenient blind for annexation, sometimes combining it with spurious elections for spurious representative bodies, as, for example, in the seizure of the Baltic states (1939). It remains a moot point whether the communist fondness for the device is of a doctrinaire origin, perhaps transmitted from the French Revolution, or merely a technique for imparting to forcible territorial aggrandizement the fiction of the democratic choice, or whether it is motivated pragmatically because of the convenient manipulation of the popular vote.

Finally, the territorial plebiscite has a legitimate place where boundaries of the subdivisions within a federal state are to be reorganized in accordance with the manifested will of the population affected. In this sense, both Weimar (the controversial Art. 18) and Bonn (Arts. 29 and 118) resorted to the *Volksabstim-*

mung. Under Bonn, the technique was used to straighten out some of the most glaring anomalies of German territorial logic caused by the haphazard regroupment of the German *Länder* under the western occupation regimes. The unification of three territorial segments in the *Südweststaat* (1951/52) was confirmed by the Federal Constitutional Court.[3]

The Electoral System and the Will of the People

The discussion of the role assigned to the electorate in the power process would be academic without taking into account the overriding importance of the electoral system which mobilizes it for action. Unless the electoral techniques, by which the voters express their preferences for the candidates and parties to represent them in parliament and government, are designed in such a manner as to permit the honest and accurate reflection of their will, the concept of the people as the sovereign power holder remains a sterile hypothesis. The electoral system and the laws embodying it must be devised with impartiality toward all and without malice toward any of the contestants. This postulate is fulfilled only if all candidates and parties are granted equal chances to enlist the support of the voters. Strict political neutrality must govern all stages of the electoral process: the conditions of suffrage and eligibility for office, the demarcation of election districts, the nomination of the candidates, the conduct of the election campaign, the polling operations, the tabulation of the votes, the distribution of the mandates among the competing parties in accordance with the popular vote, and the decision on contested elections.

The perfect electoral law, giving all competitors equal chances without discrimination, still has to be devised, and its prospects have not improved with the mass electorate of our time. To be impartial and neutral, the electoral system must preclude undue advantages for the prevailing government and the parties supporting it. The defect inherent in most electoral laws lies in the fact that they offer a convenient leverage for the power holders government and parliament to twist the outcome of the election contest in their favor. Often they can play it, as the virtuoso plays his instrument, to obtain the political tonality they desire. Past and present experience tends to confirm what may seem an oversimplification—that those who draft the electoral law have the power to make and break the political process and, with it, the prevailing political regime. In the manner in which the electoral law is fashioned and the election techniques are manipulated lies one of the basic distinctions between the autocratic and the constitutional political systems. But the choice of the proper electoral law and the operation of the electoral process also have become a crucial dilemma of the constitutional-democratic state.

THE CONTROL OF THE ELECTORAL PROCESS IN AUTOCRATIC REGIMES

The slanted electoral law and the rigged election procedure are characteristic of autocratic and authoritarian regimes, old and new. Where permitted to function, elections are nothing but the pseudodemocratic cloak that is meant to hide, often without success, the management of the electoral process from above. This is the standard practice of all totalitarian and most authoritarian states. Examples of it abound, from Mussolini's Acerbo law of 1924 to the "election plebiscites" of 1929 and 1934 under the legislation of 1929,[4] through Hitler's single-party elections of 1933 and 1938, to the various "elections" staged in the Soviet orbit and in neopresidential regimes. Nomination by the government or the single party equals election. The electorate being deprived of alternatives, the personnel of the assemblies is actually appointed by the government. In some of the "People's Democracies" the situation is superficially camouflaged by the proviso that other political parties tolerated by the government are joined together with the official party on a single "National Front" ticket: the seats obtained are distributed among them by a prearranged key under which the government party takes the lion's share.[5]

Of the other equally effective devices autocracies have developed to obtain the monolithic election results they desire, the following may be mentioned by way of exemplification: wholesale exclusion from the election, under various pretexts, of the parties and candidates disfavored; granting privileges to the government party in the campaign and withholding campaign facilities, in particular, the telecommunication media, from the opposition; and intimidation and outright terrorization of the voters at the polls. In addition, certain less transparent manipulations of the electoral process serve the same purpose: the open vote is the surefire proof that the regime wishes to influence the result; this was exemplified by Guatemala in 1956. The compulsory vote identifies the stay-at-homes as adversaries; fear of reprisal stifles opposition. And, where these devices still prove insufficient, wholesale "doctoring" of the election results, uncontrollable by the opposition, is resorted to.

ELECTORAL ABUSES IN CONSTITUTIONAL STATES

Peccatur intra muros et extra. Manipulation of the electoral system and techniques is not confined to autocracies. Most of the cruder methods for falsifying the electoral outcome have disappeared in constitutional democracies, though still practiced, for example, in Mississippi and other states of the American South.[6] But, even if the electoral mechanics are scrupulously honest, there exist, in all stages of the electoral process, numerous legitimate loopholes through which discriminatory practices can infiltrate. Even suffrage and eligibility can be used as leverage for coloring the popular will in advance. Raising the minimum age for the voter tends to benefit the more conservative parties and classes, while lowering it is considered advantageous for the more radical groups, allegedly more appealing to youth. The disenfranchisement of entire classes of citizens on racial grounds, as was universally practiced, until recently, against the colored population in the American South and is officially legalized in South Africa, testifies to the ease with which states otherwise conducting themselves as constitutional democracies use the electoral process to intrench their ruling classes. The right of the parliament, instead of an independent electoral court, to determine the legality of contested elections is a constant invitation for the majority parties to discriminate against an obnoxious opposition, as was drastically demonstrated by the efforts of the French National Assembly in 1956 to trim the representation of the Poujadists. But the broadest avenue for governmental influence on the outcome of the election has been opened by the techniques of proportional representation.

PROBLEMS OF ELECTORAL TECHNIQUE

The integration of the mass electorate.—The electoral technique has become, in our time, a veritable science in its own right, demanding in equal measure the professional skills of the lawyer and politician, sociologist and social psychologist, statistician and mathematician. Space forbids a fuller discussion of the influence the electoral practices have on the faithful reproduction of the will of the sovereign people, or the lack of it.[7] The following selected aspects must suffice.

Three issues have contributed to the immense difficulties of designing, if not a perfect, at least an approximately fair and impartial electoral system and the laws implementing it.

1. As long as the suffrage was restricted to the propertied classes, the problem of the equality of the electoral chances was a political and not a technical one. With the extension of the vote to the entire adult population the political implications appeared in the disguise of the electoral technique. The advent of mass democracy drew millions of voters into the vortex of the electoral process. How to organize the mass electorate in viable electoral districts and territorial circumscriptions? How to establish the electoral quota, that is, the proper relation between the mass of the ballots cast and the necessarily limited number of parliamentary seats to be assigned to the contending parties? How to secure fairness in

counting and tabulating the results? All this required an elaborate state-operated and state-controlled election machinery.

2. The unprecedented increase in the voting public necessitated new techniques for acquainting the voters with the personalities and programs of the rivaling political parties. The issue had not posed itself with the same cogency in the idyllic period of early constitutionalism, when the suffrage was confined to the relatively limited class of privileged citizens believed to possess a modicum of political education. Directed to the mass electorate of today, the election campaign has become a gigantic contest of party propaganda machines. The election laws of the classical period, focusing merely on the honesty and impartiality of the election mechanics, were wholly unprepared to cope with this issue.

3. Mass democracy, with its proliferation of political parties, added a new problem. The election should lead to the installation of a parliament and government capable of attending to the policy-deciding and policy-executing functions and should not result in the emergence of power holders irretrievably stalemated and paralyzed. Though not confined to it, this novel problem was sharpened by the introduction of proportional representation.

The majority system.—Once the democratic ideology had won out against the resistance of the vote based on corporate or class privileges, democratic logic demanded that, in the individual territorial circumscription, the straight majority should prevail. The majority principle supplanted the medieval tradition of the *pars sanior*, the elite of the community, counterbalancing the mere numerical accumulation of votes. Since, under the majority system, it is technically impossible to treat the entire country as a single electoral unit, it had to be divided into electoral districts within each of which the majority principle was to prevail. The delineation of constituencies offered wide and readily used opportunities for the vested interests to tilt the electoral law to their advantage at the expense of other social classes and the parties representing them. Since democratic justice required a division into separate districts in which an approximately equal number of voters were entitled to a seat, the more conservative rural classes insisted on an over-all division which permitted them to hold their own against the numerically superior urban electorate believed to be more progressive or radical. A celebrated case of an election law slanted in favor of the conservative plutocracy was the so-called "law of the three classes" governing, until 1918, the elections in Prussia, at that time a constitutional, if authoritarian, state. It was deliberately and successfully fashioned to offset the numerical weight of the common voters in Class III by the propertied elements assembled, with superior voting strength, in Classes I and II. But it is hardly necessary to travel afar to find electoral laws brazenly rigged in favor of specific parties or vested interests. In Rhode Island, Connecticut, Georgia, Illinois, New York, and California, to quote a competent observer, they "make a farce of representation and all but guarantee minority control of the state legislatures."[8]

Another troublesome problem arose with the increasing mobility of the population. Citification resulted in vast population shifts from the rural areas to the urban centers. How should these fluctuations be accommodated in the electoral cadres? From the viewpoint of a politically neutral electoral law the periodical redistribution of seats has become no less important than the nominal equality of the suffrage. Everywhere the vested interests proved a formidable obstacle to reform. Crass inequalities are common.[9] Only the United Kingdom succeeded in approximating a fair solution: recent legislation, by an all-party agreement, established four permanent boundary commissions (for England, Scotland, Wales, and Northern Ireland, respectively) to recommend to parliament at intervals of between three and seven years a redistribution of seats in conformity with the uniformly prescribed "electoral quota," that is, the figure obtained by dividing the entire electorate by the number of seats.[10] The periodical revision has hardly been set in motion, however, and already complaints have arisen that it interferes with the normal party dynamics of the electoral process.

Proportional representation.—While the electorate was confined to the upper strata of a relatively homogeneous society, the straight majority technique worked tolerably well. With the advent of mass democracy it revealed a glaring injustice: the winner takes all, the loser gets nothing. Minorities are discriminated against to the point of being disenfranchized. The remedy was sought in proportional representation, which, at long last, recognized the facts of political life, namely, that elections are operated by the political parties. By theoretical logic, proportional representation is beyond challenge: each party should obtain the number of seats equivalent to the number of votes cast for it in the entire nation. In practical application the system proved a cure more afflicting than the sickness to be healed. Its adverse effects are too well known to require elaboration: the alienation of the voter from politics through the domination of the electoral process by the political parties, the monopoly of the party oligarchies in the selection of the candidates and their sequence on the party list, the mechanization of the political process, the fragmentation of the electoral will by the proliferation of factions, and the difficulties in the party-fragmented assembly of forming a stable government which must depend on the support of small and smallest groupings. Remedial measures to eliminate the so-called "splinter parties" either were ineffective or are at variance with the democratic tenets, quite aside from the fact that they are likely to benefit the older and established parties at the expense of new groups. Moreover, proportional representation tends to freeze the political alignments and the relative strength of the existing political parties. Landslides, reflecting ground swells of the electoral will, have become increasingly rare; exceptions such as the successes of the Nazis in 1930 or the Poujadists in France in 1955 rather confirm the rule. Lately, proportional representation has also been challenged by the contention, as yet unproved, that the straight majority technique facilitates the development of the two-party system.[11] In short, the magic of proportional representation, so vaunted as the panacea for the ills of the crude majority technique, has visibly paled; it is in a serious crisis.

No less alarming is the recent experience that proportional representation lends itself most readily to the influence of the prevailing government and its supporting parties on the composition of the parliament. It is susceptible to endless manipulations to the benefit of the parties that happen to design the specific variant to be applied. Though heavily borrowing from the authoritarian book—Mussolini's Acerbo law of 1924—the premium or bonus system of proportional representation is considered thoroughly respectable in constitutional democracies. By this system, the party with the plurality of votes automatically obtains the majority, and even the qualified majority, of all seats in parliament. The French election law of 1951 and its Italian counterpart of 1953 were brutally rigged in favor of the government parties; the former discriminated successfully against the extreme right (De Gaullists) and the extreme left (communists), and the latter failed, by the breadth of a hair, to put all power into the hands of the Christian Democrats.

Campaign finances and the electoral competition.—To conclude from the preceding material that the manipulated electoral process is the rule in constitutional-democratic states would be misleading. It can be assumed that the majority of them strive for a fair and impartial electoral system and that the conduct of the election mechanics leaves little to be desired. Yet the development of the mass society in the technological age introduced a novel element of disparity of the electoral chances. Modern election campaigns, by which the voters are acquainted with the personalities and programs of the contending parties, depend to a decisive degree on the impact of party propaganda on the mind of the individual voter.* Propaganda reaches the mass electorate by the mass-

* For a fuller discussion see below, pp. 336 ff.

communication media—press, radio, and television—and no longer, as was the rule in the period of classical constitutionalism, by personal contacts and meetings. Montecuccoli's famous words about the three necessities for warfare hold equally true for elections: money, money, and again money. In the totalitarian states the single government party monopolizes and exploits, for its exclusive benefit, the means of propaganda by mass communication. But the disparity in their utilization has become no less crucial in the constitutional-democratic state. For a long time either ostrich-like ignored or complacently condoned as the unavoidable corollary of a free society, the inequality of the campaign expenses and what they can buy of the media of mass communication has become of cardinal importance. To say that the financially best-oiled party invariably wins the election would not be true. But from the start it has an advantage over its less affluent competitors, who will have difficulty overcoming it with the most cogent counterarguments. To neutralize, in a free society, the inequalities of the press preferences may seem impossible without destroying freedom itself. But the British[12] and, to a lesser extent, the French[13] have succeeded in restraining the laissez faire anarchy of certain aspects of the electoral campaign. By setting rigorous ceilings for the election expenses of parties and candidates and by enforcing strict non-partisanship in the use of the telecommunication media, a degree of equality is secured. Contrariwise, in the United States parallel legal regulations remain wholly ineffective because more honored by breach than by observance.[14] The American example is assiduously copied by Germany. The injunction of the Bonn constitution (Art. 21, sec. 1) to the effect that "the political parties must give public account of the sources of their income" remains a dead letter; the bourgeois majority parties would never consent to surrender the financial edge they hold on their socialist competitors.

To sum up: the existence of the democratic suffrage and the honest observance of the mechanics of the electoral process do not by themselves guarantee the impartial reflection of the electoral will. Through the manipulation of the electoral system and the laws implementing it, the Powers That Be may poison the electoral will at its source and surreptitiously deflect it from its course. This defect tends to vitiate the function of the electorate as the supreme power holder in the political process and blunt its theoretically recognized right to control parliament and government.

Postscript: Deadlocks among the Power Holders

The foregoing analysis of the four patterns of interorgan controls among the several power holders cannot be concluded without some comment on political deadlocks between them that cannot be solved by constitutional processes. The following observations present merely the barest outlines of a phenomenon little explored in constitutional literature and as yet not fitted into a comprehensive constitutional theory.[15] It is the hallmark of a well-balanced constitutional order to prevent the dynamism of the political process, operated by reciprocal controls of the power holders, from leading to constitutionally insoluble stalemates and deadlocks, either within one and the same or between the several power holders. The fathers of the American constitution were wholly conscious of this problem when, in devoting intense thinking to the election of the president by the Electoral College (Art. II, sec. 3), they resolved that, in case no person should obtain the absolute majority of the votes of the electors, the final decision should be given to the House of Representatives.

Once again: the maximum of reciprocal controls assigned to the several power holders does not necessarily coincide with the optimum required for the efficient operation of the political process. That excessive sharing of functions can lead to the self-destruction of constitutional government was demonstrated by Napoleon's shrewd arrangement by which the assemblies were deliberately stalemated against one another,* with the intended

---

* See above, pp. 63 ff.

result that, with the assistance of the Council of State and the Senate he established his authoritarian domination over the paralyzed assemblies.

Deadlocks may also arise when the several power holders are so evenly matched that, if they cannot co-operate, a constitutional crisis will evolve that can be resolved only by resorting to illegality, force, and even revolution. To continue the political process, one of the power holders who feels himself the strongest, either by virtue of his assumed popular support or of his disposal over the armed forces, necessarily will establish his ascendancy over the others. He will take command of the deadlocked state machinery either by an arbitrary extension of his constitutional prerogatives or by an extra-constitutional *coup d'état*. Grave constitutional crises have arisen in different states because the constitution failed to provide for the constitutional resolution of deadlocks between matched power holders.

The following case material may illustrate deadlocks within one and the same power holder, which are relatively rare, and between the several power holders, from which the majority of constitutional crises derive. The former category pertains primarily to the parliament stalemated by party dissensions; the latter, to conflicts between the parliament and the government or between both joined together and the courts.

The constitutional crisis in Britain in 1910/11 was caused formally by a deadlock between the Liberal majority of the Commons and the overwhelmingly Conservative Lords; substantially, however, it became a conflict between the Lords and the people, who, in two successive general elections (January and December, 1910), had heavily indorsed the Liberal cabinet. The deadlock was resolved by the threat of the cabinet, as such constitutional, to appoint through the crown enough Liberal peers to break the resistance in the Lords. The permanent result was the Parliament Act of 1911 (1 & 2 Geo. V, c. 13), once and for all establishing the ascendancy of the Commons. A pertinent interorgan deadlock, although in an authoritarian state, occurred in Honduras in 1954:

after elections congress was unable to muster the quorum of the absolute majority of its members to declare the president elected (constitution of 1936, Art. 101, Nos. 8 and 9). The acting president, Julio Lozano Díaz, thereupon assumed the position of the chief of state illegally by presidential decree and dissolved parliament. A parallel situation arose in Pakistan in the same year. The Constituent Assembly proved incapable of framing a constitution. The governor-general, on the basis of the Government of India Act of 1935 (25 & 26 Geo. V, c. 42) and the Indian Independence Act of 1947 (10 & 11 Geo. VI, c. 30, secs. 8 and 9), dissolved parliament, without, however, providing for new elections, and temporarily established authoritarian government.[16]

To illustrate deadlocks between government and parliament, the famous constitutional conflict between Bismarck and the Liberal majority of the Prussian diet (1862–66) may be mentioned. The Prussian constitution of 1850 failed to determine what should be the solution if the governmental budget was not passed by the diet. When the diet refused to approve his rearmament budget, Bismarck filled the constitutional gap by wholly illegal emergency measures under the prerogative of the crown,[17] supported by the army, police, and the civil service. His successful policy of might over right broke the backbone of German liberalism for generations. The repercussions were still felt by Weimar Germany in the fateful misconstruction of the constitution (Arts. 53 and 54) which permitted the emergence of the "presidial" cabinets in opposition to the Reichstag and granted the Reich president and Reich government the vast emergency powers under Article 48, even before the parliament had become internally paralyzed by party disunity.* The collapse of constitutional democracy in eastern Europe—Poland, Yugoslavia, Rumania—in the twenties was likewise caused by deadlocks between the government and the dissension-ridden parliament, enabling the strong men to seize the reins.

* See above, pp. 222–23.

Constitutional conflicts in which government and parliament are deadlocked against the judiciary, if relatively rare, likewise are apt to lead to dangerous constitutional crises. President Roosevelt attempted to break the deadlock created by the hostility of the Supreme Court against the New Deal legislation by his famous "court-packing" plan. Similar to the threat of the crown in 1911 to appoint additional peers and equally legal, the bill submitted to congress failed when disapproved by the preponderance of public opinion and the most respected members of the legal profession. By contrast the Nationalist Government in the Union of South Africa succeeded where Roosevelt had failed: to break the constitutional deadlock caused by the opposition of the Court of Appeal against the white-supremacy legislation, additional judges were appointed in 1956 who duly supported the government policies.

The criterion of a good constitution, thus, is not only that adequate interorgan controls he built into it to prevent an individual power holder from gaining ascendancy over the others; it also must provide constitutional remedies for deadlocks that, in the normal course of the political process, can arise among them. In the constitutional-democratic state the *ultima ratio* for the solution of conflicts between the instituted power holders is the decision of the electorate as the supreme power holder, to which all others must bow.

Part III

The Control of Political Power II
Vertical Controls

X. Federalism

Our systematical analysis of the process of political power proceeds from the discussion of the horizontal controls that operate
either within one and the same power holder (intra-organ controls) or between the several power holders (interorgan controls)
to a different type of control instrumentality, here called "vertical controls." By this term are understood those patterns of
action and interaction that function between the totality of all
instituted power holders—parliament, government, courts, and the
electorate—and society as a whole. Seen structurally, horizontal
controls pertain to the level of the state machinery; vertical controls, to the level on which the state machinery confronts the
society. Expressed graphically or visually, horizontal controls
move sideways, vertical controls upward and downward.

Under the heading of "vertical controls" three different areas
of reciprocal action are grouped together:

1. Federalism—the juxtaposition and counterbalance of two
territorially differentiated sets of state sovereignties. The existence
of interfederal barriers restricts the power of the central state
toward the member states and vice versa.

2. Individual rights and fundamental guaranties. These are established for the benefit of the power addressees as limits beyond
which none of the instituted power holders can proceed. They
are created as zones of individual self-determination inaccessible
to them.

3. Pluralism. Plural groups—the "intermediary powers" of Montesquieu and de Tocqueville—interpose themselves between the
mass of the power addressees and the instituted power holders.

These vertical controls of the power process may seem heterogeneous. Federalism and fundamental guaranties are institutionalized in legal terms; pluralism, a sociological phenomenon, is not. The verticalism of federalism pertains to the relation between two different sets of governmental institutions; the verticalism of the plural stratification is different: it operates between society as a whole and the instituted power holders. What ties these three situations together is that, within their frame and context, the power process moves between the "upper" and the "lower" levels. What they have in common is that they function as a sort of shock absorber within the power process. Either they are intended to restrain the state Leviathan, as are federalism and individual guaranties, or, in the case of the plural groups, they tend to reduce the impact of state power exercised by the legitimate power holders on the socioeconomic and political status of the individual in the state society.

The Essentials of Federal Government

Next to the written constitution and the establishment of the "republican," that is, the non-monarchical, form of government in spatially extended state societies, federalism[1] is the major American contribution to the theory and practice of modern government. Quasi-confederal associations of states had existed in previous historical periods: in ancient Greece the Delian, Amphictyonic, Hellenic, and Achaean symmachies or "leagues";[2] the permanent alliances of the Swiss cantons from the fourteenth and fifteenth centuries onward; the Union of Utrecht (1579) between the seven northern provinces of the Netherlands. None of these qualifies as a genuine federal state, partly because of the absence of common organs with direct jurisdiction over the citizens of the associated states and partly because of the preponderance of a hegemonial state. Other associations of states, like the Holy Roman Empire of the Germanic nation, were either vassalries or, at the most, combinations of a semiconfederal nature. After the transitional stage of the "Articles of Confederation," the thirteen American states achieved, for the first time in history, the organizational structure of full-fledged federalism in the federal constitution of 1787.

The historical-pragmatic motivations which induce the peoples of several independent territorial entities to choose the federal form of government need no elaboration here. In general, the incentives for federalization parallel those for national unity, with the difference, however, that for specific reasons the federal pattern is preferred to the unitary. National unity is sought through regional diversity. Next to geographical, or rather geopolitical, propinquity, these conditions are decisive: a community of political, economic, or military-strategic interests; common traditions and common aspirations for the future; and, sometimes, consanguinity and common descent, though not necessarily common language. In the past also the excessive size of the territory discouraged the unitary solution as, for example, in Brazil, which only after the fall of the monarchy (1889) transformed itself from a unitary into a federal state. However, as evidenced by some state creations of recent times, the territorial obstacles may be overcome by modern communications. But the principal reason for the preference of the federal organizations remains the conviction that, in spite of the recognized need for national unity, regional traditions militate against fusing the state individualities into a unitary organization and that their cultural diversities require the federal structure.

Certain essential characteristics distinguish the federal state from the confederation, the latter most frequently the antecedent stage. These characteristics are: the central or "federal" entity possesses a sovereignty of its own, strictly separated from, and sharply limiting, the sovereignty of the member units; the central state exercises, by power holders of its own—the "federal" organs —direct control over the citizens of the entire territory without the intermediary of the member states; the jurisdictional distribution of the state activities between the central and the member states is such as to permit the operation of the federal entity independently from the member states and to allow the latter that independence from the central state deemed proper for the continuation of regional identity; and, finally, these essentials of interfederal relations are formalized in a written instrument of government. No federal organization can dispense with a written constitution. It is the treaty of a permanent union by which the heretofore sovereign member states agree to divest themselves of certain sovereign rights in favor of the central state, in compensation for the protection of their existence by the totality of all members and the benefits derived from participating in a larger state society. The federal organization is predicated on the assumption that the compromise contained in the federal constitution provides for the happy equilibrium between the interests of national unity and regional autonomy. The discovery and first application of the federal principle by the American states is another product of the mechanistic philosophy of the Enlightenment, the attempt to transpose Newtonian physics to the sociopolitical realm.

There is nothing more delicate in constitutional technique than the initial assignation of the state functions to the two areas of jurisdiction of the federal and the member states. In it lies the key to the interfederal power structure. There is an irreducible minimum of federal functions necessary to genuine federalism. These reside in the following areas: foreign relations; national defense; currency and money; weights and measures; citizenship; interstate trade and communications; and the financial wherewithal to perform the federal services. But the catalogue may be further extended to accommodate within the federal organization the needs of the social service and welfare state.

In federal constitutions the jurisdictional delineation between central and member states is accomplished by enumerating the functions assigned either to the former or to the latter, allowing an intermediary zone of concurrent powers of both and inserting a "residuary clause" that stipulates that the non-enumerated functions belong either to the central or to the member states. Frequently the correlation of the enumerated functions and the residuary clause indicates the character of the federal structure—whether it tends toward the prevalence of the central state or of the individual states. The more encompassing the enumeration of the attributes of the central state, the less important the residual jurisdiction of the member units. Examples of constitutions with an ample catalogue of federal attributes are those of the United States, Switzerland, Australia, and Germany from the Empire to Bonn, with the residual powers operating in favor of the states; Canada and South Africa—if the latter is considered a federal state—illustrate the opposite technique. However, if the residual clause operates to the benefit of the member states, the danger arises that, with the impact of the technological age on state activities, the federal government will be hampered or even incapacitated in the performance of new federal assignments. The way out of this crucial dilemma, which no federal state is spared, lies either in constitutional amendment enlarging the federal jurisdiction, as practiced, for example, in Switzerland but often impossible elsewhere, as in Australia, or in the expansive interpretation of the federal attributes by the courts, as in the United States. Where these two avenues are closed, the dynamism of the federal power process becomes static and stagnant.

Federalism within the Context of Shared Power

In contradistinction to the "monolithic" unitary state organization, federalism presents a system of territorial pluralism. The various state activities are distributed between the central and the member states and among the latter; they are, therefore, shared. The phenomenon of shared functions appears in its purest form when both the central and the member states possess concurrent jurisdiction on one and the same field of specified activities. However, here a dilemma arises which sooner or later confronts every federal organization: unless the constitution explicitly stipulates that, in case of concurrent and competitive action, the federal entity prevails over the member units—the theory of "pre-emption," consistently formulated, for example, in Germany (constitution of 1871, Art. 2, sec. 1; Weimar, Art. 13, sec. 1; Bonn, Art. 31) and in India (constitution of 1948, Art. 254)—the facts of federal life will necessarily assign priority to the central state.

The principle of shared powers is often expressed in constitutional theory by the concept of the dual sovereignty, ascribing to the federal state as well as to the member units supreme or sovereign power in their spheres of jurisdiction. The concept is misleading and even dangerous, as evidenced by the gravest constitutional crisis of the United States, the Civil War, which was conducted, on the part of the rebellious South, under the flag of state sovereignty. Actually, the federal organization possesses only one, indivisible sovereignty, that of the central state which absorbs, within the limits of the constitution, the original sovereignties of the member units. Shared power, in a federal organization, must not be equated with a system of dual sovereignty. What the federal organization accomplishes from the viewpoint of shared power is that the states' rights are protected, as effectively as may seem compatible with the sovereignty of the central state, against unconstitutional usurpation and absorption by the central state and that, correspondingly, the latter is sheltered against unconstitutional intervention of the former on the fields assigned to its jurisdictional monopoly.

The principle of power shared between the central and the member states is permanently anchored in the constitutional procedures for the formation of the will of the federal state. The customary instrumentality for the participation of the member units in policy decision and policy execution by legislation is the upper house, which, in the federal state, as a rule has escaped the general devaluation of bicameral institutions.* The member states

* See above, pp. 177 ff.

are granted representation in the upper house that is either equal regardless of size and importance—the principle prevailing in the United States, Switzerland, Australia, Argentina, and Brazil—or quantitatively in line with the population, as is traditional in Germany and, in an attenuated manner, in Canada (in the latter case equality is preserved between Quebec and Ontario).[3]

Elements of states' rights are reflected also in certain federal structures in the election or composition of the government. In the United States the intended basis of the presidential election is reflected by the federalistic interposition of the Electoral College, whose electoral votes correspond roughly to the size of the population of the member states. In Switzerland, according to constitutional usage, each of the three linguistic groups—a traditional bulwark of regional self-identification—and also the two most important cantons of Berne and Zurich are represented on the Federal Council. Under Bonn, the participation of the *Länder* in the designation of the federal president—a state organ of most limited political influence at that—is performed by the Federal Assembly (Bundesversammlung), which is composed of the members of the lower house (Bundestag) and an equal number of delegates of the legislatures of the *Länder* chosen by proportional representation (Art. 54, sec. 3). Regional interests are also often represented in the membership of the Supreme Court, in federal organizations an indispensable institution for the arbitration of interfederal disputes.

Finally, the member units share also in the modifications of the original compact by constitutional amendment, either through their participation in the upper house (Germany) or by the requirement that their majority has to consent to it directly, as in the United States, Australia, and Switzerland.

Whatever machinery may exist, however, for the member states to share in policy decision and policy control, it should be noted that states' rights are submerged or obliterated by nation-wide parties except in the very rare cases when regional interests are represented by special regional parties. Examples are the ephemeral states' rights parties in the United States in 1948 and in Bavaria, Hanover, and Schleswig-Holstein under Weimar and, to a much lesser extent, under Bonn. The "splinter parties" in Canada—the Social Credit party, governing British Columbia and Alberta, and the Co-operative Commonwealth Federation, holding sway over Saskatchewan—in spite of their local concentration, can hardly be considered regional parties based on ethnical or historical motivations.

Federalism in the United States

HISTORICAL DEVELOPMENT

Patriotic semanticism in the United States exalts the inalienable and imperishable federal structure.[4] As recently as in 1936 the Supreme Court took pains to emphasize the dual sovereignties under the American governmental system (*United States* v. *Butler*, 297 U.S. 1). Yet in the country of its origin, federalism has been on the defensive from the start, and today it is in full retreat. The great invention of divided sovereignty, written into the constitution of 1787 to limit power by sharing it between two sets of government, carried within itself the seeds of disorder and decay. Since the constitution is what the courts say it is, the development can be followed best by the jurisprudence of the Supreme Court. Hardly was the ink dry on the constitution when (1790) the issue of the First National Bank arose between the strict constructionists of the Jefferson Republicans—to whom the best government was that which governed least—and the national expansionists under Hamilton and Madison. The entering wedge was the theory of the implied powers in the sweeping clause (Art. I, last section), which once and for all terminated the assumption that the federal functions were exhausted by the enumeration in Article I, section 8. After their advent to power (1801) the Jeffersonian Republicans copied many a leaf from the Federalists' book. But the decisions of the Supreme Court under John Marshall between 1809 and 1823 placed the official seal on the new centralizing trend.

McCulloch v. *Maryland* (4 Wheat. 316 [1819]) stands out as the landmark, legalizing, by the concept of the implied powers, the expansion of federal powers at the expense of states' rights. The expansionist drive was reversed under Taney's chief justiceship (1836–64); states' rights were protected against federal encroachments. Here the Dred Scott case (*Scott* v. *Sanford*, 19 How. 393 [1857]) is the high-water mark. But the final showdown between the exigencies of a national economy and the vested rights of the states, delayed for a generation by the frontier situation, came with the Civil War. Calhoun's nullification theory was countered by Lincoln's winged words that the nation cannot be half-free and half-slave; they served as the moral justification for dismantling the original constitutional misconstruction of the dual sovereignties. The victory of the federal supremacy was consummated by the imposition of the Fourteenth Amendment (1868).

After Reconstruction an uneasy truce prevailed. The court, largely Republican and wholly conservative, invalidated most of the accomplishments of the Civil War, laying the groundwork for the subsequent legal discrimination against the Negroes. With its insistence on the freedom of contract, it defended the capitalist structure of society against the legislation of socially more progressive states. But, after some hesitation (the famous Sugar Trust case, 156 U.S. 1 [1895]), it let the Sherman Antitrust Act stand (*Swift* v. *United States*, 197 U.S. 175 [1905]), thus supplying the federal government with one of its most cutting weapons.

Another wave of retrogression of the federal power followed under Taft and Hughes. In this period the great dissenter, Brandeis, the Sigmund Freud of American constitutionalism, with his penetrating understanding of socioeconomic realities, assumed Marshall's mantle of the great centralizer. The target of an overwhelmingly Republican court was the protection of the freedom of contract and private enterprise, but states' rights benefited from it. The decisive breach of the states' rights dam came with the

Sixteenth Amendment (1913). A federal income tax which surrenders the priority of the main financial source to the central government is the death knell of genuine federalism everywhere. Irresistibly, if not without judicial reverses, as, for example, *Adkins* v. *Children's Hospital* (221 U.S. 525 [1923]), the federal jurisdiction narrowed the range of states' sovereignty.

Finally, as the New Deal battled the Great Depression, federal supremacy swept like a tidal wave over the states' autonomy, using the welfare, commerce, and due process clauses for the aggrandizement of the national government. The Supreme Court, with its conservative majority, was at first bitterly hostile, but at long last the Roosevelt court became attuned to the new federal realities. Almost two decades of concordance among congress, public opinion, and the Court followed, which again induced the Court to move the federal front forward into the inner sanctum of states' territory by the various desegregation cases of 1954 and after.

In retrospect, what differentiates the American development toward federal supremacy from other federal organizations confronting identical situations of national emergencies is the fact that, by and large, it was accomplished primarily by judicial interpretation of the constitution rather than by direct constitutional amendment. But the result was the same: federal power grew; states' power shrank.

THE INSTITUTIONALIZATION OF
FEDERAL SUPREMACY

An appraisal of contemporary American federalism must include consideration of the following institutional elements of federal supremacy:

1. The president has become the strongest pillar of national power. With the withering of the federalistic Electoral College, he is carried into office by the vote of the national electorate through the action of nationwide parties. The rise of the presi-

dent to undisputed political leadership was bound to weaken the importance of the states in the political process. National politics, focusing on the presidency, completely overshadow the interest of the citizens in their own states.

2. The Senate, intended to be the citadel of states' rights reflected by the equal membership of every state—inalienable except by consent—has lost its original character as the defender of the sectional divisions. Long before the Seventeenth Amendment (1913), which brought the popular election of senators, the Senate had come under the influence of the national parties; thereafter, the parties dominated it. The protection of states' rights has become relegated to the twilight of backstage patronage and favoritism. No longer does the Senate speak for the states; it speaks the language of the nationwide parties.

3. Under the impact of industrialization and urbanization, sectionalism was deprived of its original organic quality of representing coherent socioeconomic entities different from others. The American way of life is a standardized product, placing its indelible stamp of uniformity on the entire nation irrespective of state lines and, thereby, stamping out the identity and individuality of the states. Moreover, and even more decisively, citizens are no longer loyal to their states or sections, except in some of the backwoods of the South or high up in New England. Remnants of the once flourishing state consciousness are being destroyed by the extreme mobility of a congenitally restless population.

4. The erosion of the states' sovereignty is accentuated by the increasing reliance of most of them on federal grants-in-aid without which they would be unable to maintain even their constitutionally assigned functions, let alone the services necessitated by the approximation to the welfare state. The federal government is not inclined to assist the states without attaching centralizing strings to the grants.

5. The political parties operate on a nationwide scale. Internally they are curiously tenacious in retaining their federalistic struc-

ture and are little more than loosely federated state parties. But in the national power process they function as homogeneous and concentrated machines; the interests of the states may be reflected in personnel selection but have largely disappeared in platforms and policies, which are national and not sectional, even though the voting in congress may often be colored, for re-election purposes, by the economic interests of the constituents. But this is also inherent in the representative process of the unitary state.

6. All other plural groups of the American commonwealth—business, labor, the professons, the bureaucracies—are organized and operate on a nationwide scale. The interests of the power industry are practically identical in Idaho and in Maine. At long last American federalism has caught up with the implacable facts of socioeconomic life. However large the territory of the technological state may be, it cannot be fragmented to conform to artificial state lines. A progressive nation would not tolerate territorial differentiation of public services and social justice. Economic oases and deserts cannot live side by side; a single-market economy cannot be frustrated by regional barriers or vested sectional interests.

The net result of these accumulated centralizing pressures is that American federalism has undergone a process of erosion and retrogression to the point where it can no longer set any effective limit to the political power of the national government. Supporters of the theory of dual sovereignty may still fight rear-guard actions: the Bricker amendment was to inject federalistic safeguards into the foreign-policy process, and the laboriously revived concept of "interposition" is designed to delay the encroachments of the federal power on the hallowed preserves of racial discrimination. But the original *telos* of federalism as the vertical control of political power through territorial pluralism has lost much of its significance; it restrains the federal power holders only to a limited extent.

REGIONALISM AS THE NEW FEDERALISM

A future counterweight against the progressive concentration of power in the federal government may well lie in the emergence of a rationalized regionalism. Geographically contiguous and economically affinite sections would be grouped in new territorial and quasi-political entities, New England, the Pacific Northwest, the southern Atlantic seaboard, and others. To a very minor degree the new orientation manifests itself in the compacts between adjacent states for limited purposes. But not even the dimmest outlines of this revision of traditional state lines are discernible at this time. Comparative experience indicates that there is nothing as stationary and conservative as the vested interests within established state boundaries in a federal organization. In Germany only a victorious war (1866) or a lost war and the dictation of the occupation authorities (1945) could accomplish a modicum of streamlining of the territorial status quo. In India the realignment of state boundaries was possible, with greatest difficulties, only because the personalities of the member states had not yet jelled. There is no immediate prospect of a rationalization of the territorial structure in the United States. What the economic revolution of the atomic age might accomplish in industrial and social relocation nobody can foretell.

The preceding observations concerning the realities of American federalism should not suggest that the United States would be better off as a unitary or a decentralized unitary state. Even if this were desirable, the sheer size of the country would utterly defeat it. True, the loyalty of the people to their state is waning, and the socioeconomic importance of the states has declined. Yet they remain indispensable for the conduct of the political process and have shown considerable resilience in the face of the strongest centripetal pressures. Constitutional self-determination allows much useful experimentation; the states, within their jurisdiction, serve as laboratories in legislation, administration, and scientific research. However, not all residues of states' autonomy are unmitigated blessings. They include also the electoral systems and laws; in spite of affinities, there exist forty-eight diverse techniques of federal elections. Whether the disparity of civil and criminal law, another domain of states' rights, is conducive to an effective administration of justice is arguable. Other federal organizations possess at least a minimum of uniform private law.

On the other side of the ledger are the new techniques of interfederal co-operation through which the federal government uses the state machineries for federal tasks and services benefiting the states. And, finally, the cultural life of the American people is still largely conditioned by the frame of the state and dissociated from the Union. The spirit of local self-reliance down to the last village and hamlet, traditional on the Atlantic seaboard and fostered by the early pioneer spirit in the central and western parts of the nation, has been unimpaired and even strengthened. The local district remains the civic center, and communal self-government, now confronted with increasing responsibilities, challenges, and burdens, is as vigorous and healthy as anywhere else. These are values inherent in the federal system, and its "nationalization" would be a serious loss to the nation.

Federalism outside the United States

In the mid-twentieth century the retrogression of the federal organization is a near-universal phenomenon. Exceptions lead to crisis situations that tend to confirm the rule. This conclusion is derived from a survey of state societies reorganizing themselves under new constitutions and of the recent experience of long-established federal states.

NEWLY ORGANIZED STATES

The independent states emerging after the Second World War were reluctant to resort to the federal pattern when they made their first hesitant steps along the difficult path of democratic self-government. This generalization may seem disproved by the fact that India, Pakistan, and Burma, in their new constitutions, explicitly profess federalism. The hybrid and semantic character of this federalism is revealed, however, by the factual situation. In India the sheer size of the territory, a subcontinent, and the immense diversity of cultural, religious, linguistic, economic, and technological standards allowed no other choice but a pluralist pattern. Moreover, the Indians had substantial experience in territorial pluralism; while the constitution of 1919 had been merely British tutelary rule with a devolution of certain functions to the territorial entities, the Government of India Act of 1935 (25 & 26 Geo. V, c. 42) had to be quasi-federal because of the co-existence of states and provinces. The constitution of 1950, likewise, is, at most, quasi-federal in concept, and certainly not more in actual operation. The states are deprived of constitutional autonomy in selecting their pattern of government, cabinet government being prescribed uniformly by the federal constitution. The Seventh Schedule contains three lists of jurisdictions. The first enumerates no fewer than ninety-seven matters of exclusive federal jurisdiction—far more encompassing than is usual in other federal organizations; the second, sixty-six under exclusive jurisdiction of the sttaes; and the third, with forty-seven headings, matters of concurrent jurisdiction. But in the latter category the principle prevails that federal legislation has precedence over those of the states, except in the unlikely eventuality that the president will permit a state law conflicting with federal regulation to remain in force (Art. 254). No wonder there are serious doubts as to whether India is an authentic federal state.[5]

The constitution of Pakistan (1956), enacted after long years of labor, likewise establishes a federal state (Art. 1), composed of the provinces of West and East Pakistan (Bengal). The solution was geographically imposed, since the two parts are separated by the land mass of India. The interfederal organization (Arts. 105–11) follows rather closely the Indian precedent, with three lists pertaining to federal, concurrent, and provincial jurisdictions and, again, with the clause guaranteeing federal priority in the field of concurrent legislation (Art. 110). The hybrid character of the federal organization derives also from the fact that only two territorial units participate in it.

Burma's federal structure is strictly nominal and without foreseeable prospect of becoming normative. As yet the central government has proved incapable of effectively controlling the entire territory, much of which remains in the hands of more or less autonomous governments in rebellion against the centralized rule of Rangoon.

For the sake of completeness, a number of interterritorial arrangements in colonial environments should be mentioned, all of them associations of territories established for utilitarian and political reasons rather than motivated by a genuine desire for federalization: Eritrea, by a decision of the United Nations (1950), is to be federated, after a transitional period, with Abyssinia. The pseudo-federalism in the Kingdom of Libia, tying together the territories of Tripolitania, the Cirenaica, and the Fezzan, is devoid of reality.[6] Three associations were established in the British empire: the Central Africa Federation between the two Rhodesias and Nyasaland in 1953, the British Caribbean Federation in 1956, and the Malayan Federation in 1957. Plans are under way to federate the Gold Coast, a new member of the Commonwealth (1957), with neighboring British Togoland, heretofore a trust territory.

A cantonal solution on the Swiss model is often advocated for older or new states with a mixed population whose component parts refuse to come under the control of other ethnic groups. It was proposed in vain for Czechoslovakia before the Nazis temporarily took over the state, in Palestine before the establishment of an independent state of Israel, and in Kenya. It is also under discussion in Algeria. In every case it is too artificial and provisional a scheme to stand up against the integral nationalism of the individual ethnic groups.

None of the score of other newly created states preferred the federal to the unitary organization. Even Indonesia, where the geographical situation of separated islands with indigenous cultural traditions invited federalization, after an initial attempt at it, turned to the unitary form.[7]

FEDERAL EXPERIMENTS IN
UNITARY STATES

The ill-starred Spanish constitution of 1931 explicitly rejected the federal pattern (Art. 13) but set forth plans for regional autonomy (Art. 12).[8] These did not materialize except faintly in Catalonia (autonomy statute of 1932) and disappeared completely under Franco.

A bolder strategy of regional autonomy is envisaged in the Italian constitution of 1947 (Arts. 114 ff.).[9] It was planned to create five regions with special status—Sicily, Sardinia, Trentino–Alto Adige, Valle d'Aosta, and Friuli–Venezia Giulia—and fourteen regions with ordinary status, comprising all other provinces of the Italian mainland. All regions were to be equipped with their own parliaments and governments in charge of a substantial measure of self-government under continued supervision by Rome.

The special status was intended to preserve local traditions and satisfy autonomy aspirations in the five specified regions. To date only four of them have been established. In Sicily regional autonomy was granted after the collapse of the fascist regime to counter a strong separatist movement. Similar motivations prevailed in the French-speaking Valley of Aosta, where it was granted to prevent union with France. In Sardinia, always a stepchild, it was intended to stimulate local enterprise. In the Alto Adige—the former South Tirol—where a majority tenaciously adhere to the German language and customs, regional self-government was to compensate for the desired *Anschluss* to Austria, frustrated by the peace treaty which, however, guaranteed local autonomy. Since the former South Tirol was joined with the wholly Italian district of the Trentino to form a single region, the German-speaking population remained a minority whose desires for genuine self-government were not fulfilled.

Of the special-status regions, only Sicily was able to develop a reasonable degree of local autonomy. For example, the control of natural resources assigned to the region permitted private enterprise to exploit the oil deposits, while on the mainland they are owned and managed by the state. In neither case is regionalism more than administrative decentralization; centralized control by Rome continues through the prefects. Except in South Tirol, no local parties have emerged, an indispensable prerequisite for genuine self-government; the existing parties are merely branches of the national organizations. Moreover, neither the special-status region of Friuli–Venezia Giulia nor a single one of the ordinary status regions has been established, and the injunction of the constitution (Transitional Provisions VIII) to the effect that the regions had to be set up within a year was permitted to lapse.[10]

THE DECLINE OF ESTABLISHED FEDERALISM

The recent experience with federalism in states where it is firmly established is no less indicative of the decline of the federal solution than the failure of the new and the traditionally unitary states to adopt the federal organization.

Germany.—To study federalism in its ultimate sophistication, one has to turn to Germany, living with it for centuries. In the Bismarckian Reich genuine federalism was thwarted by the hegemonial position of Prussia. Not only did she possess two-thirds of the territory and population of the entire Reich; the king of Prussia was the constitutional incumbent of the office of the emperor, and the Prussian minister-president was ex officio Reich chancellor. By the Prussian veto in the Federal Council any constitutional amendment could be prevented. The lip service paid in the constitution notwithstanding, the net result of hybrid federalism was the progressive Prussianization of the Reich. Weimar accelerated the irresistible trend toward a unitary state. Industrialization and urbanization undermined the states' rights elements. The financial centralization under the reform of Erzberger (1919) became the foremost vehicle of centralization. Even the constitutional organ representing the *Länder*, the Federal Council, turned out to be, against expectations, an instrument of federal administration.

The Bonn constitution, on the other hand, is strong in pretensions of *Land* autonomy, spurred by the rather naïve assumption of the American occupation authorities that federalism is a guaranty of democracy and centralization an invitation to authoritarian government. The center of states' rights is the Federal Council (Bundesrat). Its role in the legislative process is twofold. The Basic Law distinguishes two categories of bills. In one are those for which the concurrence (*Zustimmung*) of the Federal Council is indispensable because they pertain to the federal structure affecting in one way or the other the status and interests of the *Länder;* references to such bills are strewn all over the constitution.[11] In these cases the veto of the Federal Council is absolute. In the other category are all other bills—the vast majority. For these the Federal Council is granted merely a suspensive veto (*Einspruch*). The council's objection, if carried by a simple majority, can be overridden by a simple majority of the Bundestag. If the objection is adopted by a two-thirds majority, the final passage of the bill by the Bundestag likewise requires a two-thirds majority (Arts. 77 and 78). Practically the objection can be effective only if the opposing parties in the Federal Council, composed of appointed representatives acting under the instructions of party-controlled *Land* governments, find enough support among their party friends in the lower house. The protection of the states' rights, thus, is subject to, and often submerged by, the dynamism of the nationwide parties. Nonetheless, the Federal Council is considerably stronger than its counterpart under Weimar.

Conscious that who pays the piper calls the tune, the Bonn constitution sought the reinforcement of the *Länder* rights in a novel system of distributing the revenues. Under Weimar the taxes with the greatest yield—personal and corporative income and property levies, estate, excise, and communication taxes—were assigned to the federal government, which then was obligated to share them with the *Länder* through grants-in-aid. The present, very complex and still provisional, regulation of interfederal finances differs. It involves two different aspects that are spoken of as the vertical and the horizontal "financial compromise" (*Finanzausgleich*). The vertical distribution of revenue consists in the assignment, by the constitution itself, of certain classes of taxes and other revenues excluively to the *Länder*, of others exclusively to the federal government, and of others again to joint or concurrent utilization. As in all industrialized states, the most important sources of revenue are the income and corporation taxes. Of these, under the legislation of 1955,[12] two-thirds are assigned to the *Länder* and one-third to the federal government. On March 31, 1957, the percentage was slightly increased in favor of the latter, and every two years thereafter a new distribution is to be enacted by ordinary statute. The horizontal arrangement, enacted likewise in 1955,[13] serves for the equalization of burden between the "rich" and the "poor" *Länder*. Under this share-the-wealth arrangement the rich states must pay an agreed percentage of their income into an equalization fund for the benefit of their poorer sisters. Direct grants-in-aid by the federal government, however, are not excluded. The net result of this complex scheme will be, in the opinion of competent observers, that the tug-of-war under way between the rich and the poor *Länder*, on the one hand, and between them all and the federal government, on the other, will be intensified. The winner in the competition for the pocketbook will be none other than the central state. If and when a split Germany is united, the liquidation of the communist heritage and the betterment of living standards in East Germany necessarily will be the burden of the central state. There are additional tendencies deflating the protestations for states' rights of the ambitious *Länder* constitutions and the Bonn instrument. The causes are psychological rather than constitutional. Economic reconstruction of West Germany, since 1948 rising phoenix-like from the devastation of the war, was accomplished by national legislation even though it was carried out by local initiative. The *Länder* have shown little eagerness to press their legislative prerogatives at the expense of the Bund and are satisfied with attending to the *Land* administration of federal legislation. Their statute books are correspondingly sterile unless one considers a Bavarian law against "reckless skiing" a major accomplishment. With Prussia's disappearance as a geographical and political entity—which may well be temporary only—particularism, once so strong in southern and western Germany against the colossus of the north, has lost its emotional target. Even the Bavarians, congenitally the most vocal among the German tribes in anti-Reich sentiment, no longer kick against the federal prick. Moreover, the redrawing of the interstate boundaries in the wake of the lost war and the occupation and the emergence of new territorial units could not fail to de-emphasize traditional state loyalties. Inveterate *Land* egotism has been overridden by the hard facts of economic life. As elsewhere, the plural groups are nationwide, as are the problems that beset the people. Local parties have almost disappeared. In short, the German people indulge in less sectional divisions and live together more harmoniously than ever before. This is all to the good, but federalism foots the bill.

Austria.—The curious situation in Austria merits a brief comment. Federalism under the constitution of 1920, restored after the war, never amounted to much because of the narrow range of provincial autonomy. Under the coalition government of the Christian People's party and the Socialists, the federal contours have become blurred. Instead of power shared vertically between the federal and the provincial entities, the two parties divide the booty horizontally on both levels. Interfederal rivalries are adjusted to the bipartisan exploitation of the spoils and patronage.

Switzerland.—Even in Switzerland, venerable bastion of living federalism, the federal jurisdiction has grown consistently at the expense of the cantons for a generation and more. Federal control over natural resources, national defense, communications and transportation, the multitude of government regulations of the economic process, and social legislation in line with the trend toward the welfare state could not fail to hollow out cantonal self-government. Centralization was accomplished by federal implied powers as well as by constitutional amendment, ratified by the majority of the people and of the cantons. The host of articles added to the text of the constitution of 1874 reveals the rapid expansion of federal powers. To this trend the enlightened Swiss electorate offered little resistance. Two out of three proposals for constitutional amendments passed by the legislature were accepted by the electorate and the cantons; the rate of rejections of popularly initiated amendments is much higher. But the crux of any federal system, the federal income tax, still awaits a permanent solution. The original arrangement of the fiscal supremacy of the cantons has been superseded, by the force of economic circumstances, by a fiscal system that alternates between outright constitutional illegality and emergency measures of doubtful legality, because the electorate is still unwilling to grant the federal government sufficient direct taxation, which alone would enable the government to cope with the federal tasks. The improvisation of fiscal conduct, in the words of a competent observer, "is a fixture of Swiss public life in the same way as cabinet instability has become a feature of French public life."[14]

Latin America.—Organized as federal states are also some of the major nations in Latin America—Argentina, Brazil, Mexico, and, at least on paper, Venezuela. However, the *ambiente* was not auspicious for the evolution of genuine federalism for two reasons: the natural hegemonial position of certain member units and federal intervention. In Argentina and Brazil a single-member unit, Buenos Aires and São Paulo, respectively, occupies the predominant position by its economic strength and population. In all states the federal government is constitutionally authorized to intervene, allegedly for the maintenance of constitutional processes and "the republican form of government," at its discretion and without judicial control, in the domestic affairs of the member units. Intervention allows the substitution of the fiat of the federal government for the autonomy of the states; it often replaces what in other federal organizations is the peaceful compromise of conflicting interests by the judicial process. The practice of federal intervention, constantly resorted to and often for the flimsiest of reasons, has rendered Latin American federalism wholly fictitious and largely cancels out the reciprocal verticalism of the federal structure.[15]

Canada and Australia.—Two federal organizations remain in which the interfederal structure has successfully withstood the near-universal trend toward centralization; these are Canada and Australia. Under the constitution of the Dominion of Canada (British North America Act of 1867), the protection of states' rights was carried to such an extreme that only the parliament of the United Kingdom, and no authority in Canada itself, can amend the constitution. Of the twelve amendments passed to date, only that of 1940, on federal unemployment insurance, concerned the distribution of functions between the Dominion and the provinces.[16] The danger to the maintenance of genuine federalism lies in the fact that the British parliament acts on the request of the Dominion parliament without being bound, by convention or otherwise, to consult the provinces. At the present time it is doubtful whether Westminster would still amend the British North America Act at the request of the Dominion parliament alone or whether it would require the consent of the provinces. Actually no one knows precisely who has the power to amend the constitution. However, centralization failed to develop because of the unbreakable opposition of the linguistically and ethnically coherent minority in Catholic Quebec. As yet the situation has not seriously impeded the national economy, partly because Canada is in a frontier situation similar to that of the United States in the nineteenth century and partly because Quebec prefers the maintenance of its traditional aloofness to participation in the technological progress of the other provinces.

But Australia remains the real island of intransigent states' rights. It is the only federal state from which a member unit recently wished to secede (Western Australia, 1935) but failed. Under the constitution of 1900 the Commonwealth government had been assigned jurisdictions adequate to cope with the economic needs of a federation of primarily agrarian states. During the last decades they proved insufficient for the exigencies of increasing industrialization. New South Wales and Victoria, in which lie the greatest population concentrations, are adamantly opposed to any substantial extension of federal powers. Between 1901 and 1955, of twelve constitutional amendments submitted, only four were supported by the constitutionally required majority (sec. 128) of the electorate and the states. Of these amendments, the transfer of the bulk of social services to the Commonwealth was the most important. Because of the rejection of a comprehensive reform program of the Labor government by the voters (1944), Australia had to face economic reconstruction after the war with inadequate federal powers. The Commonwealth, for example, cannot stop the steadily rising inflation by uniform legislation on prices, wages, and instalment buying, control capital investment, or outlaw communism.[17] Competent observers agree that, for the future prosperity of the Australian continent, the constitutional machinery must be overhauled to permit uniform direction of the Commonwealth socioeconomic policies. For the time being, with the Liberal-Country party in firm control and Labor on the downgrade, there is little prospect of it, unless a depression forces the issue.

The foregoing observations on the near-universal decline of the federal organization are not meant to minimize the values local self-government retains and will retain for a healthy state society, particularly on the municipal level. It certainly cannot be denied that local autonomy frequently does little more than provide the home politicians with spoils and patronage. But federalism tends to preserve and strengthen the cultural identity of a territorial group and, on a higher, spiritual level, it constitutes an indispensable antidote against standardization in a world increasingly headed toward uniformity and conformity. In the Swiss cantons local customs and loyalty are as strong and robust as ever. In certain other areas likewise—in southern and western Germany, in Quebec, in a few of the American states—federalism has helped to preserve a considerable degree of territorial cultural identity. But even on the most sacrosanct domain of local autonomy, education, the dam against the federal flood is about to break, if only because the training of scientists has become too heavy a burden to be carried by the states. What the industrial revolution of the atomic age will do to federalism remains to be seen. The realistic observer of its present stage is driven to the conclusion that, as an institutionalization of powers vertically shared, federalism, after a short life-span of hardly two centuries, is becoming a victim of the technological age. It has little chance of ultimately escaping the centralization of the state Leviathan.

Federalism and Autocracy

Federalism, an application of the principle of shared power, is incompatible with autocracy, signifying concentrated power. The single power holder—an individual person, an assembly, a committee, a junta, or a party—cannot tolerate areas of autonomy not accessible to its control, because they may serve as potential nuclei of opposition to the autocratic exercise of political power. This is fully confirmed by the history of autocracy. The first task Hitler undertook upon his seizure of power was to destroy federalism. After the initial stage in which the *Länder* were politically co-ordinated (*Gleichschaltung*) and placed under the control of a Reich regent responsible to the "Führer" alone, their autonomy was abolished altogether and they served merely as the territorial subdivisions of a completely unitary Reich under uniform central-ization. Vargas in Brazil, Perón in Argentina, and the dictatorial *dei minorum gentium* in other federal states of Latin America re-mained faithful to the pattern. In Spain Franco has eradicated all vestiges of provincial autonomy.

Federalism in the communist orbit is no exception to the rule. During Stalinism the U.S.S.R. was federal only in name. If theo-retically recognized, national self-determination of the member units had to be subordinated to proletarian interests. The leveling impact of technological materialism made short shrift of the mul-tinational diversity of the immense Soviet empire. The single party dominates the union republics through their central committees and the communist government apparatus, and the territorial party organization in turn is subservient to the central party agen-cies in Moscow. As an impediment to a uniform direction of the national economy, genuine federalism could not be tolerated. Political centralization, economic equalization, and cultural con-cordance, according to a competent student,[18] are the characteris-tics of what the Soviets understand by federalism. Whether the liberalization process under way will extend to relaxing the mono-lithism of centralized control and permit a larger degree of eco-nomic and cultural autonomy of the member units within the U.S.S.R., as foreshadowed by Khrushchev in his address to the Supreme Soviet in May, 1957, remains to be seen. After a genera-tion of Marxist indoctrination, it may even be considered unde-sirable by the people.

Communist China, where the extension of the territory and the diversity of the population would invite a federal structure, is rigidly centralized and directed by the Peiping central bureaucracy, consonant with the communist program of nationwide economic planning and industrialization. Of the Soviet satellite states, none except East Germany and Yugoslavia had any federal tradition whatsoever. Characteristically, the leveling-down of federalism inherent in the communist system did not spare the German Democratic Republic. Under the constitution of 1949 it consisted of five *Länder* with their own governments and legislatures. By the legislation of 1952[19] they were replaced, without being formally abolished, by fourteen districts whose administrative organs, the councils, are institutions of a centralized and unitary state.

The only possible exception to the rule that federalism does not fit into autocracy is offered by Yugoslavia: after the rigid centralization under the constitution of 1946, the new instrument of 1953 seems to have veered toward a larger degree of territorial flexibility. In the terms of the constitution, Yugoslavia is a Federal People's Republic (Art. 1). The member units composing it are organizationally brought together in the Council of Nationalities (Arts. 45 ff.). This is composed of those deputies of the legislature (the Federal Council) who were delegated to the Federal Council by the legislatures of the several member republics from among their own members (Art. 25). These deputies assemble as the Council of Nationalities only when legislation affects the constitutionally determined interfederal relations (Art. 46). Reliable information on the operation of this arrangement is still lacking. But, in line with the new technique of Titoism aiming at the decentralization of the executive function, it may well be assumed that such neofederalism is more than a mere paper declaration of intentions; it may also be motivated by the realization of the continued ethnical diversities of populations with a long tradition of self-government. Since Yugoslavia is in the fortunate position to pursue her own road to socialism, it appears possible that she may also evolve her own variant of controlled federalism.

Federalism and International Organization

Prima facie it may seem a curious anachronism that, at a time when intrastate federalism has entered a period of decline, the ideology of federalism is assiduously promoted in the field of interstate relations on both regional and global levels. The contradiction, however, disappears when it is realized that, in the interstate relations, the term "federalism" is a semantic *quid pro quo* for a greater desire, or need, of interstate centralization. What federalism amounts to internationally is the effort to replace the heretofore isolated sovereignties of independent states by a supranational organization in which certain functions are centrally vested, although exercised with due co-operation of the state entities. But this type of interstate federalism is not genuine, for it lacks the essential criteria of reciprocal verticalism. In any authentic federal structure the central state limits the power of the member units in the fields jurisdictionally assigned to it, just as the member units are protected against encroachments of their jurisdictional assignments on the part of the central state. In its present stage interstate federalism is centripetal, without the counterweight of centrifugal elements. Interstate federalization, therefore, may seem the reversal rather than the imitation of intrastate federalism.

Interstate federalization on the regional level has made only modest beginnings. At one time after the First World War the British considered a federal institutionalization of their empire. But, because of the strong centrifugal forces among the Dominions, they had to content themselves with the Commonwealth of independent states loosely linked by the symbolism of the common crown, and not all members of the Commonwealth have accepted even this symbolic bond. The French union, too little and too late, remained a paper concept incapable of stemming the disaffection of French territorial holdings abroad. Neither Pan-Americanism in the Organization of the American States nor even the geographical invitation to federalization of the Central American region has brought any tangible result.

The review of past and present efforts to achieve European

unification or, more accurately, a union of selected states of western Europe,[20] indicates that what is commonly called "federalism" is actually only a desire for more centralization without the vertical reciprocity between central state and member units necessary for genuine federalism. The waxing and waning efforts of the European movement during the last ten years have resulted in the Council of Europe, a consultative forum of little political significance; some limited-purpose associations without any federal ingredients; and quasi-federal organizations for equally limited purposes. The Organization for European Economic Cooperation (OEEC) is the most successful of the non-federal associations. It did more for common European interests than all others taken together. Of the quasi-federal organizations, only the European Coal and Steel Community,[21] in operation since 1952 between the six states of "little Europe" (France, Western Germany, Italy, and the three Benelux states), still in the trial stage, has even chances of permanent integration in the European economic process. The position of the Community within the structural pattern of federalism is not easy to define. It corresponds to authentic federalism in that it possesses common "supranational" organs—the High Authority, the Court, the Assembly—established by, and from among, the member states for the promotion of common interests. But the novel feature of the structure is what might be called its vertical, instead of territorial, pluralism: the decisions of the Community are binding on the individual plants and enterprises without the intermediary of the national governments, not dissimilar to the manner in which the acts of a federal government obligate directly the citizens of the member states. The project of the western European common market, agreed on by the governments in March, 1957, is still too indefinite in both its goals and the time for its realization to allow any conclusions as to its potentialities as a vehicle of genuine federalism. The joint venture in the field of atomic energy, Euratom—a limited-purpose enterprise likewise agreed on in March, 1957, by the six states—may well become the most successful pilot project of European co-operation because, in contrast to others, it has a concrete goal of attainable proportions, it is unencumbered by federal ingredients, and it is seemingly devoid of political overtones.

Political unification of western Europe within the federal frame, however, did not proceed beyond overambitious plans, although some of the elements of successful federalization do exist, such as geographical propinquity, common fear of Soviet domination, common disinclination toward American hegemony, and a common cultural heritage. Other equally relevant factors are lacking, such as common language, traditions, and, most important of all, the will to merge the state sovereignties in a supranational entity. Nonetheless, given time and continued effort, a federal union of western Europe will ultimately be accomplished.

Far less encouraging is the outlook for federalism on the global level. The concept of federalism as a system of vertical controls is wholly inapplicable to the associations of states in what are called "international organizations." In the League of Nations power was shared to the extent that the League was powerless. The United Nations Organization, based on the sovereign equality of its members and endowed, into the bargain, with the absolute veto of the five permanent members of the Security Council, proved, in its brief career of interminable deadlocks on all major power conflicts, that the maximum of shared powers does not produce the optimum of effective exercise of power. No higher sovereignty exists in which those of the member units can be merged for mutual benefits. A "world federation" and a "world government" remain strictly semantic terms of utopian visionaries, unless one realizes that genuine federalism is a vertical and reciprocal power configuration. It requires the protection of the central state from intervention of the member units as much as the immunity of the latter from transgressions of the former. Moreover, its advocates have never satisfactorily explained what a global federation could achieve that could not be achieved by mutual agreements and treaties between sovereign states, provided the will to mutual co-operation exists.

XI. Guaranties of Individual Liberties

Fundamental Rights as Restraints on Power

Of all restraints placed on the power of the state, the most effective is considered the recognition by law and the protection by observance of certain areas of individual self-determination into which the Leviathan cannot penetrate. These forbidden zones are inaccessible to all power holders—government, parliament, and even, since they are "inalienable," the electorate. These spheres of privacy within which the power addressees are immune to state intervention coincide with what has come to be known, for the last three hundred years, as the "rights of man" or the "fundamental liberties."[1] Some of these—family, marriage, religion, education—are the basic institutions of the western liberal society. Others, particularly those referring to life, personal liberty, and property, are concretized in the various constitutions into legally protected and enforcible rights of the individual. Constantly exposed, with changing environments, to variable interpretations, these fundamental guaranties have remained the solid core of the political system of constitutional democracy, which has come to consider them suprapositive principles even when they are not formulated in constitutional norms. Collectively, these fundamental liberties incarnate the dignity of man.

To the classification and delineation of these fundamental liberties a considerable effort has been devoted over the years. Some of them, for example, freedom of opinion and of association, at first unequivocal, had to be redefined and refined in the light of experience; freedom of opinion is useless unless coupled with freedom of information; freedom of association has been expanded to include political organization. Others have lost much of their previous significance, for example, free assembly, because political propaganda is conducted by the telecommunications and the press rather than by meetings.

It is customary to distinguish the freedoms attached to the person—the civil liberties in the proper sense—from economic and from political freedoms. The border lines are often fluid. To the first category may be assigned freedom from arbitrary confinement—in Anglo-Saxon tradition habeas corpus; inviolability of the domicile; freedom from unauthorized searches and seizures; privacy of correspondence and other means of human intercommunication; freedom of circulation and movement; and also the free choices stemming from the individualization of family relations. The second class of liberties embraces all that comes under the heading of economic self-determination: free pursuit of economic activity in general; choice of profession; free competition; free disposal over property and freedom of contract. Political freedoms, finally, refer to the individual's participation in the political process; the most significant of them are those pertaining to the formation of public opinion: freedom of assembly and of association and organization of group life and the right to vote and to have equal access to office. The Universal Declaration of Human Rights of the United Nations (1948) raises the right to participate in one's government (Art. 21) to the rank of a key freedom in the free society.[2]

Within the dynamism of the power process these protected areas operate as vertical controls of political power. Sheltered by these breakwaters against the action of any and all power holders, the power addressees can freely conduct their individual pursuit of happiness, provided the exercise of their rights does not conflict with those of others equally endowed with self-determination. These protected zones set the limits beyond which the power of the state may not proceed. But, conversely, they are also the staging areas within which the political action of the power addressees can be mobilized and from which it is carried forward into the political process. They are instrumental to the creation of the will of the people from below, so that it can be effective in the political process.

The recognition and the protection of fundamental liberties are the essences of the political system of constitutional democracy. They signify shared power without which it cannot function. The wider these areas and the better their protection, the less the danger of concentrated power. Their existence and observance separate the political systems of constitutional democracy from autocracy. Autocracy, based on concentrated power, cannot tolerate zones of individual autonomy, because they would interfere with the formation of the will of the state from above. As a matter of fact, the reality of individual liberties is the only reliable—indeed, the infallible—criterion that differentiates the two political systems, since the institutional apparatus of both—government, assemblies, elections, parties, bureaucracies—have become stereotyped to the point of identity. Recognition or non-recognition of fundamental guaranties are closely related to the ideological *telos* of either system. In the constitutional democracy they crystallize the supreme values of human self-realization and dignity; in autocracy they are denied legitimacy not only because they may function as foci of opposition against monolithic power but also because they could obstruct the ideology of economic planning under collectivism.

Individual Liberties in Historical Perspective

The origins of individual liberties and of constitutionalism do not coincide. Areas of private autonomy recognized by, and immune to, the state were wholly unknown to ancient constitutionalism. The concept that the citizens—let alone the mass of non-citizens—should possess rights of their own, different from their obligations to the community, was alien to the Hebrew theocracy, the Greek polis state, and the Roman republic. The Greek political philosophers and social practitioners insisted that the human personality can fulfil itself only by being integrated in, and subordinated to, the omnipotent state, and the Roman political pragmatists did not disagree. Individual claims outside the state have their roots in the Hellenistic philosophy of the Stoics (Panaetius and Cicero): the law of nature, reason, equality, and human dignity are values above and beyond the reach of the state. A second source was the religious enthusiasm of the early Christians, likewise of (Judaeo-)Hellenistic inspiration. The gospel of the self-governing individual rising above and even against the state received its baptism of fire in the resistance of the early Christians against pagan conformism. Subsequently, after the victory of the Catholic church, individualism was again submerged in the singleness of a religious order which knew well why it called itself "catholic."

Civic liberty in the modern sense made its first appearance in the antifeudal charters and the social practice of the medieval city-states in Italy and western and northern Europe; however, their complete recognition was foiled by the corporative organization of the guilds. After centuries of oblivion in a world bipolarized between Christianity and the infidels, the concept of religious self-determination re-emerged in the Protestant rebellion against the totalitarianism of the church, first in the Hussite doctrine, thereafter, most persuasively formulated by the Monarchomachs, in the right of resistance against the monopoly of the true faith. The revolutionary Protestant doctrine necessarily uncovered the root of secular individualism when it claimed the right of resistance against unlawful political authority.[3] However, it was the Puritan rebellion against the religious despotism of the Stuarts that, nurtured by the tradition of common law, carried religious self-determination into the political realm and to its epochal triumph in the statutory formulations of individual liberties in the Glorious Revolution.[4]

From then on the two roots of constitutionalism and individual liberties were united to grow the mighty tree of the modern constitutional-democratic state. To have perfected their union is the immortal merit of the political theory of the Enlightenment. Rationalizing the concepts of natural law and the social contract, it supplied the philosophical justification for the rising ascendancy of the middle classes. For Locke, witness of their victory in alliance with the Whig aristocracy, the accent of individual rights was on property. In contrast, Rousseau raised liberty, created and guaranteed by the general will, to the supreme value. Constantly engaged in trying to resolve the antimony between society and individuals, he found no place for individual liberties in his totalitarian system of the general will, and he seems wholly oblivious that, if Hobbes's omnipotent Leviathan were replaced by the no less despotic general will which brooks no opposition, liberty would suffer its final destruction. The pragmatic Montesquieu built the concept of liberty into the process of political power itself* by the technique of the "separation of powers": liberty is safe only if the several power holders, to whom the state functions are assigned separately, restrain themselves mutually and reciprocally. Again, there is no hint of individual liberties recognized by, and immune to, the state. But Locke's credo found its lasting incarnation in the great documents of the American Revolution: the Declaration of Independence and the bills of rights of the constitutions of the American states and of the federal Union. The concepts of Montesquieu and Rousseau were imbedded in the Declaration of the Rights of Man in France. Says its Article 16: "Toute société dans laquelle la garantie des droits n'est pas assurée, ni la séparation des pouvoirs déterminée, n'a point de constitution."

Henceforward, down to our day, fundamental guaranties became wedded to the constitutional-democratic state and imbue the constitutions of the nineteenth and twentieth centuries with the liberal-democratic ideology. The classical triad of individual liber-

* See above, pp. 34 ff.

ties admirably served the spiritual beliefs and economic needs of the bourgeois middle classes, firmly in the seat of power at the start of the industrial revolution. Religious freedom corresponded to the desire of the autonomous individual to be free from clerical regimentation and compulsion of the conscience. The sanctification of the right of property and the freedom of contract justified the economic order of the laissez faire society, protecting it against state intervention, whether mercantilist or collectivist. Political liberty, finally, in all its time-conditioned manifestations, proved its usefulness against the lingering feudal privileges and royal prerogatives as well as in the defense against any socialist or ochlocratic competitors in political power. The classical catalogue of civil liberties ideally fitted and benefited the aspirations of the self-confident, socially and intellectually homogeneous ruling class. An environment-conditioned social product, the catalogue of individual rights claimed, in the magisterial paraphrase of John Stuart Mill, universal validity as the decalogue of the good society. Subsequently, no constitution could aspire to be a real constitution unless it allied with the frame of government the bill of classical liberties. Constitutional government became identified with the acceptance, by power holders and power addressees alike, of the classical register. Its global sweep was fittingly climaxed by the Universal Declaration of Human Rights by the United Nation (1948).

The Challenges to Individual Liberties

Yet with the transfer of constitutionalism, indigenous in the milieu of western bourgeois capitalism, to states without the intellectual traditions of the West and its ambitious middle classes, the classical catalogue of fundamental rights underwent a significant erosion, paralleling the retrogression of federalism, that other instrumentality of the vertical control of the power process. It is not only autocratic regimes that deny recognition to areas inaccessible to the power holders as incompatible with the concentrated exercise of political power. In the constitutional-democratic state, likewise, grave conflicts have arisen between man's urge for self-realization and the imperatives of collective existence. The conflict between liberty and security is sharpened by the deep ideological cleavages of a bipolarized world.

The attack against the classical fundamental rights moves forward on four fronts: (1) they are subject to abridgment by legislation; (2) they are narrowed by the emergence of social and economic rights; (3) they are not respected in autocratic and authoritarian regimes; and (4) they suffer in the current conflict between liberty and security in a bipolarized world. The following discussion is confined to the bare outlines of these issues.

INDIVIDUAL LIBERTIES AND RESTRICTIVE LEGISLATION

In spite of the near-universal acceptance of the classical fundamental liberties since the great revolutions of the eighteenth century, their recognition and observance greatly vary in the practice of the different states. Much, indeed everything, depends on the technique of their formulation in the constitution, that is, whether they are absolutely inviolable or only allowed "within the law." The problem does not arise in Great Britain, where there is no written constitution. The fundamental guaranties are rooted in the convictions of the common law and enforced by the courts, subject only to such legislative restrictions as public order in peacetime or emergency situations may require. A similar situation prevails in France of the Third and Fourth republics, where the bill of rights is considered superconstitutional law. In the United States, on the other hand, individual liberties, whether stipulated in the bill of rights proper or proclaimed in other places within the frame of government, are guaranteed unconditionally. The First Amendment is categorical: "Congress shall make no law . . . abridging the freedom of speech or of the press. . . ." No exceptions or reservations are added. Yet, when public order or national security would require limitations in their exercise, the Supreme Court strikes the balance between the absolutes of individual freedoms and the congressional legislation limiting them.[5] A well-traveled avenue for legalizing restrictive legislation is the "clear and present danger" formula elaborated by Justice Holmes[6] and now even written by congress into the legislation itself, for example, in the McCarran Internal Security Act of 1950 (64 Stat. 987).

In the majority of European and other constitutions, however, individual liberties are constitutionally guaranteed in form rather than in substance. They are hedged in by limiting clauses in that they may be exercised only "within the limits of the general laws" or that exceptions are permissible "by statute." The practice appeared as early as the French Declaration of Rights, for which the statute was the Cartesian rationalization of the general will. Subsequently—the influential Belgian *charte* of 1831 was a notable exception—the technique proved convenient for monarchical regimes forced to make concessions to the democratic trend, and it retained its usefulness for all states in need of administering democracy in well-measured doses. As a result, while the shingle of inviolability was nailed to the façade, the legislator and, with his authorization, the censor and the police could enter the protected zones through the back door. Judicial review (where existing) offered no remedy because the constitution itself legalized the legislative inroads. The protection of fundamental liberties, thus, depended on the good will and self-restraint of the power holders, a weak protection indeed. Even states otherwise fully conforming to the rule of law were satisfied with such more or less hybrid guaranties. Weimar Germany is an outstanding illustration.

Learning from bitter experience, the Bonn Basic Law takes great pains to narrow the range within which the legislator may interfere with the untrammeled exercise of fundamental freedoms, without, however, being able to cut itself loose from the tradition. A praiseworthy attempt is made to square the circle by various devices: the government can no longer suspend the fundamental rights in emergency situations; specified human rights are absolutely untouchable even by constitutional amendment (Art. 79, sec. 3); any statute which abridges individual rights must explicitly refer to the article of the constitution affected by it (Art. 19, sec. 1); in no case can legislation infringe upon the essential core (*Wesenskern*) of an individual liberty (Art. 19, sec. 2).[7] These regulations certainly are an improvement over Weimar. Whether they will stand up in times of stress remains to be seen. The only safety of fundamental liberties lies in the spirit of the people and not of the laws.

THE SOCIAL, ECONOMIC, AND CULTURAL RIGHTS

The triad of human freedoms of classical liberalism, protecting the individual self-determination against state intervention, served the interests of the bourgeois middle classes of early capitalism. With increasing industrialization and urbanization its monopoly of political power was challenged by collectivist and antiliberal ideologies, Marxian socialism foremost among them. The laboring masses attacked liberal capitalism on two fronts: the industrial proletariat fought for, and ultimately obtained, equality of political rights through the suffrage, believed to be the means by which its legitimate claim to a share in political power could be fulfilled. On the other hand—and this is the lasting merit of Marxism—the underprivileged masses were no longer content with the formalism of liberty and equality that the liberal constitutions and their bills of rights offered them. To them they were mere abstractions, because the reality of the power process was dominated by the plutocratic ruling classes. The formal frames had to be filled with the substance of public services granting them a minimum of economic security and social justice. The working masses of the capitalist societies, exposed to the market fluctuations of supply and demand and their inevitable booms and busts, demanded economic security to make the most of political rights. The economically weak had to be protected against the economically strong. Public services and social legislation were needed to protect them against misery and want. The scourge of unemployment had to be eliminated. Moreover, organized plural groups—labor unions, professional associations—for which there was no room within the cadres of liberal fundamentalism, claimed their recognition as participants in the socioeconomic process.

Yielding to mounting pressure and anxious to forestall a violent explosion, free-enterprise capitalism was compelled to grant, in instalments, the demands of the masses for economic betterment and social justice. The result of the long-drawn struggle is, in the mid-twentieth century, the emergence, or rather the re-emergence, of the state as the regulating, managing, directing, controlling, and supervising agency of socioeconomic life. In all industrialized state societies, the social service or welfare state or approximations to it were established.

In this momentous transformation state control over the socioeconomic process assumes proportions closely resembling, and even surpassing, the role it played in mercantilism. Public authority was compelled to maximize its intervention in the private life of its citizens, instead of minimizing it as under classical laissez faire capitalism. The more equitable distribution of wealth profoundly influenced the range and importance of the classical individual liberties. Government intervention in the economic process and state regulation of business limited freedom of contract* and even the holiest of holies of classical liberalism, the autonomous exercise of property rights. In the formulation of the Weimar constitution (Art. 153, sec. 3) "property is obligation. Its use should at the same time serve the commonweal." Consequently, if property is guaranteed by the constitution, "its content and its limits are determined by the laws." The main pillar in the temple of classical liberalism has crumbled. But the new concept of the social control

---

* For the even more decisive restrictions on the freedom of contract by the plural groups see below, pp. 360 ff.

of life in the interest of the entire community penetrated also into other assiduously protected areas of individual self-determination. One remembers the momentous experiment of the United States to limit, in the prohibition amendment (XVIII), the sacred right of the individual to get drunk. But one also remembers that American individualism won out over social control.

If for classical individualism the state was the enemy against whom the protected zones of private autonomy were to be defended, under the new philosophy the state has turned into the friend. The state must satisfy the collective needs of the community. Collectivism is no longer the monopoly of the socialist doctrine; it is no longer incompatible with individualism; both collectivism and individualism are living side by side and often peacefully in modern society. This change could be accomplished only at the expense of the sacrosanctity of individual liberties. Under the impact of the technological mass society, another vertical control of the power process and a barrier to the Leviathan is being dismantled.

The visible result of this process is the concretion of the demands for economic security and social justice in the form of social and economic rights.[8] These new "rights" differ from those in the older liberal catalogue. They are not intended to guarantee freedoms *from* the state and protection *against* the state, but they are claims of the individual or the collective group *on* the state. The state must act to fulfil these rights. They are not rights in the legal sense, because they cannot be enforced against the state by judicial process. They depend on the antecedent action of the state to institutionalize them.

As formulated postulates socioeconomic rights are not entirely new; some of them, such as the right to work, found their place in the French constitutions of 1793 and 1848. But only in this century, after the First and even more after the Second World War, did they become the standard equipment of constitutionalism. They were first proclaimed in the constitution of Mexico in 1917, which went the whole length of the road to implement them by nationalizing the natural resources and by establishing, at least on paper, an all-round repertory of social obligations of the state toward the individuals. They were popularized by the Weimar constitution, still a curious blend of modern collectivism and classical liberalism. Among them are the right to work and to social assistance in the case of unemployment; minimum wages and maximum hours of work; paid vacations and time for leisure; the right to unionize; the right to social betterment by adequate housing and access to education, including higher education for everyone; and the host of what is known as social legislation, including protection against sickness, care for the aged, maternity care, and benefits for families with many children. All these have become the familiar implementation of the welfare state. Of the recent constitutions, possibly the most encompassing catalogue of social and economic rights is found in that of Italy of 1948 (Arts. 29–47). At their zenith of universal recognition the classical fundamental liberties have encountered a competitor, of tremendous emotional appeal to the masses, whose very existence is bound to undermine and restrict them.

In technologically advanced state societies much of the new philosophy of social and economic rights has been translated into positive legislation. Contrariwise, in technologically underdeveloped countries they remain, and will remain for a long time to come, strictly nominal blueprints to be lived up to by the state society if and when socioeconomic conditions permit. But they are stimuli for the power holders and hopes for the power addressees.

INDIVIDUAL LIBERTIES
AND AUTOCRACY

Since the First World War and with acceleration after the Second, vast territories containing more than one-third of the world's population have come to live under autocracy. However, the two principal variants of contemporary autocracy, fascism and communism, differ in their attitudes toward fundamental liberties. The ideology of the fascist regime—if its opportunistic justification of naked power can be dignified by this term—was elitist, antiliberal, and anti-intellectual. Individual liberties were ruthlessly suppressed to prevent any challenge to the power monopoly of the ruling clique. An undiluted political tyranny could not but close the power circuit lest it fall from power.[9] Its single party was the straight negation of all political liberty. But in fairness it has to be admitted that some of the fascist regimes tried their ineffective best to grant the laboring masses social benefits, if for no other reason than to broaden the basis of their power.

The attitude of Marxism in the U.S.S.R. and the so-called "People's Democracies" toward fundamental liberties is altogether different. First, all constitutions in the Soviet orbit contain elaborate statements on fundamental rights of the citizens, characteristically coupled with provisions concerning their duties toward the state and the community. Second, civil liberties in the classical sense, which the constitution of the U.S.S.R. merely summarizes (Art. 123), are overshadowed by the new social and economic rights; these are spelled out in great detail and implemented, in every case, by statements of what the state will undertake to secure them. Third, the guaranty of the civil rights proper—freedom of press, speech, and assembly—is hedged in by the rubber clause that they are guaranteed "in conformity with the interests of the working class" and "in order to strengthen the socialist system," a restriction just as convenient for state intervention as the guaranty "within the laws" in the West. The technique of conditional guaranty is slavishly copied by most satellite constitutions (e.g., Art. 15 of the Hungarian constitution of 1949). Finally, to secure the civil liberties, the state places at the disposal of the working people and their organizations "the materials requisite for the exercise of these rights." Their enjoyment, thus, is denied to other social groups which the Communist party, as the spearhead of the state ideology, wishes to exclude from the power process. In addition, the range of individual self-determination is severely curtailed by the economic order in a managed economy where state capitalism replaces western laissez faire capitalism.

Moreover, the ideological foundation and functional purpose of classical fundamentalism underwent a far-reaching transformation in the Marxian society.[10] The Russian Revolution preaches and practices the primacy of the collectivity over the individual. Instead of being "inalienable" in human nature, rights and liberties are created and granted by the socialist order and interpreted as obligations of the state toward the laboring masses. Their extent and exercise are determined in conformity with the interests of the Communist party. The secret police see to it that no opposition against the regime develops, even though administrative criticism is tolerated and even encouraged. Political rights of the suffrage are converted into compulsory mass participation in the political process directed by the party hierarchy. Exposed to the institutionalized violence, at least prior to the de-Stalinization process, all civil liberties inscribed in the constitutions remain strictly semantic. Least affected, perhaps, is religious self-determination. Religious intolerance is also found, however, in authoritarian regimes of the West; for example, hostility existed against Protestantism in Colombia, and it is still rampant in Spain.

Measured by western standards, classical liberties are completely negated in the Soviet orbit. It should be borne in mind, however, that Russia lacks any tradition of freedom; that the rigidly regimented economy has accorded the masses more security and higher living standards than their fathers possessed; and that equal chances of self-advancement and social prestige may compensate them for the absence of liberties in the western sense. Whether their negation will remain a permanent feature of the Soviet society cannot now be surmised.

THE CRISIS OF INDIVIDUAL LIBERTIES
IN CONSTITUTIONAL DEMOCRACY

The basic dilemma.—Another chapter of the distressing story of fundamental guaranties in our time is being written in the constitutional democracies proper. Invented by their prophets, the totalitarian ideologies of our time have grown into veritable political religions. The organized movements promoting them are masterminded by professionals reared in the climate of the technological mass society and trained in the science of propaganda dissemination. To be effective, the new gospel must cater to the masses and be carried into power by the masses. Like all religions, the totalitarian creed by nature is missionary, transnational, and world wide. Impelled by quasi-religious enthusiasms, both fascism and communism are destined to spread to other nations. Both movements utilize identical techniques for the ultimate conquest of power. If frontal attack by violence against the constitutional-democratic order is not immediately feasible, they infiltrate into its state machinery and penetrate into its social fabric to prepare for the "legal" seizure of power when the target has been sufficiently undermined and subverted. To create the mass basis for the final assault, the legitimate techniques of constitutional democracy—propaganda, party organization, elections—are brought into action. The secret of the success of totalitarianism is that it attempts to beat democracy at its own game. As long as western society was agreed on the fundamentals of its existence, the power process could be conducted by peaceful competition among the rivaling social forces in the open power circuit of ideologies. Now the rules of the game have fundamentally changed: the totalitarian aggressors are prepared to avail themselves of the democratic instrumentalities only until they have seized power; thereafter the open power circuit will be permanently closed.

In trying to meet the totalitarian challenge to its own values and its very existence, the constitutional-democratic state finds itself at the horns of the gravest dilemma since its inception. If it resolves to fight fire with fire and to deny the totalitarian invaders the use of the democratic liberties for the ultimate destruction of all liberty, it runs counter to the very tenets of liberty and equality on which it is predicated. If it maintains the democratic fundamentals for the benefit of its sworn enemies, it courts disaster.

The defense of the democratic state.—With the *vestigia terrent* of the meek surrender of Italy and Weimar to totalitarianism, democracy in self-defense at long last chose to become militant. On the battlefield, however, remained the fundamental liberties. Beginning in the thirties many democratic states placed on their statute books an extensive array of legislative restrictions known as legislation for the defense of the state, directed against persons and groups proclaiming and practicing the totalitarian ideology.[11] The novel epithet of "subversive," attached to ideologies and the parties and groups promoting them, made its appearance on the political scene. In the last decade the term, formerly confined to isolated instances of violent non-conformism, has become a permanent fixture in the political repertory also of constitutional democracies.

Such restrictive and repressive legislation refers to the entire compass of the political process: formation of public opinion and propaganda; group organization, association, and assembly; the participation in the electoral process and access to public office; and even citizenship. After the First World War these legislative measures were directed primarily against the danger of fascist aggression. More often than not they were applied by the law-enforcement agencies without vigor and conviction, because fascism caters primarily to the appetites of the propertied classes, for which the mass basis was merely a means toward an end. Since the defeat, for the time being, of fascism in the Second World War, the defense was shifted against communism.[12] At first, legislation for the defense of the state was enacted by parliament and, when necessary, sustained by the courts. More recently, the outlawing of totalitarian ideologies or their equivalents—those disapproved by the ruling majorities—was legalized also in the constitutions themselves,[13] thus removing any doubt about the constitutionality of their prohibition. The techniques of prohibition vary considerably, ranging from the establishment of general criteria of subversiveness to the naming of specific ideologies. Catholic states are particularly emphatic in their proscription of communism. The degree of restrictive legislation differs from state to state also in accordance with the potential danger to which the state society believes itself exposed.

Pertinent measures for coping with "subversive" parties are the arrangements the German republic, once bitten, twice shy, found proper to insert into the Bonn Basic Law. While no restrictions exist concerning the establishment of political parties, their internal organization must correspond to democratic principles (elective procedures for intraparty government [Art. 21, sec. 1]). Parties which "in view of their aims or the conduct of their adherents are aiming at the impairment or elimination of the constitutional-democratic order" are unconstitutional, the unconstitutionality to be declared by the Federal Constitutional Court (Art. 21, sec. 2).[14] Moreover, the constitution, visibly inspired by Article 30 of the Universal Declaration of Human Rights of the United Nations, stipulates (Art. 18) that persons abusing the fundamental guaranties for the subversion of the constitutional-democratic order forfeit these rights, the forfeiture likewise to be decided by the Federal Constitutional Court.[15]

The conflict between liberty and security.—Whatever the justification of such liberty-restricting legislation, the conflict between liberty and internal security—and, in a bipolarized world, domestic cannot be divorced from external security—has plunged the constitutional-democratic state society into a serious conflict. The universal recognition of, and the scrupulous respect for, fundamental guaranties have suffered heavily. Everywhere such legislation necessarily narrowed the areas of individual self-determination, impingement of which, under the classic concept of liberty, should be forbidden to the state. The open power circuit is no longer open for political beliefs held at variance with those of the ruling majority. The democratic fundamentalist may be accused of legalistic pedantry, or worse, if he contends that democracy is more than the rule of the majority openly arrived at in honest elections. It must be, at the same time, the protection of minorities, even of minorities holding unpopular political opinions. In the light of the democratic tenets it is submitted that the proscription of any political creed, whatever its professed or real political objectives, is untenable. A state society which outlaws political opinion as such is no longer fully democratic.

The dilemma between democratic freedom and national security is by no means beyond a reasonable solution. Participants in the political process must conform to the general laws. A firm line must be drawn between opinion, which must be free, and "overt acts" of illegality and violence, which are subject to repression. Every organized state has at its disposal the criminal laws, which are legitimate means for the defense of the state and the protection of public order against "overt acts." It cannot too strongly be emphasized that as yet no totalitarian ideology or subversive movement has come into power by legitimate, that is, nonviolent, methods, provided the legitimate power holders who controlled the enforcement apparatus of the state possessed a will to prevent it. Successful defense of the constitutional-democratic state, of course, is conditioned on the assumption that the enforcement agencies—police, armed forces, courts, and bureaucracy—remain loyal to it and have not become subverted to the point that they suborn the totalitarian assault as happened in Italy and Weimar. The political conduct of the members of these groups necessarily is subject to standards more exacting than those valid for the citizenry at large. These intricate and difficult problems are beyond the scope of our discussion. By outlawing political opinion, as such, without measuring the potential danger of the overt action into which it may be translated—the clear and present danger—the constitutional-democratic state distinguishes itself only by degree from the closed power circuit of autocracy. "Qui mange du Pape en meurt."

The western record.—The record of civil liberties, and, in particular, of political freedom, in the free societies of the West during the last decade can be summarized here only in the most general terms. It was best in Great Britain, the Lowlands, and the Scandinavian countries, which were least exposed to the temptation to sacrifice the liberal patrimony to political expediency. The record of civil liberties protection in the British Dominions is uneven. It is good in Canada, with the exception of Quebec, dominated by the Catholic hierarchy, in New Zealand, and also in Australia, which is one of the few states not possessing a bill of rights; here the Communist Party Dissolution Act of 1950 was invalidated by the High Court because of its incompatibility with the interfederal structure rather than because of conflict with liberal fundamentals.[16] The subsequent referendum on a constitutional amendment that granted the federal government the requisite powers was rejected (1951) by both the majority of the states and the voters. In the Union of South Africa, finally, no civil liberties whatsoever exist for enemies of apartheid or sympathizers with the plight of the Negroes. Under the Suppression of Communism statute (1950), whoever has been declared by the government a "statutory" communist is placed under police surveillance and practically deprived of the enjoyment of all fundamental liberties.

France, burdened with a strong Commuinst party, refrained from outright proscription of political beliefs, but the ruling majority parties resorted to discriminatory measures through the medium of the electoral laws.* After the liberation, the recurrence of the venality of the press was to be forestalled by the confiscation of all press instrumentalities and their redistribution, with initial government funds, among proved democratic journalists.

* See above, p. 296.

Nonetheless, the press is no longer free from the control of the financial interests; *Le Monde* is the exception, and it is constantly exposed to government harassment.[17] Moreover, the Algerian crisis is beginning to cast its liberty-obliterating shadow also over metropolitan France. The special powers granted by a reluctant National Assembly to the cabinet of Bourgès-Maunoury in July, 1957, with their potential abrogation of civil liberties for Frenchmen in France proper, are viewed with deep alarm by many inside and outside the county where once the Declaration of the Rights of Man was born. Under the new constitution of Italy no political party can be outlawed, with the exception of the Fascist party. Its reconstitution is prohibited, and for five years ranking functionaries of the dissolved Fascist party were subject to restrictions in voting and in access to office (Transitional Provisions, XII). These precautions did not prevent the emergence of a neo-Fascist party (Movimento Sociale Italiano).

Germany-Bonn, on the basis of the constitutional authorization (Art. 21, sec. 2), proceeded to outlaw, by decisions of the Federal Constitutional Court,[18] both the neo-Nazi Social Reich party (1952) and, after five years of hesitancy, the Communist party (1956), in both cases correctly applying the constitutional intent. On the whole, western Europe's record of fundamental freedoms, if spotty at times and in certain places, did not fail her bills of rights. But it is hard to forecast whether the prosperity of civil liberties will last much longer than the current economic prosperity.

Contrariwise, in the United States, it must be noted with regret, the people's respect of, and the power holders' solicitude for, the civil liberties were exposed to a devaluation unprecedented in peacetime since the Alien and Sedition Acts of 1798. England had her crisis of liberty in the Chartist unrest; France in the Dreyfus case; and the United States in McCarthyism. Set in motion by the impact of the cold war on the public mind, exploited by both parties for political reasons, and aided and abetted by the courts, the deterioration of political freedom, accomplished by legislation and administration alike, is still too much with us to be judged merely a passing interlude in a nation proud of its liberal patrimony. The Communist party was banned by federal legislation, an action unheard of in our tradition.[19] There was no lack of valiant defenders of our freedoms.[20] The roll of honor is headed by the Columbia Broadcasting System's Edward R. Murrow. But perhaps the most significant aspect of this distressing situation is the apathy and indifference of the vast majority of the power addressees while all three power holders made inroads into zones of individual autonomy previously held inaccessible to them. The crisis of fundamental liberties symbolizes the crisis of the democratic mind. And it cannot be ignored that American resistance to being bound by an international convention modernizing our bill of rights played a large part in keeping the "universalism" of human rights from proceeding beyond a paper declaration in the United Nations.

The deeper causation.—From the foregoing material it may seem that the fundamental guaranties of individual self-determination protected against the state and its power holders, which embody the second pattern of vertical controls in the power process, have been exposed to a process of retrogression and erosion similar to that of federalism, the first area of vertical controls. This recession of fundamental guaranties, noticeable in autocratic and constitutional-democratic states alike, may be merely a temporary phenomenon conditioned by the ideological tensions of a bipolarized world. Whether the guaranties will be reaffirmed if and when the world accepts the coexistence of peaceful competition is impossible to tell at this time. But it is submitted that the real causes for the devaluation of individual liberties in our time lie deeper. It may well be that the reason the mass of the power addressees now prefer economic security at the expense of personal liberty has its roots in the sociological transformation society has undergone since the beginning of the industrial revolution.

Like all other human institutions, the catalogue of classical human freedoms was conditioned by its historical period and environment, the transcendentalist *mystique* of its inalienability to the contrary notwithstanding. The dynamics of the modern mass society has inevitably narrowed the range within which the individual can exercise his liberties without impinging on those of others. With more people in each nation, the individual loses elbowroom. Within most societies the frontier situation, paradise of individualism, has vanished. Intensified competition necessitates more stringent rules for the orderly conduct of the social process. The individual has become more dependent on the state, and the state exacts, as the price for its support, the surrender of individual sovereignty. More wealth is being produced, but more people claim a share in its distribution. The moral climate of society has radically changed. Human dignity and conformity, for the philosopher mutually exclusive, have become almost interchangeable values. The problem is no longer, "How lonely is man in the crowd?" It is rather, "Can man in the crowd still be lonely?"

Political Liberty and Propaganda

THE CIRCULATION OF POLITICAL IDEOLOGIES

The Powers That Be have always insisted on securing the status quo benefiting them and on denying their rivals both the legitimation and the means to alter it. Only with the advent of constitutionalism has the peaceful change of the location of political power become possible. But the emphasis on the defense of constitutional democracy against ideologies deemed subversive of it is a phenomenon of our time, commensurate to the width and depth of the ideological attack directed against it. Intrinsically responsible for the bitterness of the struggle is a technological fact: the effect of the mass-communication media, as instruments of political propaganda, on the individual mind.

Political systems and their institutions are disseminated primarily by disseminating their underlying ideologies.[21] The diffusion of ideologies—their "circulation" or "mobility"—depends on the "receptivity" of the power addressees—their willingness to accept and be guided by them. Political civilizations of the past—the Byzantine empire, the republic of Venice, the Islamic monarchies, the Chinese empires—reveal an amazing intranational stability in spite of frequent, and frequently violent, changes of the persons at the top of the power pyramid in all except Venice. This was largely due to the slow mobility of the political ideologies and the low receptivity of the power addressees for them. The range of ideological circulation was limited. There were no receptive masses, and, if there had been, the technical devices were lacking to reach and influence them.

Since the Renaissance and Reformation the tempo of ideological circulation has become vastly accelerated. The invention of the printing press, popularizing knowledge and education, created the open door for the penetration of non-conformist and revolutionary ideologies, whether religious or secular. With the Enlightenment they acquired a transnational character. The foremost transmission belt was at first the intellectuals and later the political parties. Only the political party could mobilize the masses and integrate them into the political process.

What the printing press, through book and pamphlet, did for the mobility of ideologies was repeated, on a larger scale, by the newspaper press in the nineteenth century, and, on a truly gigantic scale, by the electronic mass-communication media in the twentieth. Today all barriers to the penetration of ideologies into the remotest corner of the state have disappeared. Government in the modern society, whether democratic or autocratic, depends on the linotype machine and on radio and television. Through them the political parties condition the masses for their participation in the political process.

POLITICAL PROPAGANDA AND THE MASS-COMMUNICATION MEDIA

Political propaganda, in one form or another, has existed since the inception of the organized state society. Its influence, however, on the individual mind as the cell of the mass mind became overwhelming when it appropriated the communication media. "Propaganda" is commonly understood to mean the utilization of persons, words, objects, symbols, or other "representations" to guide the mind and the action of those to whom it is addressed toward the objectives of those who dispense it. More realistically, propaganda is nothing but a facet of power; it is an attempt to limit the freedom of will of the addressee, so that he feels induced to act according to the directives of those who control the propaganda apparatus. The degree of psychological compulsion varies according to the personality of the addressee.

Political propaganda in the contemporary mass society can no longer rely on the technique of personal contacts—through canvassing and meetings—of early constitutionalism. Almost all propaganda is conducted by the mass-communication media. Among these, the telecommunications are far more effective than the press—books, newspapers, pamphlets, and magazines. The average citizen no longer forms his political opinion by reading the newspapers, even though their tabloid technique may facilitate the process. More people listen to the radio and its commentators or sit in front of the television screen than digest editorials of the daily press. Reading consumes more time and effort than listening.

However, the degree of competition among the various communication media for the access to the individual mind varies considerably from country to country. Electronics occupy the prominent place in America and also in nations with a high degree of illiteracy, while the press is still holding its own as the most important vehicle for the formation of public opinion in most states of western Europe.

Political propaganda is an attempt to impress the masses of the adressees. It therefore depends more on emotional reactions than on persuasion by rational arguments. To reach the mass audience, political issues and ideas disseminated by propaganda are externalized, superficialized, simplified, and even vulgarized. Destined for mass consumption and mass digestion, political propaganda does not present the pros and cons to inform and educate the addressee and to allow him to form his independent judgment. Propaganda is generated by emotion and generates emotion. By evoking the emotional responses, it pre-empts the individual's decision.

The apparatus of political propaganda through mass communication can no longer be serviced by amateurs. Its management has shifted to the professionals of public opinion formation. In the idyllic past of classical constitutionalism ideas circulated freely, by their natural weight, among the relatively restricted elite of the educated classes. Nowadays, only specialists in the mass-communication media are capable of diffusing issues of unprecedented complexity among a mass audience unparalleled in size. The advertising techniques of competitive private enterprise, attuned by scientific consumers research and market analysis to the stimuli and responses of the public, are being applied to the political process, predicated on an equally refined inquiry into the attitudes of the consumers of propaganda. The public opinion poll, for example, indigenous in the American milieu, has become an indispensable tool for the public policy-maker. That the technique has often been discredited by subsequent experience seems to have had little effect on both its manipulators and addressees.

What the propaganda specialist does, or tries to do, is to predigest the information material for the consumption of the recipient; to sell him a political opinion as a commodity; to stimulate or to stifle, as the case may be, his appetite by emotional incentives; to dull his individual reasoning; and to overcome his sales resistance until he is persuaded to accept the political nostrum as if he had chosen it by his own volition. Under the impact of mass communication, the political climate has changed drastically during the last decades, at least in the United States. The political boss of yesteryear has vacated his commanding position in the political process to the Svengalis of Madison Avenue, the scientific molders of the public mind. Already it is not uncommon to sell a candidate or a referendal issue to the public like toothpaste or soap. To the public relations specialist it does not matter what kind of political merchandise he sells.[22] He is hired to build up as well as to wreck a person or an issue. More and more, the issues and personalities become less important than the conduct of the campaign. The professional behind the limelight performs a job for which he is paid; he remains anonymous and outside political responsibility. He is the Mephistopheles of the political process, beyond good and evil.

In our pluralist society the Leviathan speaks with many voices. He who speaks loudest, longest, and at the most convenient hours of radio and television reception has for his message the ear of the greatest number of potential customers. He who fries the political bacon with the most appetizing smell carries it home. Or, to paraphrase the geopolitical "law" of Sir Harold MacKinder: he who controls the mass-communication media controls the electorate; he who controls the electorate controls the political process.

CONCENTRATED AND SHARED POWER IN THE PROCESS OF PUBLIC OPINION FORMATION

Conscious of the spell cast by political propaganda over the individual mind, one may well ask: How free is political freedom? How much self-determination is left to the individual under the propaganda barrage? How much value attaches to the freedom of political will when the information on which it rests is filtered through the sieve of propaganda? It is at this point that the dichotomy of shared and concentrated power must be brought into the focus of political liberty.

Autocracy.—The issue at stake stands out clearly when techniques af public opinion formation in modern autocracy are compared with those of the constitutional democracy. Faithful to their operational principle of the closed power circuit, the totalitarian regimes completely, and the authoritarian regimes to the largest possible extent, monopolize all media of public opinion formation and particularly the telecommunications. Only the radio makes dictatorship in the modern mass society possible. Propaganda favorable to the power holders is instilled into the power addressees; adverse information is withheld from them. Endless brainwashing by scientific propaganda persuades them to believe in the wisdom and benevolence of their power holders and the wickedness of all within and without who disagree with them. Social consent is engineered. In the monolithic state society which denies recognition to the competitive plural forces, the exercise of control over the propaganda apparatus is concentrated. Perhaps the most comforting aspect of the Polish and Hungarian rebellions against the Soviets and their stooges is the demonstration that, in the long run, even the most rigid indoctrination cannot permanently stifle the innate will of a people to judge for themselves.

Constitutional democracy.—In constitutional democracy, on the other hand, operating with the open power circuit, it is assumed that access to the mass-communication media is equitably shared by the competitive ideologies and the plural groups promoting them. A free society requires not only the right of free speech but also the means to realize it: freedom of propaganda, a free press, a free radio, and free television.

This, at least, is the underlying theory. But the grave question poses itself: Does the practice live up to the theory? No unbiased observer would be willing to offer an unqualified affirmation. It would be as unwise to generalize the recent American experience as it would be unfortunate to minimize its portents for the future of constitutional democracy everywhere. The symptoms are ominous. If the impact of political propaganda is deepest in the United States and, perhaps, less manifest in other western democracies, the difference obviously lies in the different economic theories applied to the media of public opinion formation. The United States occupies an almost unique position in this respect. Here the communication media are considered the legitimate domain of private enterprise in a capitalist society; private enterprise necessarily prefers profits to public service or camouflages profits as public service. Political propaganda is a salable commodity distributed by those who are willing and able to pay for it. Propaganda is an object of legitimate trade, and the communication media serve those who pay the highest price for them.

Is there anything that can be done? It is obvious that in a free society the press cannot be regimented. The most licentious press is better than one controlled by the government.[23] But no press organ can live on subscriptions alone. It depends on the advertisers who, as a rule, prefer a political and economic system protecting private enterprise and the political parties defending it to their competitors. Without destroying the freedom of the press, little can be done to reform it.[24] However, rival political propaganda can be given something approximating equal access to, and use of, the telecommunication media. Great Britain and other nations following her example point the way. Since 1926 the British Broadcasting Corporation, an agency independent from the government, has been universally acclaimed for its equitable dispensation in the use of the radio. It performs a public service with impartiality and without malice. But even in an economy in which private enterprise controls the mass-communication media, a remedy of the present laissez faire anarchy may be feasible. The issue is intimately related to the freedom of the electoral process discussed before,* without, however, being confined to it.

There is no occasion to present a detailed plan here. Merely the principle is suggested: at the beginning of an election year the political parties, by statutory regulation, would have to agree on the ceiling they could spend on radio and television time, and the ra-

* See above, pp. 269 ff.

dio stations would not be allowed to sell more time to either party than the maximum amount allotted to them would permit.[25]

To some such forebodings of the potential perversion of political liberty by unequal access to the communication media may seem exaggerated. They will point to the presidential election of 1948, when the people broke through the sound-and-fury barrier of press and radio propaganda heavily loaded in favor of a specific candidate and elected his opponent to office. But this hopeful experience was largely canceled out by the presidential campaign of 1956. The skill of public opinion managers was able to ward off all rational counterarguments against the second term of President Eisenhower and turn his unquestionable popularity—in itself the product of masterly public opinion management—into a landslide far beyond the will of the electorate demonstrated in the congressional and gubernatorial elections.

Political liberty, like economic liberty a century ago, finds itself at the crossroads.* It is endangered by the concentration of the power to mold public opinion in the hands of the few who are able to pay the expenses. As in the economic field, the maximum of political liberty may not equal the optimum of political equality. If the present trend continues unabated, a degree of governmental control of the free-market economy of public opinion formation, similar to the government regulation of business, may become imperative, or constitutional democracy will reach the point of no return on the road to self-destruction. Whether the American people, either blissfully ignorant of the danger signals or even proud of them, will in time put the brakes on their invisible power holders is open to question.

---

* The concurrent dilemma of economic liberty will be discussed in the next chapter (see below, pp. 360 ff.).

XII. Pluralism

Plural Groups and the Power Process

The third vertical control interposing itself between the power holders and the power addressees is the multitude of plural groups, which collectively represent the infinite variety of the interests of the members of the state community. If there exists a single predominant characteristic of the mass society of the technological age, it is its plural basis and dynamism.[1] True, the conduct of the power process is constitutionally vested in the power holders—government, parliament, and electorate. What the official power holders are presumed to do is to harmonize, in their policy decisions, the conflicting interests of the plural groups for the common benefit of the community. But the plural groups, by influencing their policy decisions, influence the power process itself. Depending on the degree of their interaction in the specific political environment, the plural groups function as the unofficial or invisible power holders.

From the viewpoint of the vertical stratification of the power process, the interposition of the plural groups operates as an effective restraint on the power holders. By joining with others of similar interests, the individual is able to offer more resistance to the Powers That Be than he could if he had to confront them in isolation. United with others, he wields an influence on the policy decisions commensurate to the strength of his group. Plural groups, thus, serve as a barrier to, and a brake on, the omnipotent Leviathan.

The following discussion of plural groups—a subject of increasing prominence in political science here and abroad—necessarily will focus on their relations to the governmental process.

In the attitude toward the plural stratification of society another criterion may be found for the differentiation of the political systems of the constitutional democracy and autocracy. The absolute monarchy of the French *ancien régime* tried to accomplish the subordination of all plural groups. Francis I's Concordat of Bologna (1516) even attempted to establish the domination of the state over the church. Hobbes, the Leviathan's most forceful apologist, warns of the "private societies" in the body politic as "the worms in the entrayles of natural man." The monolithic power structure of contemporary autocracy insists not only on the monopoly of political power concentrated in the official power holders and the single party; it also excludes the operation of plural groups outside the machinery of the state and the state party. The power holders cannot tolerate fragmentation of, let alone opposition to, their power monopoly. All associative impulses of the power addressees are controlled and directed by the state and its single party. Under the iron fist of the police state all organic group life is extinguished, and its revitalization encounters stern retribution. This was fully demonstrated in Nazi Germany by the fate of the traditionally most powerful interest groups—the army, the churches, big business, and labor. None of them was able to exert any influence on the policy decisions of the ruling clique.[2] The single attempt of the army to assert itself against the regime (conspiracy of July 20, 1944) was abortive.

Likewise in the communist orbit of the U.S.S.R. organic group dynamics have ceased to function and are replaced by the artificial mobilization of party-controlled group action. It may be assumed that the recurrent purges were aimed as much against the re-emergence of pluralism outside the pale of the state and party as against individual deviationists and dissenters. A genuine liberalization will require the revival of the organic plural stratification. When an authoritarian regime does not feel strong enough to suppress group life altogether, it tries to canalize it into state-controlled institutions.*

The essence of constitutional democracy, on the other hand, is the unfettered participation of the most diversified plural groups in the political process. All relevant social forces are granted, in the open power circuit of values, the freedom of competition. The free interplay of the plural groups corresponds to the principle of shared power. The policy decisions of the constitutional power holders are the compromise of the conflicting aspirations of the plural interests of society. By a variety of techniques, their policy goals are brought to the recognition of the government, the parliament, the electorate, and public opinion. The principle of the plural organization of society is constitutionally guaranteed by the civil liberty of free association, limited only by the requirements of public order and the security of the state. However, in spite of their overriding importance for the reality of the sociopolitical process, the plural groups still lack commensurate legal institutionalization, let alone constitutionalization. In no other aspect has the philosophy of the classical laissez faire continued so anachronistically as in the relationship between the official power holders and the extra-constitutional plural forces guiding and molding them.†

At this point a clarification of terms is imperative. A plural group, in the widest sense, is any conscious association, in organized form, of people linked together by common interests. These interests may be political—the political party is the most important of all plural groups; religious—the churches; economic—business and labor; occupational and vocational—the crafts and the free professions; or cultural—devotees of folk dancing or nudism.

In the American multi-faceted society, more conducive to plural stratification than other nations, plural groups are usually identified with pressure groups, and pressure groups, in turn, with lob-

* See below, pp. 378 ff.

† On this important subject see below, pp. 362 ff.

bies. This, however, appears to be an oversimplification of a most complex situation and is not generally applicable elsewhere. Any organized plural group is potentially a pressure group. But a plural group may exist, and even wield considerable influence, without engaging in the techniques commonly resorted to by a pressure group. Tending merely to the interests of its adherents, it may remain wholly neutral toward the power prócess. Such quiescent plural groups, however, have become rare. Or, the other extreme, a plural group may be so firmly intrenched in the power process that it need not conduct itself as a pressure group. Controlling the personnel of the power holders, it is satisfied to hold what it holds and to ward off competitors. Illustrations are the Catholic church, for example, in Ireland; the military establishment in imperial Germany and in pre-1945 Japan; the bureaucracies in Prussia or of the mandarin class in Manchu China. By a pressure group, therefore, should be understood a plural group that deliberately sets out to promote the interests of its affiliates by influencing the power holders and public opinion. A lobby, finally—an American figurative term derived from the primitive technique of "buttonholing" legislators in their lobby—is the action squad of the plural group, its spearhead devised to carry the fight for the interests into the public arena. Lobbies may, but rarely are, identical with the plural group at large. They function as the mobile commandos for the more slowly advancing pressure group they represent.

The Group Basis of the State Society

Plural groups are organic in the biology of the state society. They were inherent in the power process long before Montesquieu and de Tocqueville, calling them the *corps intermédiaires*, raised them to scientific respectability. A comprehensive study of their historical role in the power process seems not to have been written; Mosca's and Max Weber's observations were merely incidental to the systematic analysis of the group phenomenon in the social process. To be meaningful, such a study would have to distinguish between the social classes and the plural groups proper. The concept of the social class has been recognized since Aristotle and his successors rationalized the coexistence of classes in the pattern of the "mixed" government. A social class has frequently controlled the power process. Illustrations are the senatorial oligarchy in the mature Roman republic, the capitalist equestrian order in the centuries of republican decline, the shogunate of the Tokugawa period in Japan, and the monasterial class in Tibetan Lamaism. All of them dominated the political process by appropriating the state apparatus as the official power holders.

On the other hand, history is equally rich in illustrations of genuine plural groups which, without necessarily being identified with the official power holders, operated as restraints on them. The bureaucracy in the late Roman empire and during the entire life-span of the Byzantine state functioned as a quasi-autonomous corporation under its own laws and regulations for recruitment, promotion, and tenure; its members constituted, by virtue of the rationality and impartiality of their office conduct, the counter-weight of legal security against the violent fluctuations at the apex of the caesaropapist power pyramid. Class interests, on the other hand, transcending those of a mere plural group, were organized in the estates—nobility, clergy, burghers, and peasants—of European feudalism. Contrariwise, the guilds in the medieval cities of Europe were originally organized plural groups which afterward, as is often the case, gained political power as a social class. Similarly, the *parlements* of the *ancien régime* in France operated as a plural group of professionals, again with the result, almost unavoidable in the case of a long-continued power position, that they acquired all the traits of a social class, although their membership was restricted. The republic of Venice, in turn, represents a sociopolitical configuration in which a plural group, the merchant aristocracy, fashioned the entire state machinery for the exclusive benefit of their class interests.

If, thus, the group phenomenon in the power process is nothing new, it grew to full maturity only with the industrial revolution and the rise of the technological mass society. No modern state society can be analyzed in terms of its constitutional and legal arrangements alone without reference to the role the plural groups play in the political process. The roots of the contemporary plural structuration are too well known to merit more than a summarization: industrialization under capitalism resulted in an unprecedented increase in the population and the corresponding division of labor and specialization of occupational activities. These, in turn, progressively produced competitive tensions between the various productive, distributive, and consumptive sectors of the national economy. In the brutally competitive world of early laissez faire capitalism the isolated individual, in order to survive, was compelled to combine with others of an affinitive occupational status. Concomitantly with the victory of the democratic ideology that broadened the basis of the power process, political democracy implemented itself by plural democracy.

While all state societies engaged in industrialization are bound to develop similar traits of organized pluralism, the private-enterprise milieu of the United States provided the most favorable climate for the plural stratification of society. The plural diversification reached its maximum here because of several special factors. Functional pluralism could grow Topsy-like in a basically classless and equalitarian society, without being grafted on the residues of the traditional class stratification that persisted in Europe; the abundance of natural resources and the natural resourcefulness of the population created new needs to be satisfied by production; racial and ethnical heterogeneity formed the natural nuclei of plural diversity. The political structure tended toward decentralization. Finally, the American typifies the social animal par excellence. By nature gregarious, we are a nation of "joiners." Group impulses, thus, are indigenous in the American habitat.

All these factors—and others not mentioned here—combine to create in the United States the most complete and complex network of correlative and competing interest groups which, by force of circumstances, have had to conduct themselves as pressure groups. Their penetration into the social fabric has reached the point that one may justly speak of the "collectivization" of the individual. The vast majority of the power addressees is integrated in, or affiliated with, at least one and frequently several plural or interest groups. It is understandable that, on the basis of a century's pragmatic experience with democratic pluralism, the United States developed a pioneering interest in the science of plural structuration. So far, however, it has not been able to integrate the vast empirical material into a comprehensive functional theory of the state, as has been attempted abroad, for example, by Tönnies and Laski.

Another significant feature of technological pluralism, not confined to the United States, is that the border lines between the economic and political interests have become obliterated. Marxism deserves the primary credit for having called attention to the economic basis of the political process, even though the political religions of our time have sufficiently disproved the doctrinaire oversimplifications of historical materialism. However, economics always have constituted and will continue to constitute the infrastructure of political power. No political issue can be divorced from its economic implications, and no economic problem can be solved without political means. In accordance with this transubstantiation, the core of every political ideology of our time consists in the economic eschatology it has to offer. Politics have become a function of economics, and vice versa.

This development could not fail to be reflected in the relations of the plural groups to the political process. The majority of these groups are economically oriented, but they seek to promote their interests by action or pressure directed toward the political power holders. By influencing them, they advance their group interests. Moreover, with the advent of the welfare and social service state —in itself a product of group pressure—only the concerted action of the weaker members of the community is able to wrest benefits from the stronger. Finally, the development of the political mass parties hastened plural stratification. Unless the organizational *telos* of a political party is the promotion of a specific class or other interest—as in the case of labor or religious parties—the nationwide parties are reluctant or even incapable of identifying themselves with the needs of a special-interest group. Catering to the mass electorate, regardless of the vocational status of the voter, their sociopolitical philosophies have to be wide and indefinite enough to accommodate all interests; they cannot run the risk of offending some interest groups by openly favoring others.

The Dynamics of the Interest Groups

It is not accidental that the modern version of the pressure group emerged at about the same time—toward the middle of the last century—as did the political parties, nor is it surprising that their organizational structures closely resemble each other. In the period of early industrialization interest groups were *ad hoc* affiliations for limited purposes; they disappeared once their initial goal had been achieved. Cobden's Anti-Corn-Law League, one of the first modern pressure groups, is a pertinent illustration.[3] Nowadays plural groups, like political parties, usually establish themselves as permanent organizations. Like political parties, they are highly bureaucratized, under expert managerial direction, and engaged in continuous operation; they enlist all known techniques of public relations management to attract, on the largest possible scale, adherents sharing their interests. No longer are they strictly voluntary, loosely affiliated organizations. In many instances membership is mandatory, as the prerequisite of engaging in a profession. Often they have at their disposal considerable financial means, raised either by voluntary contributions or by assessed dues or both. Since the rank and file of their members remain largely passive, their internal structure—again like that of the political party—reveals little evidence of intragroup democracy. The government of the group is left to a professional and a mostly self-appointed oligarchy, which justifies itself by the results achieved for the common group interests.

Valid classifications of plural groups based on a comparative orientation are unavailable. But the material supplied by the United States, with the most articulate plural stratification, may serve as a convenient typological pattern for the country-by-country variations. By numerical standards, the most important plural groups are the churches; by standards of political influence, the most important are the political parties. The larger categories of economic interest groups are industry and business, immensely subdivided and the subdivisions often at loggerheads with one another. By contrast, labor, organized in the trade unions and their affiliated associations, presents more of a common front, though here, too, subdivisions existed for a long time in the United States and are still common in Europe. Relative homogeneity and unity in relation to competitive plural groups distinguish the farmer groups, which are often connected, at least in Europe, with the co-operatives. Possibly the closest internal cohesion exists among the group organizations of the professions—physicians, lawyers, architects, and the like. These are integrated to such an extent that the professional group functions as a quasi-autonomous corporation or guild, with vast disciplinary powers over the enrolled members.[4] Exclusions from the group is tantamount to inability to exercise the calling. Other categories of interest groups are the war veterans, usually a particularly virulent pressure group; racial and ethnic groups in all multinational states; and reform groups which aim at changes of public policy. The three last-mentioned categories are plural affiliations without specific occupational orientation. Finally, surprising as it may seem, organized pressure groups and lobbies are also frequently maintained, within the governmental structure proper, by the bureaucracies. These exist, with a varying degree of articulateness, in all countries with a civil service system. A singularity, however, of the American milieu and common also in Latin America are pressure groups of the armed forces, subdivided according to the branches of the service and often engaged in lusty warfare against one another. Of all plural groups the least organized and effective are still the consumers, partly because the universality of the membership defies organization, partly because the housewife, singly the most important member of the community, is more resistant to organization than any other vocational group. In Europe the gap is filled, at least to some extent, by the consumers' co-operatives, a plural group understandably disfavored in the business community of the United States.

Practically all these classifications overlap and are split into innumerable subgroups with often conflicting policies. Moreover, the relationship between the most powerful plural groups, the political parties, and the more vocationally oriented interest groups still has not been meaningfully analyzed.

Obviously, the foregoing schematic categorization, largely based on the American experience, is not uniformly applicable to all contemporary states, even though the universal trend toward mass technology cannot fail to develop plural structurations on similar lines elsewhere. Moreover, outside the United States the systematic evaluation of the immense empirical material is still in its infancy.[5] The following observations, therefore, are strictly exemplificatory.

Plural integration of labor is most advanced in Australia and New Zealand; co-operatives in Scandinavia, Holland, and Switzerland; clerical and religious interests in the Catholic regions of Europe; bureaucratic interest groups are best organized in France. The civil service in Britain and Switzerland lacks conspicuous group integration. In Britain, on the other hand, the teachers are thoroughly organized, while they lag behind in Germany. Agricultural interests are most powerful in France and Scandinavia. Everywhere business manifests the maximum of plural integration.

The Operational Techniques of the Interest Groups

The operational techniques by which the interest groups gain influence in the power process depend to a large extent on the prevailing pattern of government and vary according to the national environment. Generally, they are directed, through all available devices of information and education, persuasion and propaganda, to all official power holders—government and its bureaucracy, the legislature and its parliamentarians, the mass of the power addresses in their capacity as voters. Not even the allegedly neutral courts are immune, if for no other reason than that their personnel consists of members of the general public. "Class justice" is a common slogan of the opposition in Continental Europe and is often more than a slogan, considering the class origin of the judicial personnel. But, even where crude class prejudices are absent, to resist the subtle plural pressures requires a strong judicial personality. This aspect has been given proper attention by the "realist" school of American jurisprudence.

More specifically, either the interest groups try to infiltrate into the official power holders—government and parliament—to bore from within or they work on the individual governmental and parliamentary personnel from without. Where possible, both approaches are used.

INFILTRATION INTO THE POWER HOLDERS

The foremost instrumentality for gaining access to the policy-making function by infiltration into the power holders proper is the political party. Here the operational strategy, however, differs. In the multiple-party system an interest group sufficiently large to command a mass following can mount a political party of its own—the "economic interest" party differentiated from the "ideological" party. The deputies elected on its ticket represent the interest group which delegated them into parliament. Economic interest parties were common in central and eastern Europe between the two world wars. Even the sober Swiss are afflicted by them.[6] Lately they have lost favor with the electorate, though the Expellee party in Germany-Bonn (bloc of the "Homeless and Victims of Injustice") and the Poujadists in France are recent examples. Their entrance into parliament is facilitated by proportional representation, provided they can overcome the restrictions on splinter parties. Once in parliament, they may reap benefits for their special cause far beyond their numerical strength. If included in a coalition government with a narrow majority basis, they function as pressure groups and exact their price for their continued support. The separate political party is also commonly used in Europe for the promotion of religious interests. Such parties are traditional in all states with a Catholic population. In the States General of the Netherlands, no fewer than five parties represent both denominations. Proportional representation offers the interest groups an additional advantage: all major parties see to it that known spokesmen of influential interest groups are prominently placed on the party tickets.

Under the two-party system, on the other hand, interest groups are hardly ever in a position to compete with the traditional parties. The regionally limited Farmer-Labor party in the American congress during the twenties and thirties is the exception confirming the rule. Nor can the major parties afford to pander openly to the prides and prejudices of specific interest groups, lest they alienate the electoral weight of other vocational groups; all are invited to join. The interest groups, therefore, put their spokesmen into the hall of parliament on the tickets of the two parties to promote, when occasion arises, the group interests from within. Again, this is a common practice in all European parliaments. The occupational analysis of the parliamentary personnel has become a legitimate study of the sociology of representation. A favorite device is to delegate into the assemblies officials of the respective interest groups: the syndics of business associations, the secretaries of farmers' groups, the functionaries of trade unions. This explains why, in Europe, the majority of the parliamentarians are professionals, no longer belonging to the elite of politically interested amateurs. Their election campaign is often financed by the sponsoring group, and their salaries as employees continue during their mandate. The practice makes a mockery of the prohibition of the imperative mandate and the constitutional fiction that the deputy represents the entire nation. Sporadic efforts to eliminate their influence by establishing incompatibilities between the parliamentary mandate and certain economic positions have proved wholly unavailing. However, exclusion from parliament of the members of certain professions, for example, public officials,* clergymen, and active officers of the armed forces, has been customary in many states.[7]

Far more effective and equally difficult to meet by statutory regulation is the infiltration of the interest groups, be it labor, agriculture, or big business, into the governmental personnel proper. The situation was sharply brought to the attention of the American public when a prominent member of the first Eisenhower administration was reluctant to sever his economic ties with the mammoth corporation he had headed, of which, incidentally, the government happened to be the largest customer. And the executives of big business do not enter public service as dollar-a-year men exclusively for the common welfare. Similarly, the influence of the trade unions on any Labor government in England, Australia, and New Zealand is well known and practically unavoidable.

THE LOBBIES

The two-party system in the United States discourages the direct infiltration of interest groups into congress, and the technique of delegating representatives of interest groups into the American legislatures is far less conspicuous than in western Europe. Labor, for example, is hardly represented at all. The

* See above, pp. 189 ff.

operation of insiders representing them is at best intermittent and uncertain. The interest groups, therefore, prefer to work on the personnel of the official power holders from outside. This phenomenon, almost as unique as the senatorial filibuster, takes the form of the lobbies the pressure groups maintain in Washington and the state capitals. Elsewhere, the practice is conducted with more subtlety, if it exists at all. Lobbies have become too favorite a target of American political science to require much discussion here. The lobbying activities are directed to both the members of congress and the key officials of the government because, under the American pattern of government, both participate in the policy-making function. Nor is the president immune to the lobbyist who approaches him through his advisers and personal contacts and even on the golf course. Some of the lobbies' work is conducted in the open; the congressional hearings and investigating committees are their favorite haunts. But, like icebergs, most of their bulk is hidden below the surface.

In addition, a major part of the activities of pressure groups and lobbies is devoted to converting public opinion to their aims. Lobbies are rigidly bi- or, rather, multipartisan. The dazzling fireworks of the most sophisticated public relations techniques are staged for the education, if not always the edification, of the American public, as every wastepaper basket in the country eloquently testifies. The public is inclined to accept the propaganda flood as a sign of a healthy plural democracy, unaware that its invisible government is manipulated by high-powered hucksters for the benefit of high-pressurized interest groups, among which, in fairness, are many causes worthy of its attention.

Legislative efforts to control lobbying by registration and disclosure have been entirely ineffective, partly because of lack of judicial enforcement but primarily because the practice is condoned by the public as inherent in American democracy.[8]

Again, the comparative material does not lend itself to generalizations. According to the pattern of government in which they function, the activities of the pressure groups either are more limited than in this country or have to seek out more respectable avenues of approach. Since in Great Britain policy decisions are monopolized by the cabinet, with the Commons merely confirming them, it would serve no purpose for the interest groups to try to influence, as lobbies, the individual member of parliament. Parliament and public would strongly disapprove if a member of parliament were "entertained," like his American cousin, by a lobbyist to "educate" him on legislative policies. There is no lobby in the American sense in England. But group pressure, if not in the form of the open pressure group, is common also in England. It is directed toward the ministerial bureaucracy and the country at large in the expectation that it will filter through the constituencies into the policy-making process.

Pressure groups in Germany, from the Empire to Bonn,[9] come closest to the situation in the United States, though the more blatant aspects of American lobbying are as yet absent. They prefer the twilight behind the scene to the limelight on the stage. But the major plural groups—industry, agriculture, and trade unions—wield enormous influence, at both the federal and the *Land* levels, on policy decisions and on implementing legislation. They operate through their spokesmen in parliament, through lateral contacts with the key men in the government and ministerial bureaucracy, and through their press organs.

PARTICIPATION IN GOVERNMENTAL ADMINISTRATION

Moreover, it is an unwritten constitutional usage in all constitutional-democratic states for the interest groups to consult with the administration on legislation and to be consulted by it. They bring the expert knowledge into the legislative process; not even the most omniscient ministerial bureaucracy could possess the technical know-how required by the complexities of regulating the life of a technological society. State paternalism has been largely replaced by voluntary co-operation with the interest groups. This is the common practice of most states. But the situation is best exemplified by one of the smaller European states with a higher degree of pluralistic stratification.

In Sweden and also, to a somewhat lesser extent, in Switzerland the interest groups are officially if extra-constitutionally integrated into the policy-making process. The various advisory councils and committees, on which the interest groups and the political departments of the government are represented, attend to the joint elaboration of legislative projects by which the interest groups are affected. Sweden's renown as the model of a pluralistic democracy is well established: the government, the major plural organizations of labor, industry, agriculture, the free professions, the co-operatives, and even the churches share, on equal footing, in the preparation of legislation. The subsequent parliamentary action merely puts the official seal on legislation previously agreed on between the government and the plural groups.[10]

Finally, the practice of unregulated contacts of the interest groups as pressure groups and lobbies with the official power holders has been recognized in recent years by statutory regulations; herein lies one of the most momentous implications of the transformation of the legislative into the administrative state. These arrangements legalize the official participation of the plural groups in the administrative process. England and the Continent have gone farther in this direction than the United States. They at long last provide the interest groups with official and legitimate access to the actual administration of wide areas of public policy by which they are primarily affected. The situation has been aptly called "administrative pluralism."[11]

A plethora of administrative agencies, variously styled "boards," "authorities," and "commissions," has sprung up like flowers in the spring, sometimes connected with the regular departments of the government, more often wholly detached and independent from them. These agencies are charged with the most varied administrative functions (often including that of lawmaking), dealing, for example, with the self-government of the professions, with marketing and price regulations, with cultural matters, and, in particular, with the administration of the social services. Perhaps the most interesting and important among them are the public corporations managing the nationalized industries in Britain and France (coal, gas, electricity, transport, airways, and, before 1953, steel in Great Britain; coal, insurance, railroads, and banking in France). The purpose of these independent agencies is to keep the actual administration outside government management, the parties, and also parliamentary or congressional control. In many cases, the major categories of the plural groups are officially or unofficially represented on these boards. For the nationalized industries in France a complete tripartism has become standard practice, in which employees, consumers, and the government are represented.[12] The Labor Relations Board in the United States is similarly constructed. One may well judge these developments, as yet haphazard, pragmatic, and unsystematized, as the beginnings of the legal integration of the interest groups into the administrative process. For the time being, however, they cannot be considered a contribution to the reduction of the plural groups' traditional practices of influencing the legislative process at its source.

The Individual in the Plural Society

How has the individual fared in the pluralist society? Affiliating himself with others engaged in the same occupational pursuit, he has certainly gained in socioeconomic security. His group shields him against the unfair competition of other group members as well as against the pressure of competing groups. But the price is heavy: he has exchanged one master for another. The sovereignty of the group is incompatible with the sovereignty of the individual. His professional freedom, instead of being strengthened, has become more precarious. Being a member of the group made him subject to its regulations, conditions, and standards, to its social and moral codes, and, often enough, to its discipline. His freedom of action is severely restricted by the policies of the group. What he has gained in economic security he has lost in individual self-determination. Enmeshed in the network of the plural society, the individual is in danger of becoming collectivized.

There is little need for documentation. Suffice it to refer to the restrictions imposed on management and labor by unionization and collective bargaining or on industry and trade by cartel practices, compulsory price levels, and fair-trade regulations. In particular, the labor union has assumed the role of the government in controlling the life of the millions of their members and has developed loyalties and allegiances similar to, and even stronger than, those demanded by the political government. Government by the state, on an ever increasing scale, is being replaced by government by private groups. They have attained the rank of a quasi-official government exercising lawmaking functions over their members and, beyond this, by their mere existence, over all members of the same occupational pursuit not affiliated with them.[13]

No longer is the state alone to be feared; the despoiler of individual freedom is the despotism of the plural groups. In this unrelenting process of the collectivization of the individual, that pillar of classic liberalism, the freedom of contract, has been undermined. Only in isolated cases, because of his specific bargaining power, can the individual emancipate himself from the group-dictated terms governing his socioeconomic existence. And from the group regulations of his daily life there is no escape. Contractual self-determination has been superseded by the collective and compulsory contract in the form of the contract of adhesion,[14] the standardization of contractual relations in mass production, mass distribution, and mass dispensation of the public and private services. The regulatory powers of the interest groups stretch their tentacles into all aspects of daily life: transportation and insurance, entertainment and rents, services and commodities.

Anticartel legislation in Europe, nowhere undertaken with determination, was unable to change the ingrained cartel habits of the people. All over Europe the guild system has returned with a vengeance, duplicating the social controls of the neomerchantilistic state. In the American environment the individual is fighting a war on two fronts: he is confronted by the monopoly practices of the powerful corporations and trusts and he is hedged in by the regulatory practices of the interest groups to which he professionally belongs, and even by those to which he does not belong. Antitrust legislation, intended to curb group domination but first used in the United States to prevent the destruction of free competition, may have had sporadic successes,[15] but it was unable to stem the tide, because the judicial injunctions for economic deconcentration do not benefit the consumer. Even where the enforcement of antitrust legislation has reached a certain degree of effectiveness, the consumer is always on the receiving end of the stick. He may choose among cars of different colors, or cigarettes in different packages, but the price he has to pay remains the same. And he can derive little comfort from what has been described by the corporate romanticists as the benevolence of the self-generating "countervailing" forces,[16] by which, in the free-market economy of the United States, the dominant plural groups are alleged mutually to neutralize and cancel out themselves. It makes little difference that the few Brobdingnagians "countervail" while the myriads of Lilliputian small businessmen are trampled underfoot. It is the consumer who foots the bill for higher prices, higher wages, and higher profits in an unending spiral of inflation.

The Legal Integration of the Plural Groups in the Power Process

This section is concerned with the relations of the plural groups and the law. It starts with the empirical observation that, while practically all other aspects of social life are subject to legal regulation, the plural groups remain largely *hors de loi*. The questions are: Is it desirable, and, if it is desirable, is it feasible, to establish legal rules for the functioning of the plural society? How can the factual role the plural groups play in the power process be rationalized by legal—constitutional or legislative—norms?

The desirability is conditioned by the political philosophy of the observer. If he believes, with Dr. Pangloss, that we live in the best of all possible worlds and should let nature take its course, he will accept the domination of our life by plural groups as an unalterable fact of the political biology of man. Since nothing can be done about it, nothing should be done. If, contrariwise, he is deeply alarmed by the relentlessly progressing collectivization of the individual, his mind will be open to legal remedies to curb the excesses of the laissez faire anarchy in which plural groups operate and into which they have forced us. In either case, the summary analysis of the efforts undertaken to date to bring the plural groups within the compass of the law and to integrate them thereby into the political process, submitted on the following pages, may not be wholly unwelcome.

Empirical as well as theoretical reasons suggest the distinction, for the purposes of this discussion, between the two kinds of plural groups: the political parties and the socioeconomic interest groups.

THE LEGAL INSTITUTIONALIZATION OF POLITICAL PARTIES

Political parties and the constitution.—The indispensability of political parties for the power process in constiutional democracy as well as modern autocracy is self-evident. Without them none of the patterns of government of the former could function, nor would totalitarian autocracy be possible without the mass-mobilizing and mass-controlling agency of the single party. Yet it is striking that the vast majority of the constitutions, old and new,

altogether ignore the existence of parties, let alone their participation in the formation of the will of the state and the process
of political power in general. Political parties operate in a complete constitutional vacuum.

The American and the French revolutionary constitutions understandably failed to mention them. As eloquently expressed by
Madison in the *Federalist* (No. 10), they were stigmatized by the
founding fathers as pernicious factions. The French Revolution,
inheritor of the aversion of the *ancien régime* against *les corps
intermédiaires,* rejected them because they were held incompatible
with the ruling dogma of the sovereignty of the general will. For
both political philosophies the exercise of political power was
delegated exclusively to the constituted power holders. The constitutions of the nineteenth century were no less discreet on the
political parties, which, in many instances, had been midwives at
their birth. It was deemed sufficient that the liberal right of free
association implied freedom of political organization.

The constitutions of the twentieth century at first continued the
conspiracy of silence. Weimar, so articulate in most other respects,
mentioned the party only in passing (Art. 130) by enjoining the
public officials to conduct themselves as servants of the community and not of a party. After the Second World War when
the importance of the political parties for the process of constitutional democracy could no longer be glossed over, the taboo was
broken, and references to them occurred. They are, however,
cautious and marginal. Italy included an elaborate section on
political relations in her constitution of 1947 but confines herself
(Art. 49) to the declaratory statement that "all citizens have the
right to organize themselves in political parties to co-operate, in a
democratic way, in determining national policies." None of the
three references to parties in the French constitution of 1946 is
more than strictly utilitarian, pertaining to their role in certain
elections.[17] More recently the existence of political parties is constitutionally honored, at least by negation, for example, in Latin

America, where political parties deemed subversive by the ruling classes are constitutionally outlawed.

None of the constitutions even remotely touches on the over-riding influence of the political parties in the dynamics of the power process by the designation, maintenance, and removal of the power holders government and parliament. Ostrich-like, they treat the legislative assemblies as though they were composed of sovereign and self-determining representatives functioning in a party-disinfected atmosphere. The fact that the deputies are dele-gated into the assemblies on the tickets of the parties and, accord-ing to the pattern of government, subject to their dictates and discipline is ignored. The spurious *mystique* that the member rep-resents the entire nation is tediously repeated, with the practical result that he may change his party allegiance at will without the risk of having to meet his constituents. It is readily admitted, how-ever, that, to subject the interplay of the parties under parlia-mentary government to constitutional rules would encounter near-insuperable difficulties of the normative technique. Not even the most felicitous verbal formula could match the realities of the give-and-take of the parties and the preponderance of the party leadership in the process of public policy formation.

The Bonn Basic Law and the constitution of the German Democratic Republic penetrate somewhat deeper into the constitu-tional no man's land of the political parties. Bonn (Art. 21, sec. 1) recognizes the political parties as "participants in the formation of the political will of the people." Similar declaratory statements are strewn over a number of the *Land* constitutions; that of the (now extinct) *Land* Baden boasted a veritable catechism for party be-havior in government and opposition that would satisfy even the most meticulous Emily Post of political etiquette.[18]

Of all constitutions—including that of the U.S.S.R., which ex-plicitly refers to the Communist party as the vanguard of the working people (Arts. 126 and 141)—only that of the German Democratic Republic (1949) comes to grips with the participation of the parties in the governmental process (Arts. 91, 92). But the pungent odor peculiar to "People's Democracies" robs it of any didactic value for other nations. The political party (*"Fraktion"*) with the greatest number of seats in the Volkskammer designates the minister-president, who, in turn, appoints the cabinet. All parties with at least forty members participate, in proportion to their strength, in the cabinet. The Socialist Unity party, the camouflaged communists, takes the lion's share after rigged elections, and the opposition is constitutionally the prisoner of the majority party, since rejection of the offer to join the government, permissible under Article 92, section 2, is considered illegal obstruction. From this disingenuous arrangement derives the by now famous "block system": the parties represented in the cabinet agree in advance on the policy decisions, and the Volkskammer has only to confirm them.[19]

To this writer's knowledge, the constitution of Uruguay is the only instance of constitutional democracy attempting the direct incorporation of the political parties into the governmental process. Under the constitution of 1952, of the nine members of the National Council of Government,* six are constitutionally assigned to the winning majority party, three to the minority party, or, if there are several, distributed among them in proportion to their voting strength. The opposition party (or parties), thus, is joined with the majority in the government. In addition, the participation of the parties in the designation of all elective offices is anchored in the constitution itself (Art. 79), based on a very complex regulation concerning the legal possession of the party emblem (*lema*), known in French legislation as *étiquette*. Only groups in legal, that is, judicially controlled, possession of a *lema* or *sub-lema* can participate in the elections.[20]

Political parties and the legislation.—Because of the reticence of the constitutions toward the political parties, regulation of their legal status is left to ordinary legislation. If regulated at all, parties

* See above, p. 120.

are treated as associations under private law, permissible under the guaranteed freedom of association and as such subject to implementing legislation. They may have the right or the duty to register and incorporate. But even this minimum formalism is neither mandatory nor voluntarily complied with everywhere.

The situation may be exemplified by France.[21] Political parties do not possess or enjoy any special legal status. Like all other associations, they are subject to the regulations, most liberal at that, of the law of July 1, 1900, on the freedom of association, the first in French history which recognized the complete liberty of group formation. All that is required is a declaration before the prefecture and the deposition of the association's bylaws. As voluntary non-profit organizations, parties do not have a legal personality, and their capacity to own property is limited.

However, this indefinite legal status of political parties is confounded by the interest the legislator otherwise takes in them, primarily in connection with the mechanics of the electoral process and of intraparliamentary management. The electoral laws necessarily have to accept their existence. Since the introduction of proportional representation, which cannot be operated without organized parties, they have become a legitimate object of legislation, although it is curious to note that many election statutes, in maidenly reticence, still refer to "lists" and "candidates" instead of to parties and party nominees. The nomination of candidates is practically everywhere the monopoly of the organized parties. The legal recognition of political associations formed *ad hoc* for the nomination of candidates is most sporadic. For example, the *Wählervereinigung*, provided by the law of 1949 for the election of the German Bundestag, which was intended to counterbalance the nomination monopoly of the established parties and to give a break to "independents," remained academic and was not included in the law of 1953. The formation of new parties is generally discouraged. Political parties are also indirectly recognized in legislation incidental to the election process—legislation against corrupt and illegal practices and dealing with the regulation of campaign expenses and election propaganda, where such regulations exist.

The gap left by the constitutions with regard to the participation of the parties in the political process proper is partly filled by the Standing Orders of the assemblies. Often their influence on the prevailing pattern of government is as great as that of the constitution itself. Again the situation may be exemplified by France. The long historical process reveals that political groups steadily, if slowly, progressed toward recognition as instruments of the governmental process. At first their existence within the assemblies was strictly *de facto*, based on custom and utility. Intraparliamentary elections for the officers of the assembly were conducted on the hypothesis that the deputies voted personally for whomever they wished, and the members of the commissions were even designated by lot. But the parties crashed the door of the political process even without official invitation. In a cabinet crisis the president was compelled to consult with the party leaders. Formal recognition was the next logical step. By a resolution of 1910 the Chamber of Deputies, followed by the Senate in 1920, granted the political groups official status under the Standing Orders. The members of the commissions are now appointed according to the proportional strength of the parties instead of by lot. The supreme intra-assembly authority, the Conference of the Presidents, is composed, in addition to the president and vice-president of the legislature, of the chairmen of the commissions and the chairmen of the political groups within the parliament. The parties, thus, have acquired a legal status, at least for the purposes of their participation in the parliamentary business.

On the other hand, in Europe next to no legislative effort was devoted to regulating the intraparty structure, except in the negative sense that parties which, by their aims or techniques of conduct, tend to violate the constitutional-democratic order may be dissolved. This may be done either by judicial process, as in Germany-Bonn, or by government decree, as was permissible under the exceptional legislation directed against the paramilitary fascist "leagues" and other groups in France in the thirties.[22]

A fundamental charter for political parties.—Much of this legislation either is merely utilitarian or is marginal to the political process. The core of the problem, the standards for the intraparty structure, is left untouched. Regulation of party structure can be accomplished, if at all, only by an organic law or charter prescribing certain minimum standards, to which all parties have to conform, for party organization and for intraparty government. European and Latin American constitutional theorists show an acute consciousness of the facts that the state of the twentieth century is a party state and that the sovereignty of the people actually has been superseded by the sovereignty of the parties. This is reflected by the search for an organic law for political parties. The results *de lege lata* are negligible. The Constitutional Committee of the French National Assembly, when drafting the first constitution of 1946, adopted by a small majority (22 to 17), in the session of December 7, 1945, a plan for a "Fundamental Party Charter" to be included in the constitution. It set forth the following principles: plurality of political parties, adhesion of every party to the tenets of the Declaration of the Rights of Man, democratic intraparty government, and public control of revenues and expenditures. Far from being popular with the parties themselves, and received with complete indifference by the public, the plan failed to become incorporated in the first constitution and was silently dropped in the second. In Argentina an ambitious "Organic Statute for Political Parties" was placed on the statute book by the Farrell regime in 1944 but failed ot be applied by Perón.[23] The party statute prescribed by the Bonn constitution (Art. 21, sec. 3) did not proceed beyond the government project stage and has no chance of being enacted.

Legislation on political parties in the United States.—In contrast to the unregulated liberty of political parties in Europe, parties in the United States[24] are subject to a high degree of legislative control, resulting in their formal integration into the political process. Political parties are mentioned neither in the state nor in the federal constitutions. Nonetheless, political practice and the courts have firmly established their right to exist and to operate, on the basis of the constitutional guaranties of free assembly, petition, and vote. The right to organize in political parties is assumed to be inherent in democratic government. Under the federal constitution (Art. I, sec. 4, clause 1), elections for federal offices are subject to state legislation. The authorization (second sentence of clause 1) that congress may legislate on federal elections has been used most sparingly.

At first and for a long time political parties were considered private, voluntary, non-profit associations with complete freedom to regulate their internal affairs, including membership conditions. In addition, the parties enjoyed the undisputed right to nominate candidates for elective office and to determine the methods of nomination. After the introduction of the Ballot Acts—the Australian ballot under which the names of all candidates are printed, at state expense, on one and the same ticket—the initial stage of the party unregulated by legislation was followed by a great deal of state legislation concerning membership qualifications, illegal and corrupt practices, and campaign expenditures; on the last two subjects also federal legislation was enacted. But the decisive limitation on party autonomy was brought about by the primary legislation enacted since the beginning of this century. This deals with the procedure for the nomination of candidates for elective office, both federal and state. Intended to protect party autonomy, it factually transformed the political party from an extra-constitutional private organization into a state organ. Nomination by party primary or convention was turned into a statutory right, with the proviso that the parties had to observe the legislative requirements. Other measures deprived the parties of the previously claimed right to determine the qualifications of membership. Since the primary is an integral part of the electoral, and of the governmental, process, legislation may prescribe standards and conditions. Different from the French legal theory under which membership in a party is established by contract,[25] the American political party cannot set standards of admission designed to exclude any person. The right to join a party of one's own choosing is an individual right under law. In a series of epochal decisions the Supreme Court asserted this principle on behalf of the colored citizens previously excluded from the "white" primary.[26]

Much less successful was a secondary aim of the primary legislation, namely, to secure by elective procedures the democratic designation of the intraparty government. The party leadership remains a largely self-appointed oligarchy, and the elective procedures, where prescribed, are used merely to confirm antecedent decisions of the party hierarchy.

This accomplishment—the establishment of the party as a legislatively controlled instrumentality of the political government—strangely contrasts with its continued status as a non-incorporated, non-profit association; the only exception, seemingly, is in California, where the party is legally considered a corporation.[27] This is all the more anachronistic, since the large parties are business enterprises with considerable staffs, funds, and often property; they engage in important financial transactions and incur debts and liabilities. The recognition of the governmental status of the political party would require implementation by granting it a legal personality of its own.

Finally, the United States has also felt that it could not spare itself the need of special legislation against subversive parties. The original restrictions directed against individual activities deemed subversive were extended to a specifically named political party collectively.[28]

The over-all result of the comprehensive legislation is that the political party in the United States—and this again is a distinguishing singularity—has been accorded the status of a recognized instrumentality of the political process, a legal institutionalization which otherwise only totalitarian regimes have found necessary to undertake.[29]

While none would advocate a totalitarian solution for the constitutional-democratic state, the foregoing material on the regulated liberty of American parties may well be worthy of the attention of other states in search of a solution of one of the most crucial problems of their political existence. It may suggest the conclusion that the complete laissez faire of the parties in the governmental process could well be replaced by state regulation securing intraparty democracy and formalizing their role in the political process. Such rudimentary beginnings as do exist are stymied by the inertia of public opinion and the resistance of the party hierarchies to any legislative rationalization which would endanger their hold on the party machines and, through it, on the governmental process.

FUNCTIONAL REPRESENTATION AND THE LEGAL INSTITUTIONALIZATION OF INTEREST GROUPS

Since the formal integration of the political parties, ubiquitous as they are, made little headway against the indifference of public opinion, one would assume that the institutionalization of the socioeconomic interest groups, equally omnipresent but much more elusive, would find even less attention. The opposite is true. The claim, and often clamor, to bring the interest groups into the state machinery proper is being supported by a powerful intellectual pressure group. Various practical attempts also have been undertaken, from Napoleon's Acte Additionnel (1815)[30] down to recent times. Centering on the theory of corporativism and the technique of functional or vocational representation, they aim at the inclusion of the interest groups in the legislative process.*

The intellectual sources of corporativism.—Under the individ-

---

* The issue is basically different from the participation of the interest groups in the administrative process, discussed above, pp. 358 ff.

ualistic-equalitarian flood of the French Revolution all previously existing landmarks of the organic structure of society were submerged. The democratic ideology rode to victory on the mechanistic concept of manhood suffrage: one man, one vote, without regard to his intellectual and economic qualifications. The political process was anchored in the weight of the numerical vote cast and the number of seats obtained in the assembly. The mechanics of the representative system worked tolerably well as long as the political parties were merely different wings of an otherwise homogeneous ruling class. With the extension of the suffrage to the masses and the proliferation of ideologically conflicting parties, parliamentarism ran into stormy waters. Political parties, managed by professional politicians, became discredited and, with them, parliamentarism itself. Moreover, the highly organized interest groups, within and without parliament and parties, turned the major policy decisions to their benefit. The cleavage between the pluralist reality and the fiction of parliament's political monopoly became manifest.

All these factors combined to create in Europe, at the beginning of this century, a widespread malaise toward parliamentarism and parliamentary democracy among substantial sections of the intellectuals and the masses. The legal integration of the interest groups into the parliament in the form of functional or vocational representation was proclaimed the panacea. Inorganic and chaotic was to be replaced by organic and rationalized pluralism.

The pragmatic reaction against the mechanization of the political process by parliaments and parties allied itself with a powerful ideology—organicism and corporativism. It drew its persuasive strength from different sources. Democratic parliamentarism had hardly been born when Edmund Burke pitted against the artificially created state of the French Revolution his image of the organically grown, and growing, society. He was rediscovered by the neopluralists. Particularly in Central Europe, political romanticism, more often than not the respectable disguise of conservativism and reaction, indulged in gilded reminiscences—frequently presented in brilliant literary form—of the happy equilibrium of the social forces in the corporate organization of the estates (*Stände*).[31] In England guild socialism and in the Latin countries revolutionary syndicalism traveled the same road, if for different destinations. The corporate ideology derived its major prestige, however, from the Catholic church. Since the papal encyclicals of Leo XIII (*Rerum Novarum*, 1891) and Pius XI (*Quadragesimo Anno*, 1931), the church had presented a new social philosophy to exorcize the blandishments the Marxist eschatology held out for the laboring masses. Corporativism, consequently, found its most fertile soil in Catholic nations: Italy, Spain, Portugal, Austria, Eire, and Brazil. In France the organicist reform could draw on such varied inspirations as Saint-Simon, Louis Blanc, the Paris Commune, and Léon Duguit's social solidarity. But to proceed from romantic conservativism "à la recherche du temps perdu" to antidemocratic activism was a small step indeed. Contemporary autocracy, thus, opened the door wide to corporativism, primarily in fascist Italy and falangist Spain. A different but no less influential contribution was made by Russian bolshevism in the form of the Soviet principle, replacing the mechanical territorial structuration of the parliament.

Since the second half of the nineteenth century repeated attempts have been undertaken to translate the theory into practice. Bismarck's antiliberal and antidemocratic genius could not fail to play with corporativism in the short-lived Economic Council of Prussia (1880–86), as a first step toward the abolition of the Reichstag. Proposals for functional representation were introduced, in vain, in France and Belgium. But the practical institutionalization of functionalism had to wait for the antiparliamentarian impulses of the twentieth century.

The actual efforts to integrate economic and vocational interests into the legislative and political process are reflected by the following patterns: (1) economic interest parties within the parliament (this subject has been discussed before);* (2) functional representation in the second chambers; (3) division of the legislative function between the political and an economic branch; (4) implementation of the political parliament by an economic council; and (5) integral corporativism.

Functional representation in the second chamber.—The most obvious place for the formal incorporation of the interest groups in the legislative process may seem to be the second chamber. Dating back to the nineteenth century, such efforts continued intermittently in both constitutional and authoritarian states, the former exemplified by the Rumanian Senate under the reform of 1923, the latter by the House of Magnates in Hungary in the legislation of 1926. Among the recent streamlined functional upper houses the Senate of Eire under the constitution of 1937 (Arts. 18 and 19) is noteworthy. Of its sixty members, forty-three are elected from panels of candidates representing the different vocational strata—culture, industry, labor, agriculture, public administration—in addition to eleven members appointed by the prime minister and six elected by the universities. The practical results are disappointing:[32] Only in a remote sense does the Senate conduct itself as a functional representation. Since the parties of the Dáil Eireann (lower house) and the local authorities are in charge of the actual selection of the candidates from the panels, the senators act and vote on party lines.

Generally speaking, the inclusion of vocational representatives in the upper house may benefit the quality of the debates, but, in view of the limited importance of second chambers in most states, it does not give the plural groups an influence commensurate to their position in a pluralist society, nor does it detract one iota from their extra-constitutional operations.[33]

Combination of the political with a functional assembly.—Under this pattern the legislative body consists of two houses. Two systems are theoretically possible. Either the political assembly,

* See above, pp. 352 ff.

elected by the people at large, deals with political legislation, and the economic branch, designated by the interest groups, with economic legislation; or both houses, of equal rank, deal uniformly with both types of legislation. The first-mentioned scheme could nowhere proceed beyond the blueprint stage for the simple reason that politics and economics are no longer separable, if they ever were. A labor-management act, for example, has vast political implications.

The way out of this dilemma was thought to be the juxtaposition of a political lower and a vocational upper house. The device is attractive to authoritarian regimes desirous of a respectable constitutional disguise. Antonio de Oliveira Salazar's constitution of 1933 in Portugal is the best illustration because it offers twenty years of practical experience of neocorporativism.[34] The benevolent dictatorship of Salazar enjoys an excellent reputation abroad, and not undeservedly. It is a non-fascist, thoroughly Catholic, and, therefore, thoroughly ideology-resistant authoritarian regime under an exceptionally honest and efficient leader, with a minimum of political oppression and a maximum of governmental paternalism. But the corporative laurels cannot be justly claimed. The Corporate Chamber (Arts. 103–6) is a curlicue on a regimented and planned economy, and the vocational interests are organized outside in effectively managed co-operatives—fisheries, cork, general agriculture—with the upper house retaining such advisory functions as the state managers allow it.

The Austrian example,[35] under the "Ender" constitution (1934) of the Dollfuss regime, was a product of clerical fascism, boasting no fewer than five different branches of a pseudocorporative legislature. Whatever Hitler's sins, the extinction of this specious specimen of neocorporativism was not the least of his accomplishments.

Economic councils.—A more fruitful course for the integration of the vocational groups into the legislative function is pursued by the institution of the economic council. Among the countries to establish such bodies were Weimar Germany, Czechoslovakia after 1920, and the French Third and Fourth republics. The feature common to all is that they participate in legislation in a strictly consultative capacity only. They appear in different operational patterns: the economic council either is linked with the parliament as a separate advisory agency, is at the disposal of the government alone, or is available to both. The Economic Council of the Third Republic was attached to the cabinet (to the office of the president of the council) until the reform of 1936 linked it officially with the parliament. Weimar Germany, faithful to the new accent on socioeconomic matters, anchored the Reichswirtschaftsrat in the constitution itself (Art. 165) as the apex of a never completed pyramid of functional organizations. It served as a consultative body to the Reichstag. The National Economic Council of the French Fourth Republic likewise was provided by the constitution (Art. 25); authorized "to examine all bills of socioeconomic character," it serves both government and parliament.

The crucial problems of all such institutions are to delineate the various vocational groups to be represented and to assign to each the numerical weight commensurate to its economic importance for the community. No arrangement is wholly free from arbitrariness. In the German and French variants the consumer element was badly underrepresented. As to the designation of the members, the German and the French Third Republic patterns relied on government appointment, while the members of the Economic Council of the Fourth Republic are elected by the professional groups themselves, the far preferable method.

The result of the experiment differs in Germany and in France. The Reichswirtschaftsrat,[36] after an initial spurt, soon became moribund; Bonn did not resurrect it. In France the Economic Council was found to be sufficiently useful to be strengthened in the constitution of 1946.[37] It renders advice on economic and social issues to the government and the parliament; publishes, under the reform of 1951, valuable annual reports similar to those of the American Council of Economic Advisers to the president; and makes large-scale studies on important socioeconomic subjects, in much the same way as the American Hoover commissions. In both instances the councils proved a wholesome antidote to the policy-planning monopoly of the ministerial bureaucracy and supplied solid information for the parliamentary bodies. However, they suffered from the defect that, in the plenary sessions, decisions were made on management-labor divisions rather than on the merits of each case, with the result that the best work was done by small committees. No real *esprit de corps* could develop. If the purpose was to provide for a forum of the plural interests, it was reached only to a very limited extent. The councils could not canalize the extra-constitutional plural forces into the legislative process. The political parliaments, jealous of their legislative monopolies, did not allow them any measurable influence on the policy-making function. As vehicles of organic pluralism these institutions fell far short of the expectations.

Integral corporativism.—The complete realization of the corporate ideology is integral corporativism: the replacement of the political parliament, elected on a territorial basis, by a functional assembly whose constituencies are the plural groups. In a remote sense this pattern resembles the guild structure of the medieval cities in which the representatives of the trades and crafts organizations constituted the political government and regulated the economic process. Recent applications of integral corporativism are the organization of fascist Italy and the "soviet" structure of the U.S.S.R. prior to 1936.

The consummation of Italian corporativism[38] developed slowly on the basis of the syndical organization, a near-gapless system of labor-management relations under state control, climaxing in the much-vaunted Labor Charter of April 21, 1927. The second stage led to the creation of the so-called "corporations," twenty-two allegedly autonomous vertical frames embracing the major segments of the national economy. Membership in one of the subdivisions was compulsory for any person engaged in an economic pursuit or profession. In their completed form these bodies constituted pyramidal service frames stretching from production to distribution and consumption and controlling all phases of management-labor relations. At the apex resided the National Council of Corporations, a wholly fascist body of some five hundred members, rigidly supervised by the National Ministry of Corporations. The final stage was reached (1939) with the supersession of the political parliament by the Chamber of Fasces and Corporations, integrating the syndical and corporative stratifications. Its members, some six hundred hand-picked fascists, were appointed by the government. It never came to assume the political functions of the defunct parliament which, under the fascist dictatorship, had been negligible anyway.

The Italian experiment, undertaken in an economy precariously balanced between underdeveloped industrialism and still largely primitive agrarianism and hampered by the general pressures of the time, was nothing but a gigantic apparatus for the control of socioeconomic life by party and state. It offers little didactic value for the constitutional-democratic states. A playground for party politicians, captains of industry holding the whip hand over labor, and some ambitious and corrupt labor bosses, it contributed nothing to raising the standards of living or preparing for the crucible of war. From the comparative viewpoint, however, it is regrettable that the only corporative experiment undertaken to date in a western state was fatally blighted by its character as an instrument of totalitarian control.

That the indigenous habitat of contemporary corporativism is the authoritarian regime is also confirmed by its attempted institutionalizations in the Third Reich and in Franco Spain. In the former[39] the elaborate estates (*Stände*) and "service frames" (*Dienstordnungen*) were exclusively used to co-ordinate and subordinate the plural groups under the control of state and party. For the totalitarian domination they proved indispensable; earning a living was conditioned upon membership in one of the groups. The same holds true, with less rigidity corresponding to lesser administrative ability, for the syndical organizations of Spanish falangism.

Finally, the functional structuration of the early Soviet state,[40] under the constitutions of 1918 and 1924, cannot be passed over in a survey of contemporary corporative experimentation. To Lenin's fertile brain, stimulated by the Paris Commune of 1871, the activists of the abortive revolution of 1905 proved serviceable for an organizational principle altogether original in the political process, the "soviets." The councils of workers and peasants, in the Bolshevik revolution of 1917, were to assume simultaneously the roles of the executive and legislative agencies on the local, intermediary, and national levels. Lenin's conceptions were dictated by tactical as well as theoretical reasons: free elections could not have brought victory to the activist minority of the Bolsheviks, and Bolshevik theory rejected the separation of functions along with their rejection of western parliamentarism. Consequently, in the pre-1936 period the soviets were the official power holders. The vertical pyramid culminated in the All-Union Soviet Congress, roughly comparable to the parliament in the West. The soviet technique was dropped by the westernized Stalin constitution of 1936. Once again, what the Soviet "functional" representation accomplished was not genuine functionalism of freely operating plural forces but an instrument for the totalitarian control of socioeconomic and political life by the Communist party. While great emphasis was placed on mass participation in the soviets of the different levels and discussion in them was encouraged, the soviets themselves remained annexes of the Communist party and its Politburo.

Neocorporativism in Yugoslavia.—The corporative organization under the constitution of 1953 in Yugoslavia, however, may come to be of considerable interest to the West. Likewise operating in an authoritarian environment, it appears less obnoxious as a camouflage of state control, and its democratic overtones are far more authentic than in any one of the patterns discussed before.

Specific circumstances impelled the Tito regime toward a socio-political pattern which combines features of industrial democracy with the techniques of functional representation. To hold the allegiance of the people after the break with the Cominform (1948), Marshal Tito committed himself to the reduction of the rigid Stalinist centralization and bureaucratization and the retrenchment of the state activities in economics by what may be called an attempt to produce the grass roots of collective democracy. The decisive step was taken by the Workers' Councils Law of 1950. The representatives elected by the workers and employees in the individual enterprises and no longer exclusively chosen from the communist ranks were given the right of active participation in the plant management, similar to the codetermination in the German coal and steel industry (1951). Plant management was withdrawn, to a considerable extent, from the state and party managers and transferred to the workers and employees themselves.

This trend toward decentralized socialism was continued by the constitution of 1953. The new philosophy called for new techniques of government and administration; these were accomplished by the introduction, on all administrative levels, of the bicameral system: a lower house elected on the territorial-numerical basis and an upper house which serves as a functional representation of workers, employees, peasants, and artisans. The horizontal decentralization was vertically capped by the Federal People's Assembly, the center of political and economic government. It consists of two houses (Arts. 24 ff.), namely, the Federal Council and the Council of Producers—or, rather, of three, if the Council of Nationalities is added, the latter reflecting the federal structure in member republics. While the members of the Federal Council, as the political parliament, are elected on the traditional territorial basis, those of the Council of Producers derive their mandate from an authentic corporate suffrage conducted within the framework of the three vocational divisions of workers and employees of the individual economic enterprises, agricultural co-operatives, and other occupational associations and organizations. To determine the relative strength of the various segments of the national economy, three large categories were established: industry (including transportation), agriculture, and crafts. These categories have one hundred and forty, seventy, and six representatives, respectively, in the Producers' Council. The two houses are unequal in jurisdiction, the Federal Council being the more important. But to the Council of Producers are assigned (Art. 40) specific rights in line with its special economic objectives; it may, in addition to recommendations, pass binding decisions on the work of the economc units, state organs, and self-governing institutions.

The operation of the Council of Producers has to be considered in relation to the novel construction of the executive function, residing in the Federal Executive Council. It appears to be a curious blend of the Soviet-invented presidium and the customary cabinet or council of ministers, a sort of, collective executive integrated with the legislature. The entire system, original in several aspects, may be classified as assembly government into which the plural groups have been built.

Hailed by its inventors as a trail-blazer toward democratic socialism and genuine functional representation, the scheme is commented on with more skepticism by a foreign observer.[41] It is still on trial. But if it succeeds at all, or even moderately, it will be the first time that functional representation has been integrated into a state society intended to be democratic.

Evaluation of functional representation.—With the exception of consultative economic councils, of limited importance and success, and of the Yugoslav reform, still in the experimental stage, all efforts legally to integrate the plural groups into the legislative process have occurred in authoritarian regimes, where they have been alibis for the unrelenting control of socioeconomic life. As yet it does not seem feasible in constitutional-democratic states to canalize the laissez faire dynamics of the interest groups into the frame of state regulation. The failure to date is not due to lack of public interest. Although the United States is inhospitable[42] to any rationalization of the pluralist reality, the issue continues to claim public attention in most other nations. The discouraging results must be traced to deeper causes: (1) There are no viable categories to serve for the delineation of the plural groups. Labor, industry, agriculture, and commerce are not homogeneous entities; each comprises subdivisions with often irreconcilable policies. How could one find, for example, a common denominator within the over-all category of transportation, which includes rail, plane, truck, and shipping interests? (2) Even if agreement could be reached on the basic divisions, the specific voting weight attributed to each of them would have either to be calculated by mechanical standards—number of employees, investment capital, etc.—or to be determined arbitrarily. (3) According to the corporative mythology, the functional representation will bring the elite of the vocational experts into the legislative process; can they, however, be found by electoral procedures? Elected, within each category, will be those who know how to pull the strings. (4) Even the best experts in their chosen field will be no better, and often much worse, equipped than the professional politicians in parliament to deal with questions in which they are not experts. Decisions in a multimembered body would always have to be taken by majority, and the majority technique defies and defeats the very purpose of functional representation, namely, policy-making by the experts. Wild lobbying and logrolling inside the assembly would be the inevitable result. (5) The great division of plural stratification is still between management and labor. A new two-party system would emerge, with certain groups that do not fit into either category tipping the scales. (6) To enable all citizens, including the consumers, to be represented would require the compulsory unionization of the entire community. Everybody would be tied up in the strait jacket of collectivization. (7) Even the most sophisticated technique of functional representation would not eliminate and, perhaps, not even measurably relocate the free-for-all struggle of the interest groups for power.

Again the Shadow of the Leviathan

To dismantle the corporate *mystique* is not difficult. But the problems of the interest groups in the power process and their relations to the official power holders are left as unresolved as before, and the correlative issue of the interaction of the political parties and the socioeconomic interest groups is not even touched. Yet, unless human ingenuity in politics, which invented the representative technique, the separation of functions, and the political party, devises a new approach, the danger threatens that the immensely delicate and complex plural mechanism will get stalled and break down; moreover, individual liberty and self-determination will become further eroded and destroyed and, with it, constitutional democracy. Ultimately—this can safely be predicted—the superbly organized anarchy of the intermediary bodies, political parties as well as socioeconomic interest groups and "oligopolies," will have to be brought under social control. It is this writer's considered opinion that one of the crucial issues confronting the state society in the mid-twentieth century is that of overcoming the untrammeled laissez faire pluralism of our age by integrating the plural groups, parties as well as interest groups, into the political process through effective and socially enforcible legal arrangements. How this fundamental reform of our contemporary state society can be brought about is beyond his knowledge or even his imagination. But one thing appears certain to him: a supreme arbiter between the competing plural forces that dominate the power process and choke the individual must move in, and this be none other than the State itself. The only alternative to more private government is more public government.

Only the political government, installed in power by democratic processes uncontrolled by the interest groups, is able to function as the custodian of the individual against his collectivization by the plural forces. To save the ultimate values of political democracy, plural democracy will have to be regulated.

But this development carries with it the incalculable risk that the individual, rescued from the tyranny of the free-wheeling plural forces, will have to submit to the authoritarian direction of the state. And—is it possible to open the road toward the neo-paternalism of the "neutral," "objective," "benevolent" state if it is blocked by the realities of the power process prevailing in our technological society, where the major interest groups (or one of them) are so deeply intrenched in the official power holders that they cannot be peaceably dislodged? What will be the influence on this development—retarding or accelerating—of the impending revolution of the atomic age or, if solar energy is harnessed, of the solar age? The unregulated liberty of the plural forces, political parties no less than interest groups, will constitute the major problem of statecraft in the second half of the twentieth century. Once again it will focus on the eternal conflict of any state society, the reconciliation of freedom and authority. More than one hundred years ago de Tocqueville warned: "On ne peut se dissimuler que la liberté illimitée d'association, en matière politique, ne soit de toutes les libertés la dernière qu'un peuple puisse supporter. Si elle ne le fait tomber dans l'anarchie, elle la lui fait pour ainsi dire, toucher à chaque instant."[43]

Postscript

Postscript

This book was first published in 1957 and was reprinted in 1962. A considerably enlarged translation, under the title *Verfassungslehre* (for which no English equivalent exists) appeared in Germany in 1959. The Spanish and the Japanese translations followed in 1965.

A postscript to the first edition may be useful to guide the reader through the manifold changes that have occurred on the political scene since the book was first published.

Constitutions

When this book was first published, approximately seventy states were members of the United Nations. Now this number has increased to some hundred and fifteen; as yet, no end is in sight. All newcomers have given themselves new constitutions by various procedures, through national assemblies, governmental action, or plebiscites. Constitution-making has become a veritable industry. Being put to an almost daily test, the tripartite division of constitutions (*supra*, pp. 147 ff.) into normative, nominal, and semantic documents has been fully confirmed. Few of the recent instruments of government are normative in the sense that, in the reality of the political process, they are applicable as they were intended. The majority remain nominal at best, holding out the hope that some distant day they may become truly normative. Others, in the expanding orbit of autocracy, remain strictly semantic, camouflaging nothing more than the existing power structure which could be changed only by revolution.

So-called Separation of Powers

Within the widening area of autocracy endowed with a nominal or, more often, a semantic constitution, the concept of the separation of powers (*supra*, pp. 34 ff.), so cherished by classical constitutionalism has become meaningless in spite of the lip service paid to it by all constitutions. Where political power is concentrated in the hands of a strong executive, whatever its name, the concept of shared political power that the separation idea implies is so clearly incompatible with the reality of executive ascendancy that the concept is flouted in practice. Likewise in established constitutional democracies, the theoretical divison of state power into executive, legislative, and judicial functions has been superseded by the new trinity of decision-making, decision-executing, and decision-controlling phases of the political process. Where the government controls a disciplined majority of the parliament and is safe from being overturned by the opposition (as at least normally in Great Britain, the German Federal Republic, and the French Fifth Republic after the election victory of the Gaullists in November, 1962), legislatures merely execute the legislative program of the cabinet and have little if any leeway for independent action. Only where classical presidentialism prevails, as in the United States, does the legislative body possess enough independence from the executive leadership to preserve the separation of powers. This situation was illustrated as well by the failure of the late President Kennedy to obtain the enactment of his legislative program as by the success of President Johnson in persuading Congress to do so, although both Congresses had a strong Democratic majority.

But even in the United States, where the separation of powers scheme is still valid, the borderlines have become obliterated; Congress is constantly encroaching on the presidential prerogative, for example, in foreign policy by the powers of the purse. The president usurps congressional functions, for example, by initiating, guiding, and vetoing legislation.

Totalitarian and Authoritarian Government

The terminological distinction between totalitarian and authoritarian government (*supra*, pp. 58 ff.) has proved its usefulness within recent years. Although generally the area of authoritarianism has become significantly enlarged, no new totalitarian regimes have installed themselves, if this term is properly understood as denoting a pattern of rule under which the power holders can inculcate an ideology as the dominant way of life into the power addressees and society. The creation of a genuinely totalitarian society requires organizational and educational efforts of such magnitude that recently only Communist China seems to have achieved it. In the Soviet satellite countries and even in Russia itself, the totalitarian aspects of social and political life are reported to have become visibly diluted. Obviously the economic stabilization has resulted in a weakening of the totalitarian incentive in most Communist regimes. In a period of universal prosperity the socioeconomic climate conducive to the emergence of genuine totalitarian fascism does no longer exist.

Similarly an ideological approximation or even reconciliation between the political systems of Western constitutionalism and Communism seems to be in the making. Although assiduously maintained by both sides as a propagandistic device, the Iron Curtain has practically ceased to exist. The once-rigid bipolarization imperceptibly has given way to a flattening out of what formerly appeared to be unbridgeable differences. State ownership of industry as well as state management of social services has increased in the West; individual initiative has returned, although on a smaller scale, to the East. One may even assume that the previously dominant ideologies nurtured by mutual exclusiveness have begun to converge into a single quasi-universal ideology, namely, increasing the living standards of the mass of the people. The means of reaching this goal differ in line with the prevailing dogma or philosophy; but once again the dogmas or philosophies approximate one another as increased national productivity—the economic shibboleth of this era—as improved social services for the aged and disabled, and as better educational opportunities for the under-privileged are being provided for. In short, what a current slogan describes as the "war against poverty" has risen to the rank of an all-embracing ideology, beside which all seemingly irreconcilable ideological ingredients of official dogma shrink to insignficance. Possibly the Communist world is ahead of Western endeavors in this effort. Even Western emphasis on individualism has had to yield to a more and more collectivist society which is indivisible—not being capable of existing half affluent and half poor. More and more, the individual has to surrender to a pluralist-enmeshed society. Today East and West differ only in the degree of progressing collectivization, or, speaking economically, in the relative size of the public and the private sector.

Techniques of the Political Process

The approximation which is under way between Western constitutionalism and Communism extends beyond the ideological framework even to the techniques of the political process. The Soviets themselves, not to speak of the Eastern European Communist regimes, found it convenient and prudent to substitute, in the operation of the governmental process, a definite measure of calculated orderliness, which may be spoken of as the Communist version of the rule of law, for the former arbitrary methods of violence and lawlessness. Persons considered enemies of the state are no longer dealt with summarily; they merely are removed from office. Purges of nonconformists have ceased. The gap between the ruling elite and the mass of the power addressees has been narrowed. The pattern of a single man's unchallengeable dictatorship, which was the characteristic of Stalinism, has been discarded in favor of collective leadership and ruling-group responsibility that are vested in the official positions of the Council of Ministers and the Central Committee of the Communist party (*supra*, pp. 171 ff.). Consequently, the replacement of Nikita S. Khrushchev by Kosygin and Brezhnev in October, 1964, was conducted by orderly processes which, incidentally, do not compare too un-favorably with the arbitrary methods by which the Earl of Home was installed as Prime Minister in Great Britain (October, 1963).

Authoritarian Government and Neopresidentialism

Probably the most conspicuous development of the past ten years is the increased prevalence of authoritarian government, in particular the more frequent use of the use of neopresidentialism (*supra*, pp. 65 ff.) which has become fashionable as a pattern of government. The establishment of Gaullism in France and its in-fluence on governments elsewhere may be the single most im-portant event since this book was first published.

During May and June, 1958, the French Fourth Republic, under the pressure of the Algerian impasse, was driven into a lethal crisis resulting in the complete disintegration of state authority. From this crisis General Charles de Gaulle emerged as the leader because only he alone was believed capable of resolving the Al-gerian dilemma gnawing at the vitals of the country. He fashioned his political concepts into a new instrument of government; the French Fifth Republic has lived under his constitution of October 5, 1958, ever since. Originally the constitution attempted to strike a balance between the strong and undisputed executive leadership vested in the president and his hand-picked cabinet, on the one hand, and a "domesticated" parliamentarism in which the political responsibility of the cabinet before the National Assembly was still implied. Subsequently, Charles de Gaulle was elected president for a seven-year term by an electoral college of some 80,000 "notables."

De Gaulle upheld the trust placed in him by the majority of the French people by solving the Algerian issue in spite of repeated rebellions of the military leaders. He also had the majority behind him when, contrary to expectations, he permitted Algeria to be-come independent. Within six years, however, the original intent of the instrument of government was distorted beyond recognition. The National Assembly, at first demonstrating a degree of independence from the presidency, carried a successful vote of non-confidence against Premier Georges Pompidou, leading to its dissolution (October 5, 1962). The following elections for the National Assembly (November 18 and 25, 1962) gave a strong victory to the Gaullist party which, for the first time in French parliamentary history, achieved an absolute majority. Simultaneously, by a procedure considered unconstitutional by all responsible constitutional lawyers, the method for electing the president was changed through a popular referendum (October 28, 1962); the Chief Executive will be elected by direct universal suffrage of the voters instead of by the electoral college. The new National Assembly proved wholly subservient to the government, functioning merely as the docile instrument for converting governmental proposals into statutes.

General de Gaulle was able to play havoc with his own constitution because of his undisputed personal prestige as a leader who had raised France's stature in the world, and the complete governmental control of state-owned telecommunications which are the primary means for forming public opinion. The government's monopoly will make the emergence of a popular leader to compete in the forthcoming elections with the incumbent (provided de Gaulle will have chosen to run again) next to impossible.

Characteristic of this type of *régime personnel*, by no means novel in France, is the use of the referendum or plebiscite (*supra*, pp. 263 ff., 267 ff.)[1] as a conspicuous demonstration of the people's acclamation of the leader's policies. The existing representative techniques were completely disregarded. Moreover, since the president can use his constitutional emergency powers (Art. 16) of ruling without constitutional limitations for lengthy periods, the neopresidential regime created a republican monarchy wholly in line with the personal style of de Gaulle. Compared with the government's monopoly in the control of telecommunications, which in turn were largely responsible for the outcome of the referenda, the press remained relatively free, although individual liberties were interfered with when the government believed it necessary for the paramount interests of the regime. Gaullism in France is a perfect pattern of neopresidentialism in the twilight zone between constitutionalism and autocracy.

Few expert observers are willing to concede that Gaullism will endure in France once its originator has departed from the political scene, either by natural causes or, most unlikely, by voluntary withdrawal. Given the notorious cyclicity of French political regimes, the demise of the Fifth and the advent of the Sixth Republic—possibly reverting to a reformed parliamentary system— may safely be expected.

The French pattern of streamlined neopresidentialism exerted a tremendous influence not only on the new African states formerly under French colonial control—recent illustrations are Tunisia (1959), Senegal and the Ivory Coast (1960), and Algeria (1963)— but also in other parts of the globe where the power holders believe it advantageous to disguise outright authoritarian rule as quasi-constitutional government. Because of its influence on other countries with a traditional instability or with the difficult tasks of incipient nationhood, Gaullism may well be considered to have created an "original" constitution (*supra*, p. 140).

The borderline between neopresidentialism and outright dictatorship cannot be drawn easily. Consequently, many of the new nations emerging from colonial rule have adopted a pattern of government in which a tribal chieftain who has risen to leadership in the process of statehood formation assumes dictatorial rule. Although constitutionally camouflaged as presidentialism, the power structure is actually tantamount to an unbridled dictatorship. This development may seem inevitable; it is illusory to expect that primitive peoples who are accustomed to a predominantly communal or tribal social structure and who are captives of traditional superstitions and taboos, unmitigated by mass literacy, would be capable of managing democratic self-government by Western-style electoral processes. As the emancipation from the previous benevolent colonial rule progressed, tribal chieftains who had been trained in the West rose to power as the natural elite of their people and the establishment of a dictatorship presented itself as the only viable method of integrating a tribal society into a state. As experience during recent years teaches: the assumption of dictatorial powers, in the disguise of a strictly nominal or even semantic constitution, seems to be the only feasible solution. Transitional dictatorship is operated sometimes by civilian, sometimes by military men. On the other hand, constitutionalism or constitutional democracy so far has gained few recruits from among the underdeveloped nations in Africa. It is hoped that the transition to constitutional government will ultimately be accomplished, but the process will be a time-consuming one at best. Its success is hampered by the near-universal fact that new African states are either non-party or single-party structures.[2]

Military Dictatorships

A noteworthy phenomenon of recent years, although by no means novel in history, is the rapid spread of the military dictatorship.[3] Its habitat is either in countries that have tried constitutional government and found it wanting or in those new nations which soon after birth, without the intermediary of constitutional government were plunged into military rule as the only way toward national survival. So many states in Africa, Asia, and last but not least, Latin America are being subjected to military rule that the mere enumeration would be tedious.

A definite pattern of seizure of power from civilian government has evolved. Since no single general controls the entire military establishment, usually a group of dissident high-ranking officers—generals or also occasionally colonels—form a collective revolutionary group, for which the Spanish term *junta* has become familiar. Group government, however, never lasts long; from the power struggle within the ruling clique an individual, more often than not different from the original initiator of the revolt, emerges as the single leader. Frequently, rather than submitting to a single leader, the various branches of the military engage one another in the struggle for supremacy, as amply demonstrated by events in Argentina. In this country the Air Force, considering itself the military elite for technological reasons, has an edge over the others. No military leader, however, is safe in the seat of power since he is constantly exposed to the rivalry of other generals. There are also instances in which the military, reluctant to directly assume power and responsibility, prefers a pseudo-civilian in control and enforces its policies through him, as was the case in the military take-over in Brazil (1964). Constitution and civil liberties are suspended for an indefinite period; political parties are dissolved and their re-formation prohibited. Large-scale purges of enemies, actual and potential, are conducted, and hostile civilian politicians are exiled or deprived of political rights. After a period deemed sufficient for the entrenchment of the military rule, the return to constitutional government through elections under a new constitution is held out as bait both for recognition by foreign countries and for the appeasement of the opponents within the country itself. If such elections—heavily manipulated from above—are actually held, the successful military ruler may shed his uniform and continue to rule as a civilian as did Colonel Gamal Abdel Nasser in Egypt (1956) and General Park Chung Hee in South Korea (1963). A convenient substitute for rigged elections by a manipulated parliament to determine the Head of State is confirmation by an equally manipulated plebiscite. This pattern was successful when Ngo Dinh Diem in South Viet-Nam (1956), a civilian, maintained his dictatorial regime with support from the armed forces and a special praetorian guard until his deposition by the army in November, 1963. Since then South Viet-Nam has experienced a succession of military dictators and the return to a kind of civilian control (October, 1964 to January, 1965) proved to be only a fleeting interlude.

Usually these military power cliques are strictly pragmatic and without ideological underpinnings, unless their mere protestations of wanting to replace corruption by honesty and chaos by order can be considered a sufficient substitute. So far no evidence has been forthcoming to prove that military officers are better administrators, or more immune to corruption than civilian politicians, or better qualified to rule than leaders chosen by popular elections, although legends to that effect persist to be propagated. Military dictatorship may provide a considerable degree of security and order, and socially progressive programs may emerge if the officers in control stem from the people proper instead of exclusively from the conservative ruling classes as was the custom a generation ago. A revolt of the masses against military dictatorship, however, is difficult if not impossible because of the ruler's monopoly in disposing of the armed forces. It can succeed only when a potent military group sides with the masses. The transition from outright military rule to a legalized government under a president makes it difficult to draw the line between military dictatorship and neopresidentialism.[4]

Constitutional Democracy

Even though the political system of constitutional democracy (*supra*, pp. 70 ff.) has not gained new members in recent years, it has held its own remarkably well. In the old, established democracies of Western Europe—Great Britain, the three Benelux countries, Scandinavia (including Finland), and Switzerland all riding the crest of unprecedented prosperity—the political process has taken its normal course, with regular elections conducted under a free party system and with a scrupulous preservation of civil liberties. No crisis has arisen when parliamentary bodies have been dissolved before their legal legislative term expires. Nor have major disturbances occurred in the British overseas dominions of Australia and New Zealand, although Canada, owing to a progressing disintegration of the traditional two-party system, and the increasing cleavage between the Catholic and French-speaking Quebec and the other parts of the Dominion, went through a period of violent political shifts; nevertheless, even these were accomplished by the proved democratic techniques: vote of non-confidence, dissolution of parliament, and new elections.

Italy also was remarkably free from interruptions of the normal political process, although plagued more than the other constitutional democracies by governmental instability. Lately (1963) this has been overcome by the much-debated *apertura a sinistra*, the attempt to broaden the narrow basis of the Christian Democratic rule by a parliamentary alliance with the moderate Socialists.

In Austria the Catholic Peoples Party and the Socialists, almost equal in strength over the years, have continued their coalition government, if not without major difficulties. It has proved mutually profitable for sharing the spoils since its beginning in 1945.

Israel—the lonely democratic outpost in a sea of military dictatorships and authoritarian rulers—was likewise able to preserve a British-style parliamentary government, even in the face of the threat to her very existence by the continued hostility of her Arab neighbors.

On the ever-shifting political scene of Latin America, constitutional democracy has been able to recoup some of its previous losses to the authoritarian camp. Within the present cycle, Mexico, Costa Rica, Uruguay, and Chile have proved faithful to a democratically conducted political process. The Argentine people, tired of the succession of ineffective military *juntas* which have followed the overthrow of Juan Perón (1955), finally (1964) rounded the corner on the way to restored constitutional democracy by electing President Ilia. He is confronted, however, by a powerful Perónista party and is still wholly dependent on military benevolence. Venezuela, for the first time in her turbulent history, held two normal presidential elections in succession (1958 and 1964), thus changing her chief executive without outright violence—also a first in her history. An interesting experiment was undertaken in Colombia. After years of military misrule the people, supported by the army, agreed by plebiscite (1957) on the establishment, for a period of twelve years (subsequently [1959], extended by constitutional amendment to sixteen years), of an all-party regime. During this time the two traditional parties alternate in the office of the presidency and have equal representation in legislative assemblies at all levels.

So far all-party government seems to have been successful only in Austria, although recently the processes of harmonious cooperation are exposed to increasing strains. Some new African states, particularly those whose elite have been trained in England (for example, Nigeria, Sierra Leone), although hardly classifiable as full-fledged constitutional democracies, have been able to steer clear of single-party or non-party regimes.

In India, after the death of Jawaharlal Nehru (1964), whose long, remarkable leadership had held the country firmly to the democratic course, the future of democratic government seems precarious. Overwhelming economic and social odds confront the sprawling subcontinent with its multilingual and racially complex society. Nobody would be bold enough to forecast whether this largest experiment in constitutional democracy ultimately will succeed or fail.

Western Germany and Japan have successfully terminated their apprenticeship in constitutional democracy and become certified members of the family of nations adhering, at least in form, to the political processes customary in such. In the German Federal Republic, the pattern of "demo-authoritarianism" (*supra*, p. 98) continued under Chancellor Konrad Adenauer without mitigation, even after his Christian Democratic Union, having lost, in the elections of 1961, the absolute majority, was compelled to enter a coalition with a third party, the Free Democrats, under a highly specious coalition agreement. However, in October, 1962, the celebrated affair of the news magazine *Der Spiegel* shook the cabinet to its foundation; the ambitious Minister of Defense and the leader of the Bavarian affiliate of the Christian Democrats, Franz-Joseph Strauss, aided and abetted by the ministerial bureaucracy and the federal prosecution authorities, had the offices of the magazine raided under the pretext of finding proof of allegedly treasonable activities of editor and staff. The action was in violation of the rule of law to such an extent that for once the habitually docile public revolted and forced a reconstruction of the cabinet from which Strauss had to be dropped. This was the first time since the last war that the demo-authoritarian pattern prevailing had been broken. Popular dissatisfaction also forced the resignation of Adenauer (1963) after fourteen years of undisputed authoritarian rule, which had hardly been conducive to the evolution of democratic processes in Germany. The succeeding regime of Chancellor Ludwig Erhard possesses little appeal for a people engrossed in affluence, since prosperity makes them indifferent politically. Erhard's government may be considered merely a stopgap until after the federal elections in 1965.

The two-party system with its chance of alternating parties controlling the governmental machine has failed to implant itself in Western Germany. Instead of two potentially alternating major parties, the Christian Democrats and the Social Democrats, a four-party division has recently emerged with the Free Democrats and the Bavarian Social Christian Union as the minor participants. Once again the outcome of the elections of September, 1965, in which, for the first time since 1945, the Social Democrats are given, by some observers, an outside chance of victory may bring a decision.

In Japan the political process evolved in a manner curiously similar to that of Western Germany. In spite of being compelled to operate under a clumsy, ill-constructed constitution imposed by American military government after the defeat, the Japanese, novices in self-government, have achieved an unprecedented prosperity with steadily rising living standards for the masses without encountering major difficulties in operating a fully democratic political process. Civil liberties are protected with the zeal characteristic of neophytes in the art of self-government. Big business and the bureaucracy, organized in the ruling Liberal-Democratic party are firmly in the saddle. Not even the vexing problem of constitutional reform, advocated by some to eliminate the controversial constitutional injunction against armaments of any kind, could provoke more than a theoretical discussion, perhaps because the opposition parties control one-third of the votes in the Diet (parliament), thus being able to prevent the required constitutional amendment. When the postwar generation achieves political responsibility, Japan will have acquired recognized membership in the club of states that firmly adhere to constitutional democracy.

Parliamentary Government

The techniques for the operation of parliamentary government have been tested and remain intact. However, the dissolution of parliament by the executive, the principal interorgan control (*supra*, pp. 277 ff.), is no longer being practiced with the same frequency as in former, politically more controversial periods. This may be the result of widespread prosperity which deprives the political parties of real issues. In most constitutional democracies, the parliaments could outlive their entire legislative terms. In Great Britain, general elections were held in 1955 and 1959, giving the Tories an unprecedented term of office for thirteen years; but the spell was broken by the Labour victory of 1964. The pattern was repeated in Western Germany (1953, 1957, and 1961), in the Benelux countries, and in Scandinavia. Economic security under prosperity and extended social services have made party dynamics static—if not outright stale and stagnant. In countries with two alternating parties a kind of equilibrium seems to have established itself.

The popular vote in the American presidential elections (1960) gave the Democrats only a paper-thin edge over the Republicans.[5]

In Britain, Labour won its victory in 1964 with the slimmest majority of seats, which—a rarity in the capricious British electoral system—for once closely corresponded to its small majority of the popular vote. Even in multiple-party states (Switzerland, Scandinavia, and the Lowlands) elections resulted only in minor shifts. Violent landslide swings of the electorate to a different party have failed to materialize. In general, "All's quiet on the Western front."

The tendency toward the *unicameral* instead of the *bicameral* organization of the legislature (*supra*, pp. 177 ff.) has not reversed itself. The republican senate in Turkey under the new constitution of 1961 has to be evaluated as an ex post facto device for preventing the re-establishment of a single-party rule rather than as a means for improving the legislative process. Of the new African states, only Madagascar and Tanganyika preferred the bicameral system. In Nigeria, the establishment of a senate was necessary when federalism was adopted after independence.

A novel creation is the office of *ombudsman*, an independent official chosen by parliament to watch over the administrative services in whose practices the general public is interested. The office originated in Sweden, where for more than one and a half centuries a commissioner for the supervision of the administration of justice has been functioning with universal acclaim. Recently the office of commissioner was created in Finland, Denmark (1955), and Norway (1962) to handle complaints about the administration in general. New Zealand followed suit in 1962. Western Germany adopted the technique but with a more limited scope and without much success by establishing (1956) the office of the parliamentary commissioner for military affairs to keep watch over the military establishment in general and to protect the civil liberties of members of the armed forces in particular. The institution of the *ombudsman*, also under discussion in Great Britain and Switzerland, proved its usefulness in a twofold way: it allowed the adjustment of claims concerning unjust treatment by the administration without resorting to judicial proceedings, and it helps to relieve parliament of detailed administrative control for which it is neither technically prepared nor has it time.

A recently accentuated phenomenon is the replacement of representative techniques by plebiscitary and referendal ones (*supra*, pp. 263 ff., 267 ff.). Seemingly the battle between Montesquieu and Rousseau has to be joined anew by every succeeding generation.[6] Obviously, the technique is not confined to any particular pattern of government. It occurs in constitutional democracies no less than in authoritarian regimes. It is favored over parliamentary decision-making by states that have little experience in handling representative institutions. The modern plebiscite has many uses. When applied in a constitutional democracy for the popular ratification of an entire constitution or a constitutional amendment,[7] for the establishment of an all-party government (Colombia [1957 and 1959]), or for the restoration of presidential government that had temporarily been abandoned in 1961 (Brazil [1963]), the plebiscite is identical with a referendum. A referendum or plebiscite can be manipulated from above far more effectively than can the deliberation and decision of a parliamentary body, however managed and influenced by the government. In an authoritarian environment, therefore, it can also be used for the popular elevation of a leader to the presidency or for the confirmation of a constitution (South Viet-Nam [1955], Ghana [1960]). In these instances it is more of an acclamation than a genuine decision-making act. Frequently the plebiscite decides issues of national sovereignty: whether the country should join another territory or remain independent. Such plebiscites were held, for example, repeatedly in Malta to define the constitutional relationship to Great Britain. They were also held in Guinea (1958), Algeria (1962), and in Southern Rhodesia (1964). How a basically arch-democratic institution can be perverted into an instrument of self-mutilation was demonstrated in Ghana when President Nkrumah used the plebiscite for legalizing the single-party state and for other plainly dictatorial measures (1963). De Gaulle's preference for the referendum and plebiscite derives from his disdain for parliamentary institutions and from his personal mystique which believes in the value of the direct popular consent.

Federalism

Recent experience proves the thesis presented previously (*supra*, pp. 292 ff.) to wit: federalism is being progressively eroded by encroachments of the central government on the rights and jurisdiction of the member units. To evaluate this, a distinction between intrastate and interstate federalism is necessary.

In all governmental structures which are based on some degree of self-government of the member units, the freedom of movement of the latter has been narrowed by the operation of nationwide political parties and plural groups as well as by the imperative need to make political, social, and economic decisions uniform over the entire territory. The expression of wishes and interests of the component parts is confined to their participation in common federal organs. The prevailing prosperity may contribute to de-emphasizing the federal issue; when the people are doing well, as a whole, economically, they are satisfied even though dogmatic discussions about states' rights never stop.

The most cursory glance at the legislative output of the German federal parliament should convince the unbiased observer of the progressive limitations imposed on the self-determination of the German *Länder* whose people must be content, for the time being, with regional autonomy in educational and cultural matters. The situation is not much different in Switzerland, where the traditional cantonal insistence on being master in one's own house is increasingly compelled to yield to inroads by the federal government.

In the United States the resistance of the states against the federal juggernaut has been reduced to a desperate rear-guard action. After the Supreme Court, under the pretext of upholding the Fourteenth Amendment, had dictated how the states should organize and manage their schools, the recent decisions on compulsory reapportionment of the state legislatures—the key decisions were *Baker* v. *Carr* (369 U.S. 186 [1963]) and *Reynolds* v. *Sims* (366 U.S. 533 [1964])—invaded the holiest of state sovereignty by prescribing the manner of electing the state legislature. To do this the Supreme Court used the expanded commerce clause of the constitution as a wedge for dismantling time-honored social habits. Congress followed in the furrow plowed by the federal judiciary by enacting the powerful civil-rights legislation of 1964 to enforce non-discriminatory treatment of the Negro minority in daily life.

In Canada the federal solution of traditionally co-operating provinces was shattered by the silent and not-so-silent revolt of the French-speaking Catholic minority in Quebec against the English-speaking majority elsewhere. No compromise, which is necessary to preserve the national identity of the Dominion, is in sight.

Nor can current experiments in interstate federalism be considered auspicious. In Nigeria, Africa's most populous and potentially influential state, the federal solution imposed itself for welding together the economically and culturally widely divergent races and creeds—Moslems and animistic—of the territories of Eastern, Western, and Northern Nigeria and the territory of Lagos. Here, however, the centripetal forces of personalities, parties, and economic interests make themselves irresistibly felt. The break-up of the country, however, could be avoided by the counsels of moderation and compromise exhibited by the political leaders. The Federal Republic of Cameroons, composed of former British and French trust territories, is merely a marriage of convenience. Elsewhere in Africa attempts at federation have failed. The Central African Federation of Northern and Southern Rhodesia and Nyasaland had to be dissolved. Neither in formerly French nor in formerly British Africa are the new independent states as yet willing to try a confederal co-operation. Tanganyika and Zanzibar, united as Tanzania (1964), are the only—and insignificant—exception, leading, on the occasion of the general election in January, 1965, to a dangerous constitutional crisis.

The Caribbean Federation was disbanded (1962); some of its members—Jamaica, Trinidad and Tobago—went their own independent ways. The remaining scattered small islands, not viable by themselves, probably will try again to create a common organization.

In Latin America, not even the common interest in the American-sponsored Alliance for Progress could bring the individual nations closer together; in Central America, federation plans remain largely on paper.

In the Arab world, the shotgun marriage between Egypt and Syria broke up (1961). The only common bond between the Arab states is the hostility toward Israel. President Nasser's pipe dream of an Arab world united under his leadership failed to materialize, if for no other reason than this very ambition.

Only in Southeast Asia has a federal union between Malaya, North Borneo (Sabah), Sarawak, and Singapore been accomplished (1964), although it has an uncertain future because of the racial differences between Malayans and Chinese and the aggressive opposition of Indonesia. In short, interstate federalism has failed conspicuously throughout the world.

From the foregoing observations it can be concluded that none of the lines drawn by this book some years ago have become blurred, let alone erased. On the contrary, they have deepened. This practical test tempts me to believe that the substance of this book will retain its value for a considerable time to come.

KARL LOEWENSTEIN

AMHERST, MASSACHUSETTS
February 7, 1965

Notes

Notes

NOTES TO CHAPTER I

1. Guglielmo Ferrero, *The Principles of Power* (New York, 1942); Bertrand Russell, *Power* (New York, 1938); Bertrand de Jouvenel, *On Power* (New York, 1949); Charles E. Merriam, *Political Power* (New York, 1934); Gerhard Ritter, *Die Dämonie der Macht* (Munich, 1948); see also Harold D. Lasswell, "World Politics and Personal Insecurity," in *A Study of Power* (Glencoe, Ill., 1950).

2. See Robert A. Brady, *Business as a System of Power* (New York, 1943); John Kenneth Galbraith, *American Capitalism, the Concept of Countervailing Power* (Boston, 1952); C. Wright Mills, *The Power Elite* (New York, 1956). For the international field see Hans J. Morgenthau, *Politics among Nations* (New York, 1948; 2d ed., 1954).

3. For the following see Karl Loewenstein, "Political Systems, Ideologies, and Institutions and the Problem of Their Circulation," *Western Political Science Review*, VI (1953), 689 ff.

4. The term "political system" as used in this book has nothing in common with its namesake employed by David Easton, *The Political System* (New York, 1953). In the context of his penetrating study, interested primarily in the methodology of political science, the "political system" is the totality of political life (see, e.g., p. 97) and, therefore, necessarily has a much wider—and vaguer—connotation than that attached to the term in this book. Here it implies the concrete institutionalization of specific political ideologies.

5. Loewenstein, *op. cit.*, n. 3 of this chapter, p. 691.

NOTES TO CHAPTER II

1. See Karl Loewenstein, *Political Reconstruction* (New York, 1946), pp. 105 ff.

2. See Karl Loewenstein, "Political Systems, Ideologies, and Institutions and the Problem of Their Circulation," *Western Political Science Quarterly*, VI (1953), 696 ff.

3. Session of the National Assembly of August 31, 1789, quoted by Jules Laferrière, *Manuel de droit constitutionnel* (Paris, 1947), p. 630, n. 1.

4. The discussion in the text refers to the celebrated sixth chapter of the eleventh book of the *Esprit des lois*.

5. For a realistic re-examination of Montesquieu's doctrine see Karl Loewenstein, "The Balance between Legislative and Executive Power: A Study in Comparative Constitutional Law," *University of Chicago Law Review*, V (1938), 568 ff.

6. The discussion refers to *Politics* iv. 1279^b 37 and 1289^b 20. See also Hermann Rehm, *Geschichte der Staatsrechtswissenschaft* (Leipzig, 1896), pp. 84–85.

7. The issue does not seem to remain peacefully buried; see the recent discussion, learned as it is unconvincing, by J. A. O. Larsen, *Representative Government in Greek and Roman History* (Berkeley, 1955), pp. 126 ff. The great landowners and officials congregated in the provincial councils of the late Roman empire represented nobody but themselves. If their resolutions affected the power addressees not represented in the meeting, it was by the fact of their might and not by right.

8. The transformation of the feudal councils of the kings in Spain—Aragon, Castile, León, Catalonia—into authentic representative bodies is less explored, and explorable, than the analogous situation in England and France (for some material see Marie R. Madden, *Political Theory and Law in Medieval Spain* [New York, 1930], pp. 159 ff.). The emergence of representative institutions may have been connected with the contemporaneous replacement of the *fueros*—customary law in written form—by the more refined principles of the Justinian Code.

9. Rushton Coulborn (ed.), *Feudalism in History* (Princeton, N.J., 1956).

10. See Leo Moulin, "Les origines religieuses des techniques électorales et délibératives modernes," *Revue internationale d'histoire politique et constitutionnelle* (N.S.), No. 10 (1953), pp. 106 ff., esp. pp. 141 ff.; *idem*, "Le Gouvernement des communautés religieuses comme type de gouvernement mixte," *Revue française de science politique*, II (1952), 335 ff.; *idem*, "Une forme originale du gouvernement des hommes: Le gouvernement des communautés religieuses," *Revue internationale du droit comparé*, VII (1955), 753 ff.

11. See George L. Haskins, *The Growth of English Representative Government* (Philadelphia, 1948).

12. The traditional tripartism is interestingly challenged by Frank J. Goodnow, *Politics and Administration* (New York, 1900), in the first chapter, by the hypothesis that there exist only two "governmental" functions, namely, legislation and administration, corresponding to what in our discussion appears as policy decision and policy execution; however, he does not recognize policy control as a distinct and separate function. Nor does Léon Duguit (*Law in the Modern State* [New York, 1919], pp. 69 ff.) come to grips with the issue. What he distinguishes, however, are two kinds of legislation, namely, "legislation properly so-called and legislation which is really executive in character" (p. 81), the latter being the governmental ordinance-making function. The contours of the new tripartism are drawn in Loewenstein, *op. cit.*, n. 5 of this chapter, pp. 576 ff. Gentle stirrings of rebellion against the traditional tripartism are also observable in Germany; see, e.g., Peter Schneider, "Zur Problematik der Gewaltenteilung im Rechtsstaat der Gegenwart," *Archiv des öffentlichen Rechts*, LXXXII (1957), 1 ff. at 12 ff.; Werner Weber, *Spannungen und Kräfte im westdeutschen Verfassungssystem* (Stuttgart, 1951).

13. *Esprit des lois*, Book VI, chap. xi; if read in the context, the statement refers to the depersonalization of the holders of judicial power: "On n'a point continuellement les juges devant les yeux, et on craint la magistrature et non les magistrats."

14. Maurice Duverger, *Droit constitutionnel et institutions politiques* (Paris, 1955), devotes a magistral section (pp. 197 ff.) to the aspect under the title "La Limitations des gouvernants."

15. This is stressed by one of the classical treatises on parliamentarism: Robert Redslob's *Die parlamentarische Regierung in ihrer echten und ihrer unechten Form* (Tübingen, 1918), pp. 18 ff.; *idem, Le Régime parlementaire* (Paris, 1924), pp. 18 ff.

16. The official was subject not only to the *dokimasia*—the investigation in his civilian dignity and democratic reliability before assuming office—but also, upon the completion of his term, to the intense scrutiny of his conduct in office before the *logistai* and *euthynoi*, respectively (see Georg Busolt, *Griechische Staatskunde* [Part II by Heinrich Swoboda] [Munich, 1926], pp. 1072 ff., 1076 ff.).

NOTES TO CHAPTER III

1. See the convenient summary in Clinton L. Rossiter, *Constitutional Dictatorship* (Princeton, N.J., 1948), pp. 15 ff.

2. The late Franz L. Neumann, in his "Notes on the Theory of Dictatorship," published in *The Democratic and the Authoritarian State* (Glencoe, Ill., 1957), pp. 233 ff., undertook such an attempt. He based it primarily on the distinction of two major categories, namely, caesaristic dictatorship and totalitarian dictatorship, but he also considered, if only in passing, the Roman constitutional dictatorship and the absolute monarchy. However, even if he had been permitted to give his "Notes" their final shape, it is unlikely that his categorization would have attained the requisite completeness and refinement, because he fails to distinguish between the totalitarian and the authoritarian patterns. Aside from this fundamental shortcoming, many of his conclusions drawn from the historial evidence parallel the approach of this author.

3. The distinctions were first utilized by Karl Loewenstein, *Brazil under Vargas* (New York, 1942), pp. 369 ff., to establish that the Vargas regime was neither fascist nor totalitarian. Similarly, Herbert L. Matthews in his "Report on Spain, I," *New York Times*, September 17, 1956, comes to the conclusion: "In spite of these facts, Spain is not a totalitarian country. It is authoritarian."

4. This useful dichotomy was supplied, in his analysis of the Nazi regime, by Ernest Fraenkel, *The Dual State* (New York, 1941).

5. See John A. Hawgood, *Modern Constitutions since 1787* (New York, 1939), pp. 93 ff. Unfortunately little known in this country, this is a mine of information on the cross-fertilizations in history of the constitutional state.

6. See Sylvanus Griswold Morley, *The Ancient Mayas* (3d ed., revised by George W. Brainerd; Stanford University, Calif., 1956), pp. 438 ff., and J. Reid S. Thompson, *The Maya Civilization* (Norman, Okla., 1954), pp. 84 ff.

7. See the study by J. L. Talmon, *The Rise of Totalitarian Democracy* (Boston, 1953).

8. The only monograph on the monarchical establishment, still of great importance today, that has appeared during the last decades is Karl Loewenstein, *Die Monarchie im modernen Staat* (Frankfurt am Main, 1952); it attempts a sociologically oriented analysis of the various patterns of monarchy: absolute, constitutionally limited, and parliamentary.

9. For an excellent recent American discussion see Franklin Ford, *Robe and Sword* (Cambridge, Mass., 1953); the French standard work is Ernest Glasson, *Le Parlement de Paris* (2 vols.; Paris, 1901).

10. See Karl Loewenstein, "The Dictatorship of Napoleon the First," *South Atlantic Quarterly*, XXXV (1936), 298 ff.; *idem*, "Opposition and Public Opinion under the Dictatorship of Napoleon the First," *Social Research*, IV (1937), 461 ff.

11. See Karl Loewenstein, "The Presidency outside the United States: A Study in Comparative Political Institutions," *Journal of Politics*, XI (1949), 447, at 487 ff. Much of the material used in this section has been borrowed from this article.

NOTES TO CHAPTER IV

1. Lewis B. Namier, "Monarchy and the Party System," in *Personalities and Power* (London, 1954), pp. 13 ff.

2. See Crane Brinton, *The Jacobins* (New York, 1930). For the various legal, social, and doctrinal aspects of the Jacobin regime see the literature in Maurice Duverger, *Droit constitutionnel et institutions politiques* (Paris, 1955), pp. 413 ff.

3. See Karl Loewenstein, *Brazil under Vargas* (New York, 1942), pp. 141 ff.

4. For the political and social organization of the cities in the feudal period see Heinrich Mitteis, *Der Staat des hohen Mittelalters* (Weimar, 1948), pp. 259 ff. On democratic tendencies in the Florentine republic of the Renaissance see, e.g., Leopold von Ranke, "Savonarola und die florentinische Republik gegen Ende des fünfzehnten Jahrhunderts," in *Ranke's Meisterwerke* (Munich), X (1915), 1 ff., at 77 ff. For medieval Toulouse see, e.g., John H. Mundy, *Liberty and Political Power in Toulouse, 1050-1230* (New York, 1954), pp. 149 ff.

5. To the author's knowledge no systematic study of this pattern of government exists. The (mimeographed) lectures for the doctorate in law of the University of Paris (1954–55) by M. Bastid, "Le Gouvernement d'assemblée," deal with the Long Parliament in England, Switzerland (Confederation and cantons), the German *Länder*, and the various apparitions of the pattern in France, though not with the Soviet applications. See also Karl Loewenstein, "The Presidency Outside the United States: A Study in Comparative Political Institutions," *Journal of Politics*, XI (1949), 470 ff.

6. This contingency is provided for by the constitutions of some of the German *Länder* both under Weimar and under Bonn, e.g., the Prussian constitution of 1920, Art. 6; self-dissolution of the Landtag

was likewise provided for. The only attempt to recall the legislature, undertaken in Prussia in 1932, failed.

7. Even if tenable, B. Mirkine-Guetzévitch's assumption that the Convention actually, by accident, stumbled on parliamentary government would not invalidate assembly government as a pattern *sui generis*. But his thesis, disproved by the facts, is not acceptable (see his *Le Parlementarisme sous la Convention* (Paris, 1936), and, against him; R. Villars, "La Convention pratiqua-t-elle le gouvernement parlementaire?" *Revue du droit public*, LVII [1951], 375 ff.). Maurice Duverger (*Droit constitutionnel et institutions politiques* [Paris, 1955], p. 414) observes sardonically that there is a difference between the vote of non-confidence and the guillotine.

8. Most historians of British parliamentarism gloss over the fact that England almost missed the cue for it. By the end of the seventeenth century the following principles had become established: (1) certain non-ministerial offices, for example, judgeships, were incompatible with membership in the Commons; (2) officeholders in the Commons should be so restricted as to exclude an undue influence of the government over the members; (3) parliament can exercise effective control over the government only if a certain number of holders of political office, namely the ministers, are members of it. To diminish the influence of the crown over the Commons, the Act of Settlement of 1700 (12 & 13 Will. III, c. 2), sec. 6, went so far as to exclude all holders of office, including the ministers, from the Commons. If this prohibition had entered into force, it would have made responsible government and the cabinet system altogether impossible. Fortunately, the prohibition was to be valid only with the accession of the House of Hanover to the throne. Before this happened the provision was repealed by the Succession to the Crown Acts of 1705 (4 & 5 Anne, c. 16) and 1707 (6 Anne, c. 41). Under these provisions holders of the so-called "old" offices, that is, those existing on October 25, 1707, could remain members of the Commons—and this class included the ministers—while the holders of "new" offices were disqualified. Subsequent legislation exempted holders of political offices wholly from disqualification and disqualified holders of all other offices unconditionally. Had the originally planned exclusion of the ministers been permitted to stand, British parliamentarism would have been nipped in the bud. For the situation see O. Hood Phillips, *The Constitutional Law of Great Britain and the Commonwealth* (London,

1952), pp. 100 ff., and "Select Committee on Offices and Places under the Crown," *H.C. Papers*, No. 120 (1941), pp. xiii ff.

9. See Karl Loewenstein, "The Balance between Legislative and Executive Power: A Study in Comparative Constitutional Law," *University of Chicago Law Review*, V (1938), 566 ff., at 680 ff., for a historical survey of the alternating periods of parliamentary and executive ascendancy.

10. The rule is not without exceptions, however. In the Netherlands a member of parliament appointed to a ministerial office may continue to hold his seat for a maximum of three months (constitution of 1815, revised form of 1947, Art. 99, sec. 2). In Weimar Germany not infrequently non-parliamentarians were appointed as "expert ministers" (*Fachminister*); in one case even the Reich chancellor (Herr Cuno) was not a member of the Reichstag.

11. The July monarchy (constitution of 1830) could not function as parliamentary government because of the preponderant influence of King Louis-Philippe. The "cocktail" constitution of 1848 is variously classified by French constitutional lawyers as parliamentary and as presidential government (see Marcel Prélot, *Précis de droit constitutionnel* [Paris, 1955], pp. 124 ff., 142 ff.). Under the criteria submitted in the text it should be qualified as assembly government.

12. Emile Blamort, "La Mise-en-œuvre de la dissolution," *Revue du droit public*, LXXII (1956), 105 ff.; Georges Berlia, "La Dissolution et le régime des pouvoirs publics," *Revue du droit public*, LXXII (1956), 130 ff. See also the author's letter to the *New York Times*, December 11, 1955.

13. For a recent and extremely pessimistic appraisal of the Fourth Republic see Emile Gireaud, "Quatrième République, l'expérience de dix années," *Revue internationale de l'histoire politique et constitutionnelle* (N.S.), No. 21 (1956), pp. 1 ff.

14. On the situation in Finland see Denis Levy, "Les Elections à la présidence de la République finlandaise," *Revue française de science politique*, VI (1956), 115 ff.

15. For the very complicated arrangements under which dissolution is permissible see Theodor Maunz, *Deutsches Staatsrecht* (5th ed.; Munich, 1956), pp. 272 ff.

16. The term was used first by Karl Loewenstein in James T. Shotwell (ed.), *Governments of Continental Europe* (2d ed.; New York, 1952), p. 580. The identical pattern of near-irremovability of the government during the legislative period prevails also in most of the

Länder. However, in 1956 it backfired in the key state of Northrhine-Westphalia: the Free Democrats, in a surprise maneuver, defected from their coalition partner, the Christian Democrats, and joined the Social Democratic opposition, whereupon the latter took over the office of the minister-president and formed a new cabinet.

17. This situation likewise escapes the attention of most students of the history of British parliamentarism. For a fuller discussion see Karl Loewenstein, "Zur Soziologie der parlamentarischen Repräsentation in England nach der grossen Reform: Das Zeitalter der Parlamentssouveränität (1832–1867)," *Archiv für Sozialwissenschaft und Sozialpolitik,* LI (1924), 614 ff., at 666 ff.

18. See the recent study by P. A. Broadhead, *Private Members' Bills in the House of Commons* (London, 1956).

19. "Notes on the State of Virginia," Query XIII, sec. 4, Ford ed. of *Jefferson's Writings,* ed. William Peden (Chapel Hill, N.C., 1955), III, 120. Reference supplied by courtesy of the editors of *The Papers of Thomas Jefferson* (Princeton, N.J.).

20. François Goguel ("Vers une nouvelle orientation de la révision constitutionelle?" *Revue française de science politique,* VI [1956], 493 ff.) is skeptical toward recent proposals of Professors Duverger and Capitant to introduce the presidential system in France.

21. See the interesting discussion by William S. Stokes, "Parliamentary Government in Latin America," *American Political Science Review,* XXXIX (1945), 522 ff.

22. The federal constitution is silent on the issue, merely stating (Art. 43, sec. 1) that every citizen of a canton may participate in all federal elections and referendums. This was always understood to refer only to males. However, for the first time in Swiss history, on March 2, 1957, the women of a small (population, 420) mountain village in the arch-conservative canton of Berne were permitted by the local authorities to vote in a federal referendum making fire-watching compulsory for women. In three larger communities, all located in French- or Italian-speaking cantons, the women participated on a consultative basis (see *New York Times,* March 3, 1957). Meanwhile, the Federal Council submitted to the federal legislature the proposal for a constitutional amendment providing for the vote of women in federal elections and referendums and making them eligible for elective office.

23. On constitutional developments in Uruguay see A. L. Barbagelata, "Charactéristiques générales de l'organisation constitutionnelle de

l'Uruguay," *Revue internationale du droit comparé*, VI (1954), 455 ff.
On the constitution of 1952 see Eduardo J. Couture *et al.*, *Legislación
vigente en el Uruguay* (Montevideo, 1956), pp. 58 ff., 69 ff.

NOTES TO CHAPTER V

1. To Aristotle the term *politeia* implied the entire social structure
of the community, beyond its legal framework, as did Bodin's *res
publica.* "Constitution" in the modern sense was first employed by
Cicero (*De republica* i. 40). Later it came to denote enactments of the
emperor (see Ulpianus *Digest* i. 4. 1, 2). This usage was taken over by
the church and prevailed in the Middle Ages. The modern connotation
of the term, referring to the totality of the basic norms of the community even if unwritten, did not emerge before the seventeenth century
(see Charles Howard McIlwain, "Some Illustrations for the Influence
of Unchanged Names for Changing Institutions," in *Interpretations of
Modern Legal Philosophies: Papers Presented to Roscoe Pound* [New
York, 1947], pp. 484 ff., at 489–90).

2. In fairness it should be reported that Emperor Haile Selassie, one
of the most enlightened rulers of our time, on the occasion of the
silver jubilee of his ascension to the throne (1956) decreed constitutional reforms under which, in 1957, a chamber of deputies is to be
elected. While the suffrage is open to all citizens, eligibility is drastically restricted by property qualifications. The upper house is appointed by the emperor. None of the chambers enjoys real powers,
because all laws are dependent on the approval of the emperor. The
ministers remain responsible solely to him. No revision of the article
of the constitution embodying the emperor's absolute powers has been
granted. But the reform appears to be an educational step toward
ultimate constitutionalization and democratization (see *New York
Times*, February 19, 1957).

3. See K. C. Wheare, *Modern Constitutions* ("Home University
Library of Modern Knowledge" [London, 1951]), pp. 46 ff. The little
volume is an excellent presentation of the complex subject of constitutions today.

4. Charles Howard McIlwain, *Constitutionalism, Ancient and Modern* (New York, 1950), p. 41. Stasis implies internal disorder. It became a byword for the atmosphere of impending coup d'état in the
tension between the democratic and oligarchic forces after Aegos-
potami (405 B.C.).

5. G. W. Botsford, *The Roman Assemblies* (New York, 1902).

6. See the magistral classic by Léon Homo, *Les Institutions politiques des Romains de la cité à l'état* (Paris, 1950), pp. 226 ff.; see also Franz L. Neumann, *The Democratic and the Authoritarian State* (Glencoe, Ill., 1957), pp. 238 ff., on the foundations of Caesar's and Augustus' rule.

7. The famous passage is Ulpianus *Digest* i. 4. 1 and *Institutions* i. 2. 6: "Quod principi placuit legis habet vigorem cum lex regia quae de eius imperio lata est populus ei et ad eum suum imperium et potestatem conferrat." See also Egon Zweig, *Die Lehre vom Pouvoir Constituant* (Tübingen, 1909), pp. 177 ff.; McIlwain, *op. cit.*, n. 4 of this chapter, pp. 72 ff., and the criticism of Karl Loewenstein in his review of the latter book, *American Political Science Review*, XXXIV (1940), 1000 ff.

8. For a penetrating discussion of the intellectual incubation of the written constitution see Zweig, *op. cit.*, n. 7 of this chapter; for England see Walther Rothschild, *Der Gedanke der geschriebenen Verfassung in der englischen Revolution* (Tübingen, 1903); Francis D. Wormuth, *The Origins of Modern Constitutionalism* (New York, 1949). For the development in the New World see Karl Loewenstein, *Volk und Parlament nach der Staatstheorie der französischen Nationalversammlung von 1789* (Munich, 1922), pp. 44 ff.

9. Perhaps credit for the first written constitution should go to the Japanese; M. Anasaki reports on "The Text of a Constitution in Seventeen Articles by Prince Botoku in 604 A.D.," *Case and Comment*, XLVIII (1953), 20 ff.

10. For a detailed description of techniques see Karl Loewenstein, *Political Reconstruction* (New York, 1946), pp. 212 ff.

11. See, e.g., Wheare, *op. cit.*, n. 3 of this chapter, pp. 121 ff.

12. The Institute of International Public and Foreign Law of the University of Hamburg is engaged in the ambitious task of compiling one. The first issue deals with Germany (see E. Menzel, F. Groh, and H. Becker, *Verfassungsregister*, Teil I: *Deutschland* [Frankfurt am Main, 1954]).

13. See Jesús de Galindez, "La Instabilidad constitucional en el derecho comparado de Latinoamerica," *Boletín del Instituto del Derecho Comparado de Mexico*, V (1952), 45 ff.

14. For France see the well-known collection by Duguit-Monnier-Bonnard, *Les Constitutions et les principales lois politiques de la France depuis 1789*, 7th ed. by Georges Berlia (Paris, 1952). For

Greece see Nicholas Kaltchas, *Introduction to the Constitutional History of Greece* (New York, 1940). The latest Greek constitution is of 1952.

15. See Karl Loewenstein, *Brazil under Vargas* (New York, 1942), pp. 46 ff.

16. The text of this unique document is contained in *Il Popolo d'Italia*, No. 209, September 1, 1920.

17. In Germany-Bonn the need to reconcile political practice with the ideology of the Basic Law, which postulated the social-democratic state under the rule of law, social justice and the dignity of the human personality, provoked considerable effort on the part of the courts (see Julius Federer, "Die Rechtsprechung des Bunderverfassungsgerichts zum Grundgesetz für die Bundesrepublik Deutschland," *Jahrbuch des öffentlichen Rechts der Gegenwart* [N.F.], III [1954], 17 ff., at 38 ff.), as well as a voluminous literature: Ernst Forsthoff, *Verfassungsprobleme des Sozialstaats* (Münster, 1954); Hans Gerber, "Die Sozialstaatsklausel des Grundgesetzes," *Archiv des öffentlichen Rechts*, LXXXI (1956), 1 ff.; Günter Dürig, "Der Grundrechtssatz von der Menschenwürde," *Archiv des öffentlichen Rechts*, LXXXI (1956), 117 ff. On the basis of Article 1 of the constitution enshrining the dignity of men, the Supreme Court (Bundesgerichtshof) disallowed the use of the lie detector without consent of the accused (see *Entscheidungen des Bundesgerichtshofs in Strafsachen*, V [1954], 333).

18. "Bonapartism" was a common term in the nineteenth century for the *régime personnel* (see, e.g., H. von Treitschke, *Politik* [4th ed.; Leipzig, 1918], II, 203 ff.). Nowadays, with the competition of Napoleon's successors, it is no longer fashionable.

19. *Webster's New Collegiate Dictionary* defines "ontological" as referring to "the science of being or reality; the branch of knowledge that investigates the nature, essential properties, and relations of being." In systematic philosophy the term is well established since Plato's ὤντος ὄντα as the absolute reality of ideas.

20. For the following see Karl Loewenstein, "Reflections on the Value of Constitutions in Our Revolutionary Age," in Arnold J. Zurcher (ed.), *Constitutions and Constitutional Trends after World War II* (New York, 1951), pp. 191 ff., at 203 ff. The article was also published in a French translation by the *Revue française de science politique*, II (1952), 5 ff., 312 ff. Benjamin Akzin ("On the Stability and Reality of Constitutions" ["Scripta Hierosolymitana"], *Studies in Social Science*, III [1955], 313 ff.), proceeding from the classification estab-

lished by this author, distinguishes constitutions as to their respective stability or fragility. States with stable constitutions are those which continue to operate without revolutionary break; fragile constitutions are those of states in which political power is gained by processes not provided by the constitution itself. Though focusing on ontological elements, the criterion appears too mechanical. If a constitution is stable, it does not imply that it is observed; on the contrary, its stability may result from its being disregarded by the power holders. Moreover, often progress toward democratic constitutionalism is achieved only by the revolutionary break with the existing constitutional order.

21. Under this instrument of 257 beautifully phrased articles the president is designated by the council of ministers (Art. 118), but the joker is that the ministers are appointed and dismissed at the discretion of the president (Art. 120, No. 11). Constitutional amendment is carried by a two-thirds majority of the council of ministers (Art. 257). The situation was normalized, as normalization goes in Cuba, by the new constitution of 1955, modeled on that of 1940, but only after General Battista had been elected, as elections go in Cuba, in November, 1954, to a four-year term.

22. See Michel Mushkhély, "La Notion soviétique de constitution," *Revue du droit public*, LI (1956), 895 ff., at 897.

23. The Section on Public Law of the Fourth Congress of the Academy of Comparative Law, held in Paris August, 1954, devoted an entire day's meeting to this subject (see the general report by Hans Spanner, "Die Rolle der Verfassungen im gegenwärtigen politischen und sozialen Leben," *Österreichische Zeitschrift für öffentliches Recht*, VII [1955], 9 ff.). Among the other papers submitted to the meeting were: W. J. Ganshof van der Meersch, "Le Rôle de la constitution belge dans la vie politique et sociale," *Revue de l'Université de Bruxelles*, 1954, pp. 169 ff.; José Miranda Gonzales, "El Papel de la constitución en la vida politica y social contemporanea," *Boletín del Instituto del Derecho Comparado de Mexico*, VII (1954), 61 ff.

24. See, e.g., Weimar constitution, Art. 21; Bonn Basic Law, Art. 38; Czechoslovakia, constitution of 1920, Art. 22, sec. 1.

25. See Harold S. Quigly and John E. Turner, *The New Japan* (Minneapolis, 1956), pp. 317 ff. (on the disarmament clause in the constitutional debates); pp. 208 ff. (on the National Police Force); pp. 307 ff. and 320–21 (on the attitudes of the political parties).

26. See W. J. Ganshof van der Meersch, "La Constitution belge et

l'évolution de l'ordre international," *Annales de droit et de la science politique*, XII (1952), 33 ff.

27. The abortive judicial proceedings before the Federal Constitutional Court and the remedial constitutional amendment—in itself unconstitutional—to fill the constitutional gap are discussed by Karl Loewenstein, "The Bonn Constitution and the European Defense Community Treaties," *Yale Law Journal*, LXIV (1955), 805 ff. On the comparative law dealing with the incorporation into the constitutions of the participation in supranational organizations see *ibid.*, p. 830, n. 107.

28. For the following see Loewenstein, *op. cit.*, n. 20 of this chapter, pp. 222 ff.

NOTES TO CHAPTER VI

1. Julius Stone, *The Province and Function of the Law* (Sydney, 1949), pp. 705 ff.

2. New Zealand is an exception: the caucus of all parliamentary members of the party selects the members of the cabinet; see Alexander Brady, *Democracy in the Dominions* (Toronto, 1952), pp. 514 ff. See also D. McHenry, "The Origins of Caucus Election in New Zealand," *Historical Studies of Australia and New Zealand,* VII (1944), 17 ff., a defense of the system which is often attacked as a curb on the powers of the prime minister and a threat to the unity of the cabinet.

3. For a brilliant study of the techniques of the parliamentary process see "Le Travail parlementaire en France, aux Etats-Unis, en Grande Bretagne et en Suisse," *Revue française de science politique*, IV (1954), 673–868, also published as a book under the same title (Paris, 1956).

4. See W. Starosolsky, *Das Majoritätsprinzip* (Vienna, 1916), for an analysis of the intellectual history of a technique which by now is taken for granted.

5. The appellations "first" and "second" chamber have no uniform meaning. In some cases, for historical reasons, as, for example, in the Netherlands, the upper house is called the "first" chamber, while in most others the lower house, corresponding to its greater political importance, is called the "first."

6. See Harry J. Benda, "The End of Bi-cameralism in New Zealand," in Sidney D. Bailey (ed.), *Parliamentary Government in the*

Dominions (London, 1951), pp. 63 ff. Efforts under way in 1957 to revive the second chamber are not encouraged by the government and the parties and find little response in the public (*New York Times*, March 6, 1957).

7. *Esprit des lois,* Book XI, chap. vi.

NOTES TO CHAPTER VII

1. Karl Loewenstein, *Die Monarchie im modernen Staat* (Frankfurt am Main, 1952), pp. 76 ff.

2. See H. W. Ehrmann, "The Duty of Disclosure in Parliamentary Investigating Committees," *University of Chicago Law Review,* XI (1943), 1 ff., 117 ff.

3. The term was coined by B. Mirkine-Guetzévitch, *Les nouvelles tendances du droit constitutionnel* (2d ed.; Paris, 1931), pp. 1 ff.; *idem, Les Constitutions européennes* (Paris, 1951), I, 14 ff., 30 ff. In the latter discussion he exhibits considerable skepticism concerning the effectiveness. See also Joseph Dunner, "Stabilization of the Cabinet System in Western Europe" in Arnold J. Zurcher (ed.), *Constitutions and Constitutional Trends after World War II* (New York, 1951), pp. 81 ff.

4. The only two cases under the French Third Republic were those of Malvy (1918) and Peret (1931) (see Joseph-Barthélemy and Paul Duez, *Traité de droit constitutionnel* [Paris, 1933], p. 875).

5. On these two cases see Loewenstein, *op. cit.,* n. 1 of this chapter, pp. 47 ff., 58 ff. Another dethronement occurred in Tunisia in July, 1957, when the rule of the bey—strictly nominal anyway—was superseded by the declaration of the republic.

6. On the use of the *renvoi* under the Fourth Republic see Maurice Duverger, *Droit constitutionnel et institutions politiques* (Paris, 1955), p. 709.

7. See O. Hood Phillips, *The Constitutional Law of Great Britain and the Commonwealth* (London, 1952), pp. 313 ff.

8. *Wayman* v. *Southward,* 10 Wheat. 1 (1825).

9. *Panama Refining Co.* v. *Ryan,* 293 U.S. 388 (1935), invalidating the National Industrial Recovery Act, a centerpiece of President Roosevelt's New Deal.

10. The literature is voluminous. For an excellent summary (with bibliography on French publications) see Duverger, *op. cit.,* n. 6 of this chapter, pp. 442–43 for the Third Republic and pp. 529 ff. for the

Fourth. Of discussions in English may be mentioned M. A. Sieghart, *Government by Decree* (London, 1950), and Sidney B. Jacoby, "Delegated Legislation and Judicial Review," *Columbia Law Review*, XXXVI (1936), 871 ff.

11. *Avis* of the Conseil d'Etat of February 6, 1953 (published also in *Revue du droit public*, LXIX [1953], 171 ff.) To square the circle between the constitutional injunction against delegating legislative functions and the practice of *pleins pouvoirs* that had become a political necessity, the court resorted to the ingenious device called "delegalization": the sovereign parliament has complete freedom to declare which subject matters must be dealt with by parliamentary legislation and which others can be attended to by governmental decree. On the latter category, thus, the government is authorized to legislate by decree.

12. See the informative report by François Goguel, "Procédure italienne de vote des lois par les commissions," *Revue française de science politique*, IV (1954), 843 ff.

13. The dissolution of the parliament is one of the most plowed-through subjects of comparative government. For a recent monograph see Federico Mohrhoff, *La Dissolution des assemblées législatives dans les constitutions modernes* (Rome, 1953).

14. For a valuable summation of crisis government in the United States, France, Great Britain, and Germany see Clinton T. Rossiter, *Constitutional Dictatorship* (Princeton, N.J., 1948). For a recent comprehensive study see Hans Ballreich, Karl Doehring, Günther Jaennicke, Helmut Strebel, and Günther Weiss, *Das Staatsnotrecht in Belgien, Frankreich, Grossbritannien, Italien, den Niederlanden, der Schweiz und den Vereinigten Staaten von Amerika* (Cologne, 1955).

15. For documentation see Georg Meyer and Gerhard Anschütz, *Lehrbuch des Deutschen Staatsrechts* (7th ed.; Munich, 1919), pp. 676 ff.

16. See Joseph-Barthélemy, *Traité de droit constitutionnel* (Paris, 1933), p. 241.

17. 4 Wall. 2 (1866). The court was sharply divided. For a general discussion see R. S. Rankin, *When Civil Law Fails* (Durham, N.C., 1939).

18. For a systematic discussion of the state of siege in Latin America see the author's contribution in *La Legislación para la defensa política en las repúblicas americanas* (2 vols.; Montevideo: Consultative Emergency Committee of Political Defense, 1947), I, 83 ff.

19. See Z. Giacommetti, *Das Vollmachtenregime der Eidgenossen-schaft* (Zurich, 1949); Muenci Kapani, *Les Pouvoirs extraordinaires de l'exécutif en temps de guerre et de crise nationale* (Geneva, 1949).

20. For a further elucidation of the complex situation see Christopher Hughes, *The Federal Constitution of Switzerland* (Oxford, 1954), pp. 100 ff.; Hans Nef, "Die Fortbildung der Schweizerischen Bundesverfassung in den Jahren 1929–1953," *Jahrbuch des öffentlichen Rechts der Gegenwart*, IV (1955), 355 ff., at 365 ff.

NOTES TO CHAPTER VIII

1. In the early period of the United States the executive, in control of the majority in congress, tried to use impeachment to rid itself of judges with whose decisions it disagreed. The first attempt of the Jeffersonians (1805) failed because of a split in the majority. Later, the appointive power was used occasionally for similar purposes of checkmating the judiciary. In 1871 President Grant appointed two new judges to the Supreme Court for the sole purpose of reversing the case of *Hepburn* v. *Griswold* (8 Wall. 603 [1870]); the new majority complied (Legal Tender Cases, 12 Wall. 457 [1871]). President Roosevelt's famous "court-packing" plan (1937), as such wholly constitutional, failed because of the opposition of public opinion. For curiosity's sake may be mentioned a resolution introduced in February, 1957, in the legislature of Georgia calling for the impeachment of six justices of the United States Supreme Court because of their participation in the antisegregation decisions and for other subversive acts (see *New York Times*, February 14, 1957). The judges in question still officiate.

2. Nicholas Halasz, *Captain Dreyfus* (New York, 1955), pp. 188 ff.

3. 6 Wall. 318 (1868) and 7 Wall. 506 (1869). A case pending before the Supreme Court was removed from it when its appellate jurisdiction in certain habeas corpus cases was quashed by statute (15 Stat. 33 [1868]).

4. O. Hood Phillips, *The Constitutional Law of Great Britain and the Commonwealth* (London, 1952), pp. 456 ff.

5. For a convenient survey of the European situation see R.K.C. Ensor, *Courts and Judges in France, England and Germany* (London, 1933); see also Arthur T. Von Mehren, "The Judicial Process: A Comparative Analysis," *American Journal of Comparative Law*, V (1956), 167 ff.

6. For details see Georges Langrod, "The French Council of State," *American Political Science Review*, XLIX (1955), 683 ff.

7. The literature is vast. For a recent dicussion see Bernard Schwartz, *French Administrative Law and the Common Law* (New York, 1954).

8. The famous Art. 13 of the Law of August 16–24, 1790, should be quoted in full: "Les fonctions judiciaires sont distinctes et demeurent toujours séparées des fonctions administratives. Les juges ne pourront, à peine de forfaiture, troubler de quelque manière que ce soit, les opérations des corps administratifs, ni citer devant eux les administrateurs pour raison de leur fonctions." See also the identical provisions of the constitution of 1791, Art. 157, and of the Law of Fructidor 16, year III (1795).

9. Edouard Lambert, *Le Gouvernement des juges* (Paris, 1921).

10. See Paul A. Freund, "A Supreme Court in a Federation," *Columbia Law Review*, LIII (1953), 697 ff.; Stefan Riesenfeld and John N. Hazard, "Federal Courts in Foreign Systems," *Law and Contemporary Problems*, XIII (1948), 29 ff.

11. The key case is *Brown* v. *Board of Education*, 347 U.S. 483 (1954).

12. 163 U.S. 537 (1896).

13. 297 U.S. 1 (1936).

14. 1 Cranch 137 (1803), at 170.

15. *Luther* v. *Bordon*, 7 How. 1 (1849).

16. *The Constitution of the United States, Analysis and Interpretation*, prepared by the Legislative Reference Service, Library of Congress, ed. Edward S. Corwin (82d Cong., 2d sess.; Senate Doc. 170 [Washington, D.C., 1953]), p. 547.

17. A case in which congressional legislation rectified the Court is the Submerged Lands Act (67 Stat. 29), which countermanded the judicial assignation of the tidelands oil to the Union (see *United States* v. *California*, 332 U.S. 19 [1947], and *United States* v. *Louisiana*, 339 U.S. 699 [1950]).

A most recent illustration was a statute enacted by the Eighty-fifth Congress in haste at the very end of its last session (1957) to minimize the effect of the decision of the Supreme Court in *Jencks* v. *United States* (353 U.S. 617 [1957]), according to which a defendant in a criminal case before a federal court is entitled to inspect the previous reports made by agents to the Federal Bureau of Investigation on matters testified to by them during the trial.

18. The literature abroad is voluminous; see, e.g., Julien Laferrière,

Manuel de droit constitutionnel (Paris, 1947), pp. 308 ff.; 329 ff.; Segundo V. Linares Quintana, *Tradado de la scienzia del derecho constitucional argentino y comparado* (Buenos Aires, 1952), II, 251 ff. The American treatment of the subject appears unrewarding; for a convenient survey, however, see David Deener, "Judicial Review in Modern Constitutional Systems," *American Political Science Review*, XLVI (1952), 1079 ff. (not without errors in fact and in judgment).

19. See Charles Eisenmann, *La Justice constitutionnelle et la haute cour constitutionnelle de l'Autriche* (Paris, 1928).

20. See Freund, *op. cit.*, n. 10 of this chapter, p. 603. Unfortunately, no special study on judicial review in India was accessible to the present author.

21. See Theodor Maunz, *Deutsches Staatsrecht* (5th ed.; Munich, 1956), pp. 277–78; on the Constitutional Committee of East Germany see *ibid.*, pp. 303–4.

22. The case pertained only to procedural issues in relation to the rights of the Council of the Republic after deliberation by the National Assembly (see A. Soulier, "La Délibération du comité constitutionnel du 18 juin 1949," *Revue du droit public*, LXVI [1949], 195 ff.). For a general discussion of judicial review under the Fourth Republic see Jeanne Lemasurier, *Les Constitutions de 1946 et le contrôle jurisdictionnel du législateur* (Paris, 1954).

23. See Maunz, *op. cit.*, n. 21 of this chapter, pp. 182 ff., with bibliography on the subject since 1945.

24. Decision of the Reich Staatsgerichtshof of October 25, 1932, *Entscheidungen des Reichsgerichts in Zivilsachen*, Vol. CXXXVIII (1932), Appendix (pp. 1* ff.).

25. For an authoritative report by one of the judges of the court see Julius Federer, "Die Rechtsprechung des Bunderverfassungsgerichts zum Grundgesetz der Bundesrepublik Deutschland," *Jahrbuch des öffentlichen Rechts der Gegenwart*, III (1954), 15 ff.

26. See Karl Loewenstein, "The Bonn Constitution and the European Defense Community Treaties," *Yale Law Journal*, LXIV (1955), 805 ff.

27. Paolo Biscaretti di Ruffia, *Diritto costituzionale* (4th ed.; Naples, 1956), pp. 451 ff.

28. See Karl Loewenstein, "Konflikte zwischen Regierung und Justiz," *Archiv des öffentlichen Rechts* (N.F.), LXXVIII (1953), 260 ff.

NOTES TO CHAPTER IX

1. For a fuller treatment of the subjects discussed in this section see Karl Loewenstein, *Political Reconstruction* (New York, 1946), pp. 200 ff., 280 ff.

2. The author's very first publication, exactly forty years ago, dealt with this subject, which, in the intervening years, has lost nothing of its timeliness (see Karl Loewenstein, "Über Volksabstimmungen bei Gebietsveränderungen," *Annalen des Deutschen Reichs*, 1917, pp. 593 ff.).

3. *Entscheidungen des Bundesverfassungsgerichts*, I, 47 ff. See also Gerhard Leibholz, "The Federal Constitutional Court in Germany and the 'Southwest Case,'" *American Political Science Review*, XLVI (1952), 723 ff.

4. On these, see Arnold J. Zurcher in James T. Shotwell (ed.), *Governments of Continental Europe* (New York, 1940), pp. 619, 640 ff.

5. The elections for the Polish Sejm of January 20, 1957, were conducted on the same principle, with the significant difference, however, that there were more candidates on the official ticket than seats to be filled and that the voter had the choice of substituting for the candidates preferred by the regime others on the list. Of the 720 candidates, only a minority—52—were members of the Communist party; all others were of the United Peasants and Democratic parties and the Independents. No pressure was reported to have been exerted on the voters. Nonetheless, the electorate, for reasons of foreign policy, heavily indorsed the government of Władysław Gomulka (see *New York Times*, January 21, 1957).

6. New England editors and publishers, invited to visit Mississippi in the fall of 1956, were reliably told that the votes of an all-Negro town, Mount Bayou, were never counted by the election officer at the county seat (*Time*, October 22, 1956, p. 54). See also the testimony before the Subcommittee of the Judiciary Committee of the Senate on the civil rights legislation pending in 1957, as reported by the *New York Times*, March 1, 1957. For the truly staggering evidence the Federal Bureau of Investigation has collected concerning the virtual disenfranchisement of the vast majority of Negroes in the southern states see *New York Times*, August 4, 1957. Senator Paul H. Douglas, Democrat from Illinois, introduced statistics in the Senate debate on the civil rights bill indicating that of 3,750,000 potentially eligible

Negro voters in eight southern states only 850,000—about 23 per cent—were registered.

7. See the pioneering study by Maurice Duverger, *L'Influence des systèmes électoraux sur la vie politique* (Paris, 1950).

8. Henry Steele Commager, "Why about Half of Us Don't Vote," *New York Times Magazine*, October 28, 1956, pp. 14 ff., at 76.

9. A striking illustration of how antiquated election laws, protecting vested interests, make a mockery of the equal protection clause of the constitution and of constitutional democracy was offered, until recently, by Illinois. The state election law, governing the apportionment of the seats in the House of Representatives, had not been changed for a half-century, with the result that the election districts varied from as low as 112,000 to as high as over 900,000 people. The Supreme Court in *Colgrove* v. *Green* (338 U.S. 549 [1946]) refused to intervene, claiming the issue to be a "political question" to be dealt with by the political departments. The long-overdue reform was enacted by Senate Joint Resolution 32 (1954) providing for the amendment of Art. 4, secs. 6, 7, and 8, of the Illinois constitution. The amendment was passed by the voters in November, 1954. Subsequently, the legislature attended to the required redistricting of the constituencies in the state (H.B. 1123 [1955]). The redistricting is made mandatory every ten years. Under this new arrangement the election districts were equalized in three categories pertaining to the city of Chicago itself, the districts of Cook County outside Chicago, and the downstate districts, respectively. (The author wishes to express his gratitude for this information supplied by the Citizen Information Service of Metropolitan Chicago.)

10. The statutory bases are the House of Commons (Redistribution of Seats) Acts of 1944 (7 & 8 Geo. VI, c. 51) and of 1949 (12 & 13 Geo. VI, c. 66). The first reports of the boundary commissions were published in 1954 (under Cmd. 9311–14). For criticism see Hansard's *Parliamentary Debates: Official Reports* for December 15, 16, 19, 20, and 21, 1954 (information supplied by courtesy of the Home Office, London).

11. This thesis has been persistently pursued for many years by Ferdinand A. Hermens (see, e.g., his *Democracy and Anarchy* [Notre Dame, Ind., 1941]). For a critical review see Georges H. Lavau, "Une panacée politique," *Revue française de science politique*, III (1953), 167 ff.; and see also Helmut Unkelbach, *Grundlagen der Wahlsystematik* (Göttingen, 1956). Present trends in the German Federal Republic point to an eventual approximation to the two-party system in

spite of proportional representation. Whether this development, strongly supported by the further tightening of the restrictions on splinter parties in the election law of 1956, will stand the acid test of an economic reversal of the current prosperity remains to be seen.

12. The British technique, based on ample legislation in the various Corrupt and Illegal Practices Acts and the Representation of People Acts (for the present regulation see generally the Representation of People Act of 1949 [12, 13 & 14 Geo. VI, c. 68]), consists primarily in the statutory requirement of an official election agent appointed by each candidate through whom all elections expenses are paid and who is personally answerable to the returning officer and eventually the courts. The expenses are statutorily limited, calculated on the number of voters in each constituency, with a slightly higher rate in rural counties than in urban boroughs. During the last several elections the individual candidate on the average spent between £600 and £900. For details concerning the campaign of 1950 see H. G. Nicolas, *The British General Election of 1950* (London, 1951).

13. In France, under the legislation of 1914 and 1946, the principles of controlled elections amount briefly to this: The election campaign is limited to twenty days prior to the election day; posters can be exhibited only at specified places, with equal space allotted to each party; the number of circulars addressed to the voters is prescribed and equal for all contenders; the state treasury carries the financial burden for printing material, printing, and distribution; and the procedure is closely supervised by an official committee. For information see M. Prélot, *Précis de droit constitutionnel* (Paris, 1955), pp. 328 ff.; Jules Laferrière, *Manuel de droit constitutionnel* (Paris, 1947), pp. 591 ff. For a pioneering study of the election expenses carried by the state in the general elections in France in January, 1956, see Mattei Dogan, "Quelques aspects du financement des élections de janvier 1956," *Revue française de science politique*, VII (1957), 88 ff.

14. For the student of comparative politics there is no more revealing—and alarming—reading than the *Hearings before the Senate Subcommittee on Privileges and Elections of the Committee on Rules and Administration* (84th Cong., 2d sess.; Senate Doc. 93396 [Washington, D.C.: Government Printing Office, 1956]) on 1956 presidential and senatorial campaign contributions and practices.

Until recently, the cardinal issue of the campaign and election expenses has found little interest outside the United States. See, however, Dogan, *op. cit.*, n. 13 of this chapter, and, for Sweden, the official report of the Ministry of Justice (published in 1951) on the financing of political propaganda (*Om offentlig redovisning av den politiska propagandans finansiering: Partifinanisieringsakkunigas betänkande-statens offentliga utredningas* [Stockholm, 1951]). The report is based on the findings of a parliamentary inquiry commission to which the Swedish political parties voluntarily furnished all apposite information. The report is analyzed by Raymond Fusilier, "Les Finances des partis politiques," *Revue politique et parlementaire*, LV (1953), 146 ff., 258 ff. From it an appraisal of the following facts emerges: (*a*) a comparison of the sums spent by the parties in election and in non-election years; (*b*) the very small percentage of expenses devoted by the parties to party adminstration as such when contrasted with those applied to political propaganda; (*c*) the equally small amount of revenue derived from member dues; and (*d*) the contributions of labor and management to the actual election campaign. The first part of Fusilier's discussion contains a survey—the only one available to the present writer's knowledge—of the legislation existing in various states concerning the control of the state over party finances. On party finances in Germany-Bonn some material may be found in Friedrich August von der Heydte and Karl Sacherl, *Soziologie der deutschen Parteien* (Munich, 1955). See also Erwin Hielscher, "Die Finanzierung der politischen Parteien," *Politische Studien* (Munich, 1955), and, for special research into the finances of the leading majority party, Arnold J. Heidenheimer," German Party Finance: The CDU," *American Political Science Review*, LI (1957), 369 ff.

15. As usual, Georg Jellinek was cognizant of the situation; see his penetrating observations in *Allgemeine Staatslehre* (3d ed.; Berlin, 1922), pp. 355 ff., on the frequent incapability of the law to deal with the realities of political power intrinsically limited by the necessity of preserving the existentiality of the state.

16. See *New York Times*, December 6 and 7, 1954. The legality of the governor-general's action was much contested; for a favorable view see K. B. Sayeed, "The Governor General of Pakistan," *Pakistan Horizon*, II (1955), 330 ff.; see also S. Gupta, "The Political Crisis in Pakistan," *Foreign Affairs Report* (New Delhi), III (1954), 133 ff. For an authoritative discussion see Sir Ivor Jennings, *Constitutional Problems in Pakistan* (Cambridge, England, 1956).

17. For the voluminous literature at the time of the crisis and after see Georg Meyer and Gerhard Anschütz, *Lehrbuch des Deutschen Staatsrechts* (7th ed.; Munich, 1919), pp. 903 ff.

NOTES TO CHAPTER X

1. The literature on federalism, one of the most conspicuous play-grounds of constitutional jurisprudence and political theory, is immense. Among the recent over-all discussions may be mentioned K. C. Wheare, *Federal Government* (3d ed.; London, 1953); William S. Livingstone, *Federalism and Constitutional Change* (Oxford, 1956); *Fédéralisme* (Université d'Aix-Marseille, Centre de Sciences Politiques de l'Institut d'Etudes Juridiques de Nice, Paris, 1956) contains various special articles, most of them first rate; for Germany-Bonn see Theodor Maunz, *Deutsches Staatsrecht* (5th ed.; Munich, 1956), pp. 117 ff.

2. See M. G. Ténékides, "Le Fédéralisme grec du Ve au IIIe siècles avant J.-C.," in the French collection cited in n. 1 of this chapter, pp. 215 ff.; J. A. O. Larsen, *Representative Government in Greek and Roman History* (Berkeley, 1955), pp. 47 ff., 106 ff.

3. Under the British North America Act, 1915 (5 & 6 Geo. V, c. 45), Canada was divided, for the assignation of senators, into four divisions with an equal number, but the representation of the provinces within each division need not be equal.

4. There is no need to refer to the American literature. But it is often interesting to see what foreign students have to say; see, e.g., the monumental work by André and Suzanne Tunc, *Le Système constitutionnel des Etats-Unis: Histoire constitutionnelle* (Paris, 1954), Vol. I; André Mathiot, "Le Féderalisme aux Etats-Unis," in the French collection quoted above, n. 1 of this chapter, pp. 217 ff.

5. C. H. Alexandrovitch-Alexander, "Is India a Federation?" *International and Comparative Law Quarterly*, III (1954), 313 ff. For a full discussion of Indian federalism see Durga Das Basu, *A Commentary on the Constitution of India* (2 vols.; 3d ed.; Calcutta, 1955–56).

6. On Libia see Henry S. Villard, *Libya: The New Arab Kingdom in North Africa* (New York, 1956), and the review of this book by Adda B. Bozeman, *Middle Eastern Affairs*, VIII (1957), 68 ff.

7. The first constitution (1949) of "The United States of Indonesia" was federal and bicameral; the second (1950) was unitary and unicameral (see J. Leyser, " Legal Developments in Indonesia," *American Journal of Comparative Law*, III [1954], 399 ff.). The first elections were held September 29, 1955, and in December, 1955, a constituent assembly for drafting a new unitary constitution was elected.

8. See Otto Kirchheimer, "The Decline of Intra-state Federalism

in Western Europe," *World Politics*, III (1953), 281 ff. (dealing with Spain, Italy, and Germany).

9. Paolo Biscaretti di Ruffia, *Diritto costituzionale* (4th ed.; Naples, 1956), pp. 524 ff.

10. *Ibid.*, pp. 532–33.

11. For details see Theodor Maunz, *Deutsches Staatsrecht* (5th ed.; Munich, 1956), pp. 159 ff. On pp. 242–43 he enumerates the thirteen categories of bills which cannot be passed without concurrence of the Federal Council.

12. *Finanzverfassungsgesetz* of December 25, 1955. It was carried as a constitutional amendment, modifying Arts. 106 and 107 of the Basic Law.

13. *Länderfinanzausgleichsgesetz* of April 27, 1955 (see Maunz, *op. cit.*, n. 11 of this chapter, pp. 207 ff.).

14. Christopher Hughes, *The Federal Constitution of Switzerland* (Oxford, 1954), pp. 49 ff. The federal income tax was levied on the basis of a federal emergency decree of December 22, 1938, and was intrinsically unconstitutional. In 1950 people and cantons conceded by referendum a temporary legalization of the decree mentioned (and other measures of equally doubtful constitutionality raising direct taxes) until December 31, 1954. Another interim solution was adopted by people and cantons when a referendum, in 1954, ratified a decree of the Federal Council of June 25, 1954, which continued the situation under the decree of 1950 to the end of the year 1958. (Information supplied by courtesy of Professor M. Battelli, Geneva.)

15. For Argentina see Austin F. Macdonald, *Latin American Government and Politics* (2d ed.; New York, 1954), pp. 115 ff.; see also Luis H. Sommariva, *La Intervención federal Argentina comparada con la Norte Americana y la Suiza* (Buenos Aires, 1935); Santos F. Amadeo, *Argentine Constitutional Law* (New York, 1943), pp. 88 ff. For Brazil see Macdonald, *op. cit.*, pp. 196–97; the new constitution of 1946 tries to restrict the arbitrariness of federal intervention by certain conditions for its application (Arts. 7–14). On intervention in Mexico see *ibid.*, p. 276; Mexican federalism exists mainly on paper anyway (see J. Lloyd Mecham, "Mexican Federalism—Fact or Fiction," *Annals of the American Academy of Political and Social Sciences*, CVIII–CXIII [1941–42], 23 ff.).

16. See Wheare, *op. cit.*, n. 1 of this chapter, pp. 89–90, 167.

17. For details see *ibid.*, pp. 86 ff., 148 ff., 151 ff., 220–21. One of the main stumbling blocks for a sound centralization of economic policies is sec. 92 of the constitution of 1900, under which trade, commerce,

and intercourse between the states "shall remain absolutely free" from federal control. An entire literature has grown around this provision. After a long chain of decisions restricting federal jurisdiction (e.g., *Australia* v. *Bank of New South Wales* [1950] A.C. 235), some progress toward greater federal powers was achieved only very recently by the decision of the Judicial Committee of the Privy Council in *Hughes and Vale Pty. Ltd.* v. *New South Wales* ([1954] A.L.R. 1069). See J. J. Hedigen and R. L. Sharwood, "Trends in the Interpretation of Section 92 of the Australian Constitution," *Res judicata*, VII (1955), 71 ff.; E. Anderson, "Main Frustrations of Economic Government Caused by Section 92," *Australian Law Review*, XXVI (1953), 518 ff., 566 ff. See also Paul A. Freund, "A Supreme Court in a Federation," *Columbia Law Review*, LIII (1953), 597 ff., at 602, 608 ff.

18. Julian Towster, *Political Power in the U.S.S.R., 1917–1947* (New York, 1948), pp. 61 ff., 83 ff.

19. *Demokratisierungsgesetz* of July 23, 1952 (see Maunz, *op cit.*, n. 11 of this chapter, pp. 257 ff.).

20. See Clarence C. Walton, "The Fate of Neo-federalism in Western Europe," *Western Political Science Quarterly*, V (1952), 366 ff.; Karl Loewenstein, "The Union of Western Europe: Illusion and Reality," *Columbia Law Review*, LII (1952), 55 ff., 209 ff.; A. H. Robertson, "Different Approaches to European Unity," *American Journal of Comparative Law*, III (1954), 502 ff.

21. Of the considerable literature may be noted Rudolf Bindschedler, *Rechtsfragen der europäischen Einigung* (Basel, 1954); Paul Reuter, *La Communauté Européenne du Charbon et de l'Acier* (Paris, 1953); Gerhard H. Bebr, "The European Coal and Steel Community," *Yale Law Journal*, LXIII (1953), 1 ff.; Henry L. Mason, *The European Coal and Steel Community* (The Hague, 1955). The most up-to-date information is contained in *Annuaire de l'Assemblée Commune* (Communauté Européenne du Charbon et de l'Acier, Luxembourg, 1956).

NOTES TO CHAPTER XI

1. For this discussion the author is indebted to Maurice Duverger, *Droit constitutionnel et institutions politiques* (Paris, 1955), pp. 189 ff.

2. See Karl Loewenstein, "Freedom Is Unsafe without Self-government," *Annals of the American Academy of Political and Social Science*, CCXLIII (January, 1946), 47 ff. The author, privileged to serve during the last war on the Committee on Essential Human Rights of the American Law Institute, proposed a corresponding provision to this group, which included it as Art. 16 in its "Statement of Essential

Human Rights." Subsequently, the latter was submitted by the government of Panama as its official proposal to the Commission on Human Rights of the United Nations. In this process the right to participate in one's government became Art. 21 of the Universal Declaration of Human Rights of the United Nations.

3. On the right of resistance against unlawful authority see Joseph-Barthélemy and Paul Duez, *Traité de droit constitutionnel* (Paris, 1933), pp. 245 ff. Curiously, the theoretical interest of German legal thought in the right of resistance was stronger than elsewhere (see, e.g., Fritz Kern, *Gottesgnadentum und Widerstandsrecht* [Leipzig, 1915]; Kurt Wolzendorff, *Staatsrecht und Naturrecht in der Lehre vom Widerstandsrecht des Volkes gegen rechtswidrige Ausübung der Staatsgewalt* [Breslau, 1916]; and, for more recent works, Herbert von Broch, *Obrigkeit und Widerstand* [Tübingen, 1954], and Carl Heyland, *Das Widerstandsrecht des Volkes gegen verfassungswidrige Ausübung der Staatsgewalt im neuen deutschen Verfassungsrecht* [Frankfurt, 1950]).

In reaction to the lawlessness of the Third Reich a number of the German *Land* constitutions after 1945 explicitly included the right of resistance among the individual rights, e.g.: Hesse (constitution of 1946), Art. 147; Bremen (1947), Art. 19; and, strangely enough, Mark Brandenburg in East Germany (constitution of 1947), Art. 6.

4. Habeas Corpus Act, 1679 (31 Car. II, c. 2); Bill of Rights, 1688 (1 Will. III, sess. 2, c. 2); Act of Settlement, 1700 (12 & 13 Will. III, c. 2).

5. A pertinent illustration in the American legislative practice is offered by the Immunity Act of 1954 (68 Stat. 745). It authorizes the federal courts, under certain conditions, to withdraw from a witness the protection against self-incrimination guaranteed unconditionally by the Fifth Amendment, thus "perforating," in individual cases, its general validity. In *Ullmann* v. *United States* (350 U.S. 422 [1956]) the Supreme Court held the act constitutional. By contrast, the dissenting Justices Douglas and Black insisted (p. 440) that "the right of silence created by the Fifth Amendment is beyond the reach of Congress."

6. The classical cases are *Schenck* v. *United States* (249 U.S. 47 [1919]) (Holmes) and *Whitney* v. *California* (274 U.S. 357 [1927]) (Brandeis).

7. See the discussion in Theodor Maunz, *Deutsches Staatsrecht* (5th ed.; Munich, 1956), pp. 101 ff. It is not surprising that Art. 19 has become a focus of judicial and theoretical controversy.

8. The subject as such finds little interest in the United States. For

foreign discussions see François Schaller, *De la charité privée aux droits économiques et sociaux* (Paris, 1950); B. Mirkhine-Guetzévitch, *Les Constitutions européennes* (Paris, 1951), I, 140 ff.; Georges Gurvitch, *La Déclaration des droits sociaux* (Paris, 1944).

9. On the position of the individual under naziism see Karl Loewenstein, *Hitler's Germany* (rev. ed.; New York, 1940), pp. 158 ff., 202 ff.; on the same problem under Italian fascism see Arnold J. Zurcher in James T. Shotwell (ed.), *Continental Governments and Politics* (New York, 1940), pp. 702 ff.

10. Julian Towster, *Political Power in the U.S.S.R., 1917–1947* (New York, 1948), pp. 281 ff., 410 ff.

11. For twenty years and more the author has devoted much of his scientific labor to this crucial issue. See, e.g., Karl Loewenstein, "Militant Democracy and Fundamental Rights," *American Political Science Review*, XXXI (1937), 416 ff., 638 ff.; *Le Contrôle législatif de l'extrémisme politique dans les démocraties européennes* (Paris, 1938) (an American version of this study is published in *Columbia Law Review*, XXXVIII [1938], 691 ff., 725 ff.); Adolf Schönke (ed.), *Die strafrechtlichen Staatsschutzbestimmungen des Auslandes* (Bonn, 1953); Pierre A. Papados, *Le Délit politique* (Geneva, 1954). A comprehensive study for Latin America was published under the title *La Legislación para la defensa política en las repúblicas americanas* (2 vols.; Montevideo: Consultative Emergency Committee for Political Defense, 1947).

12. Unfortunately, no comprehensive study on defense legislation directed against communism, paralleling the works referred to in the preceding note, has been undertaken.

13. Illustrations are: Germany-Bonn, Art. 21, sec. 2; Brazil, constitution of 1946, Art. 141, No. 13; Uruguay, constitution of 1952, Art. 80, No. 18; Peru, constitution of 1933, Art. 53; Italy, constitution of 1947, Transitional Provisions XII (these directed against the Fascist party).

14. The regulation is copied almost verbatim by the the constitution of Costa Rica of 1949, Art. 98, sec. 2, with the difference, however, that the Legislative Assembly decides on the prohibition by a two-thirds majority on the advice of the Supreme Electoral Tribunal.

15. Similar, and even more restrictive, provisions are inserted in some of the *Land* constitutions; see, e.g., Baden, constitution of 1947, Art. 124; Rhineland-Palatinate, constitution of 1947, Art. 133; they are also found in some constitutions of the Eastern Zone, e.g., Mecklenburg, 1947, Arts. 7 and 99; Mark Brandenburg, 1947, Art. 8.

16. *Australian Communist Party* v. *Commonwealth* (1951) C.L.R. 1; see also Leicester Webb, *Communism and Democracy in Australia: A Survey of the 1951 Referendum* (Melbourne, 1954).

17. See Professor M. Einaudi's letter to the *New York Times*, December 6, 1956.

18. Decision of the Federal Constitutional Court of October 10, 1951, *Juristenzeitung*, 1952, pp. 681 ff.; *Entscheidungen des Bundesverfassungsgerichts*, II, 14; Decision of August 17, 1956, *Juristenzeitung*, 1956, pp. 596 ff.; *Entscheidungen des Bundesverfassunsgerichts*, V (1956), 58. For a competent review of the latter decision see Edward McWhinney, "The German Federal Constitution and the Communist Party Decision," *Indiana Law Journal*, XXXII (1957), 295 ff.

19. Communist Control Act of 1954 (68 Stat. 775); at the time of this writing the Supreme Court has not yet passed on its constitutionality. See also C. A. Auerbach, "Communist Control Act of 1954," *University of Chicago Law Review*, XXVI (1956), 175 ff.

20. To mention only a few among the most prominent: Zechariah Chafee, Erwin N. Griswold, Walter Gellhorn, Thurman W. Arnold, Robert E. Cushman, Lord O'Brian, and, of course, Justices Hugo L. Black and William O. Douglas.

21. For the following see Karl Loewenstein, "Political Systems, Ideologies and Institutions: The Problem of Their Circulation," *Western Political Science Review*, VI (1953), 689 ff., at 699 ff.

22. Stanley Kelley, Jr., *Public Relations and Political Power* (Baltimore, 1956).

23. The Associated Press, in a survey published in the *New York Times*, December 23, 1956, reported that, during 1956, curbs on the press had sharply increased in many parts of the world. The report distinguishes four aspects of press restrictions: (1) withholding of information at the source by government agencies; (2) domestic censorship through economic pressure (withholding of newsprint is one of the common devices) or legal threats; (3) complete censorship; and (4) governmental restrictions on foreign correspondents.

24. Two interesting experiments were undertaken recently to make the press truly independent by freeing it from the dependence on special interests. In Czechoslovakia after 1945 (but prior to the seizure by the communists) individuals were forbidden to own newspapers; only officially recognized groups, such as political parties, co-operatives, and cultural associations, could own and publish them under the supervision of an agency constituted similarly as the British Broad-

casting Corporation. No censorship existed (see Joseph H. Kaiser, *Die Repräsentation organisierter Interessen* [Berlin, 1956], pp. 229–30). The reform in France after the end of the last war, growing out of demands of the Resistance, was intended to eradicate the dependence of the major press organs on private economic interests which controlled their editorial policies, and, by neutralizing the press, to eliminate its venality. Under the legislation enacted for this purpose the press was organized as a quasi-corporate, self-governing structure. The law of April 2, 1947 (following provisional regulations under the ordinances of September 30, 1944, and January 29, 1945), provided for integration of the entire press as *Les Sociétés Coopératives de Messageries de Presse*, which, in structure similar to the Associated Press in the United States, had to admit, on equal footing, all press organs complying with the law. The state participated financially, by granting initial credits, and administratively, by being represented on the Conseil Supérieur des Messageries. The novel undertaking was made possible by the wholesale confiscation of the collaborationist press under the de Gaulle ordinance of September 30, 1944, confirmed by the law of May 11, 1946. The Société Nationale des Enterprises de Presse, created under this legislation, sold or leased the press organs to reliable persons. The experiment failed: by necessity dependence on the government which financed the enterprise replaced control by the private capitalist interests. On the development in France see Georges Burdeau, *Manuel du droit public* (Paris, 1948), pp. 209 ff., 219 ff.; Georges Ripert, *Le Déclin de droit* (Paris, 1949), pp. 87 ff.

25. For the glaring disparities in the use of the telecommunication media in the United States see *Hearings before the Senate Subcommittee on Privileges and Elections of the Committee on Rules and Administration* (84th Cong., 2d sess.; Senate Doc. 93396 [Washington, D.C.: Government Printing Office, 1956]). The evidence tallies with the report of the *New York Times*, November 2, 1956, on the attitude of the American press: 62 per cent of all papers were reported backing President Eisenhower, against 15 per cent for Mr. Stevenson, the former amounting to 60 per cent of the total circulation, the latter to 10 per cent. By contrast, under the French legislation (decrees of April 26, May 16 and 18, and October 25, 1946) all lists submitted in each *département* participate on equal footing in the allotment of radio time on the national and local stations; each party is given ten minutes' time, the sequence determined through lot by an official commission.

NOTES TO CHAPTER XII

1. An impressive effort to explain society as the counterpoint to the plural forces and their representations was undertaken by Lorenz von Stein, *Geschichte der sozialen Bewegung in Frankreich von 1789 bis auf unsere Tage* (3 vols.; Leipzig, 1850; rev. ed., Munich, 1921), a sociopolitical analysis of France not unworthy to be mentioned in the same breath with de Tocqueville's political-sociological study of the United States. In recent times, following the pioneering work by Arthur P. Bentley, *The Process of Government: A Study in Social Pressures* (Bloomington, Ind., 1908) (republished in 1934 and 1949), the American literature on pluralism has grown to ungainly proportions; among the standard discussions are David B. Truman, *The Governmental Process, Political Interests and Public Opinion* (New York, 1951); V. O. Key, *Politics, Parties and Pressure Groups* (3d ed.; New York, 1952); Earl Latham, *The Group Basis of Politics: A Study in Basing-Point Legislation* (Ithaca, N.Y., 1952); still of interest is Pendleton Herring, *Group Representation before Congress* (Washington, D.C., 1929). Practically all American discussions restrict themselves to the home environment. From the comparative viewpoint organized pluralism is approached by Joseph H. Kaiser, *Die Repräsentation organizierter Interessen* (Berlin, 1956).

2. Franz L. Neumann's *Behemoth* (New York, 1942) is fatally vitiated by the belief in the survival of the major interest groups.

3. H. D. Jordan, "The Political Methods of the Anti-Corn Law League," *American Political Science Review*, XIII (1927), 38 ff.

4. On the professional discipline of such groups in England see William A. Robson, *Justice and Administrative Law: A Study of the British Constitution* (London, 1928), pp. 176 ff., 310 ff. (on domestic tribunals). Similar powers of self-government are exercised in France by the *ordres professionnels* (e.g., lawyers and physicians); see André Heilbronner, "Le Pouvoir professionnel," in *Conseil d'Etat, Etudes et documents* (Paris, 1952), pp. 33 ff. The integrated bar with professional discipline has existed in Germany since the lawyers' code (*Rechtsanwaltsordnung*) of 1878.

5. For England see, e.g., J. Ivor Jennings, *Parliament* (Cambridge, 1939), pp. 31 ff., 171 ff., 225 ff.; Samuel H. Beer, "Pressure Groups and Parties in Great Britain," *American Political Science Review*, L (1956), 1 ff. Interest in pluralism is rapidly increasing in France (see, e.g., the symposium on elections for social and political bodies in

Revue française de science politique, VI [1955], 221 ff.; Henry Mendras, "Les Organisations agricoles et la politique," *Revue française de science politique*, V [1955], 736 ff.).

6. Karl Braunias, *Das parlamentarische Wahlrecht* (Berlin, 1932), II, 88. The Swiss example is G. Duttweiler's Independents, a consumers' pressure group.

7. For comparative material for the period before the Second World War see *ibid.*, pp. 120–21; for France see Marcel Prélot, *Précis de droit constitutionnel* (Paris, 1955), pp. 359–60.

8. Regulation of Lobbying Act, Title II of the Legislative Reorganization Act of 1946, 2 U.S.C. 261–70. The statute was sustained by the Supreme Court in *United States* v. *Hariss*, 347 U.S. 612 (1953); see also "Federal Lobbying Act: A Reconsideration," *George Washington Law Review*, XXI (1953), 585 ff. Recently two lawyers were reported (*New York Times*, December 15, 1956) as having been fined for failure to register as lobbyists in connection with the pressure of the producers for the Natural Gas Bill of 1956 (vetoed by President Eisenhower).

9. Werner Weber, *Spannungen und Kräfte im westdeutschen Verfassungssystem* (Hamburg, 1951), pp. 49 ff. and *passim;* Kaiser, *op. cit.*, n. 1 of this chapter, pp. 181 ff.

10. The "agreed bill" practice in Illinois resembles the Swedish practice: no major piece of legislation is considered by the legislature unless previously approved by the chambers of commerce, manufacturers' organizations, and the AFL-CIO (see W. W. Wirtz, "Government by Private Groups," *Louisiana Law Review*, XIII [1952–53], 440 ff.).

11. Alfred de Grazia, *Public and Republic: Political Representation in America* (New York, 1951). For England see O. Hood Phillips, *The Constitutional Law of Great Britain and the Commonwealth* (London, 1952), pp. 306 ff.; Sir Arthur Street, "Quasi-government Boards since 1918," in Sir G. Campion *et al.* (eds.), *British Government since 1918* (London, 1950), pp. 157 ff. For France see Charles Celier, *Droit public et vie économique* (Paris, 1949). For comparative institutions see Kaiser, *op. cit.*, n. 1 of this chapter, pp. 274 ff.

12. The Conseil d'Administration may serve as an example. It is the central governing authority of the national coal industry in France under the legislation of 1946. Of its nineteen members, six are appointed by the government, six delegated into it by the trade unions as representatives of employers and workers, and six represent the

consumers; of these, three are chosen by the most important coal-consuming industries, one by the head organization of the *associations familiales*, and two by the trade unions, which, thus, also take care of the consumers' interests (see Kaiser, *op. cit.*, n. 1 of this chapter, pp. 168 ff.). See also William A. Robson, "Nationalized Industries in Britain and France," *American Political Science Review*, XLIV (1950), 200 ff.; M. Einaudi, Maurice Byé, and Ernesto Rossi, *Nationalization in France and Italy* (Ithaca, N.Y., 1955).

13. See, e.g., the interesting discussion by Wirtz, *op. cit.*, n. 10 of this chapter.

14. See Friedrich Kessler and Malcolm P. Sharp, *Contracts, Cases and Materials* (New York, 1953), pp. 8 ff., 39 ff.; Wolfgang Friedmann, "Changing Functions of the Contract in Common Law," *University of Toronto Law Review*, IX (1951), 15–16.

15. See, for a recent example of judicial action against a flagrant monopoly, *United States v. United Shoe Machinery Corporation* (347 U.S. 321 [1954]) and Carl Kaysen, *United States v. United Shoe Machinery Corporation: An Economic Analysis of an Anti-trust Case* (Cambridge, Mass., 1956).

16. John Kenneth Galbraith, *American Capitalism: The Concept of the Countervailing Power* (Boston, 1952).

17. Arts. 11, 52, and 91. Characteristically, the references to the political parties in Arts. 11 and 52 were stricken out by the constitutional amendment of December 7, 1954. Only the participation of the political groups in the election of the members of the Constitutional Committee still stands.

18. Baden, constitution of 1947, Arts. 117 ff.; Bavaria, 1946, Arts. 15 and 52; Rhineland-Palatinate, 1947, Arts. 133, 135.

19. Alfons Steiniger, *Das Blocksystem* (Berlin, 1949); Theodor Maunz, *Deutsches Staatsrecht* (5th ed.; Munich, 1956), pp. 217 ff.

20. For the legislation on the *lema* see Eduardo J. Couture *et al.*, *Legislación vigente en el Uruguay* (Montevideo, 1956), pp. 64–66; P. B. Taylor, "The Electoral System in Uruguay," *Journal of Politics*, XVII (1955), 19 ff.

21. The discussion in the text is based on a paper by Maurice Duverger, "Le Statut juridisque des partis politiques en France," submitted to the Fourth Congress of the Academy of Comparative Law, Paris, August, 1954; the present author does not know whether the report has been published.

22. Under the law of January 10, 1936, a number of fascist "leagues"

were dissolved; in 1939 the Communist party was also outlawed. The criterion, under due revision by the Conseil d'Etat, was the intent of the group to impair the republican form of government by force. While the legislation removed the fascist groups from the street, it failed to prevent the undermining of the Third Republic by antidemocratic forces in anticipation of the Nazi onslaught of 1940.

23. The Statuto Organico de los Partidos Políticos was enacted by Decree 11976.45 but never applied in practice (this information was supplied by courtesy of Professor Segundo V. Linares Quintana, Buenos Aires, one of the co-authors of the project).

On the subject of an organic law for political parties, wholly ignored by American literature, see Pascal Arrighi, *Statut des partis politiques* (Paris, 1948); Pedro J. Frias, *El Ordenamiento de los partidos políticos* (Buenos Aires, 1944). The subject of the internal organization of the political parties recently has become of particular if still academic interest in Germany-Bonn; see, e.g., Gerhard Leibholz, "Der Parteienstaat im Bonner Grundgesetz," in *Recht, Staat, Wirtschaft*, III (Düsseldorf, 1951), 99 ff., 116 ff.; Günther Rabus, "Die innere Ordnung der politischen Parteien im gegenwärtigen deutschen Staatsrecht," *Archiv des offentlichen Rechts*, LXXVIII (1952–53), 163 ff. The report of the commission of experts appointed by the minister of the interior to study a future legal regulation of political parties in conformity with the injunction of Article 21, Section 3, of the Basic Law was published under the title *Rechtliche Ordnung des Parteiwesens* (Frankfurt am Main, 1957). It reached this writer too late to be considered.

24. The best description is by Joseph H. Starr, "The Legal Status of American Political Parties," *American Political Science Review*, XXXIV (1940), 439 ff., 685 ff. For a useful discussion by a foreign student see Segundo V. Linares Quintana, *Los Partidos políticosa en los Estados Unidos de America: Su ordenamiento jurídico* (Buenos Aires, 1943).

25. Art. 1 of the law of July 1, 1900 (see Joseph-Barthélemy, *Précis de droit public* [Paris, 1937], pp. 136 ff.).

26. *Nixon v. Herndon*, 173 U.S. 536 (1927); *United States v. Classic*, 313 U.S. 299 (1941); *Smith v. Allwright*, 321 U.S. 649 (1944); *Terry v. Adams*, 345 U.S. 461 (1953).

27. L. M. Friedman, "Reflections on the Law of Political Parties," *California Law Review*, XLIV (1956), 65 ff.

28. The so-called Smith Act of 1940 (54 Stat. 671) was still con-

cerned with subversive actions committed by individuals. The Subversive Control (McCarran) Act of 1950 (64 Stat. 978) and the Communist Control Act of 1954 (68 Stat. 775) struck at the Communist party collectively.

29. For Nazi Germany see the Law on the Unity of State and Party of December 1, 1933, and Karl Loewenstein, *Hitler's Germany* (rev. ed.; New York, 1940), pp. 98 ff.

30. R. Warlemont, "La Représentation économique dans l'acte additionnel jusqu'aux constitutions de l'empire," *Revue internationale d'histoire politique et constitutionnelle* (N.S.), No. 15 (1954), pp. 244 ff.

31. See Heinrich Herrfahrdt, *Die berufsständische Vertretung von der französischen Revolution bis zur Gegenwart* (Berlin, 1921); Ralph Bowen, *German Theories of the Corporative State* (New York, 1947).

32. See B. Chubb, "Vocational Representation and the Irish Senate," *Political Studies,* XII (1954), 97 ff.

33. The corporative ghost hovers also over the "new style" concept of government which Indonesia's President Sukarno is propagating in that crisis-rent country. On the basis of an "Emergency Act," published on May 8, 1957, a National Council is to be established whose members are to be chosen by the president from among the various plural groups (peasants, labor, intelligentsia, women, youth, religious groups) and the geographical regions. The relationship of this new body with the parliament elected in 1955 is still undecided, but, unless it will function as an advisory second chamber, it may well serve as a stepping stone toward neopresidentialism (see *New York Times,* May 10, 1957).

34. No critical study of the Portuguese regime is available. The voluminous indigenous literature is uniformly laudatory (see, e.g., Emilia A. Ferreira, *Corporativismo português* [Coimbra, 1951]).

35. Adolf Merkl, *Die berufsständische Verfassung Österreichs* (Vienna, 1935).

36. See Lindsay Rogers and W. H. Dittmar, "The *Reichswirtschaftsrat, De mortuis,*" *Political Science Quarterly,* L (1950), 481 ff.

37. See Maurice Duverger, *Droit constitutionnel et institutions politiques* (Paris, 1955), pp. 540 ff.; on the Economic Council of the Third Republic see Jean Cahen-Salvador, *La Représentations des intérêts et les services publics* (Paris, 1936); for that of the Fourth Republic see Maurice Aubry, *Le Conseil économique* (Paris, 1953).

38. See Arnold J. Zurcher in James T. Shotwell (ed.), *Governments of Continental Europe* (New York, 1940), pp. 874 ff.

39. Karl Loewenstein, *Hitler's Germany* (rev. ed.; New York, 1940), pp. 168 ff.

40. See Julian Towster, *Political Power in the U.S.S.R., 1917-1947* (New York, 1948), pp. 76 ff. Apparently reliable reports on the early period of sovietism are Leo Zaitseff, *Jahrbuch des öffentlichen Rechts der Gegenwart*, XI (1922), 275 ff., and N. N. Alexejew, *Jahrbuch des öffentlichen Rechts der Gegenwart*, XIV (1925), 526 ff.

41. The semiofficial viewpoint is presented by E. Kardelj, "Le Rôle du citoyen dans nôtre système politique et économique," *Questions actuelles du socialisme* (Paris), XXII (1954), 97 ff.; O. Mandic, "Il consiglio degli produttori nell'ordinamento costituzionale Jugoslavo," *Rivista di studi politici internazionali*, XX (1953), 411 ff.; for a foreign critical approach see D. J. R. Scott, "Producers Representation in Yugoslavia," *Political Studies*, II (1954), 210 ff.

42. The only practical application of organized pluralism was the National Industrial Recovery Act of 1933 (48 Stat. 195). The code authorities established under it for several hundred branches of industry were composed of representatives of the employers, labor, and the public and were authorized to issue binding regulations for all enterprises of the respective category. The experiment, whose giantism was equaled only by its amateurishness, had become a chaotic failure long before the Supreme Court, in *Schechter Poultry Corporation* v. *United States* (295 U.S. 495 [1935]), administered its deathblow.

43. Alexis de Tocqueville, *De la démocratie en Amérique*, Part II, chap. iv; ed. A. Gain (Paris, 1951), I, 305. In the recent American edition, *Democracy in America*, ed. Phillips Bradley (New York, 1954), I, 195, which uses the standard Henry Reeve text, the passage is translated—rather freely—as follows: "It cannot be denied that the unrestrained liberty of association for political purposes is the privilege which a people is longest in learning how to exercise. If it does not throw the nation into anarchy, it perpetually augments the chances of that calamity."

NOTES TO POSTSCRIPT

1. So far four such referenda were staged: on the constitution itself (September 28-30, 1958) twice; on the Algerian issue (January 8, 1961, and April 8, 1962); and on the popular election of the president (October 28, 1962).

2. The literature on African politics, presently a most fashionable subject in the United States, is substantial. Compare, for example, M. Fortes and E. E. Evans-Pritchard (eds.), *African Political Systems* (London, 1961); Gwendolen M. Carter (ed.), *Five African States* (Cornell, N.Y., 1963); Herbert J. Spiro, *Politics in Africa* (Englewood Cliffs, N.J., 1962); Lucy Mair, *New Nations* (Chicago, 1963).

3. This subject touched *incidenter* only in the book itself deserves a special discussion at this point.

4. For further information on military rule, see John J. Johnson (ed.), *The Role of the Military in Underdeveloped Countries* (Princeton, N.J., 1963). For an unusually penetrating analysis of the situation of Egypt as a military society, see Andouar Abdel-Malek, *Egypte, Société Militaire* (Paris, 1962). Concerning the situation in Latin America, see Edwin Lieuwen, *Generals v Presidents: Neo-Militarism in Latin America* (New York, 1964).

5. The sweeping victory of the Democrats in the presidential election of 1964 was largely due to the lack of popular appeal of the Republican contender.

6. See Ernst Fraenkel, *Die repräsentative und die plebiszitäre Komponente im demokratischen Verfassungsstaat* (Tübingen, 1958); see also Henry W. Ehrmann, "Direct Democracy in France," *The American Political Science Review*, LVII (1963), pp. 883 ff.

7. On the techniques of constitutional revision see Karl Loewenstein, *Über Wesen, Technik, und Grenzen der Verfassungsänderung* (Berlin, 1961).

Indexes

Index of Names

Index of Subjects

[Principal discussions are indicated by italicized figures.]

U.S.S.R.—*Continued*
  federalism, 178, 310
  individual liberties, 327–28
  pluralism, 345–46
  "soviet" system, 380
  Stalin constitution of 1936, 32, *84–85*, 117, 142, 144, 365
  use of plebiscite, 268

Venezuela, 307, 399; *see also* Latin America
Venice, Republic of, 51, 75, 337, 348
Vertical controls, 18, 164–65, *285 ff.*, 316–17
Veto
  of the government over parliamentary legislation, 206–7
  of the president of the United States, 254

Victoria (Australia), 308
Viet-Nam
  North, 82
  South, 67, 146, 178, 265
Virginia, 158
Vote of non-confidence, 89, *196 ff.*, 394; *see also* Parliamentary government

Wählervereinigung, 367
Welfare state, 43, 47, 323 ff.
Western Australia, 308
"World federation," 314
"World government," 314

Yugoslavia, 82, 94, 178, 280, 311, 380–81